Public Economics for South African Students

To Daantjie Franzsen

whose leadership over half a century as teacher, researcher,
policy adviser and commissioner in the field of economics
inspired many students of economics, influenced many
decisions and decision-makers, and knowingly and
unknowingly shaped the views of many ordinary people
and officials in government and business in South Africa.

Born in 1918 and educated at the University of Stellenbosch,
Daniel Gerhardus Franzsen was Professor of Economics at
the Universities of Pretoria and Stellenbosch, Deputy
Governor of the South African Reserve Bank, Chairperson of
the Commission of Inquiry into Fiscal and Monetary Policy
in South Africa (1967–1969), chairperson and member of
various other commissions and committees, Economic
Advisor to the Minister of Finance, President of the
Economic Society of South Africa and author of many
scientific books and articles.

Public Economics

for South African Students

2ND EDITION

Philip A Black
(Africa Institute for Policy Analysis)

Estian Calitz
(University of Stellenbosch)

Tjaart J Steenekamp
(University of South Africa)

and associates

OXFORD
UNIVERSITY PRESS

OXFORD
UNIVERSITY PRESS

Great Clarendon Street, Oxford OX2 6DP

Oxford University Press is a department of the University of Oxford.
It furthers the University's objective of excellence in research, scholarship,
and education by publishing worldwide in

Oxford New York

Auckland Bangkok Buenos Aires Cape Town Chennai
Dar es Salaam Delhi Hong Kong Istanbul Karachi Kolkata
Kuala Lumpur Madrid Melbourne Mexico City Mumbai
Nairobi São Paulo Shanghai Taipei Tokyo Toronto

Oxford is a registered trade mark of Oxford University Press
in the UK and certain other countries

Published in South Africa
by Oxford University Press Southern Africa, Cape Town

Public Economics for South African Students 2nd Edition
ISBN 0 19 578442 1

© Oxford University Press Southern Africa 2003

The moral rights of the author have been asserted
Database right Oxford University Press (maker)

First published 1999
Reprinted 2003 (twice) , 2004

Commissioning editor: Marian Griffin
Editor: Owen Barrow
Indexer: Jeanne Cope
Designer: Mark Standley

Published by Oxford University Press Southern Africa
PO Box 12119, N1 City, 7463, Cape Town, South Africa

Set in 9 pt on 12 pt Palatino by Mckore Graphics
Reproduction by Castle Graphics
Cover reproduction by The Image Bureau

Printed and bound by ABC Press, Epping II, Cape Town

Author Contributions

Abridged table of Contents

Contents

Figures and Tables

Preface

This book provides a comprehensive introduction to the study of public economics against a South African background. By explaining theory with reference to South African institutions, practices and examples, the student should find it easier to grasp the issues. In view of the interrelatedness of the economies of Southern African countries and cultural and historical links, students from neighbouring countries should also find the book accessible and the examples understandable.

The emphasis is on developing the student's understanding of the theoretical issues pertaining to the role of government in a mixed economy, as it translates into expenditure on government functions which are financed by means of various taxes and loans. Many text books offer public economics as a study in applied microeconomics. To a large extent this book follows the same line, but fiscal policy is discussed in terms of both its macro and micro dimensions. The conceptual framework is that of a medium-sized, open developing economy, exposed to the forces of democratisation and globalisation. The aim is to equip the student with basic analytical skills and to demonstrate their application to practical issues.

As lecturers at both residential and distance-learning universities, we share among us a great deal of research and practical experience in different aspects of public eco-

nomics and fiscal policy. We have therefore designed this book with different kinds of students in mind: students at distance-learning universities who will have a fairly self-contained text that the lecturer can supplement with further explanations and tutorial exercises; residential students who will be able to study on their own, leaving lecturers time to analyse and debate topical issues, discuss the self-assessment exercises and explain the more difficult material; post-graduate students who are doing a course in public economics for the first time and need to do self-study in order to digest more advanced material; and post-graduate working students who did not do an undergraduate course in public economics but who need to acquire this knowledge for non-degree purposes in order to advance their careers.

In the second edition of *Public Economics for South African Students*, we have deliberately refrained from making unnecessary changes to the text. The main purpose of our revision was to update material, a necessary exercise for a book that deals with constantly changing policy and analytical issues. In updating we have used the latest relevant data, using figures and information provided in the March 2002 issue of the Quarterly Bulletin of the South African Reserve Bank and the 2002 Budget of the South African government.

The plan of the book has been restructured in one important way. The Introduction in our first edition has been reworked as a fully-fledged Chapter 1. It now includes study objectives, self-assessment questions and important concepts for review. The numbers of all the other chapters and section headings have been changed accordingly.

Public Economics for South African Students is used by different institutions at different levels and in different semesters. The assumed microeconomic foundations are sometimes lacking or are acquired concurrently with a course or module in public economics. To bridge these gaps we have extended the use of basic microeconomic tools in the book. In Chapter 2, Section 2.2 on the benchmark model, we included the Edgeworth-Bowley box analysis of production equilibrium and consumption equilibrium. In Chapter 4 the distinction between perfect competition and monopoly is now introduced using a simple graphical illustration of imperfect competition.

In recent years we have witnessed important reforms of the tax structure and changes to specific taxes in South Africa. The base of income tax was changed from a source of income base to a residence base. In order to accommodate this change a new section on the international taxation of income was included in Chapter 11. The taxation of capital gains was implemented in 2001 which we describe and analyse in section 11.8.

In Chapter 17, the consolidated fiscal authorities are now discussed in one section (Section 17.3.5). Revisions of textbooks more often than not add rather than reduce content. In a balancing act we excluded some material. Victims were the sections on multi-year expenditure planning and the South African Government's medium-term expenditure framework which were included in Chapter 16 (Sections 16.7.2 and 16.7.3) of the first edition.

Plan and outline of the book

We have three objectives with this book:
- To provide South African students with an opportunity to study public economics with reference to South African institutions and practices, rather than having to study overseas textbooks which use examples pertaining to other countries.
- To teach public economics as a field representing the dynamic interaction and tension between macro- and micro-economic considerations, rather than only as applied microeconomics, as is found in most textbooks.
- To explain public economics with reference to the enormous challenges posed by South Africa's constitutional change in 1994 and the country's (re)integration into the global economy.

The book is divided into five main parts. **Part I** deals with various perspectives (mostly theoretical) on the **role of government** in the economy from a theoretical perspective. We begin in Chapter 1 with an introduction to the study field of public economics, in which we also discuss the nature of the public sector in South Africa. In Chapter 2 we explain the rationale for the role of government in the economy in terms of market failure, and distinguish between the allocative, distributive and stabilisation roles of government. The next two Chapters (3 and 4) examine the different dimensions of the government's allocative role, focusing on the nature of public goods, externalities and imperfect competition. Chapter 5 deals with inequality as a type of market failure and examines criteria for government intervention. Chapter 6 discusses the institutions and mechanisms of public (or social) choice and examines their efficiency and equity properties.

In **Part II**, which deals with **public expenditure**, we first discuss the phenomenon of public expenditure growth in South Africa (Chapter 7) with reference to international experience. Theories of expenditure growth are studied with a view to determining their explanatory value for South Africa. We also study the positive impact of public expenditure on economic growth, with reference to both Keynesian economics and new growth theory. The title of this chapter is thus deliberately ambiguous. Chapter 8 focuses on expenditure efficiency and the nature and use of cost-benefit analysis.

A major part of this book is devoted to **taxation (Part III)**. In Chapter 9 we examine the principles of taxation and equity, before we focus specifically on tax efficiency and related aspects of tax reform (Chapter 10). We then analyse different types of taxes, placing the emphasis on both theory and the South African experience: taxes on income (Chapter 11), taxation of wealth (Chapter 12), taxes on goods and services (Chapter 13) and benefit taxation, tax dedication and user fees (Chapter 14).

In South Africa the debate on fiscal policy and the role of government in the economy has been strongly influenced by two seemingly opposing forces. On the one hand there are severe demands on the fiscus to deal with poverty, unemployment and the skew income distribution. On the other hand there are severe constraints imposed on the fiscus by the need to maintain macroeconomic stability and at the same time promote sustained economic growth within a very competitive global economy. In **Part IV (fiscal and social policy)** we capture this debate and spell out the development of policies at the macro level, as well as sectoral policies which are sometimes referred to as social policies in books on public policy (e.g. with regard to welfare and housing). Chapter 15 deals with fiscal and social policy issues pertaining to poverty, socioeconomic development and the distribution of income in South Africa. This is not such an unusual theme for a textbook on public economics if one thinks how important these issues are in a developing country such as

South Africa and how much time politicians and government officials spend having to come up with solutions to this challenge. Economists cannot leave these issues to be dealt with by public administrators, sociologists, political scientists and engineers. The other two chapters, public debt (Chapter 16) and fiscal policy and the national budget (Chapter 17), are particularly pertinent to the second objective of this book, namely to highlight the dynamic interaction and tension between macro- and microeconomic considerations.

The last part (**Part V**) deals with **intergovernmental fiscal relations**. In the sole chapter of this part (Chapter 18) we discuss the theoretical issues pertaining to fiscal federalism. We focus specifically on the structure of government as embodied in the Constitution and the implications for inter-governmental fiscal relations in South Africa.

The book contains material that may be more than can be digested in a semester course at under-graduate level. If public economics is presented as a theoretical course in applied microeconomics, the focus could be on Parts I, II and III and Chapter 16. If the course designer is looking for a good mix of theory and practice, Parts IV and V are a must, and one could then scale down by omitting Chapters 8 and 14.

Throughout the book we have tried to present factual information about public economics in South Africa in relation to theory and international experience, rather than as separate and dull descriptions of statistical trends and superficial features. We trust that this will enhance the relevance of both empirical observation and theoretical understanding.

Our educational approach is pretty straightforward. We explain public economics theory to students with a basic understanding of macroeconomics and microeconomics at the undergraduate level. We make extensive use of diagrams and very little of mathematics. Each chapter begins with an aim and a number of study objectives. The student should use them to maintain a focus on what is essential in the chapter. We highlight important concepts in bold in the text and list them at the end of each chapter. Each chapter also contains a list of self-assessment exercises at the end which the student can do to test his or her understanding of the material. A comprehensive literature list is included at the end of the book, containing sources consulted and references which the serious reader may wish to consult.

Acknowledgements

Many keen contributors have made this book possible. We are particularly grateful to Betsy Stoltz and Rejane Woodroffe who assisted with chapters 8 and 11 respectively of the first edition.

The various associate authors were pillars of support in their professionalism and dedication. We are proud to have been associated with such a team of experts. A sincere word of thanks to various colleagues, lecturers and students who read and commented on parts of this book.

Philip Black
Estian Calitz
Tjaart Steenekamp

Contributors

Philip Black

Visiting Professor of Economics, University of Stellenbosch and University of the Western Cape and Research Director, Africa Institute for Policy Analysis (AIPA).

Estian Calitz

Professor of Economics, University of Stellenbosch; former Professor of Economics, University of South Africa, former Visiting Professor of Economics, Rand Afrikaans University; and former Director-General of Finance, South African Government

Tjaart Steenekamp

Professor of Economics and Leader of the Certificate Programme in Economics and Public Finance, University of South Africa

Tania Ajam

Director, Applied Fiscal Research Centre, School of Economics, University of Cape Town and CEO of AFREC (Pty) Ltd

Jack Heyns

Retired Professor of Economics, Rand Afrikaans University

Krige Siebrits

Senior lecturer in Economics, University of South Africa

Servaas van der Berg

Professor of Economics, University of Stellenbosch

Theo van der Merwe

Professor of Economics, University of South Africa

PART ONE

Perspectives on the role of government in the economy

Chapter one
Estian Calitz

The public sector in the economy

The aim of this chapter is to demarcate the study field of public economics with reference to key issues that face the South African economy. The nature, size and composition of the South African public sector are discussed briefly, as well as the interaction between the public, household and private sectors of the economy.

Once you have studied this chapter, you should be able to
- list key issues confronting the South African government regarding its role in the economy;
- distinguish between the main institutional categories of the public sector;
- discuss the salient features and trends of the size and composition of the South African public sector;
- discuss various aspects of the relationship between the public sector and the rest of the economy.

1.1 Introduction

In economics we study the way in which society chooses to allocate its scarce resources in order to satisfy a multitude of needs and wants. These resources are both scarce and have alternative uses, so that it becomes necessary for society to prioritise its needs and ensure that they are met in a declining order of importance. The income or budget constraint necessitates these

choices. In the process, needs are converted into effective demand and resources are allocated and used accordingly. We are therefore interested in the allocation of resources and in the distribution of the benefits derived from resource use. In public economics we study the impact of the public (government) sector on resource allocation and distribution.

In the mixed economy, the balance between the supply of and demand for resources is pursued either through the market system or the political system. In the market system prices are the equilibrating mechanism in the interplay between supply and demand which, in turn, are determined by such factors as the preferences and income of consumers, the costs of production factors, and the prevailing technology. Needs which cannot be or are not satisfied via the market system are channelled through the political process. The equilibrating mechanism between supply and demand in the political system is the ballot box; the price is the tax which people pay.

A large portion (more than a third) of South Africa's total resource use is channelled through the political process, that is, excluding the resource use in the private sector which is, of course, indirectly influenced by the political environment. The efficiency and equity with which resources are allocated in the public sector and the impact of political decisions on private economic behaviour are therefore of paramount importance for the economic performance of the country.

On 27 April 1994 South Africa became a unified democratic state under a new constitution. The new Government was faced with a number of daunting challenges reflecting the nature of South African society, its history and the diverse expectations of its citizens. These challenges have important implications for public economics and fiscal policy in South Africa. Touching on them here provides an early glimpse of the type of issues covered in this study of public economics in South Africa.

1.1.1 Legacy of the past

The South African economy has performed poorly over the past two decades. Real economic growth has not kept up with the population growth: real per capita gross domestic product (GDP) has declined by an average rate of about 0,7 per cent per annum between 1980 and 2000. Income per capita has thus been declining in real terms and, broadly defined, more than one third of the labour force is unemployed. South Africa also has one of the most uneven distributions of income ever measured internationally.

Poverty is indeed the most pressing feature of the South African economic landscape. The lack of job opportunities among millions of previously disenfranchised citizens of the new South Africa is partly the result of statutory and other regulatory measures that inhibited occupational and geographical labour mobility in the past. Likewise, the allocation of government resources on a per capita basis has historically been very skew, resulting in many of the poor having only limited access to basic social services. A large proportion of the population has had experience of undernourishment, inadequate housing and poor education, and of only limited access to basic public services such as primary health care. Generally speaking, millions of people are ill equipped to participate meaningfully in the modern (formal) sector of the economy. Under these circumstances the need for appropriate policy intervention is evidently urgent. Faced with high expectations of the citizenry, the new Government has had little choice *inter alia* but to turn to fiscal policy in an attempt to tackle the problem effectively.

The share of government in the economy has been increasing steadily over the past three decades. By the time of the first full democratic elections in 1994, many experts felt that the total tax burden, the national budget deficit (or borrowing needs) and the public debt were too high to achieve sustainable economic growth and development. Worrisome features of government finances at the time included the increasing arrears in tax collection at the national level and the tendency for government expenditure to exceed budgeted figures.

The growth of the government's current expenditure was such that it crowded out public investment, that is, ever decreasing funds were available for government investment in social and physical infrastructure such as schools, hospitals and roads. The growth in public employment, which constitutes the main component of current expenditure, is a source of alarm. Between 1990 and 1999 the number of employment opportunities in the general government sector (i.e. excluding public sector business enterprises and corporations) was 16 per cent higher than in the previous ten years. During this period jobs in the non-agricultural formal private sector dropped by 7.5 per cent. This could hardly be described as the story of a thriving economy!

1.1.2 A fresh start

The constitutional change in South Africa occurred at a time when the acquired role and functions of governments were being reviewed across the globe. A growing consensus was emerging that the efficient management of developed and developing economies required smaller rather than bigger budget deficits and lower rather than higher levels of public debt. There was also general agreement that fiscal constraints required a thorough revision of the basic functions for which government should be responsible. Along with the international shift towards market-based economies that followed the demise of communism and the command economies of Eastern Europe, key ingredients of economic restructuring included the privatisation of activities hitherto undertaken by the state, a total revision of the role and functions of the state, and a concomitant reprioritisation of government expenditure. It is important to note that the emphasis was on how the public sector could be restructured so as to free more resources for the development function of government, without jeopardising macroeconomic stability or increasing the share of government in the economy – preferably even reducing it.

Within South Africa these global developments filtered into the public debate on the future role of the government in the new South African state. This issue was fiercely debated in the process that led to the formulation of the new constitution. What kind of economic system was to develop in South Africa? What should be the basic rules of the game (or principles) regarding rights to the acquisition, use, improvement and ownership of the country's economic resources? What protection would there be for private property rights? What constituted basic government services and would citizens enjoy a right to be provided such services? Would such rights have to be qualified by what the government could afford and how was such affordability to be determined? How should the tax system be designed in order to be efficient and just? Should the new government accept responsibility for the country's foreign debt that accumulated under the previous constitutional dispensation and

also for the public debt incurred in the past? Should all decision-making be centralised in the national government or would a decentralised system of governance be more conducive to improving efficiency of resource use and equity of resource distribution in the country? What powers should be given to provinces and local governments? How should the processes of budgeting and decision-making about public resources be undertaken by governments at all levels? How should the preferences of the public be determined and reflected in decision-making in the various departments of the national, provincial and local governments? These and many related questions characterised the constitutional debate as well as the subsequent restructuring of the public sector, which is still taking place.

Countries seldom get the opportunity to thoroughly revamp all their institutions and policies at once but this has been one of the main features of the South African experience in the 1990s. The restructuring of the public sector is very important to the country's future economic success. There is hardly a more opportune and interesting time in which to study public economics in South Africa. The restructuring of the public sector affects all groups in society. It affects the way in which business is conducted in the domestic private sector, as well as the nature of our trade and investment relations with the rest of the world. It affects the nature of public goods and services to be provided by the different tiers of government. It affects the individuals and groups of individuals who are to benefit from public goods and services as well as the way in which the tax or financing burden is distributed among individuals and firms. It changes the way in which consultation takes place between politicians and the electorate and between politicians and various sectional interest groups in society, be it interest groups in business, organised labour or civil society. Finally, it affects the basis on which employees are appointed and managed in the public sector and the nature of interaction between politicians and bureaucrats and between bureaucrats and the clients of government.

It should be clear that decisions on these questions cannot be taken by government officials alone. Public choices are the domain of the public in general, which includes the electorate (voters), politicians, trade unionists, business people and other interest groups. The behaviour and interaction of all these interest groups with respect to the allocation and use of economic resources thus constitute an important part of the study of public economics.

1.1.3 The study field of public economics

Public economics is the study of the nature, principles and economic consequences of the expenditure, taxation, financing and regulatory actions undertaken in the non-profit making government sector of the economy.

Let us examine the elements of this definition. Note firstly the main areas of decision-making: expenditure, taxation, financing and regulation. These are also called the **instruments of fiscal policy**. In public economics we study the nature and impact of these instruments. The first three entail the procurement by the state of private funds and the spending of these funds. In economic terms the use of these instruments constitutes the direct mobilisation and allocation of scarce resources. Examples would be the spending of tax income on primary health care and borrowing to build an irrigation dam or a highway. **Regulation**, by contrast, entails enacting a law or administratively proclaiming an enforceable instruction that leads to a different allocation of private resources than would apply in the absence of such government intervention. The allocation of resources is now influenced indirectly. An example is a regulation by government, which forces the manufacturers of motor vehicles to install platinum catalysts in the exhaust pipes of vehicles to reduce the emission of carbon monoxide.

Different types of expenditure, taxation, government borrowing and government debt can be distinguished. In taxation, for example, we distinguish between taxes on income, wealth and goods and services. The economic consequences differ between categories of taxation or expenditure. A tax on wealth (e.g. a property tax) will affect different people in society than would a value-added tax on red meat. In other words, the distributional effects differ. The choice of a particular tax therefore depends on how the government wants to change the distribution of income or wealth in the economy, or on how an efficient allocation of resources is pursued. Several important fiscal criteria have been developed by economists on which to base economic decisions in the public sector and which may be applied when recommendations on taxes or expenditure allocations are formulated. These governing criteria are derived from the two concepts of efficiency and equity, which are paramount and distinguishing features of economics.

The study of the nature and economic consequences of decisions fall in the realm of positive economics, posing questions such as: if I take step *a* (e.g. raise income tax), what will happen to *b* (e.g. the supply of labour in the economy)? The development of criteria, on the other hand, has to do with normative economics, focusing on what ought to be. For example, if I want *c* (e.g. a more even distribution of income), what should step *d* be (e.g. what type and level of taxation should be introduced)? As part of the latter, public economics considers such diverse questions as the rationale for government involvement in the economy and how political decisions should be taken (i.e. what kind of voting system should be used) to ensure efficiency and equity in the allocation of resources.

The term **non-profit making** signifies the

absence of profit maximisation as the leading motive, or one of the leading motives, in decision-making on the mobilisation and allocation of resources. The absence of the profit motive means that other criteria for decision-making have to be employed. We will see that the nature of public goods is such that their supply does not allow for decentralised price determination in a competitive market economy. Note that the government is not the only non-profit making sector in the economy. Many welfare, church and service organisations exist as non-profit organisations. These institutions are often referred to as **non-governmental organisations** (NGOs).

Does our definition of public economics include a study of **government business enterprises** (such as the National Road Fund) and **public corporations** (such as Eskom)? If these entities were driven strictly by the profit motive, they would not fit our definition. However, as long as political appointees serve on or control the board of such entities, as long as these entities render certain socio-economic services on behalf of the government and rely on government financial support, and/or as long as they behave in a monopolistic manner, they are not pure private institutions. They then operate in the vague area between the government and the private sector. In countries such as South Africa that have embarked on privatisation, public enterprises often find themselves in transit between a public entity and a private company. Consequently their exact position on the spectrum between public and private is not easy to pinpoint, so that the criteria in terms of which to study their behaviour are not that clear. In our study of public economics we do not include a separate section on these kinds of activities. We do, however, analyse aspects of their functioning when we discuss topics such as imperfect competition, user charges, privatisation and macroeconomic stabilisation.

1.2 The public sector in South Africa

From our discussion in the previous section it is clear that public economics studies a wide range of diverse activities. In order to structure our thoughts, we take a look at the composition and size of the public sector in South Africa and briefly review the relationship between the public and the private sector.

1.2.1 Composition of the public sector

What are the constituent institutional components of the **public sector**? We present them in Figure 1.1 as a set of concentric squares. Our constitution specifies three levels or spheres of government. The **central (or national) government** (see the inner square in Figure 1.1) consists of all the national government departments, as well as various **extra-budgetary institutions**, such as the Council for Scientific and Industrial Research (CSIR), the Human Sciences Research Council (HSRC), universities and technikons. These entities are distinguished from general government departments on account of their access to additional funds over and above those appropriated through

Figure 1.1 The public sector in South Africa

the national budget. (Note that in the national accounts the universities and technikons are in fact classified as part of the public sector. The additional funds stem from user charges, levies and other non-tax income.)

At the second and third tiers of government, South Africa has nine **provincial governments** and 284 **local authorities**, as shown in the second concentric square in Figure 1.1. Together with the central government, the general departments of provinces and local authorities are constituent components of the **general government**. For the most part, general government thus represents the non-profit activities of the public sector. The allocation of resources is determined by political considerations and financed through the tax system (or loans which have to be repaid out of taxes at a later stage). The final component of the general government comprises business enterprises such as the National Road Fund at the national government level or the trade departments (for electricity, water, transport, etc.) in the local government sphere.

The next category of public entities (see the outer concentric square in Figure 1.1) consists of public corporations such as Eskom, Mossgas, the South African Broadcasting Corporation (SABC), Telkom and Transnet. These activities are managed much more along business lines and in the case of corporations like Eskom and Telkom, decisions are often taken on the same basis as in the private sector. Since and as long as these corporations are subject to government control, however, either in the form of shareholding or the appointment of directors, they are classified as part of the public sector. Note that should any public-sector activity or body (or a part of it) be privatised, it will thereafter be classified as part of the private sector.

To sum up: we refer to the three tiers of government (i.e. the general services and business enterprises of national, provincial and local government) as the general government, and to the combination of general government and public corporations as the public sector.

1.2.2 Size of the public sector

The size of the public sector differs according to the indicator used. If we are interested in the size of the burden, which the government imposes on current taxpayers, we may use the total tax income of the general government as indicator and express it as a percentage of the gross domestic product (or national income). By this criterion the government's share in the South African economy in 2001 was 27,3 per cent. We know, however, that government expenditure is not only financed through tax revenue, but by means of non-tax income (such as dividend and property income, mining leases and administrative fees) and borrowing (loans) as well. We will thus get a better picture of the total amount of **resource use** by (i.e. the final demand by, or exhaustive expenditure of) government in any year if we measure its size from the expenditure side. From Table 1.1 we note that the total spending of the public sector (consumption and investment spending – or capital formation – valued at market prices) has increased from an average of 20,9 per cent of gross domestic product over the period 1960-1969 to an average of 24,1 per cent for the period 1990-1999. In 2000 this ratio amounted to 21,2 per cent.

Even this is not the complete picture. Not all of government expenditure is in the form of final demand for goods and services (i.e. exhaustive expenditure). The government also makes transfer payments (subsidies, current transfers, interest on public debt) to targeted beneficiaries or entities. These are called non-exhaustive government expenditure. The government mobilises the resources, but they are used by the recipients who exercise the final demand. If we add interest payments and transfers to the household, business and foreign sector, we

Table 1.1 Average size of the South African public sector by different measures, selected periods (current prices as percentage of GDP[a])

Measure			1960	1960-69	1970-79	1980-89	1990-99	2001
Taxes (direct & indirect)			14,2	15,8	19,1	22,9	25,1	27,3
Resource use (1) of which			17,8	20,9	28,1	27,0	24,1	21,2
General government consumption			9,5	11,3	14,6	18,0	19,2	18,0
Investment[b]	Total		8,3	9,6	13,5	9,0	4,9	3,2
	of which General government		7,0	7,6	8,7	5,3	2,6	1,8
	Public corporations		1,3	2,0	4,8	3,7	2,3	1,4
Transfer payment (2) of which			3,9	4,2	5,9	8,9	11,5	10,6
Interest on public debt			0,7	1,0	1,9	4,0	5,8	5,5
Subsidies & current transfers			3,2	3,2	4,0	4,9	5,7	5,1
Total public sector resource mobilisation (1) + (2) of which			21,7	25,1	34,0	35,9	35,6	31,8
General government			20,4	23,1	29,2	32,2	33,3	30,5
Public corporations			1,3	2,0	4,8	3,7	2,3	1,4

Notes: Due to rounding, totals may not add up.
[a] National accounting figures.
[b] Gross fixed investment or capital formation

Source: South African Reserve Bank, Quarterly Bulletin, various issues.

get a picture of the extent of **resource mobilisation** by the government. In 2000 the South African public sector was instrumental in mobilising 31,8 per cent of the national resources.[1]

Selected changes in the composition of public sector expenditure are shown in Figure 1.2.

Because of the diverse nature of government activities and the corresponding differences in the factors that determine the allo-cation and distribution processes in the public sector, we are not only interested in the aggregate size of the public sector, but also in its constituent components. Note in particular the diverging trends of general government consumption expenditure and public investment, and the rising share of transfer payments (especially interest on public debt) as a percentage of GDP. These are recurrent themes in this book.

1. The figures in Table 1.1 pertain to current transfers only. Capital transfers, which were not readily available, are too small to significantly change the resource mobilisation figures. For example, in 1998/99 the capital transfer amounted to R1,2 bn. This would have added only 0,2 percentage points to the ratio in calendar year 1998.

Figure 1.2 Composition of South African public expenditure

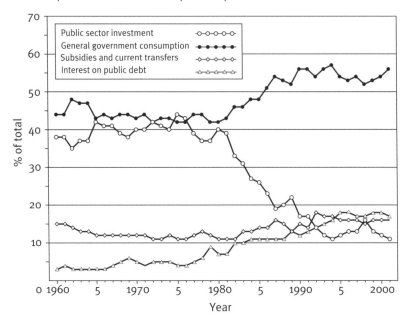

1.2.3 The relationship between the public and the private sector

What is the relationship between the public sector and the rest of the economy? A number of important aspects of this relationship may be identified with reference to the familiar circular flow of income, expenditure and goods and services (see Figure 1.3).

- Government is a supplier of public goods and services. Households and businesses pay for these goods and services through taxes, which the government then uses to acquire factors of production and purchase private goods and services (as intermediate inputs) in the process of producing public goods and services. Government departments of course use outputs of other departments as intermediate inputs as well. Government activities are relatively labour intensive, thus salaries and wages constitute the largest input cost.
- The size of government in the mixed economy is such that its purchase of goods and services exerts important influences on the economy. At the sectoral level, for instance, government spending is often decisive for the construction and engineering sectors. Often private investment cannot be undertaken unless the necessary public infrastructure is in place (e.g. roads and electricity networks). At the macroeconomic level, changes in the aggregate level and composition of government expenditure are important factors in determining economic stability and growth. Excessive expenditure growth can, for example, be inflationary or crowd out private investment, thus retarding economic growth.
- The way in which government finances its expenditure also has important economic consequences. The kind of taxes used and the rates levied influence the well being (utility) of individuals and the decisions by private businesses regarding the allocation of resources in the private sector. The tax system can promote or obstruct efficiency and equity.

Figure 1.3 The government in the circular flow of income, expenditure and goods and services

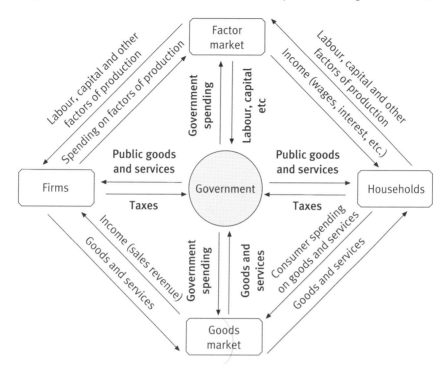

- If there is a budget imbalance (surplus or deficit), the government exercises an influence on the balance between saving (S) and investment (I), or on the balance of payments (i.e. the balance between exports (X) and imports (Z)) This is shown in Figure 1.4. In national accounting terms, a budget imbalance (i.e. $G \neq T$) is reflected in either an imbalance between private investment (I) and saving (S), that is, $S \neq I$ (internal imbalance) or an imbalance between exports (X) and imports (Z), that is, $Z \neq X$ (external or balance of payments disequilibrium).
- If there is a budget deficit, for example, tax revenue (T) is less than government expenditure (G), or $T<G$, and the government has to borrow. The size of its deficit and the way in which it is financed is very important for macroeconomic stability, depending on one's view of the impact of budget deficits on the economy. Government borrowing occurs via the financial markets and represents a use of either domestic (S_d or foreign savings $\frac{S_f}{c}$), as shown in Figure 1.4. (In Figure 1.4 T, S and M represent leakages from the income-expenditure circular flow, while G, I and X are additions to or injections into the circular flow.) Part of the savings may find their way into financing government investment, which is included in government expenditure (G). In the case of a budget surplus, the government supplements the supply of savings in the economy.
- While the government can influence the course of the economy, it is also extensively affected by what happens in the economy. In an economic recession, for instance, government revenue falls or grows at a slower rate. This may impair its ability to provide public services, especially if its

Figure 1.4 The impact of a budget imbalance on the financial sector in the context of the circular flow of income and expenditure

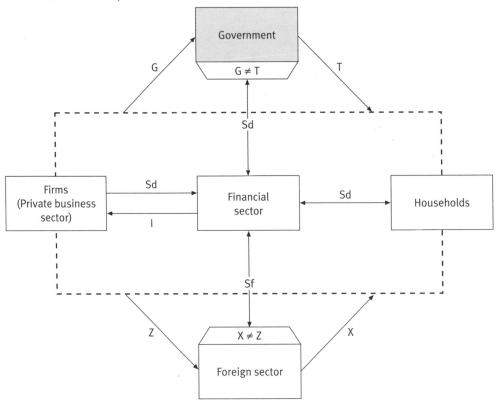

debt or budget deficit is already relatively high. Government also bears the brunt of its own decisions via their adverse effect on the economy, such as when high budget deficits result in higher interest rates, thereby increasing the government's interest bill.

Important concepts

central (or national) government
extra-budgetary institutions
general government
government business enterprises
instruments of fiscal policy
local government
non-governmental organizations (NGOs)
non-profit making

provincial government
public corporations
public economics
public sector
regulation
resource mobilisation by the public
   sector
resource use by the public sector

Self-assessment exercises

1.1 Distinguish between
   • Positive and normative economics
   • General government and public sector
   • Resource use and resource mobilisation

1.2 List the key issues which confronted the ANC government when it took office under the 1994 Constitution.

1.3 Briefly review the salient changes in the size and composition of the South African public sector during the past few decades. Which of the changes, in your opinion, are incompatible with the requirements of a thriving economy?

1.4 Give an overview of the various dimensions of the relationship between the public sector and the rest of the economy.

Chapter two

Phillip Black

Benchmark model of the economy: positive and normative approaches

We begin this part of our book with a brief review of the neoclassical theory of general equilibrium – our benchmark model. It is a benchmark model precisely because it does not presume to provide an accurate description of the real world. Rather, it should be seen as a frame of reference, or a starting point, which helps us to better understand and appreciate real-world problems. As we shall see in the chapters that follow, the model can in fact accommodate a large variety of alternative assumptions, and it is this built-in flexibility that enables it to yield alternative predictions that bring us closer to the real world.

Section 2.1 of this chapter gives a brief description of the basic assumptions of our benchmark model, while Sections 2.2 and 2.3 discuss the equilibrium properties of the model. These three sections thus provide a vision of how the world ought to work, and as such can be viewed as a good example of what some commentators refer to as "normative" economics. In Section 2.4 we begin to compare our normative model with the real world, and in so doing, enter the domain of "positive" economics. This is done by introducing the reader to the concept of "market failure" – a generic term describing broad categories of human behaviour which deviate from the ideal assumptions of the benchmark model. Sections 2.5 and 2.6 deal with the role of the public sector in coming to grips with these market failures and related real-world problems.

> Once you have studied this chapter, you should be able to
> - identify the critical assumptions of the two-sector model;
> - define what is meant by a Pareto-optimal allocation of resources;
> - articulate the three conditions for a general equilibrium;
> - distinguish between allocative efficiency, X-efficiency and "dynamic" efficiency (or economic growth);
> - discuss the broad categories of market failure;
> - explain the allocative, distributive and stabilisation functions of government;
> - distinguish between direct and indirect forms of government intervention.

2.1 Basic assumptions of the benchmark model

Our benchmark model is based on a host of patently unrealistic assumptions – set out in the accompanying box. The individual consumer or producer is assumed to be fully informed about the economy, unaffected by the actions of other consumers or producers, completely mobile in the occupational and spatial sense of the word, and always striving to maximise his or her own utility or profit within perfectly competitive markets.

Any exogenous disturbance will merely set in motion a series of more or less instantaneous adjustments that will automatically return the system to a stable equilibrium. Indeed, in such a blissful state there would be few economic problems to speak of and little need to write this and many of the subsequent chapters.

One does not have to be an economist to realise that real-world economies do not behave in the way that the neoclassical model predicts. Perhaps the only real market that comes close to it is an auction, where suppliers and demanders all come together to reveal their preferences to an independent and knowledgeable auctioneer who establishes the equilibrium price **before** any trading takes place. In the neoclassical model we simply assume the existence of such a knowledgeable and omnipresent auctioneer – also called the "Walrasian auctioneer" – and give him or her the task to establish equilibrium prices in all markets, more or less simultaneously.

Before looking at the model itself – in Sections 2.2 and 2.3 below – it is perhaps worth noting that a theory does not necessarily stand or fall by its assumptions. To be sure, if one wanted to explain and predict some real world phenomenon, assumptions are important, as are the functional relations used to make predictions and test the validity of the theory. But if one's aim is merely to develop a normative theory – such as our benchmark model of resource allocation – it is hardly appropriate to judge it in terms of the realism of its assumptions.

Box 2.1

Assumptions of the two-sector model

1. There are two individuals, A and B, who are the suppliers of two factors of production, the producers of two commodities, and the consumers of both these commodities – all at the same time! Each individual is initially endowed with fixed quantities of the two factors, capital (K) and labour (L), which are both used in the production of the two commodities, X and Y, both of which are consumed by the two individuals.

2. There are no external effects in consumption and both individuals have fixed tastes – as reflected in the existence of smooth and well behaved individual indifference curves. The latter are convex with respect to the origin, cannot intersect and exhibit diminishing marginal rates of substitution.

3. The two production processes are both characterised by unlimited factor substitutability, diminishing marginal productvities and constant returns to scale. The latter assumption rules out internal (dis)economies of scale, while there are also no external costs or benefits in production. These assumptions together ensure the existence of smooth and well behaved isoquants.

4. As consumers, A and B maximise utility, and, as producers, they maximise profit. Both are perfectly informed about their respective environments, and are also perfectly mobile in the occupational and spatial sense of the word.

5. The commodity and factor markets are all perfectly competitive, which implies that each market behaves "as if" there were a large number of individual demanders and suppliers involved, none of whom can influence price.

These assumptions together ensure the existence, uniqueness and stability of a general equilibrium.

2.2 The benchmark model and allocative efficiency

Economic efficiency is conventionally defined in terms of both allocative efficiency and technical efficiency (or X-efficiency), and can also refer to a country's ability to achieve economic growth. In this section we confine ourselves to allocative efficiency only, leaving our discussion of X-efficiency and economic growth for the next section.

Allocative efficiency refers to a situation in which the limited resources of a country are allocated in accordance with the wishes of its consumers. An allocatively efficient economy produces an "optimal mix" of commodities. Under conditions of perfect competition, the optimal output mix results from the fact that utility-maximising consumers respond to prices which reflect the true costs of production, or the marginal social costs. It is thus evident that allocative efficiency involves an interaction between the consumption activities of individual consumers and the production activities of producers.

In an economy with no public sector, and in which there are no consumption or production externalities, allocative efficiency in the general equilibrium context requires the simultaneous concurrence of three familiar conditions. These are briefly discussed below.

- Condition 1. Production activities must be Pareto optimal. This means that it should not be possible to increase the output of any one commodity without thereby bringing about a decrease in the output of at least one other commodity; or put differently, in a non-optimal situation it is always possible to increase the output of one commodity without thereby decreasing the output of other commodities. In terms of the familiar two-sector model, this condition requires that each of our two sectors, X and Y, should maximise output subject to its own cost constraint. In figures 2.1(a) and 2.1(b), each sector does exactly that. At points r and s each sector employs a combination of the two inputs, capital (K) and labour (L), for which the marginal rate of technical substitution (given by the slope of the isoquant), equals the corresponding factor price ratio, $\frac{w}{r}$ (given by the slope of the isocost); that is,

$$MRTS^x{}_{lk} = \frac{MPLx}{MPKx} = \frac{w}{r} \qquad [2.1]$$

$$MRTS^y{}_{lk} = \frac{MPLy}{MPKy} = \frac{w}{r} \qquad [2.2]$$

where $MRTS^y{}_{lk}$ is the marginal rate of technical substitution of labour for capital in sector X, MPL^x and MPK^x are the marginal productivities of labour and capital in sector X respectively, and w and r are the market-determined equilibrium factor prices; and similarly for sector Y (equation [2.2]).

Under perfectly competitive conditions, each sector will face the same equilibrium factor prices, so that

$$MRTS^x{}_{lk} = \frac{w}{r} = MRTS^y{}_{lk} \qquad [2.3]$$

Figure 2.1 Individual sector equilibria

(a)
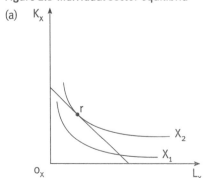

(b)
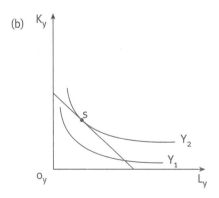

Figure 2.2 Edgeworth-Bowley box diagram

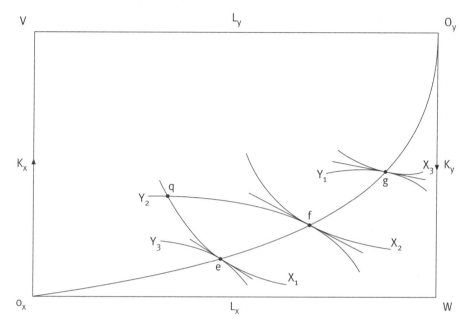

Equation [2.3] implies, inter alia, that the economy is operating at some point on its contract curve for production. This is illustrated in Figure 2.2 above in the form of the familiar Edgeworth-Bowley box diagram. The dimensions of the box are determined by the total (fixed) supplies of our two factors of production: total capital supply is given by either of the two vertical axes, 0_xV or 0_yW, and total labour supply by either of the two horizontal axes, 0_xW or 0_yV. Sector X's production function, or isoquant map, is shown with respect to the Southwestern corner, 0_x, and sector Y's with respect to the North-eastern corner, 0_y. Only three out of a large number of isoquants are indicated for each of the two sectors, i.e. X_1, X_2 and X_3 for sector X, and Y_1, Y_2 and Y_3 in the case of sector Y. The next step is to find all those points where the two sectors' respective isoquants are tangent, e.g. points e, f and g. If this exercise is repeated many times, we can derive the contract curve for production – $0_x 0_y$ in Figure 2.2.

It is important to note that each point on the contract curve represents a Pareto-optimal allocation of the two resources, K and L, between the two sectors, X and Y: at point e (or f or g), it is not possible for either sector to increase its output without the other sector having to cut back its own output. This is clearly not true of a point such as q where either of the two sectors can increase its output without causing a reduction in the output of the other. Point q is not on the contract curve and, as discussed in the next section, represents an "X-inefficient" outcome.

Not only does perfect competition ensure that our two sectors will operate at the same point on the contract curve – e.g. e, f or g in Figure 2.2 – but it also implies that the economy will find itself at a point on the production possibility curve (PPC). The latter is simply the flip side of the above contract curve: it brings together all the output combinations along the contract curve within a more conventional diagram – as is shown in Figure 2.3

below. There the PPC is depicted as the curve MN, on which the points E, F and G represent the same output combinations as their equivalents on the contract curve in Figure 2.2.

The slope (or rate of change) of the PPC in Figure 2.3 is given by $\frac{\Delta Y}{\Delta X}$, and is known as the marginal rate of product transformation, or $MRPT_{xy}$. The latter, in turn, equals the corresponding marginal cost ratio – which is easily proved with the aid of Figure 2.3.

Consider a small movement from point F to point h such that the resources gained by sector X equal the resources lost by sector Y. With factor prices assumed unchanged, this means that the increase in the total cost of sector X will equal the decrease in the total cost of sector Y; or $\Delta TCx = -\Delta TCy$. Now, since

$$MCx = \frac{\Delta TC_x}{\Delta X} \text{ and } MC_y = \frac{\Delta TC_y}{\Delta Y} \quad [2.4]$$

or

$$\Delta X = \frac{\Delta TC_x}{MC_x} \text{ and } \Delta Y = \frac{\Delta TC_y}{MC_y} \quad [2.4a]$$

therefore

$$\frac{\Delta Y}{\Delta X} = MRPT_{xy} = \frac{MC_x}{MC_y} \quad [2.4b]$$

where MC_x is the marginal cost of production in sector X. Since under perfect competition each sector will ensure that its own marginal cost equals the corresponding market price, that is, $MC_x = P_x$ and $MC_y = P_y$, we have,

$$MRPT_{xy} = \frac{MCx}{MCy} = \frac{Px}{Py} \quad [2.5]$$

which is given by the slope of a tangent drawn to a point on the PPC – for example, the slope of line tt' at point F in Figure 2.3.

The first condition thus implies a point on the PPC, according to which it is impossible to increase the output of either of the two sectors without thereby

Figure 2.3 Production possibility curve (PPC)

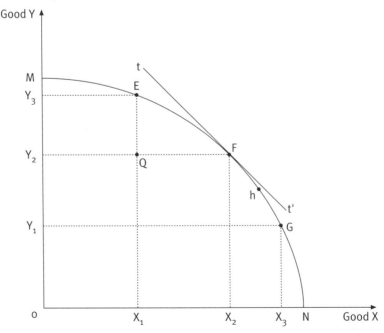

decreasing that of the other. Under perfect competition, price will equal marginal cost in each sector, so that the MRPT, which equals the marginal cost ratio for the two sectors, also equals the corresponding price ratio.

- Condition 2. Economic efficiency in consumption must occur in such a way that no interpersonal re-allocation of commodities can increase the utility of either of the two consumers, A or B, without thereby decreasing the utility of the other. Each consumer will thus maximise utility subject to his or her own budget constraint; or choose that commodity mix for which the marginal rate of substitution (or the slope of the indifference curve) equals the corresponding commodity price ratio, $\frac{Px}{Py}$ (or the slope of the budget line); that is,

$$MRS^a{}_{xy} = \frac{Px}{Py} = MRS^b{}_{xy} \qquad [2.6]$$

where $MRS^a{}_{xy}$ is consumer A's marginal rate of substitution of commodity X for commodity Y, and P_x and P_y are the corresponding equilibrium prices.

Consider Figure 2.4 (which is similar to Figure 2.3) and assume that the econo-my is producing the Pareto-optimal combination given by point F on the PPC. Our second condition simply means that the two individuals will together consume 0_aX_2 of good X and 0_aY_2 of good Y, and in the process maximise their respective utilities subject to their respective budget constraints. This is shown by the box diagram for consumption indicated as the area $0_aY_2FX_2$ in Figure 2.4, and by the associated contract curve for consumption, 0_aF (= 0_b), along which the indifference curves of the two consumers are tangent; as before, each point along the contract curve for consumption represents a Pareto-optimal allocation of the two goods, X and Y, between the two consumers, A and B.

How much each individual ends up consuming will depend on his or her tastes, or relative preferences for the two goods, and on his or her income, which will in turn depend on how much of the initial resources (K and L) he or she owns. At point F' in Figure 2.4, for example, individual A maximises her utility ($U^a{}_2$) subject to the budget constraint given by the line vv', consuming 0_aX_a of good X

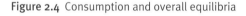

Figure 2.4 Consumption and overall equilibria

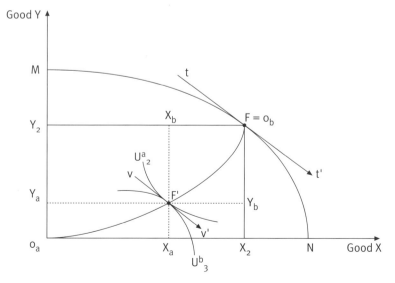

and 0_aY_a of good Y. Individual B does likewise, maximising his utility (U^b_3) subject to the budget constraint, vv', and consuming 0_bX_b of good X and 0_bY_b of good Y. Each consumer's total income is given by the distance between vv' and their respective origins, 0_a and 0_b; though both consumers face the same market determined commodity prices, P_x and P_y, the ratio of which is, of course, equal to the slope of vv'.

Pareto optimality in consumption thus implies a situation in which it is impossible to increase the utility of either of the two consumers (for example by reallocating consumer goods between them) without thereby decreasing the utility of the other.

- **Condition 3.** The third or top-level condition requires that producers and consumers achieve equilibrium simultaneously. Given that the slope of the PPC, or the $MRPT_{xy}$, equals the corresponding ratio of marginal costs, $\frac{MCx}{MCy}$, and hence also the corresponding equilibrium price ratio, our third condition can be written as:

$$MRPT_{xy} = \frac{MCx}{MCy} = \frac{Px}{Py} = MRS^a_{xy} = MRS^b_{xy} \quad [2.7]$$

indicating equality between the (marginal) rate at which each consumer is willing to substitute one commodity for the other, and the rate at which it is technically possible to do so.

Simultaneous compliance with these three conditions will ensure production of the optimal output mix – shown by the parallel lines tt' at point F and vv' at point F' in Figure 2.4 above. The slope of the line tt' equals the $MRPT_{xy}$ and the corresponding marginal cost ratio, whilst the slope of vv' equals the marginal rates of substitution for the two consumers. Points F and F' in Figure 2.4 are thus consistent with equation 2.7 above: they represent our third or top-level condition, and hence also our first and second conditions for a general equilibrium.

Point F is a **Pareto-optimal top-level equilibrium**, in the sense that it is not possible to increase the output of either of the two commodities, or the utility of either of the two consumers, without thereby reducing that of the other.

It is important to note that the precise location of the top-level point on the PPC will depend on the underlying assumptions of the model, particularly the initial distribution of resources between the two individuals, A and B. If one of the two individuals owns most of the initial capital and labour resources, and has a particularly strong relative preference for commodity Y, it stands to reason that our model will generate a top-level equilibrium lying on the PPC and close to the Y-axis in Figure 2.4.

2.3 X-Efficiency and economic growth

Technical efficiency or X-efficiency refers to a situation in which existing resources are utilised in the most efficient manner. Obtaining the maximum possible output from a given set of resources – or technically efficient production – necessarily implies a position on the PPC, such as points C_0 and S in Figure 2.5 below.

A point such as R indicates the presence of X-inefficiency. All economic inefficiencies other than allocative inefficiency fall under the term X-inefficiency. Leibenstein (1966) argued that although X-inefficiency (sometimes also termed organisational slack) derives primarily from a lack of motivation by production agents, factors such as a lack of information about market conditions, incomplete knowledge of production functions and the incomplete specification of labour contracts, can also explain the existence of X-inefficiency.

Clearly, X-efficiency alone is an insufficient measure of economic efficiency since

Figure 2.5 X-inefficiency and economic growth

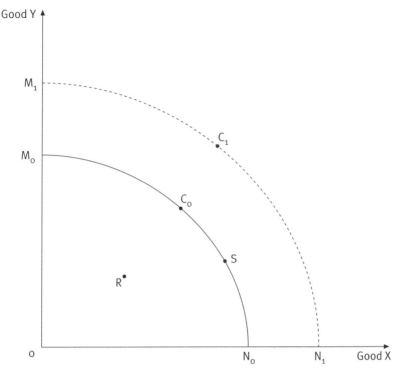

the technically efficient production of goods by itself does not necessarily reflect the needs of consumers. In common sense terms, it is pointless to produce goods efficiently if people would rather consume some other combination of goods. Put differently, X-efficiency ensures that society is on its PPC, but cannot determine where society should be on this curve.

It is possible also to define economic efficiency dynamically in terms of given increases in the quantity and/or productivity of the factors of production. The sources of growth are conventionally defined to include savings, investment in the form of both physical and human capital formation, technological inventions and innovations, and increases in the availability of labour of different skills. From a general equilibrium perspective, the net effect of sustained economic growth can be shown as an outward shift in the PPC, for example, from M_0N_0 to M_1N_1 in Figure 2.5, and by a concomitant change in the competitive equilibrium, for example, from point C_0 to C_1.

2.4 Market failure : An overview

The perfectly competitive model is nothing more than a theoretical nicety, a normative ideal against which real world conditions can be judged; and in this section we briefly distinguish between several instances of **market failure**, the most important of which are discussed in more detail in the remaining chapters of this part of the book.

2.4.1 Lack of information

Consumers and producers do not always have at their disposal the information necessary to make rational decisions. Producers may be unaware of the existence of certain resources or of the latest technologies available in their own lines of business. Similarly, consumers may be ignorant of potentially harmful properties inherent in some goods and services they consume, or of the fact that certain goods are available at lower prices than what they are currently paying for them (Bohm, 1978).

Even if consumers and producers were prepared to pay for the required information, this too would not help. It is clearly impossible for them to calculate such costs without knowing precisely what the additional information is. But if they knew the latter there would be no need to acquire it, let alone calculate the cost. They thus have no choice but to accept their lack of information as a binding constraint.

This raises the question whether governments in free societies should bear the responsibility of providing individual citizens with information for private decision-making. In some cases governments do perform this function: in South Africa, for example, virtually all consumer goods must be cleared by the South African Bureau of Standards, and must indicate their weight, mass and volume and, more recently, their ingredients, including chemical additives. On the whole, however, private institutions, being profit-driven, are better at acquiring and disseminating information than government agencies.

2.4.2 Lags in adjustments

Most markets do not adjust very rapidly to changes in supply and demand. While this may be partly due to a lack of information, it is also true that resources are not very mobile at the best of times, that is, even when the necessary information is at hand. Labour may take time to move from one job to another or from one place to another, while physical capital can only move from one location to another at very irregular intervals. It takes time for an entrepreneur to move out of textile production into comput-

er software production, or for a civil engineer to become retrained as an electrical engineer – even when they are fully aware of the new opportunities available in the market place.

2.4.3 Incomplete markets

Markets are often incomplete in the sense that they cannot meet the demand for certain public goods such as street lighting, defence or neighbourhood security on their own. Neither do they fully account for the external costs and benefits associated with individual actions. When a company pollutes the air or river water, damaging the health of consumers using that air or water, it is not usually held responsible for its action; and neither are the consumers compensated for the additional health expenses they might incur. These issues are discussed more fully in Chapter 3 below.

2.4.4 Non-competitive markets

Non-competitive markets are the rule rather than the exception. Commodity markets are characterised by the presence of monopolies and oligopolies, while labour markets are in turn constrained by minimum wages imposed by trade unions, governments and by large corporations themselves. Several of the new labour laws in South Africa, including the Basic Conditions of Employment and the Employment Equity Acts, may well raise the non-wage costs of employment, thus forcing firms either to reduce output or adopt labour-saving technologies.

Whilst a lack of competition may well undermine allocative efficiency and X-efficiency, as defined above, it may also be the net result of a competitive process in which one or more low-cost firms managed to dominate the market. In Chapter 4 below we shall look at these issues in more detail and also consider the role of competition policy in a modern economy.

2.4.5 Macroeconomic instability

At the macroeconomic level markets may be slow to react to sudden exogenous shocks to the system – witness the recent speculative attacks on the rand and the hardship they have caused domestically. Left on their own, markets may take too long to adjust to changing external conditions, and it is often necessary for domestic policy makers to take appropriate actions aimed at bringing such speculative attacks to an end (South Africa Foundation, 1998). The important role played by monetary and exchange rate policies today can be viewed as an attempt on the part of governments to deal with the problem of market failure at the macroeconomic level. We return to this issue in the next section.

2.4.6 Distribution of income

Perhaps the most important shortcoming of the neoclassical model of general equilibrium is the fact that it is entirely neutral on the distributional issue. It basically operates like a "black box": what you get out of it is what you put into it! The distributional outcome – as reflected by the precise top-level equilibrium on the *PPC* – is very much determined by the initial distribution of capital and labour between the two individuals. If the initial distribution is highly unequal, then so too will be the final distribution. In Chapter 5 we take up this issue again and also spell out some of the relevant policy implications.

These examples are but a small sample of the many things that can go wrong in a modern capitalist economy. It is clear that real-world economies are not very efficient in the conventional economic sense of the word: they do not, and probably never will, achieve a Pareto-optimal allocation of resources. And neither will they on their own produce an equitable distribution of income – or one that is acceptable to the broad community, or its representative government.

But this does not mean that any other form of economic organisation, such as a socialist or centrally planned economy, will be any better at allocating scarce resources in accordance with the true wishes of the community. Indeed, there is now enough evidence to suggest that countries which have abided by the principles of the market have generally grown more rapidly, and have spread the benefits of that growth more effectively, than those opting for an interventionist or centrally planned system. It is partly for this reason that we have witnessed the gradual encroachment of free markets in several Eastern European and other countries during the past two decades.

All the same, it is also true that in most market-based economies the public sector has played a significant role in creating wealth for their growing populations. In these economies the public sector has been charged with the task of providing certain public goods such as defence and law and order, dealing with the problem of externalities, and regulating or nationalising certain natural monopolies. It is with these issues that we shall be mainly concerned in the sections and chapters that follow.

2.5 Enter the public sector: General approaches

We have seen in the previous section that various kinds of market failure can render the benchmark model of perfect competition unworkable in the real world. These failures provide a *prima facie* case for government intervention, and in this section we briefly focus on the broad approaches that governments can follow in coming to grips with such failures.

Economists conventionally distinguish between three broad functions of government, namely the allocative, distributive and stabilisation functions, each of which is briefly discussed below.

2.5.1 Allocative function

The allocative function of government stems from the fact that market failures distort the allocation of resources in an economy. Market failures due to incomplete and non-competitive markets are particularly important sources of allocative distortions.

The problem of incomplete markets is discussed in more detail in Chapter 3, but the gist of it is that some goods and services have characteristics which prevent competitive markets from supplying them efficiently. Such market failures can take various forms. In the case of pure public goods (such as national defence and street lighting) potential consumers have a strong incentive not to reveal their demand. This makes it impossible to determine a price or to force users to pay for the benefits they derive from using the good or service. As a result, competitive markets cannot supply public goods at all, even though they are very much in demand.

A second class of goods and services, known as mixed goods, has some public good characteristics. Consumers would either not reveal their demand for such goods and services, or producers would find it impossible to enforce payment of the price. Mixed goods can be supplied by competitive markets, but neither the quantity supplied nor the price resulting from market provision would be optimal. Examples of these goods are subscription television services and certain health care services.

The existence of externalities is a third manifestation of incomplete markets. In practice, the activities of individual consumers and producers often impact on other "third parties", and failure to account for such external effects tends to create a divergence between actual market prices and quantities and their socially-optimal equivalents. Externalities can be either negative, as in the case of air or river pollution, or positive. An example of a positive externality would be the "additional" benefits that society derives from education, such as having a more literate voter population. Such benefits are additional to the private benefits accruing to individual recipients in the form of higher earnings.

As suggested in Section 2.4, non-competitive markets may take two forms. "Artificial" monopolies operate in markets where perfect competition is technically feasible, but is prevented by legal restrictions imposed by the government or professional bodies. By contrast, "natural" monopolies develop in industries characterised by large capital outlays that give rise to economies of scale over the entire range of their output. Only one firm can effectively operate in such a market. Examples include the markets for water and electricity. In both cases, firms operating in non-competitive markets maximise their profits by supplying less than the optimal quantity of the good or service at too high a price.

Governments have various instruments at their disposal for correcting the allocative distortions resulting from incomplete and non-competitive markets. We refer to some of these instruments in Section 2.6 below and discuss them more fully in Chapters 3 and 4.

2.5.2 Distributive function

In Section 2.4 we pointed out that the neo-classical general equilibrium model is neutral as far as the distribution of income is concerned. It yields a distributional outcome largely determined by the initial distribution of labour and capital between the market participants. The model can thus be used to determine the Pareto-optimal allocation of resources for a given distribution of income only; in fact, there exists a Pareto-optimal allocation for each income distribution. However, the model is silent on the fairness of that distribution.

Market outcomes tend to exhibit considerable inequality in the distribution of income. The fact that all governments use combinations of taxes, transfer payments and subsidies to alter these outcomes, suggests that no society regards the market-determined distribution of income as fair or just. Some commentators have even suggested that a redistribution of income could improve the general well-being of society, even if it carried a cost in terms of lower levels of productivity or slower economic growth. In practice, however, there is considerable disagreement about the appropriate criteria for evaluating the distributive function of government – which remains a key aspect of its role in a modern capitalist economy. These issues are investigated in more detail in Chapter 5.

2.5.3 Stabilisation function

The stabilisation function of government refers to its macroeconomic objectives, which include an acceptable rate of economic growth, full employment, price stability and a sound balance of payments (see Chapter 17). An inability on the part of competitive markets to realise these objectives would represent market failure on a grand scale, and often induces governments to correct for such failure by means of appropriate monetary and fiscal policies. Being a macroeconomic issue, however, a detailed analysis of stabilisation policy falls outside the scope of this book, though some of the fiscal aspects will be dealt with in Chapters 16 and 17. Our purpose here is mainly to provide a brief overview of the stabilisation role of government.

The notion that governments have an important stabilisation function to fulfil is associated primarily with the Keynesian school of macroeconomic thought. The Keynesian approach to stabilisation rests on three premises:

- the market economy is inherently unstable;
- macroeconomic instability is a form of market failure which is highly costly to an economy; and

- governments are able to stabilise the economy by means of appropriate fiscal and monetary policies.

Keynesians therefore propose active counter-cyclical policies to stabilise economic activity. Their proposed policies mainly work on the demand side of the economy. In times of recession, governments should reduce taxes, increase their expenditure and boost credit expansion in order to raise aggregate demand and stimulate economic activity. Conversely, inflationary overheating of the economy should be addressed by higher taxes and lower levels of state spending and credit expansion, thus moderating aggregate demand.

The stabilisation function of government – as described above – is not without its critics. Economists from the new classical macroeconomics school believe that the macroeconomy is self-adjusting and that government intervention would worsen rather than improve matters. They argue that Keynesian economics lack a proper microeconomics foundation, and fail to realise that individual agents could rationally anticipate the actions of government and act upon them even before they are executed, or at least before they have their intended effect. New classical economists thus believe that there is no need to stabilise the market economy and that, even if there were, governments would be unable to do so effectively.

In response to these criticisms, the so-called neo-Keynesian school has tried to revive Keynesian theory by providing it with a credible microeconomics foundation. Neo-Keynesian economists argue that several inflexibilities in the modern economy are perfectly consistent with rational economic behaviour, and that some of them, such as wage and price contracts, can prevent the economy from responding or adjusting rapidly to exogenous shocks. These theories provide some justification for demand-management policies, although neo-Keynesians do acknowledge some of the practical difficulties facing policy makers, such as policy lags and shifting expectations.

2.6 Direct versus indirect government intervention

A second way to approach the role of government in the economy is to look at the nature of government interventions. Viewed very broadly, it is useful to distinguish between direct and indirect forms of intervention.

Direct government intervention refers to the actual participation of government in the economy. It includes the government's constitutional right to tax individuals and companies, borrow on the financial markets, and execute its budgeted spending programmes. As far as the latter programmes are concerned, governments intervene directly when they respond to a market failure by producing or supplying a good or service, such as national defence, waste disposal or electricity; or by financing production undertaken by the private sector on a contract basis, such as school textbooks and much of the state's infrastructure.

Indirect government intervention refers to the regulatory function of government. **Regulation** entails enacting a law or proclaiming a legally binding rule that gives rise to market outcomes that are different from those that would have obtained in the absence of the intervention. Examples abound, and in this country they include the new labour laws – aimed at improving the working conditions of labour; the new anti-tobacco law through which it is hoped to curb tobacco smoking; the new competition policy which is aimed at preventing abusive behaviour on the part of monopolies; and several new environmental control measures. Indirect taxes and subsidies, which also change market outcomes, constitute indirect fiscal measures as well.

The distinction between direct and indirect interventions can make an important difference to our estimates of the size of the public sector and its effects on the economy. Conventional indicators of the size of the public sector, which are based on the total tax burden, government expenditures and the budget deficit or surplus, provide a reasonably accurate picture of the size and extent of direct government intervention in the economy (or of the "resource use" by government, as explained in Chapter 1). The problem is that regulatory interventions, whose total effect on the private sector may well be as important as that of direct measures, do not show up in the national or government accounts. Conventional measures of the size of the public sector, such as those used in Chapter 1 and in Chapter 7, may well underestimate the overall effect of public sector activity on an economy. However, as yet there is no suitable quantitative indicator which fully accounts for the economic impact of government regulations.

2.7 Concluding note on government failure

Irrespective of how we define the public sector, or how we measure its size or impact on the economy, it is important to realise that governments, like markets, can also fail. Those involved in the business of government – politicians, bureaucrats and public employees – are no different from the rest of us. They often pursue their own self-interest, rather than the public interest, and because of the protected nature of their business, they are not particularly X-efficient. They make mistakes, wittingly or unwittingly, and are even corrupt at times – just like the rest of us!

In Chapter 6 we argue that "government failure", like market failure, is nothing sinister or extraordinary. It is a perfectly natural outcome of the way in which politicians and government officials behave. Like their counterparts in the private sector, they are utility maximisers: politicians want to maximise votes, virtually at all costs, while bureaucrats often strive to maximise the size of their departmental budgets, or "empires". The net effect is usually an excess supply of public goods and services – or a government that is bigger than its optimal size.

It is therefore important – indeed imperative – for the tax-paying public, including students of Public Economics, to know how efficiently their government is performing its various functions. But to make this judgement it is necessary also to know why governments intervene in the economy in the first place – which is the focus of the rest of this part of our book – and what it is that governments are supposed to do – the focus of the remaining parts of the book. Only then will we be able to make an informed judgement of the role of government in our economy.

Important concepts

allocative function of government
direct government intervention
distributive function
dynamic efficiency
indirect government intervention
Pareto optimality (in consumption)
Pareto optimality (in production)
Pareto-optimal top-level equilibrium
regulation
stabilisation function
X-efficiency

Self-assessment exercises

2.1 Distinguish between allocative efficiency, X-efficiency and economic growth and briefly consider their relevance to South Africa.

2.2 Outline the conditions for a top-level general equilibrium and explain why they represent a Pareto-optimal allocation of resources.

2.3 Explain the meaning of market failure giving a few pertinent examples.

2.4 Distinguish between the allocative and distributive functions of government.

2.5 Should governments have a stabilisation function?

2.6 Distinguish between direct and indirect government intervention.

Chapter three

Philip Black and

Krige Siebrits

Public goods and externalities

In Chapter 2 we introduced a benchmark model which explains the allocation of scarce resources within a perfectly competitive environment. We emphasised the point that the model itself provides a normative standard against which the performance of real-world markets can be judged; and in Section 2.4 we briefly introduced the notion of "market failure", that is, the inability of real-world markets to achieve the efficient outcomes of our benchmark model.

In this chapter we provide a more detailed discussion of two important sources of market failure, namely public goods and externalities. Both sources of failure reflect the incompleteness of markets. On their own, free markets cannot meet the demand for public goods or fully account for the external costs and benefits associated with individual actions. These market failures therefore provide a rationale for complementary government actions aimed at improving the allocation of resources. In addition to the theory of public goods and externalities – discussed in Sections 3.1 to 3.7 – we also look at some of the relevant policy implications in Sections 3.8 and 3.9.

Once you have studied this chapter, you should be able to
- distinguish between private, public, mixed and merit goods;
- derive the conditions for the optimal allocation of private, public and merit

goods with the aid of supply and demand analysis;
- explain why competitive markets fail to provide public and mixed goods efficiently;
- explain the distinction between the financing of public goods and services and their physical production;
- explain the concept of an externality;
- identify the main types of externalities;
- explain the effects of positive and negative externalities with the aid of supply and demand analysis;
- discuss the policy options to correct for externalities;
- discuss the relative importance of property rights and transactions costs in market-based approaches to dealing with the problem of externalities.

3.1 Private goods and the benchmark model

We begin our discussion of public goods by reflecting on the nature of the goods produced and consumed in the benchmark model. In Chapter 2 we simply labelled these goods X and Y and gave no further information about them. We then proceeded to derive the conditions under which X and Y would be produced and consumed in a Pareto-efficient manner. The issue that we now have to consider is whether the nature of X and Y has any bearing on the outcome of the analysis. Can we substitute any actual commodity or service for X and Y and still achieve allocative efficiency? As suggested in Section 2.4, the answer to this question is "no". Not all goods and services can be supplied efficiently by competitive markets.

Efficient production under competitive conditions requires that consumers reveal their preferences (or demand) for goods and services. By doing so, they signal to producers what types and quantities of goods they prefer. And on the basis of these signals, producers decide what and how much to produce. Competition among producers ensures that they do so at minimum cost. Provided that consumer preferences are fully revealed, the market performs like a huge auction that meets the third or top-level condition for allocative efficiency: simultaneous achievement of equilibrium by producers and consumers.

Conversely, competitive markets will fail if there are no satisfactory mechanisms through which consumers can reveal their preferences. Whether or not such mechanisms exist, depends on the nature or characteristics of goods and services. They certainly exist in the case of **private goods**, which we can define in terms of the following two characteristics:

- **Rivalry** in consumption. Private goods are wholly divisible amongst individuals, which means that one person's consumption of the good reduces its availability to other potential consumers. If Thandi wears a particular dress, it is not possible for Christine to wear it simultaneously; similarly, the consumption of an apple by Christine reduces by one the quantity of apples available for consumption to Thandi.
- **Excludability.** The consumption of a private good can be restricted to given individuals, typically those who pay the indicated or negotiated price. Once private goods have been paid for, ownership (or the assignment of property rights) is cer-

tain and uniquely determined. If Charles pays for a drink in a restaurant, he gains the sole right to consume that specific drink and has legally excluded Thabo from enjoying it.

The benefits of consuming private goods are therefore restricted to those individuals who reveal their preferences for such goods. The rivalness and excludability of private goods force potential consumers to reveal their preferences, thereby setting in motion the competitive processes resulting in allocative efficiency.

We can illustrate this point by referring to the market for compact discs – as shown in Figure 3.1. D_B and D_J are the individual demand curves for two consumers, Bongani and Joan. Each demand curve depicts the quantities of compact discs that the respective consumer would demand at different prices. The market demand curve – given by D_{B+J} – is simply the horizontal sum of the individual quantities demanded at each price. Market equilibrium occurs at point E, where market demand equals market supply, thus yielding a single equilibrium price at point P. Joan and Bongani cannot affect the equilibrium price they pay for compact discs and are therefore price-takers. The equilibrium output of compact discs is $0Q$, with the quantities demanded by Joan and Bongani given by $0J$ and $0B$, respectively. Note that although $0J$ and $0B$ sum to $0Q$, there is no reason why the two should be equal. The respective quantities demanded at the equilibrium price may differ according to the tastes, income levels and other characteristics of our two consumers. They are therefore quantity-adjusters, in the sense that each one determines the quantity he or she demands in accordance with the equilibrium price.

Our compact disc example enables us to highlight two important characteristics of a private good. Firstly, recall that the area underneath the demand curve gives the

Figure 3.1 Equilibrium of a private good

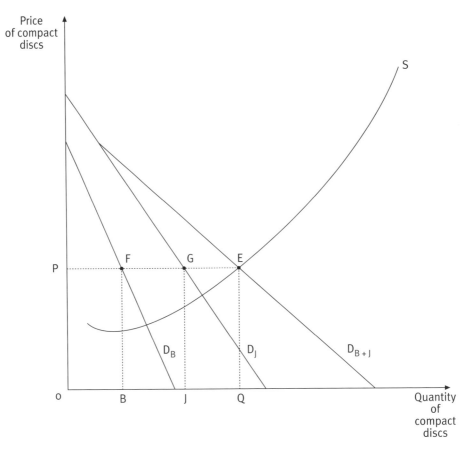

total utility derived from consuming compact discs – or the sum of the marginal utilities derived from consuming each compact disc; while the area under the supply curve gives the sum of the marginal costs of producing each compact disc. Therefore, at equilibrium price *0P*, the marginal utilities of Bongani and Joan (*BF* and *JG*, respectively) both equal the marginal cost *QE*. This is the condition for the efficient supply of a private good: marginal utility equals marginal cost for each consumer. Secondly, as is clear from Figure 3.1, the price of a private good equals its marginal cost. This is the efficient pricing rule for private goods.

3.2 Pure public goods: definition

The fact that private goods have two defining characteristics implies that there are three classes of "non-private" goods. Two of these classes each share one characteristic with private goods, but not the other. They are known as **mixed goods** and form the subject of Sections 3.5 and 3.6 below. In this section we discuss those goods to which neither of the characteristics of private goods applies. Such goods are called **pure public goods** or **pure social goods**.

Pure public goods, such as street lighting and national defence, are indivisible – that is, they cannot be divided into saleable units

– and are therefore **non-rival** in consumption. For a given level of production of a public good, one person's consumption does not reduce the quantity available for consumption by another person.[1]

If Thandi uses a street light to guide her during her walk to a post-box, Roger can use that same street light to establish whether he has found the street in which a distant relative of his lives. Similarly, the protection provided by the South African National Defence Force (SANDF) to the inhabitants of Pretoria does not reduce the "quantity" of protection available to the inhabitants of Johannesburg or Pietersburg.

Non-rivalness in consumption has two important implications that we will return to in the next section. Firstly, the fact that one person's consumption does not reduce the quantity available to other consumers implies that the marginal cost (that is, the cost of admitting an additional user) is zero. The second implication follows from this, namely that excluding anyone from consuming a non-rival good, even if it was feasible to do so, is Pareto-inefficient. The reason is straightforward: allowing Ibrahim to use the above street light, at zero marginal cost, will clearly make him better off than before; and yet it will **not** detract from the enjoyment that Thandi and Roger derive from that same street light.

In addition to being non-rival in consumption, pure public goods are also **non-excludable**, that is, it is impossible to exclude particular individuals from consuming such goods.[2]

Put differently, it is not possible to assign specific property rights to public goods or to enforce them. Let us again take national defence and street lighting as examples. The inhabitants of the Free State Province cannot be excluded from the protective services provided by the SANDF; and neither can any of the evening strollers along Cape Town's Sea Point promenade be excluded from sharing in the benefits of street lights.

The two criteria for pure public good status are quite stringent, and in practice it would seem that there are very few goods that qualify as pure public goods. For example, the protection offered by an army becomes less effective as more people or bigger areas have to be protected, and it is therefore debatable whether national defence is fully non-rival at all levels of provision.

Similarly, very few goods are non-excludable in the true or "technical" sense of the word. The development of new technologies continuously expands the scope for the application of the exclusion principle to more goods. Consider the standard case of the lighthouse. For many years, the lighthouse was the favourite example of a non-excludable public good. However, the service offered by a lighthouse is not so much a beam of light as a navigational aid. Nowadays it is technologically feasible and cost-effective to provide this service in the form of an electronic signal made available only to those willing to pay for it.

Non-excludability on cost grounds is perhaps more common. It is clearly very costly to place a policeman at every street light in Durban and expect him to chase away those who are unwilling to pay for the benefits received; or for the government to "exclude" citizens who are unwilling to contribute to the maintenance of the SANDF. However, in such cases it is possible that technologies may yet be developed that make exclusion viable in financial terms.

---

1 The use of the word "consumption" in the context of public goods could perhaps be misleading. Such goods are not really consumed; they generate a stream of benefits that can be enjoyed by all.

2 In his path-breaking analysis of public goods, Professor Paul Samuelson (1954; 1955) of the Massachusetts Institute of Technology defined public goods in terms of non-rivalness in consumption only. As we have just shown, non-rivalness is indeed a sufficient condition for public good status since it makes exclusion inefficient even when it is feasible. Some textbooks follow Samuelson in defining public goods in terms of non-rivalness only, but we shall follow the more conventional approach of using non-rivalness and non-excludability as criteria for public good status.

In spite of its limited applicability to real-life situations, the pure public good case remains an important analytical benchmark – much like the model of perfect competition. And for our present purposes, it is an extremely useful introduction to the sections that follow.

3.3 The market for public goods

Let us now consider the market for pure public goods from a partial equilibrium perspective. Our analysis is the public good equivalent of the private good case analysed in Section 3.1. The implications of the divergent characteristics of public and private goods will therefore become apparent from a comparison of the results obtained in Figure 3.2 below with those derived from Figure 3.1.

The two music-lovers we met in Section 3.1, Bongani and Joan, live in neighbouring houses. They spend many enjoyable evenings there listening to their latest purchases of compact discs, often developing a strong demand for snacks in the process. A convenience store is located nearby, but the sidewalks in their neighbourhood are so poorly maintained that street lights are essential to prevent slipping and tripping at night.

Figure 3.2 depicts the market for street lights in Joan and Bongani's street. We assume that they are the only "consumers" of the light. Their respective demands for street lighting are given by curves D_J and D_B. Note that these are what Samuelson (1954) called "pseudo demand curves", because they can be drawn only if consumers accurately reveal the quantities that they demand at different prices. As we have indicated in Section 3.1, however, such revelation of preferences occurs only with private goods. We will return to this point and its implications below, but for the moment we assume that Bongani and Joan do accurately reveal their preferences for street lighting. Given this assumption, the individual demand curves and the total supply curve S are drawn similar to those in Figure 3.1.

The fundamental difference between the public and private good cases is the manner of deriving the market demand curve. In Figure 3.1, we derived the market demand for compact discs by horizontally adding the demand curves of Joan and Bongani. But in the case of a public good, which is indivisible, horizontal summation of the quantities demanded by each consumer at each price is clearly not appropriate. The non-excludability of street lighting implies that the full quantity supplied is available to both Bongani and Joan, that is they are **quantity-takers** in the public good case. The market demand for public goods, D_{B+J}, is therefore derived by **vertically** adding the demand schedules. In effect, we are adding the marginal utilities they derive from (or the prices they are willing to pay for) different quantities of street lighting, not the quantities they demand at different prices.

The equilibrium position is defined in the usual manner as the point of intersection between the market demand and total supply curves. This occurs at point E. The equilibrium output $0Q$ is available to both consumers. Price $0P_{B+J}$ represents the total amount that the two consumers together would be willing to pay for the equilibrium quantity of street lighting, $0Q$. In the example of Figure 3.2 Bongani is willing to pay a price of $0P_B$ (equal to his marginal utility), while Joan is willing to pay a price of $0P_J$ (equal to her marginal utility). Bongani and Joan are therefore price-adjusters who can adjust their willingness to pay for street lighting.

The rules for the efficient allocation and pricing of public goods are also different from those for private goods, as stated in Section 3.1. Again, keep in mind that the areas under the demand and supply curves show the sum of marginal utilities and the

Figure 3.2 Equilibrium of a pure public good

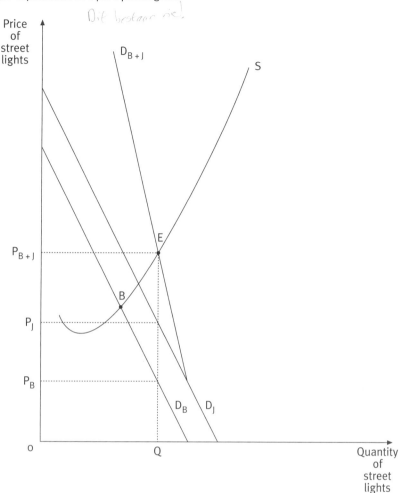

sum of the marginal costs, respectively. The equilibrium position implies that the condition for the efficient provision of a public good is equality between the sum of the marginal utilities of the individual consumers and the marginal cost. From this condition we can derive the efficient pricing rule for public goods: the sum of the individual prices should equal the marginal cost. It is important to add that the equilibrium shown in Figure 3.2 is basically a "pseudo" one, due to the inability of consumers to reveal their true preferences.

Table 3.1 summarises our discussion so far by contrasting some key characteristics of public and private goods.

3.4 Who should supply public goods?

Why do private markets fail to supply goods and services characterised by non-rivalness and non-excludability? We have already touched on the effects of non-rivalness when we stated that the marginal cost of admitting additional users of non-rival goods is zero.

Table 3.1 A comparison of key characteristics of public and private goods

	Public goods	Private goods
Property rights	Non-excludable	Excludable
Consumption	Non-rival	Rival
Aggregate demand curve	Vertical addition of individual demand curves	Horizontal addition of individual demand curves
Partial equilibrium condition for optimum provision	The sum of marginal utilities equals marginal cost $[\Sigma MU = MC]$	Marginal utility of each consumer equals marginal cost $[MU_i = MC$ with i the individual consumer]
Efficient pricing rule	The sum of individual prices equals marginal cost $[\Sigma P = MC]$	Price equals marginal cost $[P = MC]$
Source: Adapted from Freeman 1983; 482		

The condition for efficient pricing by competitive markets (P = MC) therefore requires the price to be zero as well. Clearly, profit-maximising producers cannot apply the efficient pricing rule in this case, as charging a zero price would not enable them to cover the costs of providing the good or service.

The alternative of setting a cost-covering price (equal to the sum of the individual prices) would potentially enable a competitive market to supply the good; but it would not be efficient as exclusion cannot occur. Any price other than zero exceeds the zero marginal cost of admitting additional users and, consequently, reduces consumption of a non-rival good. Such exclusion is Pareto inefficient, as its annulment would increase the welfare of previously-excluded consumers without reducing the welfare of those already enjoying access to the good. In sum, it is impossible to determine an equilibrium price for the private provision of a non-rival good.

The non-excludability characteristic of public goods and services creates incentives for "**free riding**", that is the phenomenon of misrepresenting preferences (or hiding them

completely) on the expectation that a benefit may be enjoyed without having to pay for it. Let us return to our example of street lighting. Being rational individuals, Bongani and Joan know that they cannot be excluded from enjoying the benefits once street lighting is provided. Both of them therefore have an incentive to understate the intensity of their preferences for street lighting in the hope that the other will reveal his or her demand and pay for the service. They become free riders. If Bongani reveals his preference for street lights while Joan attempts to "free ride", a competitive market will under-supply street lighting at the level where Bongani's marginal utility equals the marginal cost of provision, that is at point B in Figure 3.2. And in the extreme case where both Joan and Bongani attempt to "free ride", no street lighting would be provided at all: their true preferences would then not be revealed.

Government provision of public goods and services can improve on the inefficient outcomes of the market. But it cannot ensure an optimal provision of public goods either. Compared to the market, the government has the advantage that it can use its coercive powers to enforce payment for public goods. However, it is no more able than the market to get consumers to reveal their demand for such goods and therefore cannot determine efficient prices. These points may be illustrated with the aid of Figure 3.2. Ideally, the government wishes to apply the efficient pricing rule for public goods, $\Sigma P = MC$. To do so, however, it would have to know the demand curves of the two consumers so that it can charge each a price equivalent to his or her marginal valuation of the benefits of street lighting. In this case it would charge Bongani OP_B and Joan OP_J, thus recovering the full marginal cost (OP_{B+J}) of providing OQ street lighting. Optimal provision of a public good thus requires the application of price discrimination, that is, the practice of charging different consumers different prices.

In practice, however, the government does not have the required knowledge about people's preferences to enable it to apply perfect price discrimination. This is the reason why governments typically cover the costs of supplying public goods by collecting a "tax price" from consumers. The mandatory nature of tax payments eliminates the "free rider" option and gives taxpayers a direct stake in revealing their preferences for public goods. Once Bongani and Joan have been forced to surrender a part of their hard-earned salaries to the government, they clearly have an incentive to participate in decisions on the use of their tax contributions, for example by insisting on better maintenance of sidewalks or the provision of street lighting in their neighbourhood. Such participation could take the form of voting in a referendum on tax and expenditure measures, or voting for political parties in a democracy – as we will discuss in more detail in Chapter 6 below.

The actual production of public goods need not necessarily be undertaken by government as such – it could be done on a contract basis by the private sector. The critical difference between public and private goods lies more on the financing side. When we talk of public goods, we essentially refer to the need for **public (or collective) financing**, rather than private financing through the private financial sector. In an extreme sense one may say that all public goods could be produced privately as long as they are financed publicly. Many economists would argue that such a system is more efficient than one in which the government produces public goods, as governments are not subject to the profit and loss discipline of the market.

There are many examples of privately produced and publicly financed goods and services: school textbooks, free medicines, roads, dams, and the like. In addition, governments often use private goods and services as a means of meeting public demands, with the labour of public employees being the only significant value that is added in the "production process'". Examples include the sophisticated equipment used by the military to produce a national defence system, the equipment and buildings used by diplomats in overseas embassies, and the electronic equipment used by administrators in the public sector. It is clear that a substantial part of government activity is in a sense already "privatised'". The much-debated issue of further privatisation largely involves the service component and the important financing issue.

Of course, government financing presents its own problems, and in several subsequent chapters we will highlight some of the efficiency implications of using tax increases or debt-financing as sources of government revenue.

3.5 Mixed and merit goods

As the name suggests, mixed goods possess both private and public good characteristics. Such goods and services are common in the real world and raise several vital questions about the economic role of government.

Two classes of mixed goods and services can be distinguished:

- **Non-rival, excludable** mixed goods and services. Consider the part of the N14 highway between Vryburg and Kuruman. The exclusion principle can be applied by installing a toll gate, as is already done on the N1 and N3 highways from Johannesburg to Bloemfontein and Durban. (This is indeed an old method of exclusion. At the entry of the old Montagu pass between George and Oudtshoorn in the Western Cape, a toll house survives to remind us that the government applied it as long ago as 1849!) Yet, on an average day, there is no rivalry in getting access to the N14, as road users have no need to compete for scarce space. The public good characteristic of non-rival access to the road prevents competitive markets from providing such roads efficiently. As discussed in the case of pure public goods, the problem is the impossibility of determining a competitive price. The competitive solution of setting the price equal to marginal cost is inappropriate since the marginal cost of access to the road is zero; and similarly, charging a cost-covering price will lead to Pareto inefficient exclusion. Another example of this class of mixed goods is the subscription television channel M-Net.
- **Rival, non-excludable** mixed goods and services. On weekdays, Vermeulen Street in the central business district of Pretoria is a good example of the class of mixed good characterised by rivalness in consumption and non-excludability. Rivalry in the form of competition for the scarce road space is fierce, and the marginal cost of road usage increases with increasing congestion. Efficient price determination at the level of the marginal cost becomes theoretically possible. But the problem is how to apply the exclusion principle. Imagine the congestion effects of levying

toll charges at the entrances and exits to the central business district of a city like Pretoria! In this case market failure arises from the non-excludability characteristic of the mixed good.

Mixed goods as a group represents a "grey area" and the question of whether they should be supplied by the public or the private sector remains open. The influence of technology on the application of the non-excludability characteristic is particularly important in this regard. We mentioned earlier that technological innovation changed the status of navigational aids from a pure public good (the lighthouse) to a non-rival but excludable mixed good (electronic information signals). In the same way, congested urban roads may in future become private goods through the use of road sensors to measure traffic volumes, detect licence plate numbers and bill road users.

But political factors also come into play. In the case of some mixed and even private goods it is possible to apply the exclusion principle, but the goods in question are politically regarded as so meritorious that they are often provided via the national budget. Examples of such **merit** goods are education and health services. The reason for treating merit goods and services in a special way is that the individual who is buying or receiving them often confers certain "external" benefits on other people, and hence on the broader community – an issue to which we return in the next section.

But in many other cases, such as enforcing the use of seatbelts in cars and making primary school education mandatory, the provision of merit goods simply reflects the belief that individuals are unable to act in their own best interest. The same belief guides the prohibition of certain "bads"', for example comprehensive bans on smoking or on the use of certain drugs. There is an undeniable element of paternalism to the merit goods argument which makes it quite controversial, particularly among those who fear that special interest groups would attempt to use the government to further their own views of how people should behave.

On the whole, mixed goods can be provided either by the government alone – such as in the case of health care services in some countries; or by the private sector – as with private toll roads or subscription television services. But most mixed goods are provided by a combination of the private and public sectors. In addition to wholly owned government schools, for example, we also have a growing number of privately owned schools and training colleges in this country. Likewise, universities get their income partly from government, and partly from students in the form of registration fees. The latter split can be viewed as an attempt to share the costs of university education in accordance with the public and private good components of the service.

3.6 Externalities

Externalities, or external effects, can be either positive or negative. They are positive when the actions of an individual producer or consumer confer a benefit on another party free of charge; and they are negative when those actions impose a cost on the other party for which he or she is not compensated. Such actions can be either of a "technological" or of a "pecuniary" nature. They are **technological** when they have a direct effect on the level of production or consumption of the "other party"; and they are **pecuniary** when they change the demand and supply conditions, and hence the market prices, facing the other party. In either case, however, the beneficiary gets a windfall by not having to pay for the benefit, whilst the prejudiced party gets no compensation at all.

As far as pecuniary externalities are concerned, it can be argued that they do not have a **net** effect on society – resources are merely

transferred from one owner to another, and markets adjust efficiently to changing demand and supply conditions (Browning and Browning, 1994:49). Consider an area in which crime is rampant and house prices are falling rapidly. Current owners and sellers will be disadvantaged but buyers will get the benefit of lower house prices. There is therefore no net loss to society and no real external effect – only a redistribution from one group to another. Nonetheless, it is still true to say that house buyers enjoy a windfall while house sellers – the losers – get no compensation.

External effects drive a wedge between the private (or monetary) and the social costs and benefits associated with everyday market transactions. Social costs (benefits) are simply the sum of the private costs (benefits) and the external costs (benefits), and in what follows we shall focus on the respective marginal equivalents.

Externalities can originate on either the supply side or the demand side of the market, and it is possible to distinguish between the following four broad categories:

As far as the **supply** side is concerned, the productive activities of a producer can have either:

(a) a **negative** external effect on other producers or consumers, in which case the marginal external cost (MEC) > 0 and marginal social cost (MSC) > marginal private cost (MPC); or

(b) a **positive** external effect, in which case $MEC < 0$ and $MPC > MSC$.

Likewise, on the **demand** side, the consumption activities of an individual consumer can have either:

(c) a positive external effect on other consumers or producers, in which case the marginal external benefit (MEB) > 0 and marginal social benefit (MSB) > marginal private benefit (MPB); or

(d) a negative external effect, in which case $MEB < 0$ and $MPB > MSB$.

This four-pronged taxonomy is ideal for analysing the effects of externalities and the scope for remedial government intervention with the aid of demand and supply curves. Each of the four types of externalities can be analysed separately, but we shall consider only two cases: the negative production externality and the positive consumption externality.

3.6.1 Negative production externality

Assume that a coal-fired power station on the Mpumalanga Highveld pollutes the air and the water used by nearby livestock and crop farmers. This example of a negative production externality can be analysed with the aid of Figure 3.3. The diagram shows the normal private (= social) demand curve and the private supply or marginal cost curve ($S_p = MPC$) for the electricity generated by the power station. Recall that these curves represent the consumers' benefits from using electricity and the supplier's cost of providing it, respectively. In a typical market situation equilibrium would occur at point E_0, with OQ_0 electricity supplied at a unit price of OP_0.

But from the perspective of the community as a whole, the costs incurred by the supplier do not reflect the full cost of providing the electricity. The external costs of pollution to nearby farmers are ignored, but are in fact part and parcel of the full or social cost of providing electricity. This is shown in

Figure 3.3 External cost and Pigouvian tax

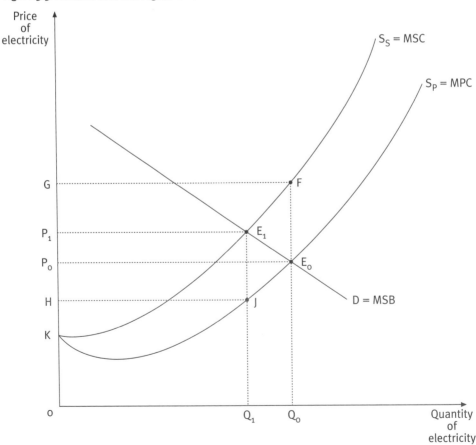

Figure 3.3 by the "social" supply curve labelled $S_s = MSC$, indicating that the negative externality raises the social costs of providing electricity above the private costs of the supplier. By producing OQ_0 units of electricity, the supplier incurs a marginal private cost equal to $Q_0 E_0$ and a marginal external cost of $E_0 F$, which together make up the marginal social cost of $Q_0 F$. At the private equilibrium point E_0, total private costs equal $OQ_0 E_0 K$ and total external costs are $KE_0 F$.

If the externality were taken into account, the "social" equilibrium would be at point E_1, where social supply (or MSC) equals demand (assumed to equal MSB). At point E_1 only $0Q_1$ units of electricity are supplied at a unit price of $0P_1$. Two points are worth emphasising here. First, OQ_1 represents a lower quantity of output than OQ_0, whereas P_1 is a higher price than P_0. Thus, from a social point of view, the presence of a negative production externality in a competitive market causes inefficiency in the form of over-provision and underpricing of the good in question.

Secondly, in moving from point E_0 to point E_1 the externality has **not** been eliminated. It has merely been reduced – from $KE_0 F$ to its **optimal** level KJE_1. The latter is an optimal level because our farming community is basically prepared to accept this negative externality from electricity generation, in exchange for the value that it adds to their personal comfort and farming activities.

The opposite case – of a positive production externality – implies the presence of negative external costs, ie a situation where the social supply (MSC) curve lies below and to the right of the private supply (MPC) curve. A good example is the classic case of a bee farmer's bees pollinating the apple blossoms on an adjacent farm.

3.6.2 Positive consumption externality

The market for education provides an example of a positive consumption externality. In Figure 3.4 the curve S represents the (social) supply of educational services, that is, the marginal social cost of providing education. Curve D_p depicts the private demand for education, indicating marginal private benefits in the form of skills accumulation, expected higher earnings, and the sheer enjoyment to be had from being more knowledgeable. The market equilibrium therefore occurs at point E_0, with OQ_0 education being supplied at a "unit price" of OP_0.

In this case the externality originates on the demand or consumption side of the market. The benefits of education are not restricted to the individual recipient. Society as a whole also derives considerable benefits from the effects of education. The educated individual may, for example, disseminate valuable information to other producers and consumers free of charge, thus enabling him or her to become a more productive or happier citizen. Higher education levels also go hand in hand with lower birth rates and lower crime rates, thus relieving the pressure on government, and hence on taxpayers, to provide additional health care facilities and policing. As a result, the marginal social benefits from additional education exceed the marginal private benefits[3] – as shown in Figure 3.4 by the social demand (or MSB) curve, D_s, which lies to the right and above curve D_p.

Taking account of the external benefits from education thus moves the equilibrium position from point E_0 to point E_1, raising the effective price from OP_0 to $0H$ and increasing the quantity from OQ_0 to OQ_1. Competitive markets thus under-provide

---

3 These benefits may be subject to a form of decreasing returns. Most empirical estimates of the returns to education indicate that the excess of the social benefit over the private benefit decreases as education becomes more advanced (Todaro, 1997: 390-93).

Figure 3.4 External benefit and Pigouvian subsidy

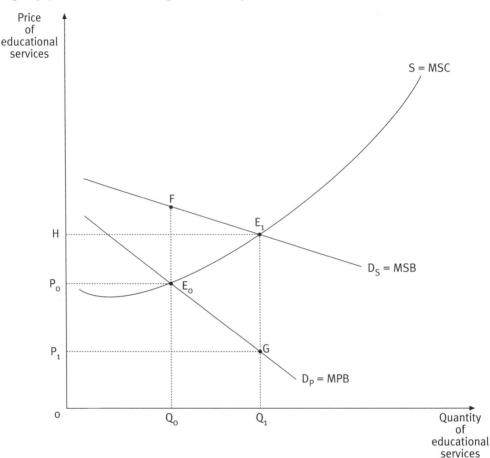

and under-price goods and services exhibiting external benefits.

The opposite case – of a negative consumption externality – implies the existence of negative external benefits, with the social demand (*MSB*) curve lying below and to the left of the private demand (*MPB*) curve. If Bongani had a particular liking for the hard rock music of Springbok Nude Girls and played their CDs into the early hours of the night, he may impose a negative externality on his next door neighbour, Prudence, who prefers the more sedate music of Bles Bridges.

3.7 Possible solutions to the externality problem

What can governments do about the allocative inefficiencies caused by externalities? There are four interventions that can be considered, namely regulation, Pigouvian taxes and subsidies, the establishment of property rights and the creation of markets.

3.7.1 Regulation

The option of regulation is particularly relevant to the case of negative production externalities such as pollution. This option entails telling each polluter to reduce pollution to a certain level or else face legal sanction. In the example used in Figure 3.3, the power station would be ordered to reduce its output from OQ_0 to the socially-optimal level OQ_1. This approach has two shortcomings. Firstly, it assumes that the government is sufficiently well-informed to determine the output level OQ_1, which in practice is very difficult to do.

The second objection to regulation would be valid even if the problem of determining the socially-optimal output level could be overcome. Regulation of this nature is simply not efficient in industries consisting of more than one firm, since it requires each firm to reduce its output by equal absolute amounts or proportions. But by doing so, individual firms may be forced into violating the efficiency criterion of producing at the point where marginal social cost equals marginal social benefit. The reason is that these costs and benefits may vary significantly between firms within the same industry, so that the application of a blanket rule would result in some of them producing too much and others producing too little.

3.7.2 Pigouvian taxes and subsidies

A second possible solution refers to the introduction of **Pigouvian taxes and subsidies** – named after the famous British economist, A C Pigou (1920). Such taxes and subsidies attempt to internalise externalities, that is, to force parties to include the external effects of their actions in their cost and benefit calculations.[4]

The effect of a Pigouvian tax can be illustrated by revisiting our case of a negative production externality – as illustrated in Figure 3.3. Recall that a negative production externality leads to an over-provision and under-pricing of the good in question. By levying a Pigouvian tax on the party whose

actions cause the externality, the government can increase the producer's marginal private cost to the level of the marginal social cost. In Figure 3.3 this would be achieved by levying an *ad valorem* tax on the price charged by the power station, that is, a percentage tax equal to the corresponding value of the externality. In unit terms the tax would equal E_0F at price Q_0F (= $0G$), and JE_1 at price Q_1E_1 (= OP_1), thus shifting the private supply curve S_p to $S_s = MSC$. But since at point F supply exceeds demand, the new equilibrium will settle at point E_1, where MSC equals MSB. Note that for this tax to be efficient it must equal the marginal external cost measured at the new social equilibrium. At Q_1 the marginal external cost is the vertical difference between MPC and MSC (= JE_1).

At point E_1 the unit tax is JE_1, and the (internalised) externality equals KJE_1 – its optimal size. The net effect of the policy is that a large portion of the original externality – given by the area JE_0FE_1 – has been eliminated.

The use of a Pigouvian subsidy to correct a positive consumption externality can likewise be illustrated by revisiting Figure 3.4. If the government subsidises education by E_0F (or GE_1) per unit, again on an *ad valorem* basis, it will bring the marginal private benefit in line with the marginal social benefit, that is, private demand D_p effectively shifts to $D_s = MSB$. At point F, the price **inclusive** of the subsidy is high enough to induce a positive supply response. At the new equilibrium point E_1, where the marginal social benefit equals marginal social cost, the price paid by consumers will be Q_1G (= OP_1), the unit subsidy will be GE_1 (= P_1H), and the supplier will receive Q_1E_1 (= OH). Again, note that for the subsidy to produce the optimal result, it must equal the marginal external benefit at the optimal output level Q_1. Clearly, the final equilibrium represents a more efficient out-

---

4 Internalisation of externalities could also be viewed as a means of conferring property rights to external effects in order to account for divergences between private and social costs and benefits.

come with more educational services being provided at a lower unit demand price.

Although Pigouvian taxes and subsidies are widely used in the real world, they are subject to the same informational constraints as the regulatory option. The Pigouvian option unrealistically assumes that the authorities are perfectly informed about the size of the externality and, hence, about the slopes and shapes of the respective demand and supply curves, all of which are supposedly costless to obtain.

3.7.3 Property rights

The third approach to the treatment of externalities reflects the view that regulation and Pigouvian taxes and subsidies are both costly to administer, and in any case not likely to achieve their purpose. The Nobel Laureate, Ronald Coase, argued that the divergence between marginal private cost and marginal social cost arises due to insufficiently defined property rights over the use of resources. **Property rights** represent the legal specification of who owns what goods, broadly defined, including the rights and obligations attendant upon such ownership. The problem of externalities thus boils down to disputes over the use of resources.

To illustrate the problem: does Prudence have the right to paint her front door a garish pink when it offends Bogani every time he passes it to enter his own adjacent front door, and when it may reduce the value of his apartment? Or returning to our earlier example: do the producers of electricity on the Mpumalanga Highveld possess the right to discharge pollutants into the atmosphere, or do farmers possess rights to unpolluted air and water? If property rights are well defined, they can be exchanged on a voluntary basis by means of a straightforward market transaction. If Prudence had the

right to paint the outside of her front door any colour she wished, then Bogani could offer to pay her a certain amount not to paint it pink (or he can offer not to play Nudies music late at night). Likewise, if our Highveld farmers had a right to clean air and water, the electricity supplier could buy that right from them by offering to compensate them for the damage caused. The externality problem can thus be resolved without having recourse to potentially unsuccessful government intervention.

The Coase theorem holds that, provided property rights are well defined and enforceable, and **transaction costs** are negligible, market incentives will generate a mutually beneficial exchange of property rights through which externalities can be fully internalised. Moreover, the outcome of such an exchange is allocatively neutral; that is, the initial endowments of **property** rights between economic agents will not affect the ultimate pattern of economic activity. In the Coasian approach, the government's role in respect of externalities mainly consists of the maintenance of a judicial system to define and enforce property rights and a market system to lower transaction costs.

The Coase theorem is crucially predicated on the twin assumptions of well-defined and enforceable property rights and zero transaction costs.[5]

As suggested above, the definition and enforcement of property rights are largely determined by the quality of the judicial system. If transaction costs are non-trivial however, they may prevent parties from exchanging their property rights and in the process internalising the externality. In general, the higher the transaction costs, the lower will be the degree of internalisation of externalities and the greater will be the resultant divergence between marginal pri-

---

5 Transaction costs are the costs of the exchange process. They comprise the resources used when economic agents attempt to identify and contact one another (identification costs), negotiate contracts (negotiation costs) and verify and enforce the terms of contracts (enforcement costs).

vate cost and marginal social cost. Transaction costs are bound to be high when large numbers of people are involved, such as the many consumers experiencing respiratory illnesses from inhaling the polluted air of Sasolburg. It may be too costly for them to take the steps necessary to have their right to clean air legally enforced.

3.7.4 Creation of markets

A fourth approach, also developed in the context of the pollution problem, consists in the creation of a market in which the government would sell legal permits giving owners the right to pollute. The government would first establish the overall quantity of pollutants which it considers to be an efficient level – for example, the area KJE_1 in Figure 3.3 – and then sell a limited number of individual permits to the highest bidders. The price of these permits (also called **effluent fees**) – eg JE_1 in Figure 3.3 – should ideally clear the market, in which case the actual amount of pollution will equal the level determined by government. Producers who are unwilling to pay the market-determined effluent fee would have to reduce their own output or shift to cleaner technologies.

The market-creation approach also assumes that the government possesses perfect knowledge about the sources of pollution and the level of pollution commensurate with the efficient level of output. Nonetheless, being market-driven, the outcome may be quite revealing: if the bidding process drove up effluent fees dramatically, it would tell government something about the value of the externality to producers; and at the same time boost its income.[6]

The market-creation approach is a comparatively new one and is likely to be the topic of much further research.

3.8 Property rights, transaction costs and the theory of market failure

We mentioned earlier that the Coasian solution to the externality problem rests on the assumptions of well-defined and enforceable property rights and negligible transaction costs among the bargaining parties. In emphasising the importance of property rights and transaction costs, Coase made a significant contribution to the theory of market failure. In fact, his contribution provides a way out of a fundamental weakness in the standard benchmark model.

In Chapter 2 we pointed out that the neoclassical theory of general equilibrium assumes rational utility-maximisation on the part of all economic agents. Such behaviour implies, among other things, that agents would exploit all mutually-beneficial opportunities for exchange. Yet the present chapter has shown that many such opportunities remain unexploited, especially those characterised by external effects. This divergence between actual behaviour and the fundamental behavioural assumption of our benchmark model suggests that the model is a poor yardstick for objectively judging the efficiency of real-world conduct.

Coase's analysis of property rights and transaction costs provides a lifeline for the benchmark model by suggesting that the model is not wrong in assuming rationality, but is merely incompletely specified. If the model of perfect competition can be expanded to include transaction costs, in particular, it would conform much better to actual behaviour. Thus agents are not necessarily irrational when they decline to undertake certain transactions; in fact, they are

---

6 Interest groups often claim that such revenue should be used to compensate affected parties, for example using a tax on tobacco products to finance the health care expenses of non-smokers who are adversely affected by tobacco smoke. This will, however, create new distortions in the economy. Such revenue should rather be viewed as part of general revenue and allocated through the budgetary process (see Chapter 14, Section 14.4).

responding rationally to the fact that the costs of undertaking the transaction are higher than the corresponding benefits.

This view has quite dramatic implications for the theory of market failure, as set out in the current and subsequent chapters of this book. Taken to its extreme, it implies that there is no such thing as market failure! Economists such as Harold Demsetz (1982), Dahlman (1979) and Toumanoff (1984) have argued that what we conventionally define as market failures, such as externalities and the formation of monopolies, can be explained in terms of the failure of the standard general equilibrium model to consider various forms of transaction costs. In their view, the problem is one of "model failure", not market failure.

Literature on transaction costs is in many respects still in its infancy, and as yet does not provide a fully-fledged challenge to the theory of market failure. From a policy point of view, it would become much more useful if it could provide a coherent framework for analysing the sources of transaction costs and their effects on market institutions. Toumanoff (1984: 538) rightly points out that to attribute all instances of unexploited exchange to the existence of transaction costs would amount to rationalising the economic status quo. If we accept that all agents behave rationally in the face of transaction costs, we are confronted with the so-called **Panglossian dilemma**: whatever is, is optimal. But if this problem can be overcome by further research on transaction costs, it may be possible to equip future policy makers with a variety of original, market-based policy instruments which could complement or replace some of the more traditional ones discussed in this chapter.

Important concepts

Coase theorem
excludability (non-excludability)
free riding (free rider)
merit goods
negative externality
panglossian dilemma
pecuniary externality
pigouvian subsidy
pigouvian tax
positive externality
private goods
property rights
pure public goods
rivalry (non-rivalry)
technological externality
transaction costs

Self-Assessment Exercises

3.1 Explain the difference between a private and a pure public good. How do their respective equilibria differ?

3.2 Who should supply pure public goods?

3.3 Explain the meaning of mixed and merit goods. Who should supply them?

3.4 Explain the concept of "externality" and distinguish between the different types of externality that one might encounter in the real world.

3.5 Is there a case to be made for taxing a good which imposes an external cost on the community; or subsidising one that confers a positive external benefit?

3.6 Discuss Coase's theorem and consider its usefulness as a means of solving the externality problem.

3.7 Do you agree with the view that "market failure" is something of a misnomer, and that the problem to which it refers is rather one of "model failure"?

Chapter four
Philip Black

Imperfect competition

The widespread existence of monopolies and oligopolies represents perhaps the best-known example of market or institutional failure in a modern economy. It is customary to distinguish between two types of monopoly: firstly, an "artificial"or statutory monopoly operating in a market where perfect competition is technically feasible and, secondly, the case of a "natural monopoly". The former refers to a situation in which potential competitors are prevented from entering the market in question, either because of certain legal restrictions imposed by the government or a professional body, or because of efforts on the part of the firm itself to limit entry by setting a price below its profit-maximising level (Harrod, 1952).

Since the practice of limit pricing is difficult to detect or control in practice, we shall confine ourselves in Section 4.1 below to the case of an artificial barrier which limits productive activity within an otherwise competitive market. Section 4.2 deals with the decreasing cost case and considers the question of whether a natural monopoly should be owned and controlled by the state. Section 4.3 discusses other forms of imperfect competition, and looks at the new competition policy in South Africa. Section 4.4, in conclusion, considers some of the modern views on monopoly, including the so-called

"efficiency hypothesis"introduced to the literature by Harold Demsetz.

Once you have studied this chapter, you should be able to
- discuss the social costs of monopoly and indicate their relevance for "deregulation";
- outline the characteristic features of a natural monopoly;
- discuss the case for and against privatising a natural monopoly;
- explain the meaning of the "structure-conduct-performance"(SCP) hypothesis and discuss its relevance for competition policy in South Africa;
- explain Demsetz's "efficiency hypothesis"and discuss its relevance for competition policy generally.

4.1 On the social costs of monopoly[1]

Our starting point is the familiar distinction between perfect competition and monopoly – as illustrated in Figure 4.1. There we assume that both the demand function, D, and marginal cost, MC, are the same for the two market forms. The only difference is that under perfect competition MC represents the sum of the marginal cost curves of

---

1 This and the following sections are partly based on Black and Dollery, 1992: 10-16.

Figure 4.1 Monopoly versus perfect competition

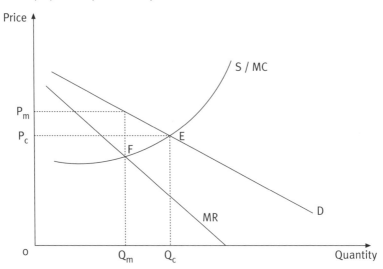

the individual firms making up the market, whereas under monopoly it represents the marginal cost of the monopolist only.

The perfectly competitive equilibrium occurs at point E in Figure 4.1, where supply equals demand and $0Q_c$ of the good is produced at a price of $0P_c$. Under monopoly equilibrium occurs at point F, where MC = MR and the market produces a smaller quantity, $0Q_m$, at a higher price, $0P_m$, than it does under perfect competition.

The above difference can also be shown in terms of the two-sector model discussed in Chapter 2. The implications of monopoly for this model are straightforward. Recall (from equation [2.5] in Chapter 2) that the marginal rate of product transformation (MRPT) equals the marginal cost ratio for the two commodities; that is

$$\text{MRPT}_{xy} = \frac{MCx}{MCy} = \frac{Px}{Py} \qquad [4.1]$$

If Y is now assumed to be a monopolist and X a perfectly competitive industry, then $P_y > MC_y$ while $P_x = MC_x$. Therefore,

$$\text{MRPT}_{xy} > \frac{Px}{Py} \qquad [4.2]$$

indicating that the first, and by inference, the third or "top-level" condition for a Pareto optimum has been violated. This is illustrated in Figure 4.2 by the difference between the slope of the production possibility curve, R_0T_0, and the commodity price line, P_mP_m, passing through point M_0. Specifically, in contrast to the competitive equilibrium at point C, the effect of introducing monopoly here is to lower the output of good Y and raise its relative price.

The difference between points M_0 and C in Figure 4.2 is often taken to reflect the degree of **allocative inefficiency** arising from the presence of monopoly in one of the two sectors. In other words, the economy as a whole is producing too little of good Y relative to good X at point M_0, and would prefer to move to point C by reallocating resources in such a way as to increase the production of good Y relative to good X.

Moreover, monopoly may entail an additional cost resulting from the emergence of **X-inefficiency**. Harvey Leibenstein (1966) believed that monopolists do not utilise their existing resources as efficiently as firms operating under the constant pressure of a competitive market. With no threat of entry,

Figure 4.2 Efficiency implications of monopoly

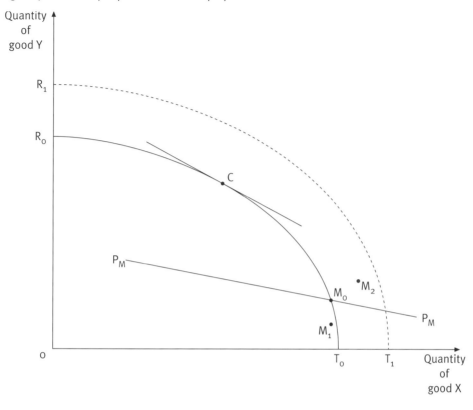

the monopolistic firm may lack the incentive to maintain a high level of labour productivity or to spend sufficient time and effort searching for and acquiring the necessary information. Such a situation can be depicted by a point lying inside the production possibility curve, such as M_1 in Figure 4.2, which has been drawn diagonally below point M_0 to indicate that sector Y is producing less output than it is capable of with its given resources. It thus indicates that resources are not being fully utilised and the economy has failed to achieve a Pareto-optimal allocation of resources. Consequently, the social costs of monopoly may result from both allocative inefficiency and X-inefficiency.

On the other hand, it is sometimes argued that monopolistic firms are in a better position to achieve **technological advancement** than their perfectly competi-

tive counterparts. Schumpeter (1954, chapter 8) believed that the typical monopolist has both an incentive and the means to initiate or imitate cost-saving technical inventions and innovations. If the monopolistic firm is to satisfy its shareholders, it will have to make a healthy profit which can then be used for research and development purposes to improve productivity within the firm. Referring back to Figure 4.2, for example, the effect of technological progress will be to shift the production possibility curve from R_0T_0 to R_1T_1. If allowance is made for the presence of X-inefficiency, the overall equilibrium may now occur at a point such as M_2 which implies that, in this example, technological progress has enabled the economy to move beyond its original production possibility curve.

This brings us to the important issue of

deregulation. As it is commonly understood, deregulation represents an attempt on the part of the authorities to promote competition by removing certain barriers to entry. These might include a prohibitive licensing fee, property taxes or inappropriate health standards. The analysis in this section suggests that the removal of such barriers will improve allocative efficiency and X-efficiency within the relevant industry, but may also entail a cost in terms of the lesser ability of competitive firms to initiate and carry out technical inventions and innovations. The economic case for deregulation will thus depend on whether the gains in terms of allocative and X-efficiency are sufficient to offset the slower pace of technological advancement amongst competitive firms.

4.2 The decreasing cost case: To privatise or not

An industry is said to be a **natural monopoly** if it is characterised by large capital outlays that give rise to economies of scale over the entire range of its output. The minimum average cost of production may thus occur at a level of output sufficient to supply the whole market. Only one firm can effectively operate in such a market, and the best known examples of this type of industry are public utilities involved in the provision of water, electricity, rail transport and postal services.

Increasing returns to scale mean that the long-run average cost (AC) of the firm diminishes as output increases. Its marginal cost (MC) curve will thus lie below the AC curve over the entire output range. This is illustrated by the curves labelled AC and MC in Figure 4.3. The condition for profit maximisation in a perfectly competitive market is that each firm sets marginal cost equal to the market price, such as at point E in Figure 4.3 where $P_e = MC$. With increasing returns to scale, however, the industry will make a

unit loss equal to ES so that individual firms will eventually close down until a natural monopoly emerges.

If the natural monopoly is not controlled by the government, it will maximise profit at point M in Figure 4.3 where its marginal cost equals marginal revenue. At point M the equilibrium price, $0P_m$, exceeds the socially efficient price, $0P_e$, while the corresponding level of output, $0Q_m$, is smaller than the Pareto-optimal level, $0Q_e$. The profit-maximising behaviour of the monopolist may thus result in too little output being produced at too high a price, giving rise to a concomitant loss of welfare. The latter refers to the difference in consumer surplus between the two equilibria. Under monopoly the total value to consumers (or their willingness to pay) is given by the area $0Q_mFA$, and the corresponding total cost by the area $0Q_mMFP_m$, with the difference being consumer surplus, or the area P_mFA. This is evidently much smaller than consumer surplus under perfect competition – given by the area P_eEA in Figure 4.3.

The question that now arises is whether something should be done about this loss of welfare. As may be expected, there is no simple answer to this question, but the government does have several options at its disposal. It can intervene by **regulating** the otherwise privately owned natural monopoly, for example, by forcing it to apply marginal cost pricing at point E in Figure 4.3, and covering the resultant loss by means of a unit subsidy equal to ES. Alternatively, the government can simply **nationalise** the monopoly and apply marginal cost pricing itself, in which case the resultant loss and required subsidy are the same as before. In either case the required subsidy would have to be paid for by government, and hence by the tax-paying public. If the government introduced a new or higher tax for this purpose, it will drive a wedge between marginal cost and marginal revenue elsewhere in the economy, implying an even greater loss in welfare due to the

Figure 4.3 Decreasing cost case

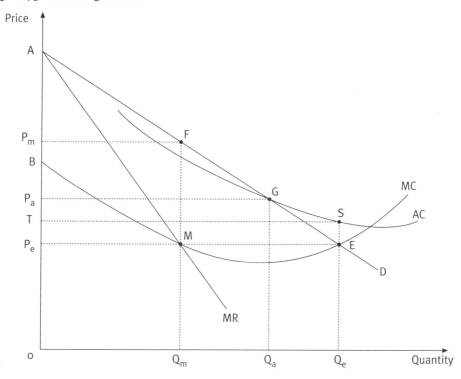

excess burden caused by such a tax wedge. And if it borrowed money to pay for the subsidy, it could put upward pressure on interest rates and crowd out private spending in the rest of the economy. Thus, whilst regulating or nationalising a natural monopoly may have an allocative advantage *vis-à-vis* the private option, it may also have a distorting effect on the rest of the economy.

The question of whether a natural monopoly should be run by the public or the private sector is clearly an important one and has attracted the attention of many economists and public officials during the past two decades. South Africa is no exception in this regard, and the privatisation drive here has gathered much momentum with the listing of Iscor on the Johannesburg Stock Exchange, and more recently with the partial sale of Telkom to two international companies. Although **privatisation** has become official policy in many countries of

the world, the issue itself is not as straightforward as its protagonists would have one believe.

As we have seen above, a natural monopoly will normally supply a greater quantity of the good or service at lower price if it is owned by the public rather than the private sector. Indeed, the main reason why such industries are often owned and controlled by the state is that they can be forced to expand output by setting price equal (or close) to marginal cost at point E. Even if allowance is made for the distorting effect of the required tax cum subsidy mix, marginal cost pricing is likely to engender a higher level of **allocative efficiency** than monopoly pricing.

This difference in allocative efficiency will, of course, depend on whether the additional benefit of having more of the one good relative to the other outweighs the additional cost arising from a higher level of taxation in the economy. In Figure 4.4, for example, sector X is again assumed to be perfectly competitive while sector Y is a natural monopoly; and similarly, the unregulated equilibrium is given by point M_0^u. The regulated (or nationalised) equilibrium is assumed to lie inside the *PPC*, at point M_0^r indicating the distorting effect of the required tax. If the regulated outcome (M_0^r) represents a higher level of social welfare than the unregulated equilibrium at M_0^u, the difference between the two can be regarded as a measure of the difference in the degree of allocative efficiency between a regulated or nationalised monopoly applying marginal cost pricing, and an unregulated private monopoly.

Whatever advantage a public enterprise may have in terms of allocative efficiency may be more than offset by the greater ability of its privately-owned counterpart to

maintain an acceptable level of X-efficiency. Most public enterprises depend on the government for financial assistance in the form of subsidies and hand-outs, and it is generally thought that this support all but destroys the incentive to keep production costs to a minimum. Although private monopolies may also experience organisational slack, labour inefficiency and the like, Leibenstein himself (1978:171-178) felt that they are less likely to be X-inefficient than subsidised state monopolies. After all, a private monopoly has little choice but to remain reasonably profitable if it is to avoid the threat of a possible take-over and, hence, continue to satisfy its shareholders. The public enterprise, by contrast, is under no such threat and can always rely on the seemingly endless resources of the state.

This difference in the degree of X-inefficiency can also be illustrated by Figure 4.4. In

Figure 4.4 Regulation versus privatisation

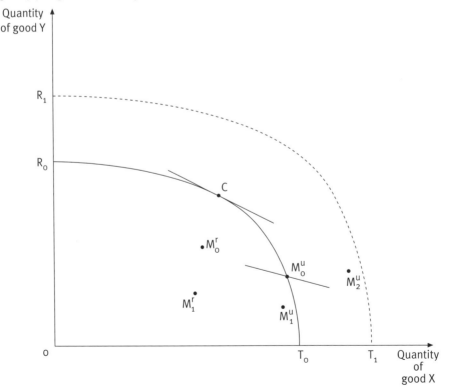

the unregulated case, for example, X-ineffi-ciency has the effect of moving the equilibri-um from point M_0^u to a point inside the pro-duction possibility curve, such as M_1^u, while in the regulated case the corresponding effect is evidently more pronounced insofar as it moves the equilibrium from M_0^r to M_1^r. If we also allow for a similar difference in the respective abilities to bring about technolog-ical advancement, the case for privatisation appears to be even stronger. We have already suggested that profit-maximising private monopolies may have a greater incentive to initiate and implement cost-saving innova-tions than subsidised public enterprises. This effect is shown in Figure 4.4 by an outward shift of the production possibility curve from R_0T_0 to R_1T_1, in which case the unregulated equilibrium may end up at a point such as M_2^u. If the latter equilibrium is deemed to be socially superior to the regulated equilibri-um at M_1^r, a *prima facie* case for privatisation will have been established. These arguments suggest that the case for privatisation depends on whether the gains in terms of X-efficiency and technical know-how outweigh the possible loss in terms of allocative ineffi-ciency that may accompany the privatisation of a state monopoly. Unfortunately it is not possible to be more precise about the relative importance of these forces, and it is partly for this reason that most commentators have done little more than pay lip service to the efficiency argument when discussing the rel-ative merits of privatisation.

Recent debates on privatisation have focused on the **financial gains** accruing to the state. These are essentially twofold. The first refers to the financial proceeds from the sale of state assets, and the second to the broadening of the tax base. As far as the pro-ceeds from privatisation are concerned, the South African government has in the past used such funds to redeem the public debt (see Chapter 17), promote the development

of small businesses, and maintain and extend the infrastructure in poor regions of the country. While these measures are strict-ly of a one-off nature only, their economic effect is likely to be felt for a long time. In the case of debt redemption, a smaller national debt would ultimately cut down on future interest payments and thereby curb the growth of government expenditure or release resources for reallocation; while the promotion of infrastructure and small busi-ness development may help to improve pro-ductivity amongst communities where it is most urgently needed.

The second benefit derives from the fact that nationalised industries do not pay taxes. When they are therefore sold to the private sector, they have to start paying taxes like any other private company. Furthermore, to the extent that privatisation improves productivity levels and profits in the economy generally, it may precipitate an induced increase in tax revenue that would not otherwise occur. These supply side effects may thus enable the government to reduce tax rates and thereby encourage sav-ings, investment and higher labour produc-tivity in the economy.

On the whole, it would appear that the case for privatisation is a pretty powerful one. The transfer of state monopolies and other public functions to the private sector is likely to boost X-efficiency and technical progress, lessen the burden of the public debt, reduce interest payments and govern-ment expenditure, broaden the tax base and, ultimately, enable the government to cut taxes and initiate a process of sustained eco-nomic growth. It is largely for these reasons that governments the world over have begun to dismantle their own empires in an attempt to restore the incentive-providing mechanisms of the market and thereby pro-mote economic efficiency in their respective countries.

4.3 Market power and competition policy

Most real world markets fall between the two extremes of perfect competition and monopoly, and are usually characterised by varying degrees of market power. In this section we briefly refer to the standard text book cases of **monopolistic competition** (where many firms produce close substitutes and each firm has some control over price), and **oligopoly** (where only a few firms produce a homogeneous product and each one has considerable control over price); after which we focus on the reasons for the high degree of seller (and owner) concentration and the related policy implications.

Monopolistically competitive markets and oligopolies generally produce equilibria that fall between the two extreme cases: that is, they tend to produce higher equilibrium quantities at lower equilibrium prices than those achieved under an equivalent pure

monopoly; but lower quantities at higher prices than those applicable to an equivalent perfectly competitive market. We can state this more formally as follows:

$$Q_{pc} > Q_{ic} > Q_m \qquad [4.3]$$

and $P_{pc} < P_{pic} < P_m \qquad [4.4]$

where Q and P represent the equilibrium quantities and prices, and the subscripts, pc, ic and m, stand for perfect competition, imperfect competition and monopoly, respectively.

The general equilibrium equivalent of these inequalities is straightforward: if sector X is assumed to be perfectly competitive and we let sector Y vary between perfect competition, imperfect competition and monopoly, then:

$$\left(\frac{Px}{Py}\right)_{pc} > \left(\frac{Px}{Py}\right)_{ic} > \left(\frac{Px}{Py}\right)_m \qquad [4.5]$$

which indicates the corresponding differences in the respective top level equilibria. These are shown in Figure 4.5 below. As

Figure 4.5 Imperfect competition

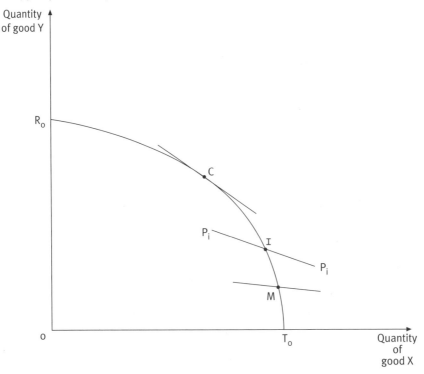

before, point C is the top level equilibrium when both sectors are assumed to be perfectly competitive; while point M is the corresponding equilibrium when sector Y is assumed to be a monopoly. Inequality [4.5] implies that our intermediate cases, where sector Y is either monopolistically competitive or oligopolistic, will generate a top level equilibrium lying somewhere between points C and M on the PPC in Figure 4.5 – e.g. at point I where the slope of the price line falls between those of the price lines at points C and M.

It is clear from Figure 4.5 that imperfectly competitive markets have a smaller negative effect on allocative efficiency than a pure monopoly; though, compared with perfect competition, they do cause at least some degree of allocative inefficiency.

The above analysis is, of course, a purely theoretical one, and in practice policy makers have been more concerned with the degree of concentration within particular markets, both in terms of the number of firms and the ownership pattern. This concern stems partly from the so-called **"structure-conduct-performance"** (SCP) hypothesis, according to which the structure of an industry determines the conduct of its constituent firms which, in turn, determines their performance. A highly concentrated industry will thus encourage collusive behaviour on the part of the few large firms comprising that industry, which will ultimately give rise to monopoly pricing. Empirically too, several observers (e.g. Leach, 1997) have found a strong and significant positive correlation between the degree of concentration and the profitability of industries within the manufacturing sector of South Africa. The latter finding can be ascribed either to the monopoly power of firms or the concentrated nature of ownership within the industry; or it can reflect the outcome of efficient behaviour on the part of low-cost firms – an issue to which we return in the next section.

Adherents to the SCP paradigm believe that the power of highly concentrated industries should be broken down in order to eradicate or avoid monopoly pricing. The instrument through which this is to be achieved is **competition policy** – a prime example of regulatory or "indirect" government intervention, as explained in Chapter 2. The need for a national policy on competition is widely accepted in the world today, and many countries have recently begun to revise their own policies, often with a view to making them less country-specific and more consistent with prevailing international trends. South Africa is no exception, and in the accompanying box we highlight some of the main features of the new Competition Act of 1998.

Competition policy should ideally be aimed at preventing or eradicating **restrictive practices** arising from the **abuse** of a **dominant** position – see the accompanying box. The issue here is not dominance as such, or the degree of market power, but rather the abuse of a dominant position. Likewise, a practice can only be deemed "restrictive" if it prevents others from entering the market while at the same time exposing consumers to unnecessarily high prices or a limited choice.

Competition policy – correctly applied – can lead to lower prices, an expanded choice, technological progress, and higher levels of fixed investment; and to the extent that it does, it will ultimately contribute to a process of equitable growth. Not only will the policy redistribute incomes through lower prices, but it will also see to it that restrictive entry barriers are dismantled, thus paving the way for new firms, including small and medium-sized ones, to enter lucrative markets.

4.4 Is competition policy necessary?

Before deciding on a competition policy, it is surely appropriate to ask whether there is a need for such a policy in the first place. Does dominance of a market necessarily result in abusive behaviour? Do high profit levels or "non-competitive" conduct necessarily imply abusive behaviour?

The answer to these questions is "no" according to the efficiency hypothesis proposed by Harold Demsetz (1973). He argued that the high degree of market power and ownership concentration in many markets across the world is merely the outcome of a competitive process in which superior low-cost firms manage to out-perform their less efficient counterparts. Prices in these markets are lower than they would have been otherwise, and any attempt to break down the power of dominant firms will undermine efficiency and put pressure on prices, thus harming the interests of consumers. He turned the conventional SCP hypothesis on its head: efficient low-cost production ("performance") goes hand in hand with competition ("conduct") which inevitably gives rise to dominance of the industry ("structure"). He was able successfully to test for the direction of causation, and found that the profitability of dominant firms was positively related to their ability to produce at low cost. In a more recent study Leach (1997) found that Demsetz's "efficiency hypothesis" also applied to the manufacturing sector in South Africa.

Box 4.1

Competition policy in South Africa

After many years of intense debate and negotiations between government, the business sector and organised labour – under the auspices of the National Economic Development and Labour Council (NEDLAC) – a new Competition Act was promulgated in 1998. The Act made provision for the establishment of a new **Competition Commission**, which consists of a governing body called the **Competition Management Board**; a new **Competition Inspectorate**, responsible for investigating alleged contraventions

---

of the Act; and a new **Competition Tribunal** whose functions include the assessment of alleged contraventions, the provisional authorisation or prohibition of existing or proposed mergers, and making recommendations to the Minister of Trade and Industry.

The main features of the new Competition Act can be summarised as follows:

- **Reason**. The main reason for the new policy stems from the Government's view that South African markets are dominated by a few large firms and that ownership and control of the economy are unusually centralised. **Abuse** in the form of non-competitive conduct (for example monopoly pricing) could result from **horizontal mergers**, where a small number of firms or shareholders end up controlling the market and selling the same or similar products; **vertical mergers** where one or a few firms own and control not only the same or a similar product, but also its suppliers and distributors, all within the same industry; and **conglomerate mergers** where one or a few firms have both horizontal and vertical control of production and distribution across several unrelated industries.

- **Objective**. The overriding objective of the new policy is to eradicate or avoid abusive behaviour and promote competition where feasible, in order to encourage efficiency and international competitiveness, provide easy access to small and medium-sized enterprises, diversify ownership in favour of historically disadvantaged people, and create new job opportunities in the economy.

- **Modus operandi**. The focus is not on dominance as such – said to exist

> where market share is at least 35 per cent – but rather on the abuse of a dominant position. The latter includes a number of potentially restrictive practices such as the fixing of purchase and selling prices, establishment of production quotas, exclusivity agreements, restriction of technical innovations, and collusive tendering. New mergers and takeovers must be authorised by the new competition authority, with the burden of proof resting with the companies involved.

It can be reasonably asked why dominant firms should use their profits to improve the quality of their products or to cut production costs, and hence prices. One reason is that dominant (even monopolistic) industries are often "contestable", in the sense that the incumbent firms are subject to potential competition, rather than actual competition. Provided there are no barriers to entry and that exit from the market is relatively costless, the mere threat of competition may be sufficient to keep incumbent firms on their proverbial toes. The South African beer market is a case in point. Even though the domestic beer market is dominated by a large conglomerate – South African Breweries – nothing prevents overseas or other local brewers from entering the market; and they might well consider doing so if local beer prices were too high, either because production costs were too high or because the profits of the incumbent brewer were deemed relatively attractive. It is therefore in the best interests of incumbent firms not to misuse their positions of power.

Contestable market theorists (e.g. Baumol, 1982) also argue that market structure depends on the relationship between the market demand and the nature of the product or service in question – as explained in Section 4.2 above. If economies of scale featured prominently in the production process, for example, then it can be expected that the market will be dominated by a few large firms. Furthermore, if the market was also globally contestable, these firms will avail themselves of the latest technologies in order to remain competitive *vis-à-vis* imported substitutes and to stay ahead of potential entrants. The optimal size of a firm depends largely on the nature of the product or service it produces and on the nature of the technology used in production.

Of course, the above arguments do not rule out the possibility that dominant firms may at times abuse their positions of power, for example by engaging in some of the "restrictive practices" mentioned above. There are many factors that may give rise to such an abuse of power – "structure" being one of them – but it is imperative that policymakers consider all the relevant facts. We have shown here that "big can be beautiful", especially if it allows one to utilise the latest technologies in order to improve quality and cut production costs. Populist intervention in the corporate structure of a country – merely on the grounds of size – could undermine efficiency, damage investor confidence and, above all, harm the interests of ordinary consumers.

It is also worth pointing out that growing global competition has already forced several dominant firms to restructure their operations, with some unbundling into smaller entities and others – especially in the financial services sector – merging into bigger ones. These dramatic changes illustrate that inefficient corporate structures are simply not viable over time – they tend to disappear of their own accord.

Important concepts

abuse of a dominant position
competition policy
contestable markets
efficiency hypothesis
increasing returns to scale
mergers
monopolistic competition
monopoly and allocative efficiency
monopoly and technological advancement
monopoly and X-efficiency
natural monopoly
oligopoly
privatisation and efficiency gains
privatisation and financial gains
regulation of monopoly
restrictive practices
structure-conduct-performance hypothesis

Self-assessment exercises

4.1 Illustrate the effect on general equilibrium of introducing monopoly into the two-sector model. What are the efficiency implications?

4.2 Should natural monopolies be regulated?

4.3 Critically discuss the case for privatising natural monopolies.

4.4 Discuss the basic objectives and nature of competition policy, with specific reference to the "structure-conduct-performance" hypothesis.

4.5 Outline the new competition policy in South Africa.

4.6 Discuss Harold Demsetz's "efficiency hypothesis" and consider its implications for the conduct of competition policy.

Chapter five
Philip Black

Equity and social welfare

Yet another potential market failure concerns the distribution of wealth or income within a community. In Chapter 2 we referred to the black box nature of our benchmark model of general equilibrium – or to the fact that its predictions are basically determined by the initial assumptions on which it is based. So too it is with the distributional issue: the model predicts a particular distributional outcome that is a mirror image of the distribution assumed initially; and if the initial distribution is deemed unacceptable, then so too will be the final distribution.

Once you have studied this chapter, you should be able to

- distinguish between the Pareto and Bergson criteria for a welfare improvement;
- discuss Nozick's entitlement theory and its relevance to the recent history of South Africa;
- explain how a redistribution of income can be justified in terms of the theory of externalities;
- distinguish between the cardinal and ordinal social welfare functions;
- discuss the efficiency implications of policies aimed at redistributing income from rich to poor people.

5.1 Introduction

In terms of the two-sector model illustrated in Figure 5.1, all points along the PPC represent maximum economic efficiency, as defined in earlier chapters. Each of these points also corresponds to a particular distribution of income between the individuals participating in the economy. This means that the distribution at point S is different from that at point C. In particular, one individual is better off relative to the other at point S than he or she is at point C.

Two important implications arising from our familiar two-sector model are relevant here. Firstly, a competitive economy producing the output mix given by point C will not necessarily also yield the most preferred distribution of income; the latter may, for example, occur at point S. Secondly, a policy-induced movement along the PPC, for example, from point C to point S, will necessarily change the distribution of income and thus make one individual worse off relative to the other.

Economists normally distinguish between two criteria when assessing the welfare effects of public policy. These are the Pareto criterion and the so-called Bergson criterion. The former implies that a policy-induced change is justified only if it

Figure 5.1 Potential top-level equilibria

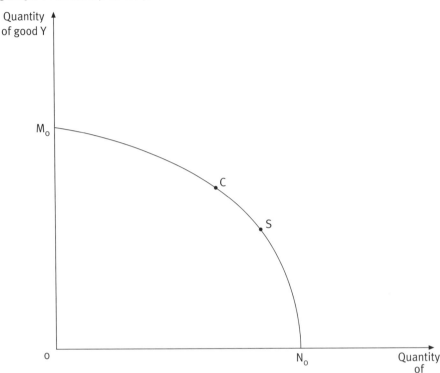

improves the well-being of at least one person without harming any other. The Bergson criterion is much broader, and allows for a welfare improvement even if one or more individuals are harmed in the process. In this chapter we shall consider both criteria: Section 5.2 looks at Robert Nozick's well-known entitlement theory, which provides a Pareto-based justification for a redistributive policy aimed at redressing past injustices; Section 5.3 examines several other Pareto criteria, and does so in terms of the familiar theory of externalities; Section 5.4 considers the Bergson criterion, and introduces what is conventionally referred to as "welfare economics"; and finally, Section 5.5 looks at some of the efficiency implications of policies aimed at redistributing income from rich to poor people.

5.2 Nozick's entitlement theory

The Pareto criterion is commonly associated with the libertarian approach to public policy according to which individual freedom is viewed as the primary goal of the community. This is usually defined in terms of the maximisation of "negative freedom", or protection of the right not to be coerced by others (Hayek 1960; Nozick 1974). The libertarian school thus advocates a *laissez faire* system in which the role of government is reduced to that of a caretaker charged with the responsibility of protecting individual freedom. Libertarians are in principle opposed to distributional policies that infringe upon the freedom of individuals.

There is however an important exception to the libertarian rule, which derives from

Robert Nozick's (1974) well-known entitlement theory. Nozick distinguished between three "principles of justice" in which he sets out the conditions for a just distribution. The first two principles can be defined as follows:
- Principle 1: **Justice in acquisition**, which states that individuals are entitled to acquire things that do not belong to others or do not make others worse off than before. Such "things" refer to property and capital goods only – not to labour income which Nozick regards as an inalienable individual right.
- Principle 2: **Justice in transfer**, according to which material things can be transferred from one individual to another on a voluntary basis, for example, in the form of gifts, grants and bequests, or through voluntary exchange.

In terms of these principles "...a distribution is just if it arises from a prior just distribution by just means" (Nozick, 1974: 58). Violating either of the first two principles gives rise to Nozick's third principle of justice:
- Principle 3: **Rectification of injustice in holdings**, in terms of which a redistribution of wealth is potentially justified only if one or both of the first two principles have been violated.

Nozick's third principle provides his only justification for a policy aimed at redistributing resources between individuals. But it is evidently easier said than done. Nozick (1974: 67) himself recognises the practical difficulties involved when he asks: "...how far back should one go in wiping clean the historical slate of injustice?" This question is clearly relevant to South Africa's recent past, and presumably formed one of the cornerstones of the investigations undertaken by the **Truth and Reconciliation Commission** (TRC). The latter limited its focus to the apartheid era, in particular to the period

between 1 March 1960 and 5 December 1993 during which the National Party was in power; though it did recognise the many historical precedents set by earlier regimes. Some of the functions of the TRC are outlined in the accompanying box entitled "Rectification in South Africa".

According to Nozick, proper rectification requires a thorough analysis of the historical events that gave rise to the violation of his first two principles. It also calls for an accurate assessment of the distributional pattern that would have emerged in the absence of the violation. While both tasks are needed to determine the extent of rectification, neither can be said to be straightforward. Both require a wealth of historical data, much of which will be largely hypothetical and based on anecdotal evidence, and neither is likely to produce outcomes that are free of human prejudice.

On the other hand, Nozick's third principle is restricted to a redistribution of improper holdings of fixed property and capital only – not to labour income. The latter reflects a person's innate endowments and cannot therefore be taken from him or her, either for equity or efficiency reasons. Whilst this restriction is perhaps highly contentious, it does at least simplify the practical application of Nozick's rectification principle.

The Pareto flavour of Nozick's rectification principle is straightforward: If Tom enriched himself at Thandi's expense, and did so against her will, the principle demands that Tom should give back to Thandi what rightfully belonged to her so that both parties would be in the same position as they would have been in the absence of the injustice.

5.3 Other Pareto criteria

Policies aimed at redistributing income from rich to poor people can be justified on Pareto grounds in terms of the theory of **externali-**

ties – as discussed in Chapter 3 above. In communities characterised by a high degree of inequality it is possible that the poor may impose certain negative externalities on the rich. High levels of crime and violence often go hand in hand with widespread poverty, and these may undermine the quality of life of the rich. Likewise, a lack of sanitation and other health-promoting services among the poor may give rise to a variety of contagious diseases, which may ultimately threaten the health status of rich people.

Box 5.1
Rectification in South Africa
The overriding objective of the Truth and Reconciliation Commission was to develop a human rights culture in the country and to bring about national unity and reconciliation. The Commission was divided into three committees whose primary functions can be summarised as follows:

- The **Committee on Human Rights Violations** was responsible for identifying victims of "gross human rights violations" committed during the period 1 March 1960 to 5 December 1993, assessing the nature and magnitude of those violations, and referring legally prepared reports on the victims to the Committee on Reparations and Rehabilitation. During its deliberations the Committee also identified alleged perpetrators, as well as persons already being prosecuted or found guilty in a court of law, and submitted reports on them to the **Committee on Amnesty.**
- The **Committee on Amnesty** considered applications from persons who had committed human rights violations and based its decision on whether these were committed for political reasons, rather than for personal gain or any other reason.

The Committee also looked at the nature and the degree of seriousness of violations before reaching a decision. Those granted amnesty could not be held liable for damages and could not be criminally charged in a court of law; whilst those who were unsuccessful were liable for prosecution.

- The **Committee on Reparations and Rehabilitation** had to submit proposals to the Cabinet for reparations in the form of monetary payments to individual victims, as well as "community rehabilitation programmes" aimed at providing a range of basic services to communities that had suffered under apartheid. The TRC Act required Parliament to establish a President's fund from which payments were to be made.

After consulting across a broad spectrum of the community, and adopting a strict legalistic approach to its deliberations and findings, the TRC concluded that an amount of R2,8 billion was needed to pay reparations to apartheid-era victims. Two other sources of rectification are worth mentioning. The Department of Land Affairs has been involved in a process of investigating and legally processing a number of land claims arising from past violations of individual and communal property rights – yet another legacy of the Group Areas Act and human resettlement programmes implemented during the Apartheid era. In addition, several politicians, including President Mandela, have appealed to the private sector to make voluntary contributions to the government's own job creation fund – aimed at "achieving racial reconciliation in South Africa".

Under these conditions, rich people may be prepared to transfer part of their income to the poor in an attempt to reduce poverty and minimise its negative external effects. But no single rich person can do so alone, and it is partly for this reason that the distribution of income is often viewed as a public good: all or most rich people stand to benefit from a reduction in poverty, and hence in the level of crime and violence or in the incidence of disease, but individuals acting on their own, cannot bring that about. Poverty relief thus calls for appropriate government action aimed at bringing down the negative external effects of poverty to an optimal level. Government policy could take the form of direct transfer payments to the poor, or it could be used to provide basic services or strengthen the security system, in which case both poor and rich people stand to benefit from a healthier and more secure environment.

A related justification for redistribution derives from the so-called insurance motive. Individuals may view their tax payments as a relatively inexpensive means of insuring themselves against a possible future loss of income or ill health. On becoming unemployed, for example, they may qualify for support from a state-run unemployment insurance fund; or if they should become ill, they could likewise avail themselves of health services provided by the state. These individuals may view tax payments as a superior or cheaper alternative to taking out private insurance.

In all these cases there is no charity involved, but rather a *quid pro quo* principle: rich people give up part of their income for distribution among the poor because they expect to derive commensurate **material** benefits from such actions.

By contrast, a redistribution of income can be justified on Pareto grounds if one or more individuals are assumed to be **altruistic**, that is, both concerned and generous (Hochman & Rodgers, 1969). Such individuals could experience a net increase in utility from a policy that taxes their own income

and redistributes it in favour of another (non-altruistic) individual; and in terms of our two-sector model, a movement along the PPC may well improve the welfare of **both** individuals.

It is important to note that the notion of altruism implies the existence of external effects in consumption. Reverting back to our earlier example, if A is an altruist but B is not, we can write A's utility function as follows:

$$U_a = f[M_a, U_b(M_b)] \qquad [5.1]$$

with the first derivatives all positive. Equation [5.1] simply says that A derives utility not only from her own income, M_a, but also from individual B's level of utility $[U_b(M_b)]$ – presumably up to some maximum level. B derives utility only from his own income, M_b.

Simplifying equation [5.1] by setting

$$U_a = g(M_a, M_b) \qquad [5.2]$$

we can state the condition for a "Pareto-efficient" redistribution of income from our altruist, A, to the non-altruist, B. Mathematically it is:

$$0 < g'(M_a) < g'(M_b) > 0 \qquad [5.3]$$

or in words: the increase in A's utility resulting from B's higher income ($g'(M_b) > 0$) must exceed the decrease in A's utility resulting from the drop in her own income ($0 < g'(M_a)$). In other words, given that B is better off, A must experience a net increase in utility.

There are presumably many real-world examples of Pareto-efficient redistributions. When people contribute towards charitable organisations, or give money to beggars, they presumably do so because it makes them feel better – which is why we view altruism as a Pareto-based justification for redistribution. Such transactions are, of course, voluntary whilst redistribution via the fiscal process is not. Nonetheless, it can be suggested that some taxpayers do derive utility from that part of their taxes earmarked for the relief of poverty and the care of old and disabled people.

5.4 Bergson criterion

In terms of the **Bergson criterion** a redistribution of income can be justified on welfare grounds even if it makes one or more individuals worse off. The Bergson criterion is best explained in terms of the familiar **social welfare function**, according to which a community's welfare is defined in terms of the utilities of all the individuals making up that community.

We can distinguish between two such welfare functions. The first is the so-called "cardinal" or **additive welfare function**,

$$W = U_a + U_b + \ldots\ldots \qquad [5.4]$$

where W represents the level of community welfare, and U_a and U_b are individual utilities. According to [5.4], community welfare equals the sum of individual utilities – assumed to be measurable on the same scale.

The additive welfare function does illustrate the Bergson criterion very neatly: it allows for the Pareto criterion insofar as W will increase if **either** U_a **or** U_b increases, or if both U_a and U_b increase at the same time; but it also allows for a welfare improvement consequent upon a decrease in either U_a or U_b – W will increase so long as the increase in U_a (or U_b) exceeds the decrease in U_b (or U_a). In addition, if a poor person, say individual A, derives greater additional utility from an extra R10 than does his or her rich counterpart, individual B, then the stage is set for a welfare-improving redistributive policy: taking R10 away from B and giving it to A will raise U_a by more than it will reduce U_b. The latter conclusion assumes that an individual's marginal utility from

income diminishes as his or her income increases.

Equation [5.4] represents a very restrictive welfare function. Apart from the measurability issue, it assumes that individual utility functions are identical and depend only on their incomes. It is also highly debatable whether increases in income engender smaller increases in utility at higher levels of income.

It is partly for these reasons that economists prefer the more generalised welfare function,

$$W = W (U_a, U_b) \qquad [5.5]$$

which is ordinal in nature and does away with the assumption of measurability. By letting W take on different (constant) values, it is possible to derive a set of **social or community indifference curves**, such as those labelled W_1, W_2 and W_3 in Figure 5.2. These functions have the same properties as individual indifference curves: they are convex with respect to the origin, cannot intersect, and exhibit diminishing marginal rates of substitution.

Also shown in Figure 5.2 is a familiar possibility frontier (also known as the "grand utility possibility frontier"), which is slightly different from the more conventional PPC. The utility possibility frontier, QR, gives the **utility** combinations associated with all the top-level equilibrium points along a conventional PPC. In the example of Figure 5.2 the community prefers the combination at point H – the welfare maximum – to any other point along the frontier.

The above analysis crucially depends on two closely related assumptions. Firstly, the community is assumed to be **able** to choose between different points along the utility possibility frontier, for example, point H as opposed to point G. The question of **how** a community makes such choices has given rise to a huge literature – referred to as public choice theory – and we shall return to this issue in the next chapter.

Secondly, when choosing a particular point on the frontier, the community is making an explicit value judgement about the relative worthiness of the two individuals, A and B. This is illustrated in Figure 5.3 where two alternative sets of welfare functions are shown, one labelled W_1, W_2, ..., and the other W_1', W_2', ...; and where the similarly numbered subscripts indicate the same level of social welfare. It is clear that the former function embodies a relatively strong preference for individual A, generating a top-level equilibrium at point I; whereas the function W_1', W_2', ..., embodies a strong relative preference for individual B. Individual A is better off at point I than at point J, while the opposite is true of individual B, and yet the two social indifference curves, W_2 and W_2', represent the same level of welfare.

It is but a small step to show that the difference between the two welfare functions in

Figure 5.3 also implies a difference in the community's assessment of the worthiness of the two sectors, X and Y. All we need to assume is that the individuals have different tastes. Thus if individual A has a strong relative preference for good X, and individual B has a strong relative preference for good Y, then it follows that the function labelled W_1, W_2, ... indicates, by implication, that the community has a strong relative preference for sector X. Similarly, the function W_1', W_2', ... would indicate a strong relative preference for sector Y.

Consider the two individual utility functions,

$$U_a = U_a (X_a, Y_a)$$ [5.6]

$$U_b = U_b (X_b, Y_b)$$ [5.7]

Given that $X = Xa + X_b$ and $Y = Y_a + Y_b$,

Figure 5.2 Utility possibility curve and welfare maximum

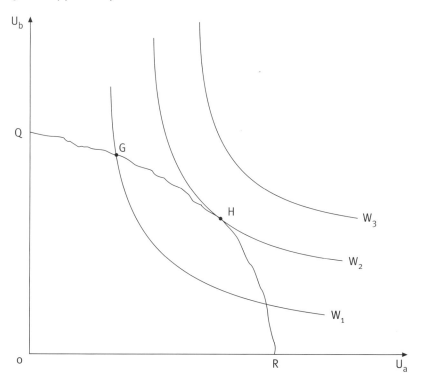

Figure 5.3 Alternative welfare functions

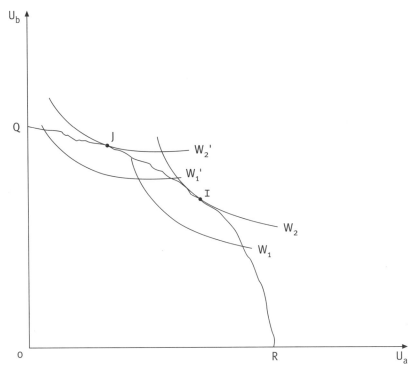

application of the "function-of-a-function" rule to equation [5.5] gives:

$$W = V [(X_a + X_b), (Y_a + Y_b)] \qquad [5.8]$$

$$W = V (X,Y) \qquad [5.8a]$$

where V indicates a different functional relationship from our earlier function. Equation [5.8a] simply states that the welfare of society depends on the production levels of the two commodities, X and Y. Equation [5.8a] is a very general version of the welfare function (defined in terms of individual commodities), and it can be specified in many ways. But most such specifications will embody the above value judgement, that is, that the community has to make a judgement about the relative worthiness of the two sectors and, by implication, of the two individuals as well.

The latter welfare function is shown in

Figure 5.4 where we assume that the top-level competitive equilibrium occurs at point C. But this does not coincide with the welfare maximum at point S: the community prefers point S to point C, thus establishing a *prima facie* case for appropriate state intervention to move the economy to point S.

The above analysis has shown that a top-level competitive equilibrium is only a necessary condition for a social welfare maximum, not a sufficient condition – as shown by the difference between points S and C in Figure 5.4. Two questions therefore arise: (a) what kinds of policy could be used to bring about an inter-sectoral or inter-personal redistribution of income, that is, a movement from point C to point S; and (b) what are the implications for economic efficiency of such policies. As far as (a) is concerned, government has several options at its disposal: it can tax sector Y and subsidise sector X, or it can tax one individual and subsidise

Figure 5.4 A competitive equilibrium versus welfare maximum

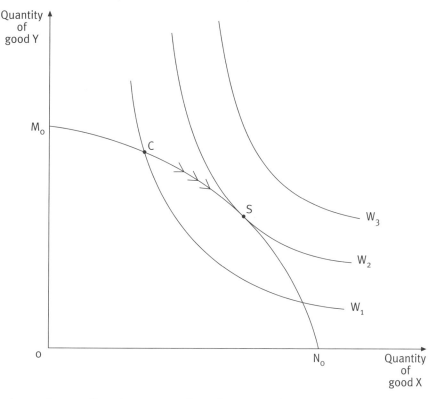

the other; or it can redirect its own spending towards one sector or individual. These options will be discussed in greater detail in subsequent sections of this book. Note, however, that a movement from C to S entails an improvement in social welfare, even though U_b may be reduced on account of the reduced supply of good Y. This is the difference between the Bergson welfare function and the Pareto criterion discussed earlier.

In the mean time we turn our focus to the second question raised above.

5.5 Efficiency considerations

It would be surprising if a redistributive policy comprising a suitable tax-subsidy mix had no effect on efficiency levels in the economy. As we shall see in subsequent chapters, most taxes and subsidies do have distortionary effects on markets, and the real question is whether the perceived benefits from such policies justify these distortions.

We shall briefly introduce two such distortions here, both of which are discussed in more detail in Chapter 10. The first is the possible effect that individual taxes and subsidies might have on the **willingness to work**. Specifically, does a new or higher tax or subsidy cause people to work longer or fewer hours per day or per month? And similarly, does a higher tax or subsidy cause people to work more or less productively, that is, produce more or fewer units of output per hour? In other words, can one expect an increase or decrease in the supply of labour or in its productivity – or, in terms of our two-sector model, a sub-optimal top-level equilibrium?

The evidence on this issue – referred to as "income and substitution effects" or the "(dis)incentive effect" – is anything but conclusive. What it does show is that, above a certain level, increased taxes tend to have a small negative effect on the willingness to work. This is illustrated in Figure 5.5 where the initial competitive equilibrium again occurs at point C_0 on the PPC labelled M_0N_0, representing an initial welfare level of W_1. Now, a policy aimed at redistributing resources from sector Y to sector X (for example by taxing sector Y and/or subsidising sector X), will move the economy in the direction of point S – the policy target. However, if the policy does have a small disincentive effect, labour productivity may fall below its potential and the economy may end up at a sub-optimal allocation lying inside the PPC – for example point F in Figure 5.5.

Although point F is inferior to point S, it nevertheless represents a higher level of welfare than the original allocation at point $C_0 – W_2$ as opposed to W_1. A stronger disincentive effect would have a bigger impact on labour productivity, and hence on the level of social welfare. Thus the policy could move the economy to a point such as E on the social indifference curve W_0, which is clearly inferior to the original allocation at point C_0.

The second possibility referred to above concerns the dynamic consequences of a distribution policy aimed at taxing the rich and subsidising the poor. The imposition of a new or higher tax (on sector Y or on individual B) may limit **savings** and investment, and hence economic growth, and, in the limit, keep the economy on its existing *PPC*, for example, at point S in Figure 5.5, representing the higher welfare level W_3 (compared to the original allocation at point C_0). In the absence of such

Figure 5.5 Disincentive and savings effects of redistribution

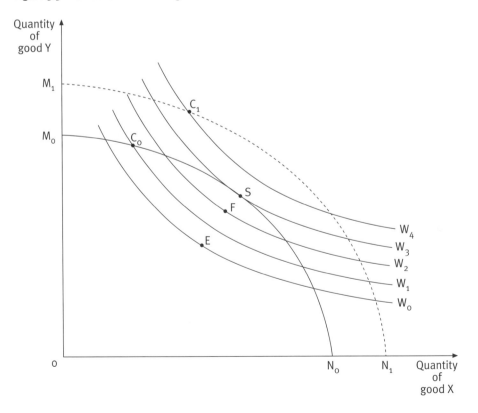

a policy, however, the economy may experience positive economic growth over time – indicated by the outward shift of the PPC from M_0N_0 to M_1N_1, and the concomitant change in the competitive equilibrium from point C_0 to point C_1. The latter change – though not achieving a welfare maximum – nevertheless represents an improvement in the level of social welfare from W_1 to W_4, and is evidently superior to the static policy-induced movement to point S.

On the whole, the above analysis indicates that there are many good reasons why societies might want to achieve a more equitable distribution of income. But whatever the justification might be, it is clearly important that the expected benefits of a policy of redistribution should be carefully weighed against the possible negative effects it might have on labour supply and on savings and investment, and hence on economic growth over the long run. We return to this theme in several of the subsequent chapters.

Important concepts
additive welfare function
altruism
Bergson criterion
entitlement theory
externality argument for redistribution
insurance motive for redistribution

justice in acquisition
justice in transfer
Pareto criterion
rectification of justice
savings effect of redistribution
social indifference curves/social welfare function
Truth and Reconciliation Commission
willingness to work

Self-assessment exercises

5.1 Discuss the proposition that Pareto optimality is a necessary but not a sufficient condition for a welfare maximum.

5.2 Distinguish between the so-called Pareto and Bergson criteria for a redistribution of income between rich and poor.

5.3 Discuss Nozick's entitlement theory and briefly consider its relevance for South Africa.

5.4 Explain why altruistic behaviour could provide a Pareto-based justification for a policy of income redistribution.

5.5 Distinguish between the "additive" and "ordinal" (or Bergson) social welfare functions.

5.6 Discuss the efficiency implications of an inter-sectoral (or interpersonal) policy of income redistribution.

Chapter six

Philip Black

Public choice theory

In the previous chapters we have looked at a range of so-called market failures, and highlighted the point that private markets cannot on their own supply public goods or make allowance for external costs and benefits. Similarly, although it is conceptually possible to regulate imperfectly competitive markets, or to evaluate the desirability of various income distributions by means of the Pareto and Bergson normative criteria, we have not as yet addressed the question of how a community can practically express its collective preferences on these matters. It is to this issue – of how communities make public choices – that we now turn.

Once you have studied this chapter, you should be able to
- discuss the Rawlsian theory of justice and comment on its relevance to recent political developments in South Africa;
- explain the median voter theory and indicate its potential strengths and weaknesses;
- discuss the meaning and importance of Kenneth Arrow's impossibility theorem;
- consider whether logrolling (or vote trading) is an efficient means of improving on the outcomes of a majority voting system;
- explain the theory of "optimal voting rules" and consider the question

whether it does indeed provide an "optimal rule" for majority voting;
- discuss the maximising behaviour of politicians and bureaucrats, and consider the implications of such behaviour for majority voting;
- explain what is meant by "rent-seeking".

6.1 Introduction

Many public issues are discussed and resolved in the **political market place**, where the quantities of public goods and services and the levels of taxes and subsidies are decided. In this chapter we study the nature and functioning of this "market" with regard to the allocation and distribution of our scarce resources. We investigate the mechanisms – or "social choice rules" – by which individual preferences are transformed into social or public preferences, and ask whether these will ensure that governments act in accordance with the wishes of the people they represent.

The most straightforward method of effecting such a transformation lies in simply imposing the ethical views of some dictator or central politburo on society and then adjusting economic policy accordingly. Viewed historically, however, dictatorial rule has often led to abusive behaviour, and clearly does not represent a desirable social choice rule. Most countries today prefer some method of collective decision-making based on and legitimised by mass participation on the part of their citizenry. Indeed, the characteristic social choice rule employed in most Western democracies is majority rule, whereby citizens elect representatives who must act within certain constitutional parameters.

Thus in the absence of dictatorial rule, the range of social choice rules varies between the unanimity rule, in terms of which a proposal requires 100 per cent support before being accepted, and ordinary majority rule, for which 50 per cent plus one vote are required. In what follows we first look at the unanimity rule, and focus specifically on John Rawls's well-known theory of justice, partly because of its relevance to the dramatic recent shift towards a full democracy in South Africa. This is followed in Section 6.3 by a discussion of the "ordinary majority rule" and the median voter theorem. Sections 6.4 and 6.5 look at some of the problems associated with majority voting, focusing specifically on its inability to allow for differences in the intensities of individual preferences. Section 6.6 deals with an important variation on the ordinary majority voting rule, i.e. Buchanan and Tullock's (1962) notion of "optimal voting rules". In the last two sections – 6.7 and 6.8 – we shift our attention to "positive public choice theory", and consider the behaviour of politicians, bureaucrats and private interest groups within a typical representative democracy.

6.2 The unanimity rule and the Rawlsian experiment

The **unanimity-voting rule** means that each member or representative group within a community must support a proposal before it becomes the collective decision. The unanimity rule is the only voting rule that will lead to a Pareto-optimal outcome, and since it requires that collective decisions be in the interest of all parties, it can be viewed as a positive sum game.

A good if somewhat unusual example of the unanimity principle is provided by **John Rawls's (1971) theory of justice**. The theory is essentially a normative one setting out the conditions under which "free and rational" persons will choose certain principles of justice that govern the "basic structure of society". These principles determine the fundamental rights and duties of individuals and regulate the institutional framework within which allocative decisions are made on a collective – and unanimous – basis. The "social contract" that ultimately emerges is described by Rawls as a case of "justice in fairness".

What sets the Rawlsian theory apart from others is its focus on the **process** by which individuals reach unanimity over the principles of justice. He thus asks his readers to imagine a situation in which the contracting parties, representing the whole community, all step through a "veil of ignorance" and enter a hypothetical "original position" – a position reached through intensive personal discourse during which all barriers are broken down and each party is able to rid itself of all prejudices and prior knowledge. In the original position, each party is wholly unaware of its "place in society" and has no knowledge of the probability distribution of expected outcomes, let alone its current well-being. They all stand as equals on the same playing field.

What is important for our purpose is that each party in the original position is assumed to be equally risk averse. All parties would thus support a risk-minimising social welfare function that effectively insures them against the worst possible outcome. Such a welfare function could take the form,

$$W = Minimum\ (U_a,\ U_b) \qquad [6.1]$$

indicating that social welfare depends on the lower of the two individual utilities. Thus if

$U_a < U_b$, welfare reduces to $W = U_a$ which implies that for W to increase, there must be an increase in U_a. The latter condition does not preclude an increase in U_b, and it is perfectly in order for U_b to increase – so long as U_a also increases in the process, or at least does not decrease. The Rawlsian welfare function is therefore perfectly consistent with a Pareto-based policy benefiting both parties.

From a Rawlsian perspective, Equation [6.1] implies that all parties in the original position will adopt a maximin strategy, giving priority to the worst off party, because it provides them with a measure of protection in case they end up being that worst-off party. All parties will therefore choose, and unanimously approve, a political constitution embodying the Rawlsian welfare function and, by implication, also an institutional system and a set of policies aimed at allocating and distributing resources in accordance with that function.

It hardly seems prudent to suggest that recent negotiations for a new constitution and democratic dispensation in South Africa even approximated a Rawlsian original position – none of the negotiating parties can be said to have been "completely impartial" while the underlying principle would appear to have been one of compromise rather than unanimity. Nonetheless, the growing concern for the poor and "historically disadvantaged" in this country, as reflected in affirmative action programmes, numerous job creating initiatives and the redistributive nature of recent budgets (see Chapters 15 and 17 below), does seem to come close to acceptance of a Rawlsian welfare function – that is, one that affords priority status to the least advantaged in the community.

The unanimity rule is not without its shortcomings. Reaching a unanimous decision may take a very long time, partly because of the divergent nature of individual preferences and the number of issues involved – witness the drawn out nature of the ("Kempton Park") negotiations that preceded the drafting of a new constitution in South Africa. The point here is that the costs of reaching consensus may be inordinately high, and it is important that cognisance be taken of the opportunity costs associated with the unanimity rule. The time spent lobbying and influencing individuals and groups of individuals can arguably be spent more productively elsewhere in the economy.

Viewed more practically, the unanimity rule could give rise to strategic actions on the part of certain individuals or groups who might want to enter into bargaining contracts with other parties in order to secure special benefits. Under such conditions parties may be persuaded to engage in "logrolling" (or vote trading) by forfeiting something they want in exchange for something about which they feel particularly strongly. We shall return to the issue of logrolling below, but suffice it to say here that the outcome of such a process is hardly likely to be Pareto-efficient.

A final objection to unanimity rule is that it gives minorities the right of veto; in the extreme case the last unpersuaded voter has the decisive vote. Exercising such a veto right will clearly render the unanimity rule obsolete, while it could also lead to a situation in which a minority effectively rules.

6.3 Majority voting and the median voter

The most common social choice rule is the "ordinary" majority rule. Every individual is given one vote, with the issue or policy receiving the most votes winning the day. Under a **direct** democratic dispensation, where each voter reveals his or her preferences directly via a referendum, the majority voting rule requires that a proposal receives "50 per cent + one vote" support before it can be imposed on the community. If South

Africa had a direct democracy and the public were asked in a referendum to vote for or against an increase in the rate of value added tax (VAT), the rate would not be increased if 4 000 001 voters out of a total of 8 million voted against such an increase.

In a **representative** democracy individual voters elect representatives who make decisions on their behalf. A representative democracy is generally less costly to administer than a direct democracy, and it is largely for this reason that the former is most widely used in the world today – although some countries like Switzerland do combine the two systems, utilising the direct method when important national decisions have to be made.

Voters' interests in a representative democracy are represented by several influential actors, including elected politicians, bureaucrats and private and public interest groups. The role of politicians is paramount, and one can reasonably ask: What are they in the "market" for? What do they want to maximise? Following Anthony Downs (1957), politicians act like any other utility-maximising consumer or profit-maximising entrepreneur, the only difference being that they are in the business of maximising the number of votes they collect in an election. In an ideal world, the vote-maximising behaviour of politicians is an important means of transforming individual preferences into a logically consistent set of social preferences.

What is required to maximise votes in a representative democracy? To answer this question we must examine the **median voter theorem**. We begin our explanation of this theorem by defining the median voter as the voter whose set of preferences divide the voting community exactly in two. Let us assume a community of five people: Ndlovo, Mary, Thandi, Johan and Ibrahim. Assume further that we know their precise preferences concerning the size of the national health budget. Table 6.1 sets out

the budgets for which each of them will vote.

Table 6.1 Voter preference for size of health budget

Voter	Amount (R million)
Ndlovo	50
Mary	200
Thandi	400
Johan	600
Ibrahim	800

Let us adopt a step-by-step approach towards discovering the majority decision on the size of the budget, beginning with a zero budget. Assuming that there are no extreme preferences (see below), all five voters will prefer a R50m budget instead of a zero budget. It will, however, be the preferred option of Ndlovo only. A movement from R50m to R200m will get the support of everyone except Ndlovo; that is, all except Ndlovo prefer a budget bigger than R50m. A movement from R200m to R400m will be approved by Thandi, Johan and Ibrahim, while only two voters will support an increase from R400m to R600m, and so on.

It is clear from Table 6.1 that three of the five options will enjoy majority support: all five voters (or 100 per cent) will support a budget of R50m, four voters (80 per cent) a budget of R200m, and three voters (60 per cent) a budget of R400m. But which is the optimal one? Which one will make our voting population happiest, or cause the least harm?

The answer is provided by the median voter theorem: the best option is that of Thandi's – our median voter – whose preference divides the voters exactly in two. The reason is that both Johan and Ibrahim would prefer Thandi's option to those of Ndlovo and Mary; while the latter will likewise have a relative preference for Thandi's option *vis-à-vis* those of Johan's and Ibrahim's. It follows that our larger-budget supporters, Johan and Ibrahim, will rather give their support to a politician campaigning for the median voter's choice than to a politician promoting any other potential majority choice.

We can now formulate the median voter theorem: under a majority voting system in which preferences are not extreme, it is the median voter's preferred option that will win the day, since that is the option that will produce the minimum welfare loss for the whole group.

The median voter model provides a simplified explanation of the rational behaviour of politicians under ideal conditions. The model suggests that politicians interact with voters to determine their relative preferences, and that by doing so they are able to identify the median voter, act upon his or her preferences, and in the process fulfil the wishes of the majority at minimum cost.

Of course, the real world of politics is a bit different from what the median voter theory would have us believe. Not all politicians are vote maximisers responding passively to individuals' demands. Some might pursue the "public interest", rather than vote-maximising strategies, while others may appeal to voters because of their vision and personality, rather than any tangible benefits they might promise. The model also presumes that the median voter can be identified. This is not easy, especially since different political issues may have different median voters. The model furthermore assumes that voters are rational and that everyone will vote. Politicians and voters are often far from perfectly informed, which renders rational choice unlikely, if not impossible – an issue to which we return in Section 6.7 below.

On the whole, the majority-voting rule – although not Pareto-efficient – does have two important advantages vis-à-vis the unanimity rule. Firstly, reaching majority approval takes much less time and is there-

fore less costly than achieving unanimous support; and secondly, under majority rule it is much less likely that a minority will be able to prevent the majority from getting their proposals accepted. On the other hand, majority rule can be criticised for its "winner-takes-all" consequences, and for its potential to ignore minority interests and even "tyrannise" minorities.

6.4 The impossibility theorem

A potentially serious shortcoming of the majority-voting rule is the fact that it can lead to logically inconsistent results. This proposition was first proved by Nobel laureate Kenneth Arrow (1951) in what is now referred to as his **impossibility theorem**. He proved that it is not always possible to derive a logically consistent set of social preferences from a corresponding set of individual preferences on the basis of an "ethically acceptable (or democratic) social choice rule". He came to the conclusion that there is not a single voting rule – not even majority voting – that would meet all the minimum "ethical" conditions he set for an "acceptable" social choice rule.

Arrow's theory crucially depends on these ethical conditions, which can be summarised as follows:

- **Rationality assumption**, according to which individuals and the community must either prefer one option (X) to another (Y), or be indifferent between the two; that is

$$X > Y \text{ or } Y > X \text{ or } X = Y$$

where > and = stand for "prefer to" and "indifferent between". The community must also adhere to the familiar **transitivity condition**, that is

$$\text{if } X > Y \text{ and } Y > Z \text{ then } X > Z$$

which means that if X is preferred to Y, and Y is preferred to Z, then X must be preferred to Z.

- **Independence of irrelevant alternatives**, which implies that if the choice is between two options, X and Y, then the effect of Z is irrelevant.
- **Pareto principle**, that is, if voter A prefers X to Y and voter B is indifferent between the two options, then the (two-person) community must prefer X to Y; or in algebraic terms:

$$\text{if } (X > Y)_a \text{ and } (X = Y)_b \text{ then } X > Y$$

- **Unrestricted domain**, that is, it should be possible for all eligible voters to vote.
- **Non-dictatorship**

Although these conditions seem very reasonable indeed, it is important to note that the Arrow problem is especially relevant to voters whose preferences are widely divergent or who choose extreme alternatives. We can illustrate such a case by considering three voters, Brenda, Christelle and Abdullah, each of whom has to choose between three alternative budgets, i.e. a large budget (denoted by L), a moderate budget (M) and a small budget (S). Let the individual preferences be as follows:

Brenda : L > M > S
Christelle : M > S > L
Abdullah : S > L > M

It is clear from this example that, if alternative budgets are voted for in pairs, a majority of the voters (i.e. Brenda and Abdullah) prefer L to M. A majority (i.e. Brenda and Christelle) also prefer M to S. Therefore, by the transitivity condition, a majority should prefer L to S – yet that is not the case: a majority (i.e. Christelle and Abdullah) actu-

ally prefer S to L; and hence we have a logically inconsistent – or intransitive – outcome.

The reason for this outcome is straightforward. Abdullah has **extreme preferences**: he prefers a small budget to a large one but also prefers the large one to a moderate one. Such a voter does not, when given the choice between any two budgets, consistently prefer a larger budget to a smaller budget, or *vice versa*. In a system of majority voting, where voting often occurs in a pair-wise fashion[1], the presence of extreme preferences[2] can have a number of consequences.

The first is that there may be a new winner every time the sequence of voting is changed. Consequently it is impossible to get a consistent winner. Whilst the preferences of individual voters may be consistent, their combined or the community's preferences (as reflected in their voting) will not be consistent if the group of voters includes people with extreme preferences. This phenomenon is referred to as the **voting paradox**. Such voting can continue indefinitely, a phenomenon called **cycling**. Furthermore, if the organisers of the election have prior knowledge of the existence of these extreme preferences, it is possible to organise the sequence of voting in such a way that a desired result is obtained. This is known as **agenda manipulation**. Any result that can be changed if the order of voting is changed, is not consistent and is not a true reflection of voters' preferences. Such a result therefore cannot claim to represent a choice for an optimal allocation of resources.

What is the practical relevance of all this? In a strict sense Arrow's theory implies that the majority-voting rule does not necessarily produce outcomes that enjoy the support of

---

1 Suppose there are three candidates for a position. Pair-wise voting entails that the first vote is between the first two candidates. The one who wins, is then paired with the other candidate in the second election. If the third candidate wins the second election, a third election will be required between the winner of the second election and the loser of the first to determine the ultimate winner.

2 In the example of extreme preferences given above, the result is quite confusing if the voter is asked to vote in a pair-wise manner. If the first vote is between large and small, small wins. In small versus moderate, moderate wins. In the final vote between moderate and large, large now beats the candidate which conquered its own superior!

the majority – which is something of a contradiction in terms! But all is not lost. The theory only proves that logical inconsistency is a **possible** outcome. In the above example of three voters choosing between three alternatives, for example, the probability of the Arrow problem arising is only six per cent (Frey, 1978:chapter 2). As one increases the number of voters and the number of alternatives, this probability rises only very gradually, reaching about 31 per cent when the number of voters becomes very large and the number of alternatives reaches six. It is thus tempting to conclude that perhaps too much is made of the impossibility theorem.

Nonetheless, the Arrow problem is compounded by the fact that majority voting does not allow for differences in the **intensity** of individual preferences, and by the attendant problem of logrolling – as we shall see in the next section.

6.5 Majority voting and preference intensities

Another major shortcoming of the majority-voting rule is the fact that it cannot account for differences in the intensity of voters' preferences, or at least cannot do so in a cost-effective way. Under these conditions it is quite possible that a small majority may have a relatively weak preference for a particular candidate, whom they nevertheless vote into power. If a large minority opposes the same candidate very strongly, it is possible that, in net welfare terms, the community as a whole will be worse off: given an additive welfare function (implying measurability of individual utilities), the cumulative decreases in individual utilities will exceed the corresponding increases.

Under majority voting there are two ways in which preference intensities can be accommodated. The first is to ask people to vote in the form of "intensity units". Instead of a straight yes-no vote, each voter can, for example, be given a total of 100 points that

he/she can allocate between competing candidates. In this way the ordering of preferences will be weighted and the weights will be taken into account in the voting procedure. It is thus possible that a candidate, who would have come last under a straight yes-no system, may fare better under the weighted system. But weighting is a normative procedure: Thandi's "80 percent" may mean something completely different from Johan's "80 percent". Weighting is also difficult to implement and administratively very costly, and it must be asked whether the additional benefits from introducing such a procedure are worth the additional costs.

Another – some would say better – way of reflecting preferences under a majority-voting rule is through **logrolling** or **vote trading**. Logrolling may occur between and among minority parties and the majority party. For example, an intense minority may trade its support for an issue enjoying strong support amongst the majority, in exchange for majority support of the minority issue; or the same exchange can be based on amendments being made to the issues involved. In practical terms, the latter exchange would only be feasible if the minority had a particularly strong preference for the "minority issue", and the majority did not feel too strongly about it. It would also not help if the minority took a minority view on each and every issue: if the majority could never count on a minority's vote on any issue, there would be no point in trading votes. Nonetheless, to the extent that such logrolling enables a better expression of consumer preferences in respect of public goods, it may increase the social welfare of society.

Logrolling can also take the form of an exchange of votes between different minority groups. Such groups could gang up against the majority by supporting each other's causes. If two minority parties in parliament each have a bill which it will never get approved on its own, they may get both passed by voting for each other's bill if the majority party had less than 50 per cent of the votes in parliament. Such vote trading may be a good thing if it leads to the approval of economically viable projects, which may otherwise not have seen the light of day. But it could equally well lead to the adoption of non-viable projects, or to projects that do not meet with the approval of the majority. While vote trading on the part of minorities does reveal the intensity of individual preferences, it can either increase or decrease the ability of a majority voting system to truly reflect the wishes of the majority.

6.6 Optimal voting rules

Is there anything in between an ordinary majority-voting rule and a 100 per cent una-nimity rule? Is there anything more efficient than ordinary majority voting? The answer can be found in the theory of "optimal voting rules", as propounded by James Buchanan and Gordon Tullock (1962).

Their main hypothesis is that the "opti-mal" voting majority varies in accordance with the particular public issue in question, and that these optimal majorities depend on the costs involved in the act of voting. Voters are faced with two kinds of costs, namely external costs and decision-making costs.

External costs arise when a community takes a decision that goes against the interest of an individual voter or group. In other words, the greater the number of people not supporting a public decision, the higher will be the external costs, or the higher will be the degree of unhappiness amongst the voting public. The expected external cost will be highest when public decisions are made by one person – a dictator – since such decisions will potentially ignore and undermine the interests of all other voters. By contrast, under a unanimity voting system, where public decisions require 100 per cent support, exter-nal cost can be expected to be zero. In other words, the closer one gets to unanimity, the

smaller will be the danger that minorities can be harmed. External costs are inherent in all decision-making rules, except the unanimity rule. In Figure 6.1, which depicts majority size as a function of cost, the external cost curve falls from top left to bottom right.

Decision-making costs refer to the costs involved in persuading voters to support a particular public issue. The smaller the com-munity of voters, the easier it will be to reach a majority decision and the lower will be the decision-making costs. As unanimity is approached, however, it becomes increasingly difficult and costly to make a decision.

One also finds that the opportunities to act as a free rider increase as the size of the group whose consent is sought, increases. Thus, as the size of the required support base increases, it becomes increasingly expensive to induce individuals to reveal their preferences accu-rately. In Figure 6.1 the decision-making cost curve rises from left to right as the number of individuals required for a collective decision increases.

We assume that voters take both types of costs into consideration when casting their votes. But since these costs will vary with the particular issue in question, the "optimal" – that is, cost minimising – voting rule will vary likewise. If the two kinds of costs are summed vertically, we obtain a total cost curve, as shown in Figure 6.1. The lowest point on the total cost curve, coinciding with the percent-age given by M^*, determines the optimal majority for the particular public issue in question. There is likely to be a different set of cost curves for each issue on which a vote has to be cast. The characteristics of the optimal majority point are as follows: the higher the external cost (curve), *ceteris paribus*, the greater M^* becomes; and the higher the decision-making cost, *ceteris paribus*, the lower M^* will be. The shape of the curves will differ accord-ing to the type of activity that is to be decided on; and the optimal majority need not be an ordinary majority (i.e. 50 per cent plus one vote).

Figure 6.1 The cost of democratic decision making

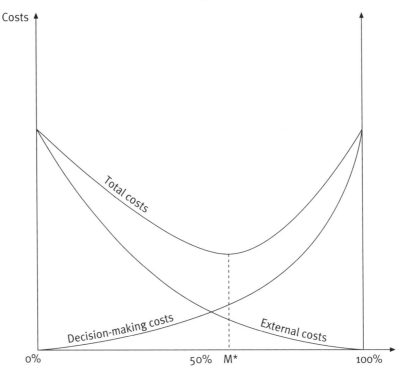

A factor that influences both decision-making and external costs, is the degree of homogeneity among the voting community. In a homogeneous community it is probably easier to achieve unanimity since there is less uncertainty about the tastes and negotiating skills of its members. The implication is that a community characterised by sharp differences among individual citizens and groups may not be able to afford the high decision-making costs involved in near-unanimity rules for collective choice. However, the potentially adverse consequences – or high external costs – for minority individuals and groups may be the very factor that will prompt such individuals to press for costly near-unanimity rules.

The above analysis can be used to determine voting rules for different kinds of collective actions. All such actions need not be organised under the same voting rule. Voters, for example, will choose a voting rule with a high majority requirement for collective actions that incur high external costs (or a major loss of utility) for them. Conversely, there are collective actions that incur low external costs, which means that a lower majority-voting rule will probably suffice. However, one should bear in mind that individuals and groups will normally not deem it in their interests to support a voting rule that may promote the interests of other groups. The customary rule when important issues such as amendments to a constitution are concerned, is that more than just an ordinary majority is required before these can be executed. Changes to the Bill of Rights in the South African Constitution, for example, require a two-thirds majority in the National Assembly.

6.7 Government failure: Politicians and bureaucrats

Even if an appropriate voting rule could identify the appropriate objectives of state intervention, **government failure** could see to it that they are not fulfilled in practice. Government failure arises from three main sources; firstly, rational behaviour by politicians pursuing vote maximising strategies – already referred to above; secondly, rational behaviour by state bureaucrats resulting in bureaucratic failure; and finally, rational behaviour by citizens and interest groups in the form of rent-seeking. In this section we focus on the first two of these sources of government failure.

As mentioned in Section 6.3, **politicians** can be viewed as entrepreneurs who engage in vote maximisation strategies in order to secure and retain political office. It is important to consider the implications for resource allocation resulting from such behaviour. The likely consequences can be more readily determined given two further characteristics of the majority-voting rule:

- Voters are rationally ignorant of much of what politicians stand for, since they usually do not have a sufficient incentive to acquire this information.
- Politicians are elected on the basis of a package of policies and therefore do not have to please a majority of voters on each separate policy issue.

These characteristics can give rise to implicit logrolling favouring special interest legislation. We can illustrate this proposition by means of a hypothetical example.

Imagine a politician standing for election in the electoral district of Pretoria East. She explicitly supports three special interest programmes, namely the relocation of Parliament to Pretoria, a rugby development programme, and a subsidised loan scheme for students in the area. Each of these special interest programmes is likely to attract strong support from a particular group within the voting population – civil servants will strongly support the relocation of Parliament, rugby lovers will likewise support the proposed development programme, and students will lend strong support to the proposed subsidy scheme. But none of the programmes will directly benefit a majority of voters in Pretoria East: the subsidy scheme will not benefit civil servants or rugby lovers directly, or at least not attract their strong support; and when faced with a choice between the three programmes, may have a weak opposition to it. They may therefore remain rationally ignorant about the full cost of the subsidy scheme.

Meanwhile, the politician in question who supports all three programmes, has an incentive to make the benefits of these policies clear to the three unrelated recipient interest groups, in order to form a coalition through **implicit logrolling**. She knows that the strong preference that civil servants have for relocating Parliament to Pretoria probably outweighs their mild opposition to the student loan scheme and the rugby development programme: they would rather have all three programmes than none. And she can make sure of this by disguising or understating the cost of each of the programmes to the Pretoria East electorate as a whole – that is, by creating fiscal illusion. Table 6.2 illustrates the nature of this implicit logrolling.

It is evident that the politician supporting all three minority programmes will defeat an opponent who opposes them, or who supports only one or two of them, by mobilising the strong preferences of civil servants, rugby lovers and students by means of implicit logrolling.

Two important consequences for resource allocation flow from this example. Firstly, we can anticipate a preponderance of special interest legislation producing a variety of relatively unpopular public goods. And, secondly, we can expect an aggregate oversupply of public goods in society.

It is clear that vote maximising behaviour on the part of politicians can lead to outcomes inimitable to the wishes of the majority of voters. Some writers, most notably Buchanan and Tullock (1962), argue that this phenomenon is a consequence of **constitutional failure** and can only be dealt with by constitutional reform which limits the proportion of scarce resources expended on public goods to some fixed percentage of national income, and specifies the distribution of these resources between alternative kinds of public goods.

A second source of government failure stems from the maximising behaviour of government employees and bureaucrats. In essence, the resulting **bureaucratic failure** comes about because of rational responses on the part of utility - maximising civil servants to the incentives presented to them by bureaucratic structures.

Thomas Borcherding (1977:xi) notes that: "Individuals in the bureaucracy, like the rest of us, do react to different incentive schemes; they do have various preferences, and have the capacity, will and desire to fulfil these preferences. They prefer more rather than less income, power, prestige, pleasant surroundings, and congenial employees."

The rational behaviour of bureaucrats can be analysed in terms of the demand for and supply of public goods. The demand for public goods in a representative democracy is generated by the decisions of vote-maximising politicians, whilst the supply of public goods is usually the responsibility of the state bureaucracy. Unlike private firms, however, bureaucracies do not maximise profit but instead receive annual lump-sum payments from the legislature based on estimates – prepared by bureaucrats – of the costs of providing specified (and usually monopolised) public goods. Consequently, bureaucracies do not face any market test. William Niskanen (1971) argued persuasively that since higher salaries, more power, greater prestige, and other favourable attributes are positively related to bureau size and hence to bureau budgets, bureaucrats have an incentive to maximise their budgets.

The resultant bias towards the excess provision of public goods is illustrated in Figure 6.2. Part (b) of the diagram shows the total social cost (TSC) and total social benefit (TSB) curves for a public good. The usual marginal principles apply here: total cost rises at an increasing rate as output expands (due to the principle of diminishing marginal productivity), while total benefits increase at a decreasing rate as output expands. The rates of change of these curves, or their slopes, determine the shapes of the corresponding marginal curves shown in the (a) part of the diagram.

Now, the socially optimal level of output

Table 6.2 Coalition forming and implicit logrolling

Policy	Strongly favoured by	Weakly opposed by
Relocation of Parliament	Civil servants (33,3%)	Rest of electorate (66,7)
Rugby development	Rugby lovers (33,3%)	Rest of electorate (66,7)
Student loan scheme	Students (33,3)	Rest of electorate (66,7)

Figure 6.2 Bureaucratic failure

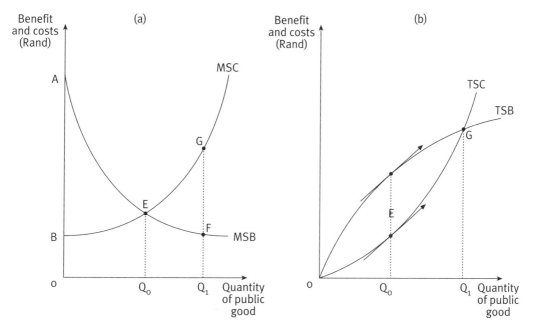

of the public good is given by $0Q_0$, where marginal social benefit *(MSB)* equals marginal social cost *(MSC)* (in the (a) part), or where the difference between *TSB* and *TSC* is maximised (in the (b) part). But a budget maximising bureaucrat would attempt to justify output $0Q_1(> 0Q_0)$, where *TSB* equals *TSC* and where *MSC* exceeds MSB by the distance FG. The result is that the total value to consumers increases from $0AEQ_0$ to $0AFQ_1$ (in the (a) part), or by the area Q_0EFQ_1; whilst total cost increases from $0BEQ_a$ to $0BGQ_1$, or by the larger area Q_0EGQ_1. The increase in total cost thus exceeds the increase in total benefits by the area *EGF* – the net welfare loss to society.

Moreover, bureaucrats can increase budget size by supplying public goods inefficiently, for example, by using more inputs to produce a given level of output. The resultant X-inefficiency stems from an excessive use of inputs rather than from excessive production by the bureau.

In essence, the problem of bureaucratic failure is simply an example of a **principal-** **agent** problem. In the public sector, bureaucrats act as agents for their principals, the taxpaying public, who are in turn represented by elected politicians. Since each individual bureaucrat benefits directly from a large budget, he or she has a strong preference for a high level of expenditure. Individual taxpayers, on the other hand, generally benefit only marginally from that expenditure, and therefore remain rationally ignorant about it. Because of the size and divergent nature of the tax-paying public, there is little individual taxpayers can do to lobby against higher levels of state spending or in favour of lower taxes. Thus, there is a poor correlation between the objectives of agents and the objectives of principals. Put differently, bureaucrats have a greater incentive to increase spending than taxpayers have to reduce taxes. It follows that one should expect spending levels on public goods to exceed their corresponding optimal levels.

Although Niskanen's model of bureaucratic failure provides a plausible explanation for excessive state intervention in the economy, it can be questioned on several grounds. Is it realistic to assume that politicians and the taxpaying public are entirely at the mercy of bureaucrats? Budgetary procedures have become more transparent everywhere, including South Africa, while the salaries and perks of senior public servants are not usually linked to the size of their budgets. In a democratic environment it seems unlikely that bureaucrats will be allowed to get away with practices that run against the public interest, at least not for long. It is thus difficult to confirm or deny the alleged empire-building motives and actions of bureaucrats.

6.8 Rent-seeking

Turning finally to the third source of government failure – **rent-seeking** – James Buchanan *et al* (1980) and others have observed that government intervention in a market economy may itself create distortions which lead to income and wealth transfers to private individuals and interest groups. These transfers constitute an additional source of economic inefficiency attendant upon government intervention.

The concept of **economic rent** is usually defined as that part of the reward accruing to resource owners over and above the payment that the resource would receive in any alternative employment. Rent is similar to monopoly profit: it cannot be competed away. In a perfectly competitive world, market forces would ensure the dissipation of rent in a manner that produces socially desirable outcomes. The existence of positive rent in a competitive market will attract resources in the same way as the existence of potential profits, and consequently result in the erosion of such rent through an efficient re-allocation of resources. However, once we adjust the mechanisms through which this process occurs, the consequence of rent-seeking behaviour can be harmful to society at large.

The theory of rent-seeking deals with the origins of, and competition for, artificially created rent. The latter usually results from government protected monopoly power, and in South Africa numerous examples abound, ranging from quantitative restrictions on licences for hawkers, liquor outlets and taxi drivers, to qualitative restrictions on purveyors of food, and people wishing to enter occupations like real estate sales, law and medicine.

The consequences of rent seeking under competitive conditions may be illustrated by means of a simple diagrammatic example. Figure 6.3 below shows a typical competitive market characterised by constant returns to scale and a demand curve which yields an equilibrium price $0P_0$, and quantity $0Q_0$. Now assume that the state intervenes to limit output to $0Q_1$. As a result, the price of the good rises to $0P_1$, causing a loss of consumer surplus equal to area $P_0E_0E_1P_1$. According to conventional economic theory, the area $P_0AE_1P_1$ denotes a socially costless wealth transfer from consumers to producers, whilst AE_0E_1 indicates the deadweight welfare loss to society. However, this may understate the net loss to society, as we explain below.

Under our present assumptions the area $P_0AE_1P_1$ is available to potential suppliers to "capture" in an attempt to boost their profits. They would thus be prepared to incur additional costs – from lobbying government, for example – in an effort to capture a share of this total rent. There are two possibilities here.

If participating suppliers – taxi drivers, say – undertook the lobbying function themselves, and the additional costs were internal to them, then marginal cost will increase – up to the critical level MC_1 in Figure 6.3. At this point the taxi drivers will have no further incentive to engage in rent-seeking activity since all rent consequent upon state intervention will have been dissipated. Given the exhaustion of $P_0AE_1P_1$, the social

Figure 6.3 Rent seeking

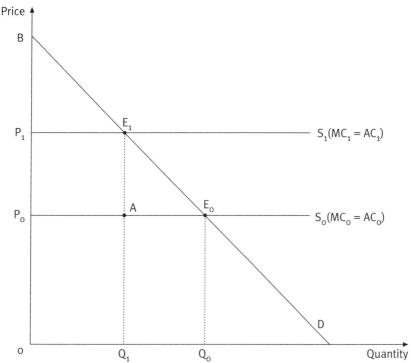

cost of state intervention will equal both areas $P_0AE_1P_1$ (or the social waste from rent-seeking) and AE_0E_1 (the deadweight loss). The point is that the taxi drivers will have transferred part of their own resources away from productive activities in favour of non-productive rent-seeking activities.

Alternatively, if a group of concerned citizens were to lobby government to reduce the number of taxis on the roads, then the additional costs will be external to them (the suppliers or taxi drivers) and the conventional theory will hold: the area $P_0AE_1P_1$ will indeed represent a wealth transfer from one group (the consumers) to another (the suppliers). The latter group will have received additional income that it can spend in the economy.

In broad terms then, the application of the microeconomic paradigm of rational maximisation provides further insight into the social costs attendant upon policy intervention by the state. In addition to the allocative and X-inefficiencies introduced into the market economy by vote maximising politicians and budget maximising bureaucrats, their efforts introduce yet another source of allocative inefficiency. Rent-seeking in response to government intervention can result in social waste.

Important concepts
bureaucratic failure
decision making costs
direct democracy
external costs
government failure
impossibility theorem
majority voting
median voter theorem
optimal voting rules

politicians and implicit logrolling
preference intensities
Rawlsian theory of justice
Rawlsian welfare function
representative democracy
rent seeking
unanimity rule
vote trading or logrolling

Self-assessment exercises

6.1 Discuss the Rawlsian theory of justice and briefly comment on its relevance to the political economy of South Africa.

6.2 Outline the median voter theorem and explain its importance to the successful application of a majority voting system.

6.3 Do you agree with the contention that majority rule does not necessarily produce outcomes representative of the majority view? Discuss with reference to the impossibility theorem and the phenomenon of vote trading.

6.4 Discuss the theory of optimal voting rules and briefly comment on its relevance to the future of majority rule.

6.5 Explain how the maximising behaviour of politicians could contribute to an oversupply of public goods.

6.6 In what way could the behaviour of bureaucrats cause "government failure"?

6.7 Explain the meaning of "rent seeking" and show how it could undermine efficiency in the economy.

PART TWO

Public expenditure

Chapter seven

Philip Black, Krige Siebrits and Theo van der Merwe

Public expenditure and growth

Part I of this book explained in theoretical terms why governments should mobilise and spend scarce resources in a typical market-oriented economy. In this chapter we turn to "real world" aspects of government expenditure in South Africa. We want to find answers to the following pertinent questions: What does the Constitution have to say about government expenditure? How much money is spent annually by government entities? What forms do such spending take and what services are provided? How has the composition of government expenditure changed over time, and how do these trends compare with those in other countries? Why has government expenditure grown so much over time? And, most importantly, how does government expenditure affect the economy in the short and in the long run?

As indicated in Chapter 1, these questions are particularly topical in view of the economic challenges facing South Africa and the global context within which they have to be addressed. In what follows, we first look at the growth of government expenditure and at the change in its composition, both in this country and elsewhere in the world, after which we discuss some of the theories explaining these changes. In the last two sections we turn our attention to a discussion of the short and long run effects of government activity on the economy.

Once you have studied this chapter, you should be able to
- comment on the implications of the Constitution for government expenditure in South Africa;
- discuss salient trends in the size, growth and composition of government expenditure in South Africa;
- identify the main similarities and differences between government expenditure patterns in South Africa and other countries;
- compare and contrast two or more of the theories that explain the growth of the government sector and indicate whether they have any relevance for South Africa;
- discuss the short-term impact of government expenditure on the economy in terms of multiplier analysis;
- consider the long-term effects of government spending in terms of "new economic growth theory".

7.1 The constitutional framework

The Constitution is the supreme law of the Republic of South Africa. As such, its provisions about taxation and government expenditure are the basic contours within which the budgetary policies of the government are formulated.

7.1.1 The Constitution and public goods

The South African Constitution contains many provisions that directly or indirectly impact upon the extent and composition of government expenditure. At a very general level, these provisions depend on how the government sector and its primary functions are defined in the Constitution. Government functions are derived from, and structured according to the constitutional distinction between the legislative, executive and judicial branches of government; the national, provincial and local levels of government; the security services and certain constitutional entitlements (discussed below); and statutory bodies such as the Public Protector, the Human Rights Commission, the Auditor-General and the Independent Electoral Commission. By granting powers and assigning functions to such institutions, the Constitution implicitly charges government with the task of maintaining them and providing for the necessary public funding. Failing to do so would indeed be unconstitutional.

In addition, the government of the day is constitutionally obliged to provide or extend the provision of specified basic goods and services. The clearest examples of such provisions are found in the Bill of Rights, which entrenches the right of each citizen to adequate housing, health care, food, water, social security and education. The Constitution is explicit on this issue: "...the state should take reasonable legislative and other measures, within its available resources, to achieve the progressive realisation of this right" (section 26(2)).

It is worth noting that these rights generally pertain to mixed and merit goods, rather than only to pure public goods (see Chapter 3), which partly confirms our earlier point that pure public goods are extremely rare in practice. But it is also indicative of modern thinking about the relative importance of the public sector in promoting sustained economic growth – a point to which we return in the last section of this chapter.

7.1.2 Constitutional entitlements

The rights to certain goods and services conferred by the Constitution could be regarded as constitutional entitlements. What are the practical implications of such entitlements for the way governments manage their own budgets? As we have pointed out, their wording in the Constitution acknowledges that governments are subject to budgetary constraints, but many economists feel uneasy about the vagueness of phrases such as "reasonable measures" and "within its available resources". They believe that such wording gives the government too much discretionary power that could threaten the macroeconomic sustainability of fiscal policy. Experts on human rights law also differ in their opinions on how enforceable these rights are in practice. To what extent can the government of a developing country like South Africa be held responsible for the provision of housing, social security and other basic services to all its citizens? And which of these rights should be accorded priority when trade-offs arise?

It is most likely that the Constitutional Court may at some stage be called upon to answer some of these very difficult questions. In an early case of this nature, the Court ruled in November 1997 that a South African kidney patient was not entitled to receiving expensive treatment at state expense. Two constitutional principles were involved in this case, namely the right to life and the right to access health care services. One of the bases for the ruling was that the latter right is subject to the "availability of resources".

From a fiscal point of view, a strong case can be made for a ruling that the government's obligations to its citizens should be extended to include future generations. This means that any current attempt at fulfilling these obligations should take full account of the impact it is likely to have on the future growth of GDP, and hence on the growth of government revenue, since the latter is clearly a necessary condition for maintaining the supply of public services over time. At the same time, however, it can be argued that the future growth of GDP depends on the current provision of services such as education and health care. The matter is therefore far from simple. A steady and consistent supply of these services, whereby backlogs and future demands are met within reasonable time frames, may help to resolve the conflict between constitutional entitlements and macroeconomic affordability. In this regard, medium-term expenditure frameworks may fulfil an important role, as we shall see in Chapter 17.

7.2 The size and composition of public expenditure

In Chapter 1 we gave some indication of the size of the public sector in South Africa. Table 1.1 and Figure 1.2 showed that the public sector had expanded considerably during the past few decades. In this section we take a closer look at trends in **general government expenditure** since 1960. The latter is defined to include the national government, provincial governments, local authorities and extra-budgetary accounts – that is, the non-profit activities and business enterprises of government – because these

constitute the broadest category for which comprehensive data on the extent and composition of state expenditure is available.

7.2.1 Size and growth of public expenditure

Trends in the size and growth of general government expenditure between 1960 and 2001 are summarised in Table 7.1. The table shows how expenditures grew relative to the gross domestic product (GDP).

Data is provided for two measures of expenditure, namely the total amount of resources used and the total amount of resources mobilised – as explained in Chapter 1. It is clear from the table that the past four decades saw sharp increases in the amount of resources used and mobilised by the general government. As a percentage of GDP it increased from 16,6 per cent to 19,8 per cent. Resource mobilisation as a percentage of GDP increased from 30,5 per cent to 33,6 per cent. Moreover, the average portions of GDP used by general government increased in each consecutive decade from the 1960s onwards.

The bottom part of Table 7.1 shows **real** average rates of growth in the amount of resources used during each decade. (Data at constant 1995 prices are not available for the resource mobilisation measure.) Although the amount of resources used grew in real terms throughout the period under review, it can be seen that the average rate of growth

Table 7.1 The size and growth of general government expenditure in South Africa, 1960-2001[a]

Measure	1960	1960-69	1970-79	1980-89	1990-99	2001
Percentages of GDP (current prices):						
Resource use	16,6	18,9	23,3	23,3	21,8	19,8
Resource mobilisation	20,5	23,1	29,1	32,2	33,3	30,5
Growth rates (1995 prices):						
Resource use		7,2	3,9	2,0	0,7	

Notes: [a] National accounting figures.
Source: Calculated from SA Reserve Bank, *Quarterly Bulletin* (various issues)

Table 7.2 The economic composition of general government expenditure (excluding business enterprises) in South Africa, 1960-2001 (percentages of total expenditure)[a]

Item	1960	1960-69	1970-79	1980-89	1990-99	2001
Remuneration of employees	35,7	32,5	27,4	31,0	40,1	41,3
Other goods and services	11,0	16,4	22,8	24,9	17,8	17,7
Consumption	46,7	48,9	50,2	55,9	57,8	59,0
Interest on public debt	3,3	4,3	6,5	12,3	17,3	18,0
Subsidies	3,6	3,8	4,1	5,6	4,2	1,8
Current transfers: households	11,8	10,0	8,5	8,2	11,3	12,9
Current transfers: rest of the world	0,3	0,2	0,9	1,5	1,7	2,4
Current expenditure	65,7	67,1	70,2	83,5	92,3	94,0
Investment[b]	34,3	32,9	29,8	16,5	7,7	6,0
Total	100,0	100,0	100,0	100,0	100,0	100,0

Notes: [a] National accounting figures at current prices.
[b] Gross capital formation

Source: Calculated from SA Reserve Bank, *Quarterly Bulletin* (various issues)

decreased in each consecutive decade since the 1960s. Despite this, the resource-use share of government in the economy increased over the period, reflecting an even larger decrease in long-term real economic growth.

The growth in general government expenditure was accompanied by significant changes in its composition, as we explain below with the aid of the next four tables.

7.2.2 The changing economic composition of public expenditure

The economic classification of government expenditure distinguishes between the current and capital components of total outlays. Table 7.2 shows that the portion of general government expenditure allocated to current expenditure increased substantially from 1960 to 2001 (from 65,7% to 94,0%), with a corresponding decrease in the capital expenditure share of total outlays. Over the period as a whole, the growing share of current expenditure mainly reflected increases

in the payment of interest on the public debt (from 3,3% to 18,0%), the value of purchases of "other goods and services" (e.g. stationery, computers, vehicles and maintenance of capital assets – from 11,0% to 17,7%) and employment remuneration (the government's wage bill – from 35,7% to 41,3%).

The share of current transfers to households (mainly social pensions) also grew during the 1990s and has returned to the share that prevailed before the sharp decreases that occurred during the 1960s and 1970s. By contrast, the expenditure share of subsidies (transfer payments to businesses, including farmers) increased during the first three decades of the period under review but shrank during the 1990s.

These trends should be interpreted against the background of the overall increase in general government spending. As Table 7.3 shows, total government expenditure increased to such an extent during this period that most categories of current expenditure also increased relative to GDP,

Table 7.3 The economic composition of general government expenditure (excluding business enterprises) in South Africa, 1960-2001 (percentages of GDP)[a]

Item	1960	1960-69	1970-79	1980-89	1990-99	2001
Remuneration of employees	7,3	7,5	8,0	10,0	13,3	12,6
Other goods and services	2,2	3,8	6,6	8,0	5,9	5,4
Consumption	9,5	11,3	14,6	18,0	19,2	18,0
Interest on public debt	0,7	1,0	1,9	4,0	5,8	5,5
Subsidies	0,7	0,9	1,2	1,8	1,4	0,5
Current transfers: households	2,4	2,3	2,5	2,6	3,7	3,9
Current transfers: rest of the world	0,1	0,0	0,3	0,5	0,6	0,7
Current expenditure	13,4	15,5	20,5	26,9	30,7	28,7
Investment[b]	7,0	7,6	8,7	5,3	2,6	1,8
Total	20,4	23,1	29,2	32,2	33,3	30,5

Notes: [a] National accounting figures.

          [b] Gross capital formation

Source: Calculated from SA Reserve Bank, *Quarterly Bulletin* (various issues)

including some whose shares of general government spending decreased.

Capital expenditure mainly consists of the acquisition of fixed capital assets, land, stock and intangible assets. It is clear from Tables 7.2 and 7.3 that spending of this nature decreased relative to both total general government outlays and gross domestic product, although this negative trend did appear to slow down during the 1990s.

7.2.3 Functional shifts in public expenditure

The functional classification of government expenditure refers to the amounts spent on the different services provided by government. Unfortunately, the relevant data is available only for the period 1982/83 to 1997/98 – not for the 1960s and 1970s. However, we can form a picture of functional trends during the earlier period from several independent studies (e.g. Döckel & Seeber, 1978; Abedian & Standish, 1984; and Calitz, 1988). These indicate that the growth of government spending during the 1960s and 1970s resulted mainly from higher outlays on general public services (especially spending related to the former homelands), defence and interest on the public debt. During this period, spending on public order and safety (policing, justice and correctional services) and social services increased only modestly.

Table 7.4 shows the functional composition of government spending for the 1980s and 1990s. The table distinguishes between the following general government services: "general public services", protection services, social services, economic services, and non-classified services.

On the whole it can be seen from Table 7.4 that while the shares of social services and non-classified services both increased between 1983 and 1998, these increases were more or less offset by corresponding decreases in protection services and economic services. Within the category of protection services, the dramatic decline in the

Table 7.4 The functional composition of general government expenditure (excluding business enterprises) in South Africa, fiscal years 1983-1998 (percentages of total expenditure at current prices)[a]

Item	1983	1983-89	1990-98	1998
General public services (sub-total)	8,3	9,0	9,6	8,3
Defence	14,2	12,9	7,4	5,1
Public order and safety	5,5	6,2	8,6	9,1
Protection services (sub total)	19,7	19,1	16,0	14,2
Education	17,6	17,8	20,4	21,4
Health	9,8	9,5	9,5	10,3
Social security and welfare	6,2	6,1	9,6	11,0
Other social services	6,5	6,2	5,1	5,2
Social sevices (sub-total)	40,1	39,6	44,6	47,9
Agriculture, forestry and fishing	3,4	3,5	2,2	1,6
Mining, manufacturing and construction	2,4	3,3	1,2	0,9
Transport and communication	10,1	7,3	5,2	4,7
Other economic services	1,7	2,4	4,5	4,7
Economic services (sub-total)	17,6	16,5	13,1	11,9
Not classified (sub-total)	14,3	15,8	16,7	17,7
Total	100,0	100,0	100,0	100,0

Notes: [a] Government finance statistics data, years ending 31 March
Source: Calculated from SA Reserve Bank, *Quarterly Bulletin* (various issues)

share of defence expenditure (from 14,2% to 5,1%) more than offset the corresponding increase in public order and safety (from 5,5% to 9,1%). As far as social services are concerned, it is worth noting that the shares of education (from 17,6% to 21,4%) and of social security and welfare (from 6,2% to 11,0%) both increased while that of health care services remained more or less the same at around 10 per cent.

Table 7.5 suggests that the total expenditure and GDP shares of the functional cate-gories correlated better than those in respect of the economic categories of spending.

Categories whose expenditure shares have decreased, including defence and eco-nomic services, also experienced reductions in their GDP shares, while public order and safety, education and social security and welfare gained in terms of both expenditure and GDP shares.

The links between trends in the economic and functional compositions of total outlays now become apparent. The increasing

Table 7.5 The functional composition of general government expenditure (excluding business enterprises) in South Africa, fiscal years 1983-1998 (percentages of GDP at current prices)[a]

Item	1983	1983-89	1990-98	1998
General public services (sub-total)	2,4	2,8	3,2	2,8
Defence	4,1	4,1	2,5	1,7
Public order and safety	1,6	2,0	2,9	3,1
Protection services (sub total)	5,7	6,1	5,4	4,8
Education	5,1	5,7	6,9	7,2
Health	2,8	3,0	3,2	3,5
Social security and welfare	1,8	1,9	3,2	3,7
Other social services	1,9	2,0	1,7	1,7
Social sevices (sub-total)	11,6	12,6	15,0	16,1
Agriculture, forestry and fishing	1,0	1,1	0,8	0,6
Mining, manufacturing and construction	0,7	1,0	0,4	0,3
Transport and communication	2,9	2,3	1,8	1,6
Other economic services	0,4	0,8	1,5	1,5
Economic services (sub-total)	5,0	5,2	4,5	4,0
Not classified (sub-total)	4,1	5,0	5,6	6,0
Total	28,8	31,7	33,7	33,7

Notes: [a] Government finance statistics data, years ending 31 March
Source: Calculated from SA Reserve Bank, *Quarterly Bulletin* (various issues)

prominence of labour-intensive and supplies-intensive functions such as public order and safety and education, partly explains the growth of the government wage bill and of spending on "other goods and services", as highlighted above. Similarly, the growth of transfers to households is closely associated with the greater emphasis on social security and welfare services. By contrast, the reduction in the expenditure share of subsidies is partly reflected in the downward trend in outlays on economic services such as reduced assistance to farmers and railway and bus commuters.

7.3 Comparisons with other countries[1]

There is compelling evidence indicating that government spending tends to grow in absolute and relative terms as per capita income increases. One time-series study (Tanzi & Schuknecht, 1995) found that general government expenditure in the industri-

1. This section draws on Siebrits (1998).

al countries increased from levels of 10 per cent of GDP or less in 1870 to between 45 per cent and 50 per cent of GDP in 1994. Similarly, a cross-sectional comparison of 1988 data found that the ratio of central government expenditure to GDP was on average significantly higher in industrial countries than in developing countries, that is, 28,9 per cent compared to 20,9 per cent (Lim, 1993). We discuss some of the theoretical explanations for the growth of government in the next section.

International cross-section evidence on the composition of government expenditure at different levels of development may be summarised as follows (Van der Berg, 1991):

• In low-income countries, the bulk of government spending is typically directed at capital investment in the infrastructure, stimulation of industrial development through export subsidies and other incentives, and the establishment of primary education and health care systems.

• Middle-income countries give priority to education, health care and research and development, and also usually begin to develop a social security system.

• High-income countries are characterised by huge increases in the share of transfer payments (especially social security-related ones), which are typically compensated for by reduced public investment.

Economic development is thus associated with a shift in the economic composition of government expenditure from capital expenditure to consumption spending, including transfer payments. The functional counterpart of this trend is a shift from protection and economic services to social services. In an authoritative study on the issue, Saunders and Klau (1985: 16) came to the following conclusion:

The structure of government expenditure has thus shifted away from the provision of more traditional collective goods (defence, public administration and economic services) towards those associated with the growth of the welfare state (education, health and income maintenance), which provide benefits on an individual rather than collective basis and where redistributive objectives are more dominant.

7.3.1 South Africa

The pattern of change in government outlays in South Africa broadly corresponds with these international trends. As indicated above, South Africa has also experienced sustained absolute and relative growth in general government expenditure, coupled with a shift from capital expenditure and economic services towards consumption spending and social services. These compositional trends have obvious distributional effects, but recent advances in the theory of economic growth suggest that government spending on education and health also brings efficiency gains in the form of higher levels of human capital (see Section 7.7 below).

However, there are also interesting peculiarities to the evolution of government expenditure in South Africa (Siebrits, 1998). These include the following:

• Some indicators, such as the ratio of general government consumption expenditure to GDP, would suggest that government expenditure in South Africa has grown to a relatively high level, especially when compared with other developing countries. In 1994, for example, this ratio was higher in South Africa than in 80 of the 98 developing countries for which data was available.

• The shift in the economic composition of expenditure from capital to current outlays was also more pronounced in South Africa than in the vast majority of developing countries. Fully 49 of the 55 developing countries for which data was available in 1994 had lower and relatively more stable ratios of central government current expenditure to GDP than South Africa.

• As far as the functional composition of expenditure is concerned, public spending on education and health is likewise higher in South Africa than in the rest of the developing world. In 1994, only 10 of the 91 countries for which data was available allocated larger portions of their national incomes to public outlays on education. Similarly, in the first half of the 1990s, South Africa's ratio of public expenditure on health to GNP was exceeded by only 26 of the 106 developing countries for which data was available.

• Similar conclusions in respect of government spending on defence and social security and welfare are less robust due to a scarcity of data. However, available evidence does indicate that South Africa is not spending particularly large portions of its national income on these government services. In fact, the level of public spending on social security and welfare is comparatively low relative to those of middle-income countries in Latin America, the Caribbean and the transition economies of Eastern Europe and the former Soviet Union.

Box 7.1
Social services: the importance of economic growth
The relative effects on per-capita government expenditure of sustained economic growth can be illustrated with the aid of an example. Let us compare public spending on education in South Africa and Spain. In 1997, the ratios of public expenditure on education to GNP were 7,9 per cent for South Africa and 5,0 per cent for Spain. South Africa's GNP per capita was US$3 400 and that of Spain US$14 510. In Spain, the public sector therefore expended US$726 per person on education, compared to South Africa's US$269. To achieve the same level of public spending on education in per capita terms, South Africa would have been required to spend more than 20 per cent of its national income on education. Since the situation is much the same for health care, social security and many other services, it is clear that South Africa (and other developing countries) cannot reach the same per-capita levels of government spending by simply increasing the portion of national income devoted to such spending. That would require extremely high tax rates or unsustainable levels of borrowing. To achieve higher levels of government spending in per capita terms, it is clearly more important to raise per capita income than to increase the share of national income devoted to government social spending.

International comparisons therefore suggest that the scope for further reallocation of resources from capital to current spending and from protection and economic services to social services is limited. Further increases in social spending would require that the burden of interest on the public debt be reduced and the crime situation be brought under control. However, it is questionable whether South Africa needs to invest even larger portions of its national income on publicly financed education and health care. Government spending on these items is already high by international standards, and the real challenge for the future is for government to utilise its existing education and health budgets more efficiently than before. Future increases in these budgets could be achieved through additional revenues obtained from sustained real growth in per capita income – as the accompanying box illustrates.

7.4 Reasons for the growth of government: Macro models

In Chapter 1 we pointed out that there are different ways of measuring the size of the government, one being to express government expenditure as a percentage of gross domestic product. We saw that over the past five decades the South African government has steadily increased its share in the economy, in terms of both the use and the mobilisation of national resources.[2]

South Africa is not unique in this regard. Both industrial and developing countries have experienced the same trend and various theories have been developed in an attempt to explain this global phenomenon. Before we discuss these theories, two important qualifications should be made. Firstly, government expenditure growth is not the same as a growing share of government in the economy. Some of the theories (for example that of Brown & Jackson discussed in the next section) provide an explanation for the phenomenon of expenditure growth, irrespective of whether it is accompanied by an increasing share. Most of the theories under discussion, however, deal with the issue of an expanding government sector relative to the rest of the economy.

Secondly, it is important to distinguish between the empirical issue of expenditure growth and the reasons for it, on the one hand, and the normative question of what the appropriate size of government should be on the other. The latter is a question about whether or not the government is too big or too small, irrespective of whether there happens to have been large increases or decreases in government expenditure or in its share in the economy. What we need to explain is not only the reasons for expenditure growth, but why there seems to have been a tendency for government to exceed its optimal size, however defined. Most of the theories discussed here try to explain the reasons for the growth of government, but the phenomenon of an exaggerated government may exist even if the government sector did not grow.

Furthermore, in addition to technical or X-inefficiency, excessive government expenditure in Paretian terms necessarily implies the existence of allocative inefficiency.

The models discussed below fundamentally provide explanations for the growth in government expenditure, as qualified in the previous paragraph. Following Brown and Jackson (1980: 120), we distinguish between **macro models** which tend to explain the broad patterns of government expenditure with regard to aggregate variables such as GDP; and – in the next section – **micro models** which focus on the decision-making behaviour of public individuals and institutions.

7.4.1 Wagner's "law"

In 1883, Adolph Wagner, a German economist, had already identified a growing share of government in the economies of industrialising European countries. He used some empirical evidence to formulate what is today generally known as Wagner's "law". In his words:

The "law of increasing expansion of public, and particularly state, activities" becomes for the fiscal economy the law of the increasing expansion of fiscal requirements... That law is the result of empirical observation in progressive countries, at least in our Western European civilization; its explanation, justification and cause is the pressure for social progress and the resulting changes in the relative spheres of private and public economy... (Wagner, 1883 – as quoted in Musgrave & Peacock 1958: 8).

In other words, according to Wagner, rising government expenditure was an inevitable feature of the developing (or industrialising) countries of his time. Rephrased to present a

---

2 Note that algebraically the increase in Government's share in the economy can come about in three ways: the economy may be growing (in real or nominal terms) but government expenditure grows faster; the economy may be shrinking, but government expenditure continues to grow or decline at a lower rate than the economy; or the economy has not grown (has stagnated) but government expenditure continues to increase.

more modern version, the "law" simply states that public expenditure will increase if the per capita income of industrialising countries increases. The implication of Wagner's "law" is, therefore, that government expenditure will increase faster than the output of the economy.

Wagner identified three factors that are responsible for the growth in government expenditure. Firstly, a country undergoing industrialisation will experience an expansion in **administrative and protective** functions. This inter alia refers to the regulatory role of government (see Chapter 2) and the complex legal relationships that need to be developed in industrialising countries. Government expenditure will therefore increase as a result of efforts to maintain internal and external law and order aimed at creating an environment conducive to economic growth and development.

Secondly, he indicated that "**cultural and welfare**" expenditure (especially education and the redistribution of income) would increase, because of his implicit assumption that these goods and services have an income elasticity greater than one, which implies that as per capita income increases, the demand for these expenditures increases by a higher percentage. Lastly, he anticipated the development of a large number of **monopolies** because of the large scale of capital investment required during the early stages of industrialisation. He thus made provision for **market failures**, which may require government intervention to promote economic efficiency. Later Wagner also identified the influence of urbanisation and high density living as factors that may put upward pressure on government expenditure.

Wagner's "law" must be assessed against the economic and social backdrop in Germany during the second half of the previous century, when industrialisation was the main source of rising incomes. According to Bird (1971: 3) the conditions for

Wagner's "law" to operate can be summarised in the following three requirements:
- Rising per capita incomes
- Technological and institutional changes
- The (implicit) assumption of democratisation

Wagner is often criticised because he had an organic view of the state, according to which society is regarded as a natural organism, which happened to consist of individuals. This is in contrast to a mechanistic view of the state, according to which individuals create the state to serve their interests in the best possible way. In addition, according to Wagner's approach, the state will increase its share of the economy if incomes increase. No allowance is made, however, for the efficiency implications of such an increasing share, or for changes in individual preferences as reflected in their public choices (see Chapter 6). Despite the limitations of Wagner's "law", it did help to explain changes in government expenditure during the 19th century.

In a study of the changes in government expenditure in South Africa, covering the period 1948 to 1975, Döckel and Seeber (1978) partially confirmed the relevance of Wagner's law for South Africa. They found high-income elasticities for most categories of government spending, which imply that government expenditures "increase more than proportionally with economic growth". However, they also found that the South African case did not unambiguously support Wagner's idea that the dominant forces influencing government expenditure are social welfare, administration and law and order. The situation has changed much since 1975 and social welfare and law and order (for a relatively short period in the 1980s) did become more important (see Table 7.4), even though real per capita income did not increase; over the last three decades real per capita income in South Africa has in fact decreased. The growth of these categories of state expenditure cannot therefore be attributed to high-income elasticities, but was more likely the result of the social unrest and political instability that characterised the economy at the time.

7.4.2 Peacock and Wiseman's displacement effect

Peacock and Wiseman (1967) used a political theory to explain the influence of political events on public expenditure. They did acknowledge a point made by Wagner, that "...government expenditure depends broadly on revenues raised by taxation" (Peacock & Wiseman, 1967: 26). Governments would thus be in a position to continue increasing their own expenditures and expanding their role in the economy – provided their economies continued to grow through industrialisation. On the other hand, individuals may not be prepared to continue paying higher taxes in order to finance such increased expenditure. In a democracy, government has to respect the wishes of the majority (50% of voters plus 1). Under normal circumstances government expenditure would therefore only increase when it is strictly necessary, and it can be expected that governments would take into account the possible resistance of voters against higher tax rates.

Social upheavals or disturbances may, however, change the established conceptions of the public. Examples of such upheavals are the two world wars and the Great Depression. National crises of such magnitude may cause a rapid increase in government expenditure, since they may convince taxpayers that higher taxes are necessary to prevent a national disaster. Peacock and Wiseman called this phenomenon the **displacement effect**, because certain government expenditures (e.g. war-related expenses) displace private expenditures as well as other government expenditures (e.g. non-war related expenses).[3]

After a crisis had subsided, government expenditure could be expected to return to its pre-crisis level. But according to Peacock and Wiseman (1967: 27) this was unlikely and government expenditure could even remain at the new post-crisis level, the reason being that taxpayers would become accustomed to the higher levels of taxation and accept them as a part of life.

The displacement effect of Peacock and Wiseman may help to explain the growth in government expenditure in South Africa, despite the conclusion of Döckel and Seeber (1978: 350) that no notable displacement effect had occurred during the period 1948 to 1975. The previous political system of South Africa resulted in a massive military build-up and excursions into neighbouring countries, amidst widespread social unrest inside the country, especially since 1975. These crises triggered rapid increases in expenditures on protective services (defence and police), and also on social services. Expenditure on protective services reached almost 20 per cent of the national budget during the 1980s (see Table 7.4), while the same share in total expenditure for education started to increase since the unrest at schools in 1976. It is, therefore, possible to argue that both social upheaval and the war situation on the borders contributed to the growth in government expenditure in South Africa during the period up to 1994. However, one may also argue that displacement pressures in South Africa were dampened by a redirecting of government expenditure (e.g. from economic services to social services).

---

3 It is interesting to note that expenditure on social services in Britain showed a marked decrease during World War I, but not during World War II, because it was considered to be an important component of the war effort.

7.4.3 Musgrave and Rostow's stages-of-development approach

The stages-of-development model of Musgrave (1969) and Rostow (1971) explains how government expenditure tends to increase when an economy develops from a subsistence or traditional economy to an industrialised economy. In the **first stage** of development it is important to get investment going. During this stage the private sector is still relatively small and as a result government may have to participate actively by providing the basic infrastructure (e.g. roads, railways and harbours) necessary to create an environment conducive to economic development. The implication of the first stage for government expenditure is that capital expenditures will feature prominently.

During the **middle stages** of development government will continue to supply investment goods, while private investment will also start to take off, partly because of the positive external effects of government investment undertaken during the first stage (see Section 7.7 below). However, the development of the private sector may cause certain market failures which government would have to address, thus giving rise to further increases in government expenditure. During the **last stage** of development capital expenditure by government, expressed as a percentage of GDP, usually decreases because most of the necessary infrastructure is already in place. At this stage, however, expenditure on education, health, welfare programmes and social security will tend to increase, because of the high-income elasticity of demand for such expenditures. The result is a continuous increase in the share of government in the economy.

During the early stages of South Africa's industrialisation, the government (through state enterprises and public corporations) was heavily involved in major capital pro-jects such as railways, harbours, roads and public works, as well as in business activities such as the creation of Sasol and Iscor, which were subsequently privatised. The growth in public investment expenditure during the 1960s and 1970s, for example, corresponds with Musgrave and Rostow's first and middle stages. The subsequent decline in public investment is not, however, an indication that South Africa has entered the last stage of development: it is perhaps better understood in terms of Peacock and Wiseman's displacement effect, or in terms of the Meltzer and Richard hypothesis which we discuss below. Note in any case that many rural areas in the country can hardly be said to have entered the first stage of development, in the sense that public investment has hardly begun in these areas.

7.4.4 The Meltzer-Richard hypothesis

Redistributional policies may have an important impact on the growth of government expenditure. Meltzer and Richard (1981) developed a general equilibrium model in which majority voting determines the magnitude of income distribution and as a result also the share of government expenditure in the economy. According to this model the most important reason for the increase in government expenditure can be attributed to an extension of the franchise, which brings about a change in the median (or the decisive) voter (see discussion of median voter theorem in Chapter 6).

Meltzer and Richard (1981: 43) argued that the median voter plays an important role in determining the size of the government sector in a democracy. For example, if all voters were ordered from left to right according to their income, with the individual with the lowest income on the far left hand side and the individual with the highest income on the far right hand side, the median voter would be the one right in the middle. Therefore, if there were for example only five voters in a country, with incomes of

R3 000, R4 000, R8 000, R15 000 and R20 000 per annum respectively, the median voter would be the individual with an income of R8 000. The median voter is important because in a two-party democracy he or she will determine which party will win the election. Both parties therefore try to gain the support of the median voter, and will need the support of three individuals (including the median voter) for this purpose.

According to the model of Meltzer and Richard, there will be pressure for redistributing income if the income of the median voter lies below the average income. Redistribution would benefit the median voter and he or she will therefore vote for the party that proposes a programme of redistribution. In our example the income of the median voter (R8 000) lies below the average income (R10 000). To gain the support of the median voter, parties will emphasise redistributional policies, which could result in higher taxes and higher expenditure on social services. The median voter thus effectively determines the tax regime.

However, Meltzer and Richard's model (1981: 916) does not allow for unlimited redistribution, because they make the assumption that voters are aware of the disincentive effects associated with high taxes and redistribution. The rational median voter will thus choose the tax rate that maximises his or her utility, while taking into account the possible impact on the economic behaviour of other individuals (i.e. their decisions to work and consume). If the median voter chooses a relatively high tax rate other individuals may decide to work less (consume more leisure), with the result that the economic "pie" may become smaller and as a result also the fiscal scope for redistribution.

The above hypothesis would suggest that the extension of suffrage (which accompanied democratisation in South Africa) should have resulted in a major increase in the share of government expenditure in the South African economy. But this did not happen, despite the fact that the election of 1994 must have been based on a new median voter with an income well below the average income. It may be argued, of course, that the median voter model does not apply to South Africa, or that a substantial degree of redistribution had already occurred earlier in an attempt to counter social upheaval (as argued above). Expenditure on social services (as a percentage of both total government expenditure and GDP) increased significantly between 1983 and 1998 (see Table 7.4), whilst defence expenditure declined dramatically both prior to and after the 1994 elections. Also, the overall fiscal restraint imposed by the need for macroeconomic stability, coupled with the shift towards medium-term budgetary planning (see Chapter 17 below), forced the government to meet many of its distributional goals by means of a **reallocation** of social spending.

7.5 Micro models of expenditure growth

7.5.1 Baumol's unbalanced productivity growth

Government expenditure may also increase disproportionately because of an increase in the prices of inputs used by the public sector relative to those employed in the private sector. This phenomenon has drawn the interest of William Baumol (1967) who developed a microeconomic model of unbalanced productivity growth to explain the growth in government expenditure. He divides the economy into two broad sectors, a **progressive sector** and a non-progressive sector. The progressive sector is characterised by technologically progressive activities, such as innovation, capital formation and economies of scale which all contribute towards a rise in the level of output. An important feature of this sector is a cumulative increase in the productivity of employees that justifies increases in wages and salaries. The inherent characteristics of the **non-progressive sector**, on the other hand, only permit sporadic changes in productivity.

The technological structure of a sector will therefore determine the increase in the productivity of the labour inputs used. In the progressive sector labour is only one of the inputs in the production process, while in the non-progressive sector labour is often the end product. Baumol (1967: 416) illustrates this difference with the aid of several examples. Consumers are usually not interested in the labour used to produce an air conditioner; they only care about the end product, that is, cold air. However, the labour input is of great concern when one has purchased a ticket to attend a one-hour concert by a Beethoven quartet. Any effort to increase the overall productivity of the concert to below four man hours, for example by doubling the tempo of the music, may upset listeners and detract from the end product, that is, the concert. In the latter case there is clearly a limit to productivity increases, which is very much determined by the labour-intensive nature of the service.

The non-progressive sector usually consists of services, which also constitute a large component of the public sector. In this sector labour plays an important role, for example in respect of functions such as education and law and order, where a certain teacher-pupil ratio or a certain number of law-enforcement officers per thousand of the population is usually the aim. According to Baumol, technological changes do not have such an important effect on productivity in the non-progressive sector as they do in the progressive sector. It will, for example, be counterproductive to try and increase productivity in health services by halving the time individuals spend in an operating theatre or hospital. As a result there are only sporadic improvements in productivity in the non-progressive sector compared to relatively rapid increases in the progressive sector.

Baumol argues further that wages and salaries in both sectors will have to move together to prevent employees from leaving the non-progressive sector for the progressive sector. This raises the relative costs of the non-progressive sector, because salary increases are not accompanied by the same increases in productivity as in the progressive sector. Baumol (1967: 426) thus came to the conclusion that "the costs of even a constant level of activity on the part of ... government can be expected to grow constantly higher." Furthermore, if production in the non-progressive sector has to be maintained relative to that in the progressive sector, it will imply that a larger share of the labour market will have to be employed in the former sector, which could have negative effects on economic growth. One point of critique, however, is that Baumol may have underestimated the opportunities for technological advancement in the public sector.

As we have seen in Table 7.2, by far the largest share of government expenditure in South Africa goes towards the remuneration of employees. Education, health services and policing, to mention but a few, all require labour inputs as an end in itself. The structure of government expenditure thus corresponds well with Baumol's notion of unbalanced productivity growth. However, the Baumol hypothesis has not been tested empirically in South Africa, so that no firm conclusions can be drawn about its relevance to government expenditure growth in this country.

7.5.2 Brown and Jackson's microeconomic model

The purpose of microeconomic models of growth in government expenditure is to study the factors influencing the demand and supply of public goods and services. Brown and Jackson (1990: 127) have developed a microeconomic model to derive the levels of publicly provided goods and services by, inter alia, taking the tastes, the income and the tax rate of the median voter – all determinants of demand – into account, as well as the costs of the goods and services in question. Since the scope of this book does not permit a detailed description of this model, we only briefly discuss some of the factors that may have an influence on the demand and supply of such goods, and hence on the level of government expenditure.

It often happens that government expenditure increases without there being a corresponding change in the level of service. Although such a state of affairs can be easily viewed as a sign of inefficiency, Brown and Jackson (1990: 137) argue that there may be other forces at work. It may in fact be the result of changes in the **service environment**. For example, an increase in the level of crime, as we have witnessed in South Africa, calls for increased policing and additional funding merely to arrest that increase and ensure that the same level of law and order as before is maintained. If the increase in expenditure did not occur, the service will be seen to have deteriorated because the service environment has become worse.

Changes in the size and density of the population and its age structure may also have an influence on the service environment. **Population growth** may lead to an increase in the demand for publicly provided goods and services. As far as pure public goods such as defence are concerned, we have seen that the marginal social cost of one additional consumer is zero by definition. However, governments do not only provide pure public goods, but also mixed and merit goods such as education and health services. In such instances increases in the population will lead either to higher levels of expenditure or to a drop in standards. On the other hand, population growth may also imply a decrease in the unit cost of such services because payment for those services will be shared by more individuals (i.e. economies of scale). If the relative price of services decreases it may be an incentive to government to supply more of those services. However, population growth and human migration may also lead to changes in the density of the population, which may cause congestion and add to the costs of government.

Another factor that may influence the level of government expenditure is the **quality of goods** demanded by the median voter. To define quality is not always easy. According to Brown and Jackson (1990: 139), however, a good is of superior quality if it requires more inputs in its production process than a good requiring fewer of those inputs, *ceteris paribus*. For example, a hospital, which has 500 patients and 100 nurses, would provide a good of superior quality to a hospital with 500 patients and 50 nurses. Increases in quality may therefore put further pressure on government expenditure if the additional costs cannot be recovered from the users.

On the whole, it would seem that the micro model of Brown and Jackson has identified and combined important and relevant factors that may influence the supply and demand of publicly provided goods and services. Their model provides a useful starting point for anyone interested in modelling government expenditure in South Africa and identifying the explanatory variables that will determine future trends in government expenditure.

7.5.3 Role of politicians, bureaucrats and interest groups

We have already discussed the role played by individual agents and interest groups in influencing government decisions and government expenditure. Politicians, bureaucrats and other interest groups are often powerful enough to pressure government in a direction that is detrimental to the social welfare of the broader community. Their behaviour may result in a larger than optimal level of government expenditure, thus contributing to the growth of government's share in the economy.

Apart from engaging in various forms of vote-trading, as discussed in Chapter 6, there are many other ways in which the vote-maximising behaviour of **politicians** can bring about an increase in government expenditure. They may grant wage and salary increases to state employees just before an election, in order to gain the support of what is often a numerically significant and powerful constituency. From a macroeconomic standpoint, the ruling party may be tempted to relax its fiscal and monetary policies in an attempt to stimulate the economy before an election. Such a relaxation may well please voters who stand to secure short-term gains in the form of lower interest rates, lower taxes and better job prospects, and they may well respond by lending their support to the ruling party. But populist macroeconomic policies are often not sustainable in the long run, giving rise to inflationary pressures and balance of payments problems, and ultimately calling for even tighter monetary and fiscal policies than had been the case prior to the election.

We also saw in Chapter 6 that **bureaucrats** tend to maximise the size of their departmental budgets, partly to help build their own personal "empires"; and that they are able to convince politicians of their actions because they are better informed about the activities of their own departments. The net result is a bureaucracy that is larger than the optimal size. In South Africa we have seen how the homelands policy of the past, and the increase in the number of provinces after the 1994 election, have contributed to a duplication of government activities which has put additional pressure on government expenditure.

Individuals with shared interests are often able to organise themselves into powerful **interest groups** and put pressure on government to implement programmes and pass legislation that will meet their own parochial interests. South African farmers have been an important lobbying group that has benefited greatly from agricultural subsidies and other forms of support over the years. The same is true of labour unions and organised business, and the government may well be tempted to grant them special favours such as tax allowances which will erode the revenue base of government. The persistent recurrence of such actions can also contribute to the growth of government expenditure in the economy.

7.6 Government and the economy: Short-term effects

In the preceding sections we have focused on the growth of the public sector in the economy, and on the reasons for this growth. We have seen that there are various theories explaining the secular growth of government in virtually all economies across the world. We now shift our focus to the economic **effects** – rather than the causes – of government activity, and distinguish between the short and the long run effects that changes in government expenditure can have on the economy.

The short-term impact of government activity on the economy depends on the value of the familiar **income multiplier**. Depending on the purpose of one's inquiry, the multiplier can be defined in many different ways, involving different levels of aggregation in respect of the relevant macroeconomic variables. One of the standard formulations is the balanced budget multiplier (BBM), which is usually the starting point in any analysis of the short-term effect of government activity on the national economy. According to the BBM, a given increase in government spending, financed by an equivalent increase in autonomous (e.g. lump sum) taxes, will give rise to a net increase in GDP equal to the original increase in government expenditure. The reason for this somewhat surprising result is that the (additional) tax is paid partly from intended consumption expenditure, and partly from savings, whereas the full amount of the tax is injected back into the economy in the form of government expenditure, and hence aggregate expenditure.

For our purpose here, however, we go a little further by including an income tax and an indirect tax (both of which are discussed in Part 3 of the book) in a simple open-economy model of the income multiplier. Consider the standard national income identity,

$$Y = C + I + G + X - M \qquad [7.1]$$

where the symbols have their usual meaning. With I, G and X all autonomous, we assume that C and M are both proportionate functions of disposable income, Y_d. Thus, private consumption expenditure,

$$C = b\,Y_d\,(1 - t_i) \qquad [7.2]$$

where b is the consumption propensity, and t_i is the indirect tax rate (e.g. VAT). Y_d is simply total income net of direct taxes, or

$$Y_d = Y\,(1 - t_d) - T^0 \qquad [7.3]$$

so that

$$C = b\,[Y\,(1 - t_d) - T^0]\,(1 - t_i) \qquad [7.2a]$$

where t_d is the direct (income) tax rate, and T^0 is an autonomous lump sum tax. Analogously, imports,

$$M = m\,[Y\,(1 - t_d) - T^0]\,(1 - t_i) \qquad [7.4]$$

where m is the import propensity. Substituting into [7.1] gives

$$Y = \frac{I + G + X - (b - m)T^0(1 - t_i)}{1 - (b - m)(1 - t_d)(1 - t_i)} \qquad [7.1b]$$

The expansionary impact of an increase in G will depend on the size of the multiplier, given by $\dfrac{1}{[1 - (b - m)(1 - t_d)(1 - t_i)]}$, and on whether it is financed by a tax increase or by increased borrowing. Similarly, the multiplier also plays an important role in determining the overall deflationary effect of a fiscal policy aimed at reducing government expenditure or raising taxes.

The size of the multiplier will vary in accordance with the size of the leakages involved, that is, the savings propensity $(1 - b)$, m, t_d and t_i. If we make the following hypothetical assumptions:

$$b = 0,8$$
$$m = 0,33$$
$$t_d = 0,25$$
and $$t_i = 0,14$$

the value of the above multiplier comes to 1,43 – a fairly realistic figure. The latter figure implies that a given increase in autonomous spending of R1 000 will, *ceteris paribus*, give rise to a multiplied increase in total income of R1 430.

Of course, "other things" do not remain constant. The impact of an increase in G will clearly be smaller if it is financed by a corresponding increase in T^0, t_d or t_i – though it will still exceed R1 000 in the above example. Likewise, if the increase in G were financed by borrowing on the open market, the resultant increase in interest rates may crowd out some private spending, thus reducing the final impact on total income. Alternatively, if government borrowing were paid for from savings rather than from private spending, or if the government secured the required funds from abroad, the final impact will be more pronounced.

It goes without saying that if the economy were operating at or near full employment, the effect of an increase in government expenditure will be felt on prices, rather than on real income. As before, the inflationary effect of such an increase in government spending will depend on how it is financed; and it is partly for this reason that most governments refrain from financing their expenditures by means of newly printed money. Of course, an inflationary macroeconomic environment would call for a relatively tight fiscal policy, according to which the growth of government spending is kept within reasonable bounds.

A final qualification concerns the time lags involved in trying to expand or contract an economy by means of fiscal policy. One can distinguish between several kinds of delays, including the so-called recognition, decision and implementation lags (see Chapter 17), but the important point to note is that these delays can render fiscal policy largely ineffectual, and even cause it to produce perverse results. In Chapter 17 below we return to the short-term impact of government activity, where we show that fiscal policy could have a pro-cyclical – rather than counter-cyclical – impact on the economy; and that partly for this reason, it is not much used as a stabilisation instrument in the world today.

7.7 Long-term effects

The long-term role of government can be usefully viewed within the context of the growing body of literature known as "new growth theory" (NGT) (Romer, 1986). Adherents to this school have all called attention to the contribution that government can make towards stimulating and reinforcing sustained economic growth. Several kinds of public investment and expenditure programmes are reputed to confer significant positive externalities on private producers (and consumers), and it is to these programmes that policy-makers should turn in their quest to promote economic growth and development.

The origin of NGT can be traced to a general dissatisfaction with the classical and neoclassical theories of growth, according to which private fixed investment, or additions to the physical capital stock, play a pivotal role in fostering economic growth. According to NGT, however, this is an oversimplification of what is really a very complex process. They adopt a much broader definition of "capital", and focus attention on the role played by each of the components of capital in the growth process.

In addition to privately owned physical capital (e.g. factories, office buildings and luxury homes), "capital" also includes the following three components:

- The existing physical infrastructure (e.g. roads, street lighting and sewerage systems).
- Accumulated human capital acquired through education, training and health care.
- The stock of technical know-how acquired through learning-by-doing and research and development (R & D).

The main thrust of NGT is that additions to any of the components of capital may yield increasing returns because they create externalities that benefit a range of sectors and industries in the economy. Investment in the physical infrastructure creates (pecuniary) externalities by lowering production costs and boosting returns in the private sector. Likewise, recipients of education may transfer their skills free of charge to third parties, healthier citizens will be more productive and limit the spread of disease, new users of electricity will boost the demand for electrical appliances, and so on.

Each of the components of capital can be influenced by government through appropriate policy intervention and, in the present instance, the case for such intervention is the standard one based on market failure. Since the marginal private benefits from investments in physical infrastructure, human capital and R & D are lower than the corresponding marginal social benefits, the untrammelled operation of the market will lead to an under-provision of these services. NGT thus provides a strong justification for government intervention in these areas because it will create favourable conditions for private investment and economic growth.

Empirically too, several recent studies have produced evidence confirming the above proposition. Although government spending as a whole tends to have a negative impact on economic growth – partly because it consists mostly of recurrent consumption expenditure – most studies show that public infrastructure investments do have a positive impact on factor productivities in the private sector. In its *World Development Report 1994*, for example, the World Bank (1994: 14) summarised the results of these studies and concluded that "... the role of infrastructure in growth is substantial, significant and frequently greater than that of investment in other forms of capital".

Much the same can be said of public investment in education, training and health care. When these spending categories are suitably disaggregated, one finds significant differences between the constituent components of each category: vocational training produces higher returns than formal schooling, and so too does primary and secondary education in relation to certain categories of tertiary education.

These findings are clearly important in helping governments to prioritise their spending programmes, especially in view of the important redistributive role that such programmes play today – a theme we return to in Chapter 15. The prioritisation of state expenditures, based on efficiency criteria, can help governments to do two things – achieve a more equitable distribution of income, and create the conditions for sustainable economic growth over the long run.

Important concepts

displacement effect
income multiplier
macro models of government expenditure growth
median voter
micro models
new growth theory
politicians, bureaucrats and interest groups
service environment
stages of development
unbalanced productivity growth
Wagner's "law"

Self-assessment exercises

7.1 Distinguish between the various macro and micro models of public sector growth.

7.2 Discuss Wagner's "law" critically and indicate its relevance to South Africa.

7.3 Explain the "displacement effect" in Peacock and Wiseman's model of government expenditure growth.

7.4 Explain how unbalanced productivity growth may affect government expenditure, and briefly comment on its relevance to South Africa.

7.5 Discuss the influence of the different stages of development on government expenditure.

7.6 Explain the median voter hypothesis of Meltzer and Richard and indicate whether it can explain the growth of government expenditure in South Africa.

7.7 Consider the implications of new growth theory for the role of government in the economy.

Chapter eight

Philip Black

Cost-benefit analysis

In this chapter we adopt a more microeconomic approach to our analysis of government expenditure. Government departments face the same basic economic problem as their counterparts in the private sector – how best to spend a limited budget. They have to make important choices between competing projects, and often do so via a public tender system. But unlike the private sector, government cannot base its decisions merely on the monetary or "private" feasibility of projects. In the case of pure public goods, for example, this is simply not possible, while in many other instances it is necessary also to consider the extent to which prevailing market prices deviate from their respective marginal social costs and benefits. It is partly for this reason that standard evaluation techniques used in the private sector will not do, and need to be modified and extended when applied to public sector projects. Some of these techniques are briefly discussed in section 8.2 below, while the required modifications and adjustments – that is, cost-benefit analysis proper – are dealt with in the remaining sections of the chapter.

Once you have studied this chapter you should be able to:
- distinguish between the private and public sector approaches to project evaluation;
- explain the Net Present Value

approach to project evaluation and compare it with the Internal Rate of Return and the Benefit-Cost Ratio;
- show why, under ideal conditions, public sector projects should strive to maximise consumer (and producer) surplus;
- explain the meaning of shadow prices and comment on some of the difficulties involved in quantifying benefits and costs;
- discuss the importance of the social discount rate in determining the net present value of a public project;
- indicate how risk factors can be taken into account in project evaluation.

8.1 Introduction

For a private business to be efficient it has to consider whether its shareholders will be made better off from engaging in one particular undertaking instead of another. Likewise, the analyst in the public sector has to decide whether society as a whole will be better off given the choice between two or more mutually exclusive alternatives. But private shareholders generally pursue a different set of objectives from that followed in the public sector, and it can therefore be expected that final choices will differ between the two sectors.

Cost-Benefit Analysis (CBA) is an analytical tool used to evaluate the relative merits of public projects financed by the state. It differs from evaluation techniques used in the private sector because it strives to maximise something other than monetary profits, i.e. the difference between private benefits and private costs. Public projects generally aim to maximise the difference between total social benefits and total social costs, that is, achieve a level of output where marginal social benefit equals marginal social cost. But this is easier said than done and, as we shall see, it is simply not possible in practice to identify – let alone quantify – all the relevant external costs and benefits associated with a particular public project.

Project evaluation in the private sector requires that a comparison be made between the expected private costs and benefits over the estimated time span of a new project. If the project is expected to yield a positive net benefit, then it can be said to be feasible and potentially acceptable. Final acceptance will depend on whether the positive net benefit exceeds the corresponding benefits associated with all other alternative projects. Standard techniques used in project evaluation include calculation of the net present value (NPV), the internal rate of return (IRR) and the benefit-cost (B-C) ratio – as discussed in the next section.

The same methodology can also be used to determine the relative merits of alternative projects in the public sector. But here it is necessary also to correct for prevailing price distortions arising from externalities, monopoly elements and indirect taxes and subsidies. In South Africa the problem is compounded by the huge inequalities that exist between individuals and communities, and by the fact that the government has taken it upon itself to correct the wrongs of the past by means of various affirmative action and other economic empowerment programmes. These include the public ten-der systems adopted by governments at all levels, according to which preference is given to tenders submitted by members from previously disadvantaged communities. In the private sector too, several large corporations have adopted affirmative procurement policies, many of which entail a loss in efficiency and profitability, at least in the short term (South Africa Foundation, 1998). In most cases, however, these institutions expect to derive additional benefits over the long run, including expanded markets and an enhanced reputation, which may ultimately outweigh the short-term losses (Black, 1993; 1996a).

The point to note is that project evaluation in the public sector is based on a different set of criteria than those used in the private sector, and it is largely for this reason that conventional evaluation techniques are usually modified and extended in accordance with the particular objectives of the public sector.

8.2 Evaluation techniques

8.2.1 Net Present Value (NPV)

Just as wages are the reward for labour services rendered, and rent is the payment received for the use of land, so interest is the return to capital. In the event that capital is employed for the development of a particular project, the net present value (NPV) approach is used to determine whether the return on such an investment will be greater than, or at least equal to, the interest that can be earned from simply putting the money into a banking account.

If you invested R1 000 in a bank at an interest rate of 10 per cent, then you would expect to receive R1 100 at the end of the first year, or R1 000 + 0,10(R1 000) = R1 000(1 + 0,10) = R1 100. After two years you would receive R1 100 + 0,10(R1 100) = R1 100(1 + 0,10) = R1 210. The latter can be written as R1 000(1 + 0,10)(1 + 0,10) = R1 000(1 + 0,10)^2.

After n years the future value, F, of your present investment, P, will be

$$F = P(1 + i)^n \qquad [8.1]$$

where i is the **market rate of interest**.

You could of course invest your money in some other financial asset, such as equity or government bonds, or in a physical asset, and after allowing for inflation and different risk profiles, you will naturally choose the one yielding the highest future value.

Conversely, it follows from equation [8.1] that the present value of your future income is simply

$$P = \frac{F}{(1 + i)^n} \qquad [8.2]$$

where i is now referred to as the **discount rate**. Thus if you knew the future value of your income, you could work out the present value. If a friend wanted to borrow from you and promised to pay you back R1 000 after two years, you would obviously not lend her R1 000 now – because you could earn 10 per cent on it each year in the bank. But how much would you lend her? The answer is given by equation [8.2]: it is simply $\frac{R1\,000}{(1 + 0,10)^2}$ = R826,45. In other words, if you invested R826,45 in the bank you would receive R1 000 after two years. There is always an inverse relationship between the discount rate and the present value of an investment. The higher the interest rate, the higher your expected future stream of income will have to be to receive a given sum in the future.

The present value concept plays a critically important role in project evaluation. It is applied to both the expected costs and benefits of a project. In addition to the initial cost of a new project, one might typically expect to derive a stream of benefits in each subsequent year, which must then be compared with the corresponding expected costs. The difference between the discounted benefits

and costs is the net present value (NPV). The NPV after, say, two years is

$$NPV = \frac{\{B(x)_1 - C(x)_1\}}{(1 + i)} + \frac{\{B(x)_2 - C(x)_2\}}{(1 + i)} - C(X)_0$$

$$= \sum_{t=1}^{2} \frac{\{B(x)_t - C(x)_t\}}{(1 + i)^2} - C(X)_0$$

where $B(x)_1$ and $C(x)_1$ are the expected benefits and costs associated with project X in the first year of operation, and $C(x)_0$ is the initial capital costs. After n years the NPV is

$$NPV = \sum_{t=1}^{n} \frac{\{B(x)_t - C(x)_t\}}{(1 + i)^n} - C(x)_0 \qquad [8.3]$$

This method can be used to determine the relative merits of two or more mutually exclusive projects. Given that the present value of two such projects are positive, the one yielding the higher net present value after a given date in the future will be the obvious choice. Higher discount rates will count against projects that yield returns further into the future, rendering the choice of an appropriate discount rate and cut off date crucial to the NPV exercise.

8.2.2 Internal Rate of Return (IRR)

The IRR method is used to determine the actual rate of return earned by an organisation when undertaking a particular project. Simply stated: a R1 000 project which yields R1 100 in a year, has an IRR of 10 per cent. If the organisation could earn 7 per cent by investing the funds in the bank, the project will be viewed in a favourable light. The actual arithmetic solves for the IRR of the project such that, when discounted, the present value of future costs and benefits equals zero. In the above example,

$$-R1\,000 + \frac{R1\,100}{(1 + r)} = 0$$

will yield an IRR (r) of 10 per cent. It follows that in general the IRR for any given project over any given time period can be solved by using:

$$-C_0 + \sum_{t=1}^{n} \frac{B_t - C_t}{(1+r)^n} - C(X)_0 \qquad [8.4]$$

Prima facie, this method appears to be a corollary of the present value method. However, the problem is that it does not allow for comparisons between two or more projects of different sizes. For example, consider project A involving an initial investment of R1 000 and yielding R1 200 in one year's time, thus giving an IRR of 20 per cent. If the opportunity cost of the investment is 15 per cent (using, say, a given bank interest rate), the firm is better off by R50. Compare this with a smaller project B for which the initial investment is R100 and which yields R130 in one year's time, thus giving an IRR equal to 30 per cent. Using the IRR method you will choose project B, and yet the firm is only better off by R15.

The IRR method clearly produces ambiguous outcomes. If the same projects are compared using the NPV method, we get a different outcome. Using the discount rate, i = 15 per cent, the NPV for project A,

$$-R1\ 000 + \frac{R1\ 200}{1,15} = R43,50$$

and for project B,

$$-R100 + \frac{R130}{1,15} = R13$$

indicating that project A is now preferred.

8.2.3 Benefit-Cost (B-C) ratio

As with the IRR method, the B-C ratio represents a simple and therefore attractive method at first glance. Hidden pitfalls, however, will lead us back to the NPV as the preferred method of evaluation. The B-C ratio also involves discounting the future streams of expected benefits and costs for a given project. Once this is determined, the ratio simply gives the (present value of) benefits divided by the corresponding costs. If the B-C ratio is greater than one, the project is admissible.

Problems arise when costs can also be classified as negative benefits, like air pollution caused by a factory; or when benefits are classified as negative costs. By reducing the numerator by the value of a negative benefit, for example, a completely different ratio will be derived than if the denominator was increased by the equivalent amount.

It follows that the only consistent and reliable method of project appraisal is the NPV one.

8.3 Valuation of benefits and costs

In a perfectly competitive environment in which there are no distortions, we already know that market prices will equal the corresponding marginal social costs and benefits. Under these conditions it is sufficient to value the inputs used by a new project at their prevailing market prices, and value output in terms of its expected market price. The outcome is shown in Figure 8.1 where the marginal cost of the project is assumed to be constant. Supply (marginal social cost) equals demand (marginal social benefit) at P_1 and Q_1, thus yielding a net willingness to pay, or consumer surplus, equal to the triangle P_1AE. The latter can be viewed as the net benefit to society (as defined in equation 8.3), and can be compared with the corresponding benefits associated with other competing projects.

Of course, real-world markets are characterised by a host of market failures, including monopoly pricing, unemployment and the presence of positive or negative externalities. Where market prices do exist, they will not reflect the true opportunity costs of the production factors and final goods in question: in an imperfectly competitive world prices will generally exceed marginal cost,

Figure 8.1 Evaluation based on social costs and benefits

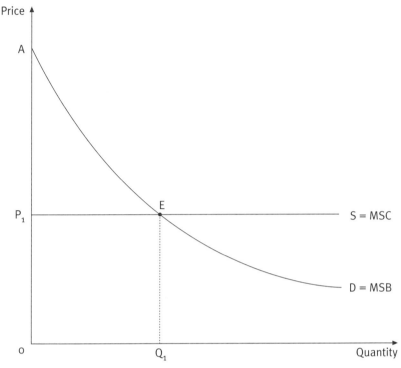

whilst technological externalities will tend to drive a wedge between private and social marginal costs and benefits. In the case of pure public goods prices do not even exist and recourse will have to be taken to alternative ways of appraising the relevant benefits and costs. In all these cases the project analyst will attempt to value the costs and benefits in terms of so-called **shadow prices**, i.e. Pareto-optimal prices based on the true opportunity costs.

Project evaluation in the public sector usually begins by utilising information based on prevailing input and output prices in the private sector. Irrespective of whether the project involves provision of a pure public good or a mixed good, it will employ a range of labour skills, capital goods and material inputs for which markets do exist. But these input prices must first be adjusted and converted into their shadow-price equivalents – as discussed below.

8.3.1 Labour

As far as **labour** is concerned, it is important to note that the existence of involuntary unemployment, experienced by many developing countries, implies that the social opportunity cost of employing unemployed labour is zero. A new public project making use of unemployed workers will not lower employment or output elsewhere in the economy, and the prevailing market wage rate cannot therefore be used to value the cost of employing labour on the project. The practice has been to set the shadow wage equal to the average unemployment benefits received by the unemployed. An alternative would be to use *per capita* income levels earned and received in the informal sector, which can be easily obtained from available household surveys.

8.3.2 Non-labour inputs

In pricing **non-labour inputs** the project analyst should ideally allow for the presence of **monopoly elements** among suppliers. Recall that the demand (or actual) price charged by a monopolist exceeds the supply (or marginal cost) price. A public project using monopolistically priced inputs can use either of the two prices, and the choice will depend on the impact that the transaction has on the relevant input market. If the increased demand for the input leads to a corresponding increase in production, then the input should be priced at marginal cost, which after all represents the value of the additional resources used in the production of the input. Alternatively, if the required inputs were simply transferred from existing users to the new project, without any increase in production, then the appropriate price would be the demand or market price – since it represents the value to current users. In the event of there being a combined response, the project analyst should devise a suitably weighted average of the two prices.

8.3.3 Indirect taxes and subsidies

The prices of non-labour inputs may also include **indirect taxes** and **subsidies**. Here too it is necessary to consider the artificial gap that exists between the demand and supply prices: under a typical sales tax, for example, consumers pay more than what producers receive, while the opposite is true of a subsidy. As before, the decision whether to use the demand or the supply price will depend on the impact that the increased demand has on the input market. If production of the input increases, then the project analyst should use the supply price and consider only the factor cost of the input; if a transfer occurs without any change in production, the demand price will suffice; and if a combined response occurs, a weighted average price should be used.

8.3.4 Price variation

A related issue concerns the first of the two possibilities raised under 8.3.2 and 8.3.3, i.e. where a new public project does give rise to increased production (of the input), and the **lower (supply) price** is used for valuation purposes. The project analyst could use the latter price or, in a more dynamic setting, a weighted average of the initial and subsequent prices. But the problem may be a lack of information about the underlying demand and supply functions. In certain instances it may be possible to obtain the necessary information directly from suppliers themselves and, after allowing for monopoly influences and indirect taxes and subsidies, price the input accordingly.

8.3.5 Pecuniary external effects

Perhaps the most important adjustment that has to be made concerns the multiplier or indirect effects that many public projects tend to have. These are usually **pecuniary external effects** that nonetheless constitute real benefits or costs (Dasgupta & Pearce, 1974: 121). Provided the economy is operating at a less-than-full-employment level of real income, a new public project could give rise to multiplied increases in output and employment in many other sectors, and it is imperative that these effects be taken into account in determining the relative attractiveness of the project. Apart from the direct impact on supplying and purchasing industries, the multiplier (and accelerator) process works its way through the spending activities of new workers on the project itself, and of workers in the supplying and purchasing industries, which ultimately add further value in the rest of the economy. Given the relevant information, including up-to-date input-output tables, it is not too difficult to estimate the overall economic impact of a new public project. Multiplier coefficients ranging between 1,4 and 1,6 are fairly common, and can make an important difference to the relative values afforded different public projects (Black, 1981; Black & Saxby, 1996).

Of course, under conditions of full employment and maximum capacity utilisation, these multiplier effects will be offset by cut-backs in output and employment elsewhere in the economy. Thus it may be that shop and restaurant owners located along or near a new rapid rail system may become more profitable as a direct result of increased traffic. But if these benefits are offset by losses experienced by shop and restaurant owners along the old routes, it can be viewed as an income transfer from one group to another, in which case total welfare will remain the same as before. In this instance we are dealing with pecuniary externalities that do **not** constitute net benefits or costs, and that should **not** therefore be included in the calculation of the discounted net benefit of a project.

If all the above adjustments could indeed be made, it should at least be possible to quantify the **adjusted marginal private cost** of the project, which, in equilibrium, is the same as the corresponding marginal private benefit. The latter equality would yield an equilibrium such as point M in Figure 8.2, where MPC – adjusted for unemployment, monopoly elements and indirect taxes and subsidies – equals the correspondingly adjusted MPB.

8.3.6 Questionnaire studies

There still remains the problem of having to quantify the technological external costs and benefits, which, as we have seen, should be added to the (adjusted) private costs and benefits in order to derive the true social value of the project. The problem here is that the analyst cannot use market prices to begin with, because there are none. Nonetheless, the basic aim remains that of estimating the net willingness to pay, or consumer surplus. Two possibilities suggest themselves, one entailing survey work and the other intelligent guesswork.

Technological externalities can be gauged by means of **questionnaire studies**. The creation of a park in a CBD will benefit some and harm others, each of whom can presumably put a monetary value on the benefit or cost. Likewise, the installation of a speed-train direct from Khayelitsha to the CBD of Cape Town will save commuters the time spent waiting for taxis and the time wasted in rush-our traffic. The challenge here is to quantify the value of time, or the value of leisure to the commuter, i.e. the amount she would be willing to pay in order to substitute the time spent in rush-hour traffic for more leisure time. Thus the benefits from the new rapid rail system can be gauged through questionnaire surveys, which ask commuters how much they would be willing to pay to reduce their current commuting time. Similarly, in addition to the (adjusted) direct or monetary costs of the project, external costs could be proxied by asking those negatively affected by the new rail line how much compensation they would need in order to put up with it.

It is important to add that we are referring here to technological externalities only – not pecuniary ones, which feature in the calculation of private benefits and costs – as discussed under 8.3.5 above. The former affect the utility functions of consumers, and the production functions of producers, and do not as a rule alter market prices.

8.3.7 Contingencies

If the above survey method should prove to be too costly, the analyst could consider using the results of similar studies undertaken elsewhere in the world. But care should be taken to adjust such findings in accordance with the particular characteristics of both the project itself and the environment in which it will be operating.

The alternative would be to treat the expected external effects as **"contingencies"** in the budget, rather than simply ignoring them altogether. For many public projects, such as a new school or health care facility, it seems reasonable to assume that they will confer a net external benefit on the community; in which case the project analyst would be justified in budgeting for a larger output at a higher price than would otherwise apply using only the adjusted private costs and benefits of the project. Such a procedure clearly involves a judgement call on the part of the decision maker, who should ideally base his or her judgement on the social preferences of the broader community as expressed through the ballot box (see Chapter 6).

The above discussion can be illustrated with the aid of Figure 8.2. S and S' are the adjusted marginal private and social cost curves, respectively, while D and D' represent the adjusted private and social marginal benefit curves. If technological externalities were entirely ignored, and the project analyst used appropriate shadow prices for all

the inputs, the adjusted private equilibrium would occur at point M, indicating production of $0Q_1$ units at price $0P_1$. But technological externalities evidently do exist, with the marginal external benefit exceeding the marginal external cost of the project at point M. Clearly the social equilibrium occurs at point E, requiring a larger output at a higher price than before.

8.4 The social discount rate

Thus far our discussion has focused on the valuation of benefits and costs. Recall that equation 8.3 had three variables: benefits, costs and the discount rate. In the private sector the profit derived from undertaking an investment (as measured by the return on capital, or ROC) must exceed the rate at which capital for the project can be obtained; otherwise there would be no incentive to begin the project in the first place. The latter

Figure 8.2 Adjusted private values versus social values

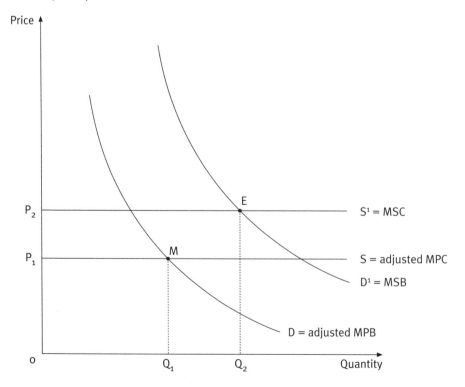

rate is simply the appropriate market rate of interest charged by the lending institution. When private firms undertake new investment projects they generally pursue their own individual interests, and it is often claimed that in doing so they choose a discount rate that does not necessarily serve the broader interests of society. Some of the reasons for this claim are briefly discussed here.

8.4.1 Insufficient investment

Private investments do not benefit investors only, but may also confer external benefits on "third" parties not involved in the initial investment activity. Investments in new technologies generally tend to benefit many more firms than only those who have taken on the initial risk of such investments. Similarly, a firm investing in the training of its own work force would indirectly benefit other firms when its trained workers change jobs (Arrow, 1962). Individual South African firms will likewise have little or no incentive to train employees belonging to historically disadvantaged groups if they expect them to be poached by other firms once they are trained. The conventional argument is that such training should become the responsibility of the public sector, which is at least potentially capable of achieving the requisite optimal level of training.

If private investments do create positive externalities, it can be expected that private markets on their own will invest too little, at least when viewed from a social welfare perspective – thus establishing the usual case for appropriate policy intervention. One option would be to lower the discount rate used in public projects below the prevailing market rate of interest. As discussed in section 8.2 above, such a downward adjustment would immediately increase the discounted net present value of all public projects, making more of them feasible and potentially acceptable. The difficulty here is again that of measuring the size of the externality. But even if this could be done, adjusting the dis-

count rate is not necessarily the most efficient means of intervention. The government could instead grant private firms an investment subsidy equal to the marginal external benefit, thus leaving it to the private sector to make up the investment shortfall (see Chapter 3).

8.4.2 Current and future generations

A second consideration concerns the relative importance of future generations *vis-à-vis* the current generation. It is sometimes argued that the community as a whole, and hence its representative public sector, places a higher relative value on the well-being of **future generations** than do self-interested private individuals and institutions. The private sector thus saves too little and applies too high a discount rate to the future returns of their investments. This preference for the current generation may well explain why private individuals do not as a rule invest large amounts in the provision of social services such as education and health care, which tend to have long gestation periods before they render positive returns. Likewise, the planting of trees in a residential suburb may only produce benefits in, say, 20 years. Such benefits are clearly unlikely to exceed the ROC demanded by private investors. But if society as a whole placed a high value on the benefits that fully grown trees could have on the next generation, it can choose a lower **social** discount rate now to increase the discounted net present value of the project.

If CBA can be used to discriminate between different generations, then it can also be used to discriminate between different groups within the **current generation**. Governments pursuing a more equitable distribution of income can do so by applying different discount rates to public projects in different regions and neighbourhoods. It is often true that the cost of investing in an established urban area is lower than the cost of the same investment in a poor and remote rural area. Given that the benefits are roughly the same, the government can avoid this distributional bias by applying a lower discount rate to the latter area; or by simply applying a higher quantitative weight to NPV in the rural area. In either case, however, the distributional gain may entail a loss in efficiency, the size of which will ultimately depend on the value judgements of the project analyst.

8.4.3 Risk

A final issue concerns the riskiness of different investment projects. Public projects are generally considered to be less risky than equivalent projects in the private sector. The reason is that project risks in the public sector are spread more widely across the taxpaying public than equivalent risks taken on by private entrepreneurs. Public project analysts could thus use a lower risk premium than that which applies in the private sector. The latter is usually included in the relevant market rate of interest, and hence in the private discount rate, thus implying that the public project analyst could use a discount rate that is lower than the prevailing market rate of interest. It goes without saying that risk premiums will vary among different public projects, and it is therefore important that such differences be duly taken into account.

All in all, it would seem that the principles of CBA, and more precisely their strict application in practice, tend to give a great deal of discretionary power to project analysts and decision-makers in the public sector. It is therefore imperative that the decisions they take should truly reflect the wishes of the community they serve. While this is clearly a tall order – perhaps a wishful one – we know from Chapter 6 that successful delivery will ultimately depend on the politi-cal system – or "social choice rule" – that is in place, and on the ability of politicians and bureaucrats to control "government failure".

> **Important concepts**
> adjusted marginal private costs
> benefit-cost ratio
> consumer surplus
> discount rate
> internal rate of return
> net present value
> pecuniary external effects
> shadow prices
> social discount rate
> technological externalities

Self-assessment exercises

8.1 Outline the net present value (NPV) method of project evaluation and briefly compare it with the internal rate of return.

8.2 Compare the different approaches to project evaluation followed by the private and public sectors.

8.3 Explain the process by which market prices can be adjusted to reflect the true opportunity cost of inputs used in a public project.

8.4 Under what conditions should the multiplier effects of a new public project be taken into consideration?

8.5 Distinguish between pecuniary and technological externalities and show how they might feature in the evaluation of public projects.

8.6 Illustrate with the aid of a diagram what you consider to be the optimal value of a public project.

8.7 How would you justify the use of a social discount rate that differs from the prevailing market rate of interest?

PART THREE

Taxation

Chapter nine

Tjaart Steenekamp

Introduction to taxation and tax equity

In Parts One and Two the role and functions of government and the nature and patterns of government expenditure were explained. The need and demand for public goods and services would appear to be varied and extensive. But like all other demands/wants and needs, the demand for public goods and services is also constrained by limited resources on the supply side. And like all other goods and services, the supply and distribution of public goods and services must be financed. John Coleman aptly remarked: "The point to remember is that what the government gives it must first take away" (quoted in Mohr & Fourie, 2000).

This chapter is about taxation as a source of finance for public expenditures. Different sources of finance are identified in Section 9.1. In the following section tax bases are identified and a distinction is made between different types of taxes (such as general taxes, *ad valorem* taxes and direct taxes). Criteria for analysing taxes are proposed in Section 9.3 after which the equity criterion is described and discussed in depth in Section 9.4 and the rest of the chapter. When the fairness of a tax is considered the effects of tax shifting are paramount. In Sections 9.5, 9.6, and 9.7 the incidence of taxes is discussed using both partial equilibrium and general equilibrium analysis.

> Once you have studied this chapter, you should be able to
> - list alternative sources of government revenue;
> - define a tax and describe the structure of tax rates;
> - distinguish between general and selective taxes, specific and *ad valorem* taxes, direct and indirect taxes;
> - list the properties of a good tax;
> - explain what is meant by an equitable tax;
> - distinguish between statutory and economic burden of a tax;
> - analyse the shifting of a tax and its impact on tax incidence using both a partial and a general equilibrium framework.

9.1 Sources of finance

The dominant source of finance of public expenditure is taxation. In 2000/01 tax revenue constituted approximately 94,4 per cent of total revenue of the consolidated general government (South African Reserve Bank 2002:S-74). Government expenditure may also be financed from alternative sources. In addition to taxation there are four other important sources of finance: user charges, administrative fees, borrowing and "inflation taxation".

User charges (also referred to as benefit

taxes) are prices charged for the delivery of certain public goods and services. The role these charges play in the allocation and distribution of resources is analogous to the role of prices in the market mechanism. The important difference is that user charges are set in the "political market". User charges can only be levied if exclusion is possible. In other words, it should be possible to exclude those who do not pay for the consumption of the public good or service in question. Examples include toll roads, public swimming pools, ambulance services and university education (see Chapter 14 for a further discussion of benefit taxes).

Administrative fees are similar to user charges but differ in the sense that the service (or benefit) received in return for the fee is defined rather broadly and imprecisely. Such fees include business licences, television licences, diamond export rights, fishing licences and motor vehicle licences. The dreaded parking ticket and speeding fine can also be added to the list. Administrative fees and fines are insignificant sources of revenue.

Government can borrow from its own citizens and from abroad. **Borrowing** is often used to finance capital expenditure. Borrowed funds must be repaid at some point and therefore amount to deferred taxes. Because lenders have to be adequately compensated for current consumption forgone, it is imperative that borrowed money should be spent on productive activities. Sometimes government uses borrowed funds to finance current consumption, a practice that cannot always be defended on economic grounds (see Section 16.2).

Government-induced inflation can also be regarded as a source of revenue. If public expenditure is financed in a manner which involves increases in the money supply, such financing may eventually raise the price level. Inflation changes the real value of public debt. If government borrows R2 000 from a taxpayer (e.g. imposes a loan levy on

all taxpayers with incomes in excess of R100 000) and inflation is 10 per cent, then in a year's time the real value of the loan is only R1 800 (R2 000 – $[\frac{10}{100} \times 2\,000]$). If the value of the loan is not linked to a price index the real value of government debt decreases. In this case it may also be said that government finances its expenditure with an "inflation tax" (also see Chapter 16, Section 16.3.1 on nominal versus real debt).

9.2 Definition and classification of taxes

In 1789, Benjamin Franklin wrote: "In this world nothing can be said to be certain, except death and taxes" (Cohen & Cohen, 1960). What then is so abhorrent about taxes? **Taxes** are transfers of resources from persons or economic units to government and are **compulsory** (or legally enforceable). There is not necessarily a direct connection between the resources transferred to government and the goods and services it supplies. In fact, government can compel one group of individuals to make payments that are used to finance activities to the benefit of another group. Taxes are compulsory because of the free rider problem. No one will pay taxes voluntarily. People have to be compelled to do so. Government has legally been granted the power to tax. This aspect distinguishes government's confiscation of resources through taxation from other involuntary transfers of resources (e.g. theft).

The power of government to tax is however not unlimited. The Constitution of the Republic of South Africa (1996) provides for money Bills, i.e. Bills that give government the legal right to appropriate amounts of money or impose taxes, levies or duties. All money Bills must be considered in accordance with the procedure established by Section 75 of the Constitution, and an Act of Parliament must provide for a procedure to amend money Bills before Parliament. Since the National Assembly must pass such a Bill it implies that, in addition to procedural limits, the imposition of taxes and changes to taxes are subject to the checks and balances of Parliament. In a representative democracy, parliamentarians must take cognisance of the preferences of voters as well as of other parties (e.g. vested interests) that may influence fiscal decisions. The influence of interest groups in this process is considered to be particularly important (see Chapter 6) and may even explain why the fear that "the numerous poor will out-vote the rich and middle classes, and tax away much of their wealth" is more apparent than real (see Becker, 1985).

Taxes can be classified in many ways. The classification used in South Africa is the one that conforms to the IMF's *Manual on Government Finance Statistics*, published in 1996. Tax revenue is grouped into seven categories and each group is then sub-divided further. The main tax categories in respect of central government (with the percentage contribution to total tax revenue net of South African Customs Union payments for 2000/01 in brackets)[1] are (National Treasury 2002a: 194):

- Taxes on income, profits and capital gains (62,4%)
- Taxes on property (1,8%)
- Domestic taxes on goods and services (34,6%)
- Taxes on international trade and transactions (0,4%)
- Other taxes (0,8%)

Income taxes were clearly the most important category of taxes in 2000/01. Taxes on the income of individuals contributed 60,0 per cent and tax on income of non-mining corporations (excluding secondary tax on companies) contributed 28,9 per cent of total taxes on income and profits.

For purposes of analysis, we next classify taxes according to tax base and then distinguish between general and selective taxes, specific and *ad valorem* taxes and direct and indirect taxes.

9.2.1 Tax base and rates of taxation

Taxes can generally be imposed on three **tax bases: income, wealth** and **consumption**. To this could be added people. An example of a tax on people is a poll tax (or lump-sum tax per head). Tax bases can also be viewed in terms of their flow and stock characteristics. **Flows** are associated with a time dimension and are measured over a period. Income and consumption are flow concepts since both are measured over a period (normally a tax year). **Stocks** have no time dimension and are measured at a particular point in time. Wealth is a stock concept. Which of the three potential tax bases is the best is a much-debated issue. Most countries have hybrid systems, exploiting three (or four) bases simultaneously. Tax systems differ according to historical and political circumstances as well as the stage of development. This aspect is considered again in Section 10.5.

Once the tax base has been identified, the **tax rate structure** can be set. The tax rate refers to the amount of tax levied per unit of the tax base. Three variants can be distinguished: proportional, progressive and regressive taxes. The rate structure can be described in at least two ways. One way is to compare the **average tax rate** to the size or value of the tax base. When the average tax rate (the total rand amount of taxes collected divided by the rand value of the taxable base) remains constant with respect to variations in the tax base, the tax is **proportional** – see Box 9.1. When the average tax rate increases as the tax base increases, the tax is progressive. If the average tax rate decreases as the tax base increases, the tax is regressive.

Box 9.1

Proportional, progressive and regressive taxes

Consider a tax on the consumption base. Suppose a tax of 10 per cent is imposed on the consumption of all grain products (e.g. mealie meal, bread and rice). Suppose further there are two households: the Peterson household with an annual income of R6 000 and the Chetty household with an annual income of R100 000. Is this tax progressive, proportional or regressive? From the 1995 Household Survey conducted by Statistics South Africa (SSA) the low-income group spends approximately 18 per cent of their income on grain products, whereas the high-income group spends 2 per cent (Statistics South Africa, 1997). The Petersons thus spend approximately R1 080 on grain products per annum and the Chettys R2 000 (almost double the amount of the Petersons). A 10 per cent tax on grain products will therefore "cost" the Petersons R108 per annum in taxes while the Chettys will pay R200 In absolute terms the Chettys thus contribute more in tax on grain products to the South African Revenue Services (SARS) than the Petersons. However, if we focus on the **average tax rate**, that is, if we divide the tax collected (R108 or R200) by the rand value of the **taxable base** (R1 080 or R2 000), the average tax rate is the same ($\frac{108}{1\,080} = 10\%$ or $\frac{200}{2\,000} = 10\%$). Our first conclusion would therefore be that the tax on the **consumption base** is proportional since the average tax rate does not vary with the size of the tax base. However, if we evaluate the tax in terms of the **income base**, as is commonly done, the picture looks rather different. The Petersons have to transfer 1,8 per cent of their income ($\frac{108}{6\,000} \times 100$) to SARS, but in the case of the Chettys it is only 0,2 per cent of their income ($\frac{200}{100\,000} \times 100$). The tax on grain products can therefore be classi-

fied as regressive because as the income base increases, the tax revenue becomes a decreasing proportion of income. Thus the consumption tax is regressive with respect to the income base but proportional with respect to the consumption base!

Another way to describe the rate structure is to focus on the **ratio of taxes paid to income**. For comparison purposes all taxes are then evaluated in terms of the income base as a common denominator, even though the tax may in practice be imposed on a different base. In this manner the distributional consequences of taxes can be determined. Taxes that generate the same proportion of income as income rises are proportional (e.g. corporate income tax). A tax with a proportional rate structure is also called a flat-rate tax. Taxes that take an increasing proportion of income as income increases are progressive taxes (e.g. personal income tax). If a tax generates a decreasing proportion of income as income increases, it is a regressive tax (e.g. a value-added tax without any zero-ratings) – see Box 9.1.

9.2.2 General and selective taxes

Taxes can be classified as general or selective taxes. A **general** tax is one which taxes the entire tax base and allows for no exemptions. General taxes are also called broad-based taxes. A value-added tax without any exemptions or zero-ratings is a general tax on consumption. Similarly, an income tax that taxes all sources of income (including capital income) without any tax deductions would be a general tax.

Selective taxes are imposed on one or a few products or only income (i.e. leisure is excluded). The whole tax base is therefore not taxed. An excise tax on cigarettes is an example of a selective tax. A selective tax is also called a narrow-based tax.

The importance of the distinction

between general and selective taxes lies in the fact that under certain assumptions[2] general taxes are similar to head or lump sum taxes that leave relative prices unchanged. Put differently, the behaviour of economic role-players is assumed to be unaffected by these taxes. In contrast, selective taxes distort relative prices by driving a wedge between the before-tax price and after-tax price of a commodity. This violates the Pareto efficiency condition. This aspect will again receive attention when the efficiency of different taxes is considered in Chapter 10, Section 10.1.

9.2.3 Specific and *ad valorem* taxes

Taxes can also be specified according to the size or the value of the tax base. The size of the tax base can be measured in terms of weight, quantities or units. When a fixed amount is imposed per unit of the product the tax is called a **unit tax** or **specific tax**. Examples of specific taxes in South African in 2002/03 were excise duties on sparkling wine (227,6c/litre), beer made from malt (R25,63/litre of absolute alcohol), and cigarettes (175,4c/10 cigarettes).

Taxes imposed on the **value** of products are called *ad valorem* taxes. Such a tax is usually levied as a rate (i.e. a percentage) of the excisable value (or price) of a commodity. VAT is an example of an *ad valorem* tax. *Ad valorem* taxes (sometimes called *ad valorem* duties) are often imposed on "luxuries". For example, in South Africa commodities such as skin care and hair preparations, perfumery, films and cameras, TV and video equipment, photocopying machines, cell phones and sunglasses are taxed at rates varying between 5 per cent and 7 per cent of the price.

9.2.4 Direct and indirect taxes

Yet another possible distinction is between direct and indirect taxes. **Direct taxes** are imposed directly on individuals and companies (e.g. personal income tax and company tax). **Indirect taxes** are imposed on commodities (e.g. excise taxes and VAT). This distinction fundamentally evolves around the issue of tax incidence (i.e. the question of who really pays the tax). Tax incidence is analysed in Section 9.4 and is a complex issue. It would suffice to say that we simply could not tell in advance what the outcome is going to be with certainty.

From the perspective of tax shifting, **direct taxes** are taxes defined as taxes that cannot be shifted readily. They are collected from individuals, households or firms and allow for the possibility of adjusting the tax according to the personal circumstances of the taxpayer (e.g. the marital status, gender, size of household, rich or poor). These taxpayers are the intended bearers of the tax burden and it is assumed that they pay over the tax to SARS. Personal income tax is nowadays mostly deducted from employees' salaries and paid over by employers. Nonetheless, the employer does not have perfect information on non-salary income (e.g. donations, interest, rent, capital gains) and the individual is therefore still responsible for the completeness and correctness of the tax assessment.

Indirect taxes are taxes which are likely to be shifted and are imposed on commodities or market transactions. Examples are excise duties and fuel levies. It is also more difficult to adjust the tax rate to the personal circumstances of the consumer. In the case of indirect taxes it is often possible to shift the burden of the tax to someone else. VAT is collected from merchants who in turn can pass – on the tax to consumers by way of a price increase. The consumer then indirectly bears the burden.

Although there are differences of opinion on the exact distinction between direct and indirect taxes, this classification is widely

---

2 The most important assumptions are that the supply of work effort and the supply of savings remain unchanged (i.e. are unaffected by the tax).

used. The relative importance of direct versus indirect taxes is much debated, also in South Africa. In 1975/76 the ratio of direct to indirect taxes was 2,7, that is, for each rand in indirect taxes collected, R2,70 was collected in direct taxes. In contrast, this ratio changed to 1,5 in 2001/02, which shows a clear shift in the direction of indirect taxes. These trends will be discussed in Section 10.5 when the topic of tax reform is considered. The merits and demerits of indirect taxes will receive attention in Chapter 13.

9.3 Properties of a "good tax"

Tax systems evolve as new taxes are introduced and others are amended from time to time. The question is whether such changes are good or bad. To evaluate the changes a list of criteria, some of which date back to the "maxims of taxation" proposed by Adam Smith in 1776, can be used. The more important criteria or properties of a "good" tax system can be classified under four headings:

- **Equity**. Taxes should promote an equitable (or "fair") distribution of income. Cognisance has to be taken of the fact that the burden of taxes can be shifted. To determine fairness the incidence of taxes, therefore, has to be examined. These topics are covered in Section 9.4.
- **Economic efficiency**. All taxes impose a burden and most taxes affect the behaviour of taxpayers (i.e. they cause an "excess burden"). Taxes should be designed in such a manner that their distorting effects on the choices made by taxpayers are minimised. This aspect is discussed in Chapter 10 (Section 10.1).
- **Administrative efficiency**. Taxes are levied to yield sufficient revenue but to be efficient, administration and compliance costs have to be kept low. This calls for tax simplicity and certainty. This topic is discussed in Chapter 10 (Section 10.3).
- **Flexibility**. As economic circumstances

change, taxes and tax rates need to adjust. Taxes should therefore be flexible enough to facilitate macroeconomic stability and economic development. This aspect is discussed in Chapter 10 (Section 10.4).

9.4 Taxation and equity: Concepts of fairness

One of the most important judgements in tax analysis is whether or not the distributional impact of a tax is equitable or fair. Fairness, however, is a subjective concept and like beauty it lies in the eye of the beholder. But although fairness is a value-laden concept, economists can help to make informed value judgements. In his first maxim of taxation, Adam Smith (1776), as quoted in Musgrave and Musgrave (1989:219) stated: "The subjects of every state ought to contribute towards the support of the government, as nearly as possible, in proportion to their respective abilities; that is, in proportion to the revenue which they respectively enjoy under the protection of the state." This statement contains a tax equity principle that is still used in theory and practice to evaluate the fairness of the impact (or incidence) of taxes, i.e. the ability to pay principle. Another principle is based on benefits received. In section 14.1 a more comprehensive review of the benefit principle can be found.

9.4.1 Benefit principle

The **benefit principle** stipulates that the tax burden of government expenditure should be apportioned to taxpayers in accordance with the benefits each receives. Take the example of a bridge. The more an individual uses the bridge, the more he or she will have to pay for this benefit. If the bridge is financed out of general revenues instead of through a benefit tax (e.g. a toll) levied on those using the bridge, those who do not use the bridge are made worse off. It seems unfair to expect non-users also to pay for the construction and maintenance of the bridge. It can also be argued that tax morality will be undermined if taxpayers do not benefit from a tax system and that a democratic society will become intolerant of such a system in the long run.

A major **advantage** of the benefit principle is that it links the expenditure side of the budget to the revenue side. In this way it serves to discipline or regulate government expenditure. A further benefit is that the allocative procedures of market behaviour are approximated. Individuals can adjust their consumption of services until price is equal to the marginal cost. In a voluntary exchange model, if the price is higher than the marginal cost, society places a higher value on an additional unit of the service than the resources required to provide the additional unit. In terms of Pareto optimality conditions, society's welfare can then be improved by allocating more resources to the provision of the service, that is, at least one person can be made better off without making anyone else worse off (Mohr & Fourie, 2000: 349). Benefit taxes assume the role of prices and can therefore ensure that resources are efficiently allocated.

Unfortunately the scope for applying the benefit principle to government funding is rather **restricted**. Governments generally provide goods and services that are public in nature. In other words, the benefits are generally non-excludable (see Chapter 3). For example, how would one apportion the benefits of protection (e.g. policing) to different beneficiaries? There is no straightforward answer. Some would argue that the rich benefit most because they have so much to lose and that they therefore have to contribute more. Others would argue that the poor are the most vulnerable (i.e. most in need of protection) and that they thus have to pay more.

Another shortcoming of benefit taxes is that they take the existing distribution of income and wealth for granted. The effective demand for public goods and services is often determined by this distribution. If the distribution is skewed towards the rich, the provision of public services might therefore be tailored largely to their needs. The benefit principle can also undermine redistributive objectives of government and result in conflicting outcomes. It would, for example, be somewhat ridiculous if old age pensioners have to bear the current taxes required to finance the transfers to themselves.

Benefit taxes (also referred to as user charges) are nevertheless levied in some cases, for example, tolls for roads and bridges, admission charges to museums and parks, licence fees and (to some extent) university tuition fees and school fees. Note that in the case of user charges the link between the financing of the use of the service and the benefit is reasonably direct. Sometimes services are financed in a way in which the link is more indirect. This occurs when charges are assigned (or dedicated) to special funds or accounts for financing services that are indirectly related to the source of the funds. In such cases the taxes are called **earmarked taxes**. Examples of earmarked taxes are levies on the sale of fuel, social security taxes (e.g. unemployment insurance contributions) and skills development levies. At the time of writing the fuel levies consisted of a general levy of 98,0 cents per litre (in respect of leaded petrol) and two other levies assigned to the Equalisation Fund for subsidisation of Sasol and Mossgas (0,0 c/l for petrol) and to the Road Accident Fund (RAF) (16,5 c/l for petrol). Together these levies accounted for 118,51 cents of the per litre price of petrol. On the recommendation of the Katz Commission (1995), government also decided that a portion of the general fuel levy would be allocated to a National Road Agency for road construction and maintenance.

The shortcomings of the benefit principle generally apply to earmarked taxes as well. In addition earmarked taxes affect the procedural fairness of the budgetary process.

Since earmarked funds have assured sources of revenue, these funds need not compete with other departments for finance. In the case of earmarked funds, accountability and the responsibility for efficient resource allocation are also shifted to the managers of these funds. Earmarked taxes also complicate fiscal policy aimed at achieving macroeconomic objectives. The Katz Commission (1995: Chapter 3) therefore recommended against a proliferation of earmarked taxes (in particular in respect of general tax revenue such as VAT where the link between benefits and costs is extremely vague).

9.4.2 Ability-to-pay principle

As mentioned above, the benefit principle cannot be applied to the financing of public goods and services that are non-excludable. Public expenditures are predominantly of this type. Total cost of such public expenditure therefore has to be apportioned according to people's ability to pay. In contrast with the benefit principle, the application of the ability-to-pay principle implies that the tax problem is viewed independently from the expenditure aspect.

The **ability-to-pay principle** calls for people with equal capacity to pay the same amount of tax, and for people with greater capacity to pay more. The first aspect is referred to as horizontal equity and the latter as vertical equity. **Horizontal equity** requires similar treatment for tax purposes of people in similar economic circumstances, while **vertical equity** requires that individuals in different economic circumstances be treated differently.

The implementation of a tax system based on ability to pay requires public consensus on an appropriate definition (i.e. measure, indicator, criterion or basis) of ability to pay. It also calls for consensus on the rate structure. Income is generally regarded

as one such measure or criterion. Other possible measures include consumption, wealth and utility. Much of the discussion concerning the appropriate measure or base is theoretical, but in practice income is commonly used.

Income, however, is by no means a perfect measure of ability to pay. Income measures outcomes and does not necessarily reflect ability or capacity. Consider, for example, two persons, Mrs. Moleketi and Mrs. Pienaar, with similar economic circumstances and the same capacity to earn income. The economic circumstances referred to here include gender, race, religion, marital status, level of education, disability, number of dependants and so on. Mrs. Moleketi, however, is much more hardworking and works 10 hours a day at a rate of R50 per hour compared to the 5 hours which Mrs. Pienaar works for the same hourly pay. Mrs. Moleketi therefore earns R500 per day against Mrs. Pienaar's R250. Using income as the yardstick of ability to pay implies that Mrs. Moleketi has a greater ability to pay and that she should therefore make a greater tax sacrifice. Is this fair? In this case, is the wage rate, instead of total wage income, not a more appropriate measure of ability? Not surprisingly, the inclusion or exclusion of the various possible determinants of economic circumstances in the search for an appropriate base for ability to pay has been hotly debated.[3]

The appropriate measurement of horizontal and vertical equity is not only a complicated issue but also requires subjective evaluations. Economics alone cannot provide unambiguous answers to the measurement of "ability" and the final decision therefore has to be taken via the political process.

Once the appropriate measure of ability to pay has been established, fairness sug-

---

3 For a comprehensive debate on whether the individual or the household should be the taxable unit as well as the constitutional implications of discrimination on the basis of gender and marital status in the South African tax system, see Margo Commission (1987: Chapter 7) and Katz Commission (1994: Chapter 6).

gests that people with the same ability should pay the same amount of tax and people with different abilities should pay different amounts. Suppose income is used to measure ability to pay. This still leaves the question of how to determine the taxes payable by people with different incomes. For example, if person A's income is double that of person B, should person A pay exactly twice as much tax as person B? This relates to **vertical equity** and is a **rate structure** issue. Various sacrifice concepts have been developed in an attempt to deal with the problem of vertical equity.[4]

Suffice it to say that most countries try to deal with vertical equity by applying the progressive tax rule to income (i.e. by taxing an increasing proportion of income as income increases). But this does not solve the dilemma. To determine whether a tax is truly progressive, proportional or regressive, one needs to know who really pays the tax. In other words, the impact of a tax on the distribution of income has to be investigated. This is what tax incidence is all about.

9.5 Tax incidence: Partial equilibrium analysis

9.5.1 Concepts of incidence

All taxes reduce the real disposable income of taxpayers. All taxes therefore involve a burden. At the outset it should be noted that only **people** bear the burden. Companies, for example, cannot bear the tax burden. Only people (e.g. shareholders, workers, landlords, consumers) bear the burden of taxation. Exactly who ultimately bears the burden is a matter for theoretical discourse and empirical evidence. To deal with this question, we first have to distinguish between the statutory (or legal) incidence of a tax and the economic (or effective) incidence.

The **statutory incidence** refers to the legal liability to pay over the tax to the revenue authorities. Economists are not really interested in who is legally obliged to make the tax payment to SARS. Since taxes affect economic behaviour, economists are more concerned with who ultimately bears the tax burden, that is, the **economic incidence** of the tax. For example, customs and excise taxes are levied on cigarettes. At the time of writing an importer of cigarettes had to pay a customs duty of 158,4 cents per 10 cigarettes to SARS. However, the importer can shift the actual burden **forward** to retailers who, in turn, can pass on the tax to the consumers (the smokers) in the form of higher prices. The tax burden can also be shifted **backward** if, for example, the importer cuts back on staff or lowers real wages. In addition to tax shifting, the tax can be **avoided** by cutting back on the taxed activity, that is, by reducing imports of cigarettes. What we notice here is that the economic incidence issue is fundamentally about how **taxes affect prices** (including wages).

Tax incidence studies may apply either a balanced-budget incidence methodology or a differential-incidence methodology. According to the **balanced-budget incidence** approach the overall distributional effect of a tax and the spending financed by the tax is considered. Income taxes lower real disposable income, but at the same time the income tax revenue is spent on education and other public services which raise real disposable income (at least for those with school-going children). The advantage of the balanced-budget incidence approach is that it relates the cost of spending programmes to who pays for it. The disadvantage is that in reality government uses a number of different taxes to finance expenditure – tax revenue is pooled in the national revenue account. Linking a particular expenditure item to a tax source is almost impossible.

---

4 For a discussion of using the sacrifice of utility as measure for determining ability to pay, see Musgrave (1959: Chapter 5).

Since not all taxes are earmarked for a particular expenditure programme the differential tax incidence approach comes in handy. The **differential tax incidence** methodology considers the distributional impact as one tax is substituted for another, holding total revenue and expenditure constant. The benchmark tax often used for purposes of comparison is a lump sum tax (e.g. head tax) that does not affect relative prices and hence economic behaviour. For example, suppose government replaces a lump sum tax on all redheads with an excise tax on beer drinkers that yields the same tax revenue. Assuming that redheads are not beer drinkers, they would gain and beer drinkers would lose. Furthermore, the owners of breweries and their employees will be affected by the tax. By comparing the total impact of the tax change on the incomes of beer drinkers to those of redheads, we are engaging in differential tax incidence analysis.

Ultimately the economic incidence of a tax depends on how the economy reacts to a tax change. The response of the economy can be determined by tracing the effect of the tax on prices. Taxes change the relative prices of goods and services. For example, if a R2,00 dairy levy on butter increases the price of butter from R11,50 to R13,50 per 500g while other prices remain unchanged, the relative price of butter also increases. If it is assumed that the initial change in the price of butter does not have significant repercussions on prices in other markets, tax incidence can be analysed in a **partial equilibrium framework**. In other words, we can then study the effect of the tax in a single market in isolation. In partial equilibrium analysis price and quantity in each market is determined by demand and supply on the assumption that other prices remain unchanged (i.e. the *ceteris paribus* assumption is used).

However, when a tax is imposed on one good it usually means that the prices of **other goods** change as well. For example, a levy on butter will affect the price of margarine, a substitute. After the imposition of the levy, butter will be relatively more expensive and margarine relatively cheaper than before. Consumers will therefore tend to substitute margarine for butter and the increased demand for margarine will probably lead to a rise in the (absolute) price of margarine. This will leave margarine consumers with less real disposable income than before. Once the secondary effects of a tax are taken into account, tax incidence is studied in a **general equilibrium framework**.

Both partial and general equilibrium analysis can be used in incidence studies. Partial equilibrium studies are less complex since all the ramifications of a tax change are not considered. It is ideally suited to studying taxes levied on goods and services which are characterised by low degrees of substitutability or complementarity. Where the secondary effects are considered to be small, uncertain or spread thinly over a number of other markets, economists would argue that these can be ignored and that the conclusions based on partial equilibrium analysis will not differ significantly from those based on general equilibrium analysis. The general equilibrium framework, however, is more suitable for studying the incidence of a general sales tax that is levied on a broad base, or a levy on an important product such as fuel that has important ramifications for the economy. Since general equilibrium analysis considers relative price changes in more than one market, it is conceptually superior to partial equilibrium analysis.

9.5.2 Partial equilibrium analysis of tax incidence

In this section we analyse the incidence effect of taxes within a partial equilibrium framework. The ability to shift the tax burden under partial equilibrium conditions depends on a number of factors but we con-

Figure 9.1 Incidence of a unit tax on consumption imposed on the supply side or the demand side

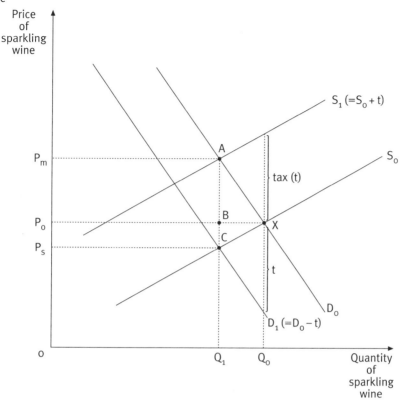

sider only two: market structure and price elasticity.

Two types of taxes are considered: a unit tax (i.e. a fixed amount per unit of a good or service sold (see Section 9.2.3)) and an *ad valorem* tax. We start by assuming that there is **perfect competition** and that the tax is levied on an increasing-cost industry (i.e. the supply curve slopes upward).

Incidence of a unit tax

In Figure 9.1 D_0 is the demand curve and S_0 the supply curve for sparkling wine. The before-tax equilibrium price is P_0 and the equilibrium quantity is Q_0. Suppose that an excise tax (a unit tax) of t per unit is imposed on sparkling wine. The excise tax is a fixed amount per unit of the product. If the tax is collected from the **seller** (i.e. the statutory

burden is on the seller) it means that the minimum price at which firms will supply the equilibrium quantity Q_0, is $P_0 + t$. Since the sellers are interested in the after-tax price, they will try to recover the full tax amount at any given quantity – they will charge a higher price (the original price + the tax) at each output level. The **supply curve** therefore **shifts up** vertically by the tax amount to $S_1(= S_1 + t)$. Note that because it is a unit tax, S_1 is **parallel** to S_0. The new market equilibrium is at point A with price P_m and quantity Q_1. The market price, which is the price paid by buyers of sparkling wine, increases from P_0 to P_m. Sellers receive the after-tax price, P_s(i.e. $P_m - t$).

What is the total tax revenue that accrues to government? The formula for total revenue is price multiplied by quantity. Total tax revenue is the tax per unit t (= $P_m P_s$ = AC) multiplied by the number of units sold, $0Q_1$ (= $P_s C$). Geometrically the total revenue is represented by the rectangle $P_m ACP_s$. The important question now is: Who pays what part of the total tax amount? The answer to this question will tell us what the economic incidence of a unit tax on consumption is.

Before the imposition of the tax, consumers paid a price P_0 for the product. After the tax they pay P_m. Note that the price that buyers have to pay did not increase by the full amount of the tax (P_m minus P_0 is less than t or AB is less than AC). The total tax amount paid by consumers is equal to the rectangle $P_m ABP_0$. What about the sellers? The before-tax price received was P_0. The after-tax price received by sellers is P_s which is less than P_0. Producers therefore also pay part of the tax. The total tax amount paid by sellers is equal to the rectangle $P_0 BCP_s$. From this analysis it is clear that the total tax burden is split between buyers and sellers, that is, the tax incidence falls on both. Uninformed observers generally assume that sellers simply pass on the total tax burden to consumers. Partial equilibrium analysis shows that this need not be the case.

Would the result be any different had the statutory burden been on **buyers** (i.e. the consumers)? The answer is no. To show this it should be remembered that the demand curve in our example indicates the maximum price consumers are willing to pay for each different quantity of sparkling wine. In Figure 9.1 the before-tax equilibrium price is P_0 and the equilibrium quantity is Q_0. At the equilibrium quantity Q_0 the consumer is willing to pay only P_0. If a tax of t is now collected from the buyer for this quantity, the buyer will still be willing to pay only P_0. The price paid to the seller, however, will be reduced by the tax amount ($P_0 - t$) that is paid over to SARS by the buyer. This will hold for each point on the **demand curve**. In this case, therefore, the effective demand curve (i.e. as perceived by the seller) **shifts downward** by the tax amount. The new demand curve is D_1 ($D_0 - t$). Since a unit tax of t is imposed, D_1 is parallel to D_0. The after-tax equilibrium is at point C with price P_s and quantity Q_1. While the original demand curve D_0 shows what price buyers are willing to pay for each quantity, the demand curve D_1 shows the price received by sellers (i.e. the after-tax price) for each quantity. Thus for quantity Q_1 buyers are willing to pay P_m and sellers receive $P_s (= P_m - t)$. The result is exactly the same as the result obtained when the tax was levied on sellers – the tax incidence is on both buyers and sellers.

Incidence of an *ad valorem* tax

An *ad valorem* tax is levied as a percentage of the price of a good or service (see Section 9.2.3). The imposition of an *ad valorem* tax (for example on video recorders) and collected from producers is now examined with the aid of Figure 9.2.

The most important difference between the analysis of an *ad valorem* tax and a unit tax is that the after-tax supply curve swivels in the case of an ad *valorem tax* (compared to the parallel shift in the case of a unit tax). Because the tax is proportional, the higher the price, the greater the amount of tax to be paid over by producers (or the higher the after-tax price paid by consumers) will be. For example, at a price of R1 000 per video recorder and an *ad valorem* rate of 20 per cent, the absolute amount of tax is R200 (= $\frac{20}{100}$ × 1 000). If the price is R2 000, the absolute amount of tax is R400.[5] Thus, when an after-tax supply curve such as S_1 in Figure 9.2 is constructed, the vertical dis-

---

5 The ad valorem tax can be levied as a percentage of the gross price (i.e. the price received by sellers). A 20 per cent tax on the gross price is equivalent to a 25 per cent tax on the net price. If the buyer pays 20 per cent on R1, the seller receives R0,80 (the net price). The tax is R0,20. Twenty cents as a percentage of the net price is equivalent to 25 per cent of the gross price ($\frac{20}{80}$ × 100 = $\frac{25}{100}$ × 100).

Figure 9.2 Incidence of an *ad valorem* tax

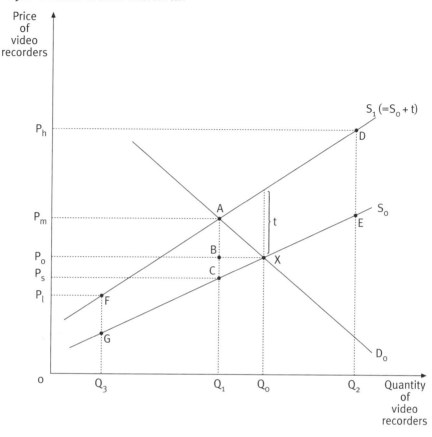

tance between S_1 and S_0 (the before-tax supply curve) at a relatively high price such as P_h (= DE) should be greater than at a low price such as P_l(= FG). The rest of the incidence analysis of an a*d valorem* tax is similar to that of a unit tax. In Figure 9.2 the total tax burden of buyers is the rectangle P_mABP_0 and that of sellers is P_0BCP_s. The *ad valorem* tax rate, expressed as the ratio of tax to the gross price paid by the buyer, equals AC/AQ_1.

Incidence and pure monopoly

So far we have investigated tax incidence under conditions of perfect competition. Pure monopoly is the other extreme form of market structure studied in this section.

It is often taken for granted that a monop-

olist, being a price maker, can always shift taxes forward in full. Under certain circumstances (e.g. where a monopolist is not maximising profit) this may indeed be the case but the conclusion does not necessarily apply. We now consider the tax shifting capacity of a monopolist which is maximising profit.

A monopolist maximises profits where marginal cost (MC) equals marginal revenue (MR). In Figure 9.3 the before-tax equilibrium of the pure monopolist is at quantity Q_0 and price P_0. The before-tax profit is the area P_0ABC. Assume that a unit tax on output is now imposed on the monopolist.

A **unit tax** on the output of the monopolist will raise the average cost (*AC*) and the marginal cost of the firm. The reason why

Figure 9.3 Incidence of a tax on a pure monopoly

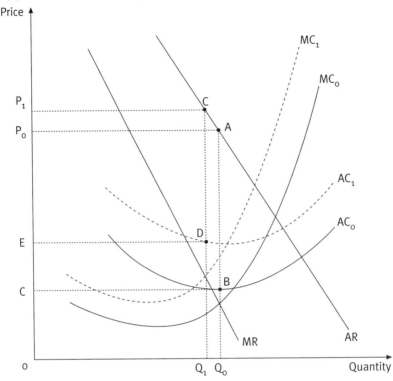

both *AC* and *MC* increase is that the tax is levied on each unit produced and is therefore viewed by the firm as a variable cost. In Figure 9.3 the average cost curve shifts from AC_0 to AC_1 and the marginal cost curve from MC_0 to MC_1. Profits are now maximised at an output of Q_1 and at price P_1. When the before-tax equilibrium is compared to the after-tax equilibrium the following is noted:

- The after-tax price is higher and the quantity is lower than before the imposition of the tax. The increase in the price from P_0 to P_1 indicates the extent of forward shifting.
- The after-tax profit (the rectangle P_1CDE) is less than the before-tax profit (the rectangle P_0ABC). The pure monopolist therefore does not shift the tax burden fully.

Monopolists can also be taxed (at least in theory) on their **economic profits**. Economic profit (or excess profit) is the difference between total revenue and total costs (i.e. both explicit and implicit costs). Implicit costs include the opportunity costs of self-owned resources (i.e. normal profit). The cost curves in Figure 9.3 represent economic costs. In other words, if average revenue exceeds average cost, economic (or excess) profits are earned. In Figure 9.3 the pure monopolist's before-tax profit (area P_0ABC) is considered to be economic profit. A tax at a rate of t per cent on the monopolist's profit of P_0ABC will simply reduce its economic profit by the tax amount. Neither the average nor marginal cost curves will be affected. The monopolist will maximise after-tax profit at the same before-tax level of output and price. Thus the tax is borne fully by the owners of the firm. In other words the profits tax cannot be shifted in such circumstances.[6]

Incidence and price elasticities of demand and supply

As mentioned at the beginning of Section 9.5.2, tax incidence is affected by market structure (e.g. perfect competition or pure monopoly) and price elasticities. When a tax is imposed, both the quantity demanded and the quantity supplied at equilibrium decreases. The magnitude of the decrease depends on the elasticity of demand and supply. Likewise, the impact on the tax burden and the relative tax shares of buyers and sellers also depend on the price elasticities.

The importance of price elasticities in tax incidence analysis can be illustrated with the aid of diagrams. We first consider the effect of demand elasticities and then the effect of supply elasticities.

Figure 9.4 shows two **demand** curves D_0 and D_1 and a supply curve S_0, all intersecting at X. The before-tax equilibrium price is the same (P_0) irrespective of the demand curve used. The intersection of the demand curves enables us to compare elasticity at this point. The demand curve D_1 is more inelastic at any price than demand curve D_0, that is, quantity demanded is less responsive (or sensitive) to price changes in the case of D_1. Suppose the taxed good is cigarettes. If a unit tax (t) is now imposed on the importer or seller, the effective supply curve shifts

Figure 9.4 Tax incidence and price elasticity of demand

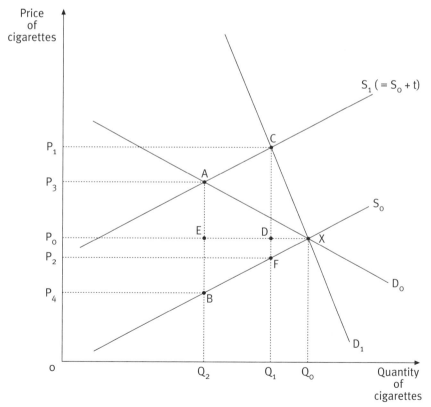

6 This conclusion holds only if the firm is maximising profit prior to the introduction of the tax on economic profits. In the case of unrealised profits or nonprofit-maximising behaviour, tax shifting is possible.

upward and to the left from S_0 to S_1 (where $S_1 = S_0 + t$). Consider the relatively inelastic demand curve D_1 first.

If the demand for cigarettes is represented by D_1, the price charged to buyers increases from P_0 to P_1. The price received by the seller (or importer) decreases from P_0 to P_2. The proportional price change for the buyers therefore exceeds that of the sellers. The tax burden (P_1CFP_2) is divided between the portion borne by buyers (the area P_1CDP_0) and the portion borne by the sellers (the area P_0DFP_2). In the case of the more elastic demand curve D_0, the proportional price changes for buyers and sellers are approximately the same in this example. The total tax burden of P_3ABP_4 is then divided between the buyers (the area P_3AEP_0) and the sellers (the area P_0EBP_4). Thus the more price-inelastic the demand for a product is,

the greater the relative portion of the tax borne by buyers, *ceteris paribus* (sometimes referred to as the **inverse** elasticity rule). Conversely, the more price-elastic the demand for the product, the greater the relative portion of the tax borne by the sellers.

We can also show that, *ceteris paribus*, the more price-inelastic the supply of a product, the greater the relative portion of the tax borne by sellers. In Figure 9.5 we have two supply curves S_0 and S_1 intersecting a demand curve D_0 at point X. The supply curve S_1 is relatively more inelastic than supply curve S_0. To simplify the analysis, suppose that the unit tax (t) on cigarettes is now imposed on buyers (i.e. the statutory burden is on smokers). This means that the effective (after-tax) demand curve shifts downwards to the left from D_0 to D_1 (where $D_1 = D_0 - t$). Let us first analyse the shifting

Figure 9.5 Tax incidence and price elasticity of supply

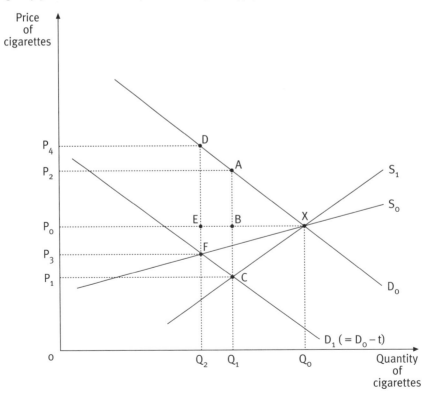

of the tax burden in the case of price inelastic supply S_1. The new equilibrium quantity is Q_1. The after-tax price paid by smokers increases from P_0 to P_2 whereas the after-tax price received by sellers decreases from P_0 to P_1. The proportional price change for sellers is greater than for buyers. Put differently, the share of sellers in the total tax burden P_2ACP_1 is P_0BCP_1 which is greater than the share of buyers (i.e. P_2ABP_0). By contrast, in the case of the elastic supply curve S_0 we notice that the proportional change in the after-tax price of sellers is less than that of buyers. The new equilibrium quantity is Q_2. The buyers pay a price P_4 per unit and the sellers receive a price P_3 per unit. The portion of the total tax burden P_4DFP_3 borne by the sellers (i.e. P_0EFP_3) in the case of the elastic supply curve is less than the burden of the buyers (i.e. P_4DEP_0).

In addition to the examples provided here there are the extreme cases of perfectly (in-)elastic demand and perfectly (in-)elastic supply. These possibilities are not considered here. From our discussion of price elasticity so far we can generalise by stating that the more inelastic the demand and the more elastic the supply, the easier it is to shift the burden of a tax forward through a higher selling price. This conclusion is illustrated in both Figures 9.4 and 9.5. By rotating the demand curve D_0 and supply curve S_0 around X in each case, we note that the buyer's portion of the burden increases as the demand curve becomes steeper (i.e. more inelastic) and the supply curve becomes flatter (i.e. more elastic).

9.6 General equilibrium analysis of tax incidence

In Section 9.5 we distinguished between partial equilibrium analysis and general equilibrium analysis. Partial equilibrium analy-sis examines a single market in isolation (i.e. on basis of the *ceteris paribus* assumption) and ignores the secondary effects of a price change. When the secondary effects of a tax are taken into account, we are studying tax incidence within a **general equilibrium framework**.

Because general equilibrium analysis considers what happens in all markets simultaneously, modelling tax incidence becomes rather complex. To make it manageable, certain assumptions have to be made.[7]

We assume that only two products are produced in the economy, shoes and reed baskets. There are two factors of production, labour and capital, which are perfectly mobile between sectors. Both factors of production are fixed in supply (i.e. the supply curves are vertical). Shoes are produced using a capital-intensive technique (i.e. the capital-labour ratio is high) whereas reed baskets are produced using a labour-intensive method (i.e. the capital-labour ratio is low). The incidence of a tax on one product (i.e. a selective tax) and the incidence of a tax on both products (i.e. a general tax) are analysed here. A selective tax on one factor of production (e.g. land) is discussed in Chapter 12.

9.6.1 A selective tax on commodities

Suppose that a tax is imposed on shoes. The price of shoes increases relative to that of reed baskets. Remember that the after-tax price does not necessarily increase by the full amount of the tax (in Figure 9.1 the tax was equal to AC but the price increase was only AB). The price increase has two effects – one is on the consumption (uses) side, the other on the factors of production (sources) side.

On the **uses side** the price increase of shoes (which is of course also a relative price

---

7 This approach to tax incidence theory was pioneered by Harberger (1962). For extensions to and limitations of the simplified model we consider, consult Boadway & Wildasin (1984: 368-374).

increase) causes consumers to demand fewer shoes (illustrated by a movement along the demand curve for shoes) and demand more reed baskets. When the demand for reed baskets increases (illustrated by a rightward shift of the demand curve), the price of reed baskets increases, *ceteris paribus*. The tax thus causes an increase in the price of both products, that is, the tax burden (and incidence) is spread to the consumers (and producers) of the non-taxed product as well.

On the **sources side** the fact that the tax on shoes results in fewer shoes being demanded implies that fewer shoes will need to be produced. When fewer shoes are produced, some of the capital and labour used in the production process become redundant. But since shoes are produced using capital-intensive technology, relatively more capital than labour is released into the market. The redundant labour and capital must now find employment in the sector manufacturing reed baskets. Since the reed basket sector is a labour-intensive sector (and technology is assumed to remain unchanged), all the redundant capital cannot be absorbed into the sector. The additional capital can only be absorbed if the capital-labour ratio increases. But with capital in excess supply its relative price will come down, so that both sectors will end up using more capital-intensive production techniques. Thus, in addition to the rise in the relative price of the non-taxed commodity (reed baskets), a tax on shoes also causes the relative price of capital (i.e. the return on capital) to decrease. The burden of the tax is therefore also spread to the owners of the factor of production used most intensively in the production of the taxed commodity.

9.6.2 A general tax on commodities

If a tax is imposed on shoes and reed baskets simultaneously at the same rate, the tax is a general one as opposed to a selective tax. The general tax is equivalent to a tax on income (e.g. a tax on capital and labour at the same rate). The tax will be borne in proportion to the consumption (or income) of each member of the economy. A general tax on commodities leaves relative prices unchanged (including the relative price of leisure[8]). The tax thus cannot be shifted and consumers have to bear the entire burden.

9.7 Tax incidence and tax equity revisited

When we introduced the topic of tax shifting and tax incidence, it was stated that most taxes alter the distribution of income. To make inferences about the equity of a tax it must be ascertained whether the tax alters the distribution in a progressive, proportional or regressive way.

In the preceding sections we examined the question of who contributes what part of the tax burden in the case of consumption taxes in particular. If the economic burden of the tax is on **buyers** and the expenditure on this good or service increases as individuals move up the income scale (i.e. if the demand is relatively income elastic), the tax is progressive. Luxuries tend to fall in this category of goods and services – as income increases individuals tend to spend more on luxuries. In contrast, expenditure on necessities tends to fall as total income rises (i.e. low-income earners spend proportionally more on these goods and services than high-income earners). A tax on necessities that is shifted to buyers is therefore regressive. A value-added tax or a general sales tax levied on a broad base will be regressive. The reason is that consumption as a percentage of income decreases as individuals move up the income ladder – high-income earners tend to save proportionally more, leaving them with a proportionally lower tax bur-

---

8 Assuming that leisure can be taxed.

den than low-income earners (since saving is exempt from the tax).

When the tax is shifted to the **seller** it also has distributional implications. If the seller has to bear the tax, his or her real factor income (wage, rent, interest, profit) is reduced. Whether the tax is progressive or regressive now depends on the factor income shares of the "sellers" and their relative positions on the income ladder. If the tax is shifted to **unskilled workers** who find themselves at the bottom end of the income scale, the tax could be said to be regressive. On the other hand, if the tax is shifted to highly skilled workers earning high incomes, the tax will be progressive.

To determine the final impact of a consumption tax on distribution, the effect on buyers and sellers should be considered simultaneously. According to Musgrave and Musgrave (1989: 254) there is no systematic relation between the distribution in consumption of a good and the distribution of the factor income that the production of a good generates. They conclude that in the absence of evidence to the contrary, the distribution of the tax burden is dominated by what happens to consumption (i.e. the extent of tax shifting to buyers) since the initial impact is on the uses side.

The incidence of alternative taxes will be addressed when they are examined in later chapters. But in addition to the impact of individual taxes on distribution we would also like to know the **overall impact of taxes** on income distribution. This is a daunting task since we need to know the incidence of each tax beforehand. Based on plausible assumptions about the shifting of different taxes, empirical studies have found the tax structure of countries to be progressive for the low-income and high-income groups and regressive for the intermediate income groups.[9] Similar results have been obtained

for South Africa.[10] It seems that not much redistribution is taking place through the fiscal system from the tax side. This conclusion has persuaded many economists to argue that if the objective is to make poor people better off, it is best to pursue the objective through the expenditure side of the national budget rather than through the tax system – see Chapter 10, Section 10.5 as well as Chapters 15 and 17.

Important concepts

ability to pay principle
ad valorem tax
administrative fees
balanced-budget
benefit principle
differential tax incidence
direct tax
ear-marked tax
economic incidence
general equilibrium framework
general tax
horizontal equity
indirect tax
inflation tax
inverse elasticity rule
lump-sum tax
partial equilibrium framework
progressive
proportional
regressive
selective tax
specific tax
statutory incidence
tax-base
tax equity
tax rate
tax rate structure
taxes
unit tax
user charges
vertical equity

9 For references see Boadway & Wildasin (1984: 384-385).
10 See McGrath et al. (1997). In the same study the authors calculated the tax share of the high-income group to be 75,7 per cent of the total tax burden, compared to the tax share of the low-income group of 2,8 per cent.

Self-assessment exercises

9.1 Distinguish between taxes and other sources of government revenue.

9.2 A R1 000 tax payable by all adults could be viewed as both a proportional tax and a regressive tax. Do you agree? Explain.

9.3 Indicate whether the following taxesare general or selective, specific or *ad valorem*, direct or indirect and explain your answer in each case:
   • personal income-tax
   • a 10 per cent tax on video recorders
   • value-added tax
   • R1,02 per litre on fuel
   • a R200 levy on all economics students

9.4 "When taxies are evaluated we need look at fairness only." Do you agree? Discuss.

9.5 Explain what is meant by tax equity.

9.6 By using the partial equilibrium framework, explain who bears the burden of an *ad valorem* tax levied on buyers (i.e. consumers) if there is perfect competition and demand is relatively inelastic.

9.7 "It is a misconception that a monopolist can simply pass on the burden of a tax on its product to consumers." Discuss this statement.

9.8 Explain what is meant by the general equilibrium analysis of tax incidence and compare it to partial equilibrium analysis. Then discuss the incidence of a selective sales tax using the general equilibrium framework.

Chapter ten

Tjaart Steenekamp

Tax efficiency and tax reform

In Chapter 9 we identified a number of properties of a good tax and considered the equity criterion in some detail. Most taxes affect relative prices and consequently also the economic choices of participants in economic activity. This chapter is also concerned with the impact of taxes on efficiency in the allocation of resources. Because tax efficiency is handicapped by the fact that people do not like paying taxes, we also examine the issue of tax compliance. Since tax systems are continuously being adjusted in response to changing economic and political influences, we also touch on the issue of tax reform.

We begin this chapter with an explanation in Section 10.1 of what excess burden of a tax is, using budget lines and indifference curves. The measurement of excess burden is discussed in Section 10.2 by applying the consumer surplus approach. Once the impact of taxes on economic efficiency has been analysed, we focus on the two remaining criteria for analysing taxes: administrative efficiency (Section 10.3) and tax flexibility (Section 10.4). In Section 10.5 international tax reform is discussed and the chapter is concluded with a brief reference to tax reform in South Africa.

Once you have studied this chapter, you should be able to
- explain what is meant by tax efficiency;

- compare the excess burden of different taxes using indifference curves;
- determine the magnitude of excess burden using the consumer surplus concept;
- explain the meaning of administrative efficiency and how it can be achieved;
- define tax flexibility;
- distinguish between patterns of taxation in DCs and LDCs;
- identify the direction of international tax reform;
- contrast international tax reforms with the major tax reforms in South Africa since the late 1960s.

10.1 Excess burden of taxation: Indifference curve analysis

All taxes place a burden on consumers, workers or producers. In addition to this direct burden, most taxes cause a burden, which is greater than what is necessary to generate a certain amount of tax revenue. This additional burden is called the **excess burden**, welfare cost or deadweight loss of a tax. An example will help to illustrate this concept.

We know from Chapter 2 that for a given set of relative prices perfectly competitive markets will allocate resources Pareto efficiently. This means that the marginal rate of substitution (*MRS*) of, say, (*x*) for (*y*) will be equal to the marginal rate of transformation (MRT) of x for y ($MRS_{xy} = MRT_{xy} = \frac{P_x}{P_y}$). Furthermore, given this set of relative prices we know the consumption of x and y yields a certain amount of consumer satisfaction (or a certain level of welfare). Suppose that a tax (t) is now levied on x. The price of x becomes $(1 + t)P_x$. Assume further that the tax is such that the consumption of x becomes zero. If this is the case, no tax revenue will be forthcoming and there will thus be no direct tax burden. But there must be some burden since consumers can now enjoy only y. Because the relative price ratio changed from $\frac{P_x}{P_y}$ to $\frac{(1 + t)P_x}{P_y}$, consumers re-alocated their resources (i.e. their after-tax income) towards y. The expenditure pattern moved away from what was previously regarded as optimal and desired and consumers therefore experience a welfare loss, even though there is no direct tax burden. This is an example of excess burden.

The theory of excess burden of different taxes can be explained using two approaches: the **indifference curve approach** and the consumer surplus approach. The **indifference curve** approach is discussed in this section and is useful for comparing the price distorting effects of different taxes. The **consumer surplus approach** is useful in measuring the excess burden and is discussed in Section 10.2.

We first focus on the impact of tax-induced changes in relative prices on the welfare of a particular consumer. We distinguish between the impact of a selective tax and that of a general tax. For comparison purposes we use a lump-sum tax as our general or benchmark tax. We thus evaluate the excess burden of a selective tax by comparing its impact on welfare with that of a lump-sum tax.

10.1.1 Lump-sum taxes

A lump-sum tax is a fixed amount of tax an individual would pay in, say, a year and is independent of his or her income, wealth or

consumption. These taxes do not distort relative prices and therefore do not affect people's choices. For example, a person will not be able to avoid a lump-sum tax by working shorter hours or by reducing consumption of a particular commodity. Put differently, a lump-sum tax does not cause a substitution effect. It reduces the taxpayer's disposable income and thus has only an income effect. Because relative prices are not distorted, lump-sum taxes have no excess burden. A head tax, levied on each member of society or on all breadwinners, is an example of a lump-sum tax.

Lump-sum taxes have one major **disadvantage**. They are regressive, since the tax as a percentage of income (i.e. the average tax rate) falls as income increases. They therefore leave the after-tax distribution of income more unequal than the before-tax distribution. For most policy makers the price tag of such a trade-off between equity and efficiency is simply too high. The perceived unfairness of the poll tax (a prime example of lump-sum tax) introduced in 1990 by the Thatcher government in Britain is widely regarded as one of the factors that led to her downfall later that year.

A head tax is not an unfamiliar tax to the fiscal authorities in South Africa. An early version of a head tax can be found in the Glen Gray Act (Act 25 of 1894), which imposed a 10-shilling tax on African men living in the district. When Cecil Rhodes introduced the Act into the Cape Parliament he argued that the tax would "remove them (the African) from that life of sloth and laziness and ... teach them the dignity of labour and make them contribute to the prosperity of the State and give some return for our wise and good government" (Nattrass, 1988: 68). A £1 poll tax was introduced in Natal in 1905 and is considered to be one of the immediate causes of the 1906 Bambatha Rebellion. This poll tax was levied in addition to hut and dog taxes and although it was payable only by all males over the age of 18, it was an onerous liability on the African peasantry. An African chief called Bambatha embarked on a war of liberation and on 9 June 1906 more than 500 warriors died in a skirmish with colonial troops. The victors hacked off the head of the chief and marched through the countryside with the trophy (see Bundy, 1988: 190 and Reader's Digest, 1994: 286-287). In later years a head tax was levied on all Black males between the ages of 18 and 65 in terms of the Bantu Taxation Act (Act 92 of 1969). In 1978 the tax was fixed at R2,50 and was payable annually before 1 June of each year. The tax generated insignificant tax revenue (R9 million or approximately 0,1% of total tax revenue in 1978/79). The tax was abolished in 1978/79,

the year in which general sales tax (GST) was introduced.

The effects of a lump-sum tax are illustrated in Figure 10.1. X is measured horizontally and Y vertically. The before-tax budget line is AB. The consumer is initially in equilibrium at point E_0 where indifference curve U_0 is tangent to (i.e. touches) the budget line. A lump-sum tax is introduced which lowers the income of the consumer and causes the budget line to shift from AB to CD. The lump-sum tax yields revenue equal to AC if measured in terms of Y, or DB in terms of X. Note that the after-tax budget line, CD, is **parallel** to AB since **relative prices are unchanged**. The consumer is now in equilibrium at E_1

Figure 10.1 The excess burden of a tax using indifference curves

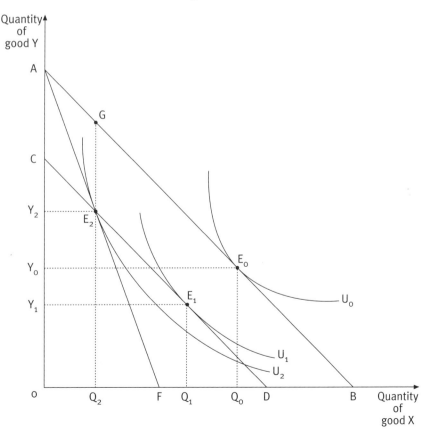

where fewer of X and fewer of Y are consumed than before.

Note that the consumer is worse-off after the tax, since consumption is on a lower indifference curve, U_1. This is due to the normal burden of the tax. The condition for Pareto optimality has not been disturbed $(MRS_{xy} = \frac{P_x}{P_y})$ and resources are allocated efficiently at the new after-tax income level. Thus a lump-sum tax causes a normal burden but it has no excess burden.

10.1.2 Selective taxes

Suppose a selective tax on X is now imposed. To analyse its welfare implications, we compare the impact of the selective tax to that of a lump-sum tax that generates the same tax revenue (i.e. AC) in Figure 10.1. We know that a selective tax on X will increase the price of X and leave the price of Y unchanged. If the consumer spends his or her entire budget on X, fewer of X can be obtained after the tax than before the tax. If the consumer spends his or her entire budget on Y, the same amount of Y can still be purchased (because the price of Y has remained unchanged). The budget line showing combinations of Y and X will, therefore, **swivel** inward (or pivot around point A). To obtain the after-tax budget line, which yields the same tax revenue as the lump-sum tax, we must find an equilibrium point, which is also on budget line CD. A budget line has thus to be drawn through A in such a way that it is tangent to an indifference curve at its point of intersection with CD. In Figure 10.1 budget line AF is such a budget line.

A selective tax on X which yields the same revenue as the lump-sum tax (i.e. $E_2G = AC$) will cause the budget line AB to pivot (or swivel) to AF. Equilibrium is at E_2 on indifference curve U_2. This is an important observation. Compared to the lump-sum tax, consumer welfare is lower (indifference curve U_2 is lower than U_1). The difference in welfare indicates the welfare cost

or excess burden of a selective tax. **Selective taxes distort relative prices and cause an excess burden.** Put in the Pareto optimality context of Chapters 2 and 3, the equilibrium condition for consumers is now where marginal rate of substitution of X for Y (MRS_{xy}) is equal to the **after-tax price ratio** $[\frac{(1+t)Px}{Py}]$. Assuming that producers shift the full burden of the tax to consumers, the equilibrium condition for producers is where marginal rate of transformation of X for Y (MRT_{xy}) is equal to the **before-tax price ratio** $(\frac{P_x}{P_y})$. Thus the **price ratios** for consumers and producers **differ** and because relative prices are distorted by the selective tax, resources are allocated inefficiently in the economy $(MRS_{xy} \neq MRT_{xy})$.

10.1.3 General taxes

In Section 9.2.2 a general tax was defined as one which taxes the entire tax base and allows for no exemptions. If a general tax is imposed at the same rate on Y and X and it is assumed that these are the only products produced in the economy, the budget line in Figure 10.1 shifts from AB to CD. Equilibrium is again at E_1. Tax revenue equals AC. A general tax does not distort relative prices. This means that the after-tax price ratio $[\frac{(1+t)Px}{(1+t)Py}]$ is the same as the before-tax price ratio $(\frac{P_x}{P_y})$. The condition for a Pareto efficient allocation of resources in the economy is therefore not distorted $[MRS_{xy} = MRT_{xy} = \frac{(1+t)Px}{(1+t)Py}]$. General taxes resemble lump-sum taxes and do not have excess burdens. These taxes have the added advantage that, from a practical point of view, general taxes at uniform rates are easy to administer. However, as in the case of lump-sum taxes, general taxes have the disadvantage of ignoring distributional implications.

Economic efficiency is considered as one of the properties of a "good tax". Efficient taxes are taxes that minimise the distorting effect on the choices of decision makers. In other words, taxes are considered efficient when the excess burden is as small as possible. This brings us to the concept of tax neutrality.

The **tax neutrality concept** must be understood in its traditional, narrow context and also in its wider, modern context. The traditional, narrow neutrality concept is mainly concerned with allocation, the idea being that taxes should not prevent consumers from maximising utility or producers from maximising profit – in other words, taxes should be neutral. The tax should have little or no impact on economic decisions about what to buy, how much to invest or save and how many hours should be worked. This view of neutrality rests on the assumption that resources in the economy are allocated optimally and that non-neutral taxes would result in a reallocation and therefore a non-optimal allocation. A broader view of tax efficiency, however, also takes account of market imperfections.[1]

In reality the market economy is imperfect (meaning it is inefficient and inequitable), and optimality is the exception rather than the rule. Hence non-neutral taxes may be beneficial or harmful, depending on whether they steer the economy in the direction of optimality or away from optimality. These two possibilities are called positive non-neutral and negative non-neutral effects respectively.

A selective tax is clearly non-neutral because it disturbs relative prices. Economic choices are affected and, according to the traditional view, selective taxes are therefore inefficient. According to the modern approach, however, a selective tax can move the economy in the direction of optimality, which amounts to positive non-neutral action. In contrast, a general tax such as a head tax, is a neutral tax and does not influence allocation decisions. From the modern perspective a general tax may well perpetuate existing distortions in the economy,

which implies that tax non-neutralities can sometimes improve allocative efficiency. Examples include levying taxes to correct for negative externalities and taxing sumptuary consumption (e.g. excises on cigarettes and liquor).

The term **optimal taxation** is derived from efforts to design tax systems to improve efficiency (minimise excess burden) and to achieve a socially more equitable distribution of income (maximise social welfare). In the following sections we will touch upon some of the "tax optimisation rules" to minimise excess burden (e.g. the inverse elasticity rule – see Section 10.2.2). Related to the theory of optimal taxation is the theory of second best. We have seen in Chapter 2 and subsequent chapters that the market sometimes fails because of certain inefficiencies (or distortions). The theory of second best is concerned with designing government policy (and therefore tax systems) in situations where some inefficiencies cannot be removed. More accurately, the theory of second best says that whenever there are distortions in several markets, removing one may not necessarily improve matters. In fact it may introduce other distortions and overall may result in lower consumers' welfare (see Lipsey & Chrystal, 1995: 414-415).

10.2 Excess burden: Consumer surplus approach

10.2.1 The magnitude of excess burden

So far we have made some progress in comparing different taxes in terms of their excess burdens. Selective taxes cause an excess burden, whereas general taxes do not. Using the indifference curve approach, we have shown that the same tax revenue can be obtained by levying a general/lump sum tax and at the same time leave the consumer better off. In this section we follow the con-

---

1 In addition, the modern approach to neutrality applies a balanced budget framework. According to this approach the concept of fiscal neutrality relates to both the revenue side and the expenditure side of the budget.

sumer surplus approach in order to measure the excess burden of a tax. To enable measurement, we employ a partial equilibrium framework and focus on the burden of a unit tax on a particular commodity or output of an industry. Let the commodity be grams of butter. We simplify by assuming that supply is produced under constant-cost conditions (i.e. the supply curve is horizontal). Furthermore we use standard demand curves. Although it is theoretically more correct to use **compensated demand** curves to calculate excess burden, we use standard demand curves. Ignoring this subtlety does not significantly affect our analysis.

In Figure 10.2 the demand curve for butter is shown as D_0 and the supply curve is S_0. The equilibrium price is P_b and equilibrium quantity is Q_0. We now have to introduce the consumer surplus. Recall that the demand curve indicates what consumers are willing to pay for different quantities. However, once the market price is determined it applies to all consumers. The difference between what consumers are willing to pay for a good and what they actually pay is the **consumer surplus**. This is represented by the area under the demand curve and above the price line. The consumer surplus measures the rand value of consumer welfare at different quantities.[2] In Figure 10.2 the consumer surplus is ACE.

Suppose that a selective tax (t) is levied on the producers of butter that increases the price of butter to $(1+t)P_b$. The supply curve S_0 shifts parallel upwards to S_1. The equilibrium quantity of butter decreases from Q_0 to Q_1, and the consumer surplus is reduced from ACE to ABF. The loss in consumer surplus is the trapezoid FBCE. But this is not the total welfare cost (or loss) to the consumer.

The tax revenue is the tax per unit (tP_b) multiplied by the quantity of butter purchased (Q_1) (i.e. FE x $0Q_1$ = FBDE). Thus the tax on butter yields revenue equal to the area FBDE. If government, which after all spends the tax revenue, were to return this amount of tax to consumers as a lump sum, the consumers are worse off by the triangle BCD (i.e. FBCE – FBDE). The triangle is the welfare loss or **excess burden** of the selective tax on butter. Put differently, the tax causes a reallocation of resources (less butter and more other goods are produced than without the tax). The triangle measures the welfare loss caused by this misallocation of resources.[3] The size of the triangle (i.e. the excess burden) is determined by the **price elasticities** of demand and supply and the **tax rate**. These determinants are discussed below.

The magnitude of the excess burden can be measured using simple algebra. We know that the formula for the area of a triangle is one half the base multiplied by the height. In Figure 10.2 the excess burden can therefore be expressed as

$$Eb = \frac{1}{2} tP \, \Delta Q \qquad [10.1]$$

where E_b is the excess burden (area BCD), tP is the *ad valorem* tax (= BD), and ΔQ is the decrease in quantity demanded (= DC). This formula can be refined by also considering two other determinants of the excess burden, namely price elasticities and the tax rate.

10.2.2 Price elasticities

Price elasticity of demand indicates how sensitive the quantity demanded is to a price change, while price elasticity of supply indi-

---

2 Assuming that the marginal utility of income is constant, the demand curve can be interpreted as measuring marginal utility. The area under the demand curve (i.e. the sum of the marginal utilities) represents the total utility (welfare) of consumers. The difference between the total utility and the actual cost of the benefits (the market price) is the consumer surplus. See Mohr & Fourie (2000: 259-260).

3 In the case of an increasing-cost industry (i.e. where the supply curve is positively sloped), the excess burden is the area below the original demand curve and above the supply curve and restricted by the after-tax equilibrium quantity. The excess burden triangle therefore contains some consumer and producer surplus.

Figure 10.2 The magnitude of the excess burden of a tax on a constant-cost industry

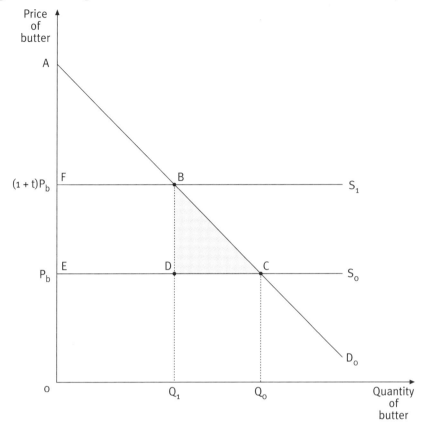

cates the same sensitivity in respect of quantity supplied. If demand is inelastic, buyers will tend not to adjust their quantities demanded by much if the price changes. In other words, they are insensitive to price changes. If demand is elastic, buyers will tend to adjust their quantities demanded significantly if the price changes. In other words, they are sensitive to price changes. What is the impact of price elasticity of demand on excess burden?

Figure 10.3 is almost the same as Figure 10.2. The only difference is that in Figure 10.3 we compare the impact of a selective tax on butter for two cases of demand. In the one case the demand curve (D_1) is relatively inelastic and in the other case the demand curve (D_0) is relatively elastic. The before-tax quantity (Q_0) and price (P_b) are the same for both. The selective tax (t) causes the supply curve to shift upwards from S_0 to S_1. In the case of demand curve D_0, the equilibrium quantity decreases to Q_1. With demand curve D_1 the equilibrium quantity decreases to Q_2, indicating that the quantity demanded is less sensitive to the imposition of the tax than in the case of D_0. Comparing excess burdens we notice that for demand curve D_0 the excess burden is BCD (the same as in Figure 10.2) and for demand curve D_1 the excess burden is GCH. This illustrates that the welfare cost of a given tax is less where the demand for a good is relatively inelastic. In other words, the more elastic the demand,

Figure 10.3 The effect of demand elasticity on excess burden

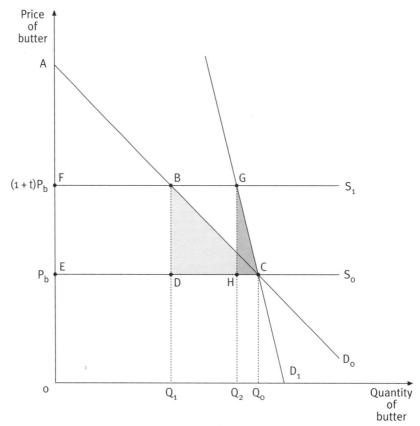

the greater the excess burden (or welfare cost).

The implication is that it is more efficient to levy taxes on price inelastic commodities than on price elastic commodities. Commodity taxes should thus be high on inelastic goods and services and low on goods and services with high demand elasticities. This tax rule, commonly referred to as the **inverse elasticity rule,** is attributed to Frank Ramsey (1927). A further implication of this tax rule is that uniform tax rates are not necessarily efficient, since the higher the elasticity of demand of good X relative to that of good Y, the lower the tax rate on X should be relative to that on Y. However, in arriving at these conclusions distributional implications are ignored. The price elasticity of demand for necessities tends to be low

(since demand is relatively inelastic) compared to luxury goods. The elasticity tax rule implies that a high tax rate on, for example, bread would be efficient (the excess burden is small). But expenditure on bread constitutes a major proportion of the income of poor people. The tax is therefore regressive and inequitable. Tax design often calls for a trade-off between equity and efficiency.

The effect of elasticity on the magnitude of the excess burden can be expressed in mathematical terms. In Equation [10.1] the term ΔQ depends on the elasticity of demand. The price elasticity of demand (ε) is defined as

$$\varepsilon = \frac{\Delta Q}{Q} \div \frac{\Delta P}{P}$$

[10.2]

which can be expressed as

$$\Delta Q = \varepsilon(\Delta P)\frac{Q}{P} \qquad [10.3]$$

The change in price caused by the tax (ΔP) is equal to the selective tax (tP). The right side of equation [10.3] can therefore be rewritten as $\varepsilon(tP)\frac{Q}{P}$. By substituting this expression for ΔQ in Equation [10.1], we obtain

$$Eb = \frac{1}{2}\varepsilon t^2 PQ \qquad [10.4]$$

Equation [10.4] tells us three things. The value of ε indicates the importance of price elasticities of demand. If the value is low (demand is price inelastic), it means that the excess burden will be small, and vice versa. PQ is the amount spent on butter before the tax. In our equation it means that the higher this original amount spent, the greater the excess burden. Finally, we notice that the excess burden is a function of the tax rate. We focus on this finding in the next section.

10.2.3 The tax rate

The magnitude of the excess burden also depends on the tax rate. As the tax rate increases, the excess burden increases by a multiple of the tax rate.

In Figure 10.4, the initial equilibrium is at price P_b and quantity Q_0. The commodity, butter, is produced under constant-cost conditions. If a selective tax of t_2 is levied on butter, the after-tax price is $(1 + t_2)P_b$ and the equilibrium quantity decreases to Q_2. The excess burden is the triangle ACH. The tax

Figure 10.4 The effect of tax rates on excess burden

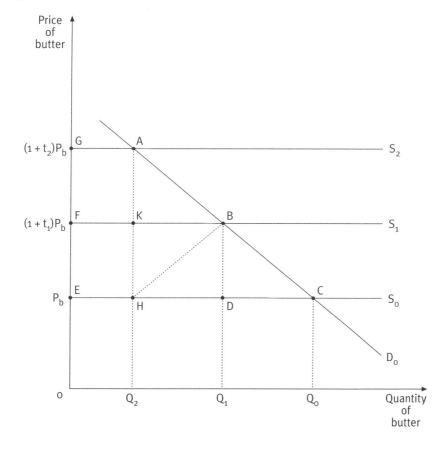

revenue is the area *GAHE*. Suppose that the tax rate is halved to t_1. The new equilibrium price is $(1 + t_1)P_b$ and the equilibrium quantity is Q_1. Tax revenue is now equal to the area *FBDE*. The excess burden is now the triangle *BCD*. We notice that although the tax rate was halved, tax revenue did not halve. More importantly, the excess burden fell by about three-quarters. This can easily be confirmed geometrically by decomposing the triangle *ACH* into four smaller triangles of equal size: *ABK*, *KBH*, *BDH*, and *BCD*.

We conclude that low tax rates on a large number of commodities will produce smaller excess burdens (and more tax revenue) than high tax rates on a few commodities that yield the same total revenue. This analysis therefore suggests that broad-based taxes such as VAT and income taxes are more efficient than narrow-based selective taxes.

Excess burden calculations are subject to theoretical and empirical limitations. When excess burdens are estimated, compensated demand and supply curves should be used. Using standard demand and supply curves overestimates the excess burden. The problems associated with attempts to make the concept operational are illustrated by its absence in public budgets. The excess burden costs of taxes are not recorded as expenditure items in public budgets. These welfare losses are nevertheless real and according to some estimates quite significant. A simple estimate of the approximate welfare losses will suffice. If for example an *ad valorem* tax of 30 per cent is levied on a good of which the price elasticity of demand is equal to one and total expenditure on the good is R200 million, it can be shown (using equation [10.4]) that the excess burden will be R9 million (i.e. 15% of the tax revenue).

10.3 Administrative efficiency

The excess burden is not the only cost of a tax. Taxes have to be administered and this generates costs. In 2001/02 the adjusted expenditure by the South African Revenue Service (SARS) amounted to R2 863,2 million which was approximately 1,1 per cent of total tax revenue collected. In addition to **administration costs** borne by government, and ultimately taxpayers, individual taxpayers incur costs in order to meet their tax obligations, called **compliance costs**. These include the cost of time spent filling in tax returns, as well as the cost of employing tax specialists (accountants and lawyers). When taxes are designed, these costs must also be considered. There is some evidence that the compliance costs are significantly greater than the administrative costs incurred by government. For example, Slemrod and Sorum (1984) estimated compliance cost in the USA at between 5 and 7 per cent of revenue collected from income taxes. In New Zealand, Sandford and Hasseldine (1992) estimated compliance costs at approximately 2,5 per cent of GDP.

Administrative efficiency entails minimising both administration costs and compliance costs. Two phenomena are related to these costs: tax avoidance and tax evasion. **Tax avoidance** is perfectly legal and includes the actions by taxpayers to take advantage of special provisions (tax loopholes) in the tax code so that their tax liability is reduced. Although tax avoidance is legal, it is wasteful in the sense that taxpayers make choices on the basis of tax considerations rather than economic considerations, i.e. it entails high opportunity costs. Avoidance practices often arise from errors or loosely drafted tax legislation. Exploiting these loopholes through careful tax planning is therefore not in the "spirit of the law". An example would be where a business is split up into smaller units to take advantage of the graduated company tax rate for small businesses.

Tax evasion is illegal and consists of actions that contravene tax laws. The most common forms of evasion are under-reporting of income and claiming more deductions than warranted. Tax evasion is quite prevalent in the informal sector (also called the unrecorded sector) and is characterised by cash transactions that are difficult to trace.

Thus, in addition to taxes having to be designed to minimise the excess burden, administration costs and compliance costs, good tax administration requires that tax evasion and avoidance be kept to a minimum. For this purpose, the golden rule in tax design is **simplification**. Simple tax laws are easy to understand and comply with. **Incentives** for "tax delinquency" should also be minimised. For example, high marginal rates should be avoided and the poor should not be taxed. **Penalties** for tax evasion should be high and actively enforced. High penalties and a high probability of being detected increase the marginal cost of cheating. Government's proposal to publish the names and particulars of persons who have been convicted of tax law offences in the Government Gazette, ranks as a measure to improve tax compliance and tax morality.

To improve tax collection, taxes should be **withheld** at source. Most taxpayers are subject to the pay-as-you-earn (PAYE) system, according to which tax is withheld at the source (e.g. by the employer) and paid over directly to the tax authorities. (Note that PAYE is a tax collection system and not a particular kind of tax.) Under the PAYE system government receives its revenue before the employee can lay his or her hands on it. Moreover, there is a regular flow of revenue that, in turn, reduces the lag in the operation of the tax multiplier and makes stabilisation policy more effective. On the other hand, the PAYE system significantly increases the compliance costs borne by the private sector. Clearly a trade-off between administrative and compliance costs is required.

When taxes are evaluated according to the criterion of administrative efficiency, a number of other issues should also be considered. One consideration is the community's level of **literacy**. For example, income

taxes require high levels of skill, while a head tax is fairly easy to understand. A further consideration is the efficiency and **expertise** of the tax administration. The importance of this was recognised in the first Interim Report of the Katz Commission (1994). Considerable attention was devoted in this Report to tax administration and it was made clear that the South African system required major structural changes. At that time the Commission estimated that at least R5 billion in additional revenue could be netted through administrative reform.

A further consideration is the **tax morality** of the community. Taxpayers' willingness to part with their hard-earned money is linked to perceptions about the vertical and horizontal equity of taxes as well as the way in which the tax revenue is spent. If taxpayers feel that the tax system is inequitable and that government is spending their tax money wastefully (or not in their interest), the willingness to pay tax will be undermined. Tax efficiency is also affected by the **political will** to enforce tax laws.

For taxes to be administratively efficient they should be **certain** and **transparent**. The tax to be paid should be certain (predictable) to ensure rational decision-making on the part of both taxpayers and the government. Both the tax collector and the taxpayer should thus be given as little discretion as possible. There should also be no uncertainty about who bears the tax burden. Personal income tax satisfies this requirement, but in respect of company tax there is still too much uncertainty as to who actually bears the burden. Transparency means that the government should not take advantage of people's ignorance. **Transparency** also means that the government has a responsibility to subject tax decisions to the political decision-making process – tax decisions should be embodied in legislation and be actively debated. Taxation through inflation is an example of a tax on income that is legislated for explicitly (see Chapter 11).

10.4 Flexibility

Economic activity is characterised by recurrent recessions and booms, that is, cyclical changes. Moreover, structural changes occur in the economy. Taxes should be flexible enough to provide for changing economic conditions. Taxes can influence economic activity from both the supply and the demand side.

On the **supply side**, economic growth can be influenced by changing the incentive to work and spend (or save). This topic is discussed in more detail in Chapter 11. For example, if the price elasticity of the supply of female labour is greater (i.e. labour supply is more sensitive) than that of males, female labour should be taxed at a lower marginal rate (according to the inverse elasticity rule). This should theoretically induce more females to enter the labour market or increase their work effort. Hence the supply of labour can be influenced.

In macroeconomics the use of **demand-side** measures to smooth out business cycles is a standard topic of discussion. This is known as stabilisation policy and a distinction is made between automatic and discretionary stabilisers. The timing of discretionary fiscal action is decisive. The problem of timing, however, is not too serious in the case of automatic stabilisers. Automatic stabilisers are characterised by built-in flexibility. An example of an automatic stabiliser is a progressive income tax system. When the economy is entering a recession, for example, the average income tax rate will automatically begin to decrease. As individuals' incomes decline they are automatically assessed at lower rates, and in this way they are left with relatively more disposable income than they would have had otherwise. By the same token, tax revenue for the government declines more rapidly than the national income. In Chapters 11 and 17 we note that inflation has largely rendered tax policy's role in automatic stabilisation ineffective.

10.5 Tax reform: International experience

The existing tax systems of countries evolved over time. Changes to tax systems are implemented through *ad hoc* reforms or comprehensive tax reform programmes. The **goals** of such reforms are varied and differ from country to country. The driving force is often a desire for more revenue. In addition, non-revenue goals, such as redistribution or equity, promotion of growth, tax simplification and a more efficient allocation of resources are also pursued.

Tax reform can be triggered by various factors. Political change is one such initiating factor. A change in government often implies different voter preferences. For example, if the new constituency is, on average, composed of relatively more low-income voters, tax reforms that redistribute income to them may be forthcoming. Political change may also be accompanied by ideological shifts (e.g. a shift away from centralised planning to a more devolved or federal-type structure). Developments in tax theory often provide new analytical insights, and attempts are then made to operationalise these through tax reforms. Some reforms are undertaken in response to international trends. For example, there is a global trend towards VAT and lower marginal income tax rates and in the current integrated world economy it is difficult for a small open economy to ignore this trend. Tax reforms have also often been the result of a fiscal crisis (e.g. short-term budget deficits) or a concerted effort to prevent future fiscal crises (e.g. chronic deficits and inflation).

10.5.1 Patterns of taxation in developed and less-developed countries

A cross-country comparison of tax systems indicates that there are vast differences in the composition of taxes between countries. As each country's tax system has been established over time by many – often unique –

forces, one should be careful of generalising about best tax practices and reforms on the basis of international comparisons alone. Nevertheless, interesting patterns do emerge when countries are grouped together, for example, according to level of economic development – as shown in Table 10.1.

Table 10.1 contains a comparison of direct and indirect central government taxes in a group of less-developed countries (LDCs), a group of developed countries (DCs) and South Africa. The percentages are weighted average shares of total tax revenue to GDP. The **total tax burden** is much greater in DCs (30,4% of GDP) than in LDCs (15,3% of GDP). A number of observations can be made in respect of the composition of taxes:

- **Direct taxes** constitute the predominant sources of revenue in DCs (69,2%) whereas **indirect taxes** are the major sources of revenue in LDCs (51,9%).
- In DCs **income tax** on individuals (28,4%)

is much more important than income tax on companies (8,3%). In LDCs these two sources are approximately equally important but company tax generates proportionally more tax revenue in LDCs (16,0%) than in DCs (8,3%).

- Social security contributions make a considerable contribution to total tax revenue in DCs. It is debatable, however, whether these contributions should be viewed as taxes.
- Property taxes are insignificant tax sources in DCs and LDCs.
- LDCs rely for much of their tax revenue on VAT and general sales taxes (27,9%).
- Trade taxes are much less utilised in DCs (0,5%) compared to LDCs (9,2%).

Explaining differences in levels of taxation (the tax burden) and the composition of tax revenue is rather tricky. A few generalisations will suffice. The high tax burden and reliance on income taxes in DCs can proba-

Table 10.1 Tax revenue of consolidated central government by type, compared for selected groups of countries (weighted averages for 1998)

Tax type	Percentage contribution to total tax revenue		
	LDCs[a]	DCs[b]	SA
Direct taxes, of which	47,1	69,2	59,2
1 Taxes on income and profit, of which	32,4	37,1	57,1
1.1 Individuals	16,1	28,4	40,9
1.2 Companies	16,0	8,3	15,8
2 Social security contributions	14,7	32,0	2,1
Indirect taxes, of which	51,9	29,5	40,0
1 Property	1,0	2,2	1,5
2 Taxes on goods and services, of which	41,7	26,8	35,8
2.1 Vat and general sales taxes	27,9	11,8	23,0
2.2 Excises	12,4	9,5	11,5
3 Taxes on trade	9,2	0,5	2,8
Total tax revenue as % of GDP	15,3	30,4	25,8

Notes: [a] The selected less-developed countries (LDCs) are Argentina, Colombia, Côte d'Ivoire, Hungary, Indonesia, Thailand, Turkey, Zambia and South Africa

          [b] The selected developed countries (DCs) are Australia, Germany, Italy, New Zealand and the United Kingdom

Source: Compiled from International Monetary Fund (2000 and 2001)

bly be attributed to their level of development. Not only does the level of development determine the size of the tax base, but it also has an effect on a country's capacity to administer taxes. In addition, taxpayers are more sophisticated in DCs, enabling tax authorities to levy relatively complex taxes and thereby broadening the tax base even further. The greater reliance on company tax and trade taxes in LDCs can be explained by the administrative ease with which a few companies or points of import and export can be targeted.

When South Africa's tax composition is compared to those of the DCs and LDCs, mixed results are obtained. In some respects the South African pattern mimics the pattern in LDCs – taxes on goods and services, property taxes and income tax on companies show roughly similar ratios. However, in two respects South Africa's pattern is very similar to that of DCs – trade taxes are unimportant sources of revenue and income tax on individuals is an important tax. The contribution to total tax revenue of personal income tax for South Africa (40,9%) exceeds the average ratio for DCs (28,4%) by a large margin. However, if social security contributions are added to personal income tax, "personal income tax" for DCs increases to 60,4 per cent and that of South Africa to only 43,0 per cent. It should also be recognised that in South Africa the social security needs of whites in particular are financed largely by individual contributions to private sector schemes (see Chapter 15).

10.5.2 International tax reform

A number of countries have reformed their tax systems in recent years. Given South Africa's developing country status, we are particularly (although not exclusively) interested in reforms undertaken in less-developed countries (LDCs). A detailed discus-

sion of tax reform in LDCs falls beyond the scope of this chapter, however. We therefore focus on a selection of prominent tax issues in tax reform debates. The lessons for reform of specific taxes will receive attention in the chapters on specific taxes. In the discussion below the emphasis is on **directions of tax reform**.[4]

There has been a reappraisal of the redistributive role of taxes. The importance of using the tax system for redistribution purposes is on the wane. Both vertical and horizontal equity have proved to be elusive goals. Nonetheless, the contention is that the tax burden on the poor should at least be reduced or removed altogether. In this way a levelling-up process can take place. Bird and De Wulf (quoted in Brown & Jackson, 1990: 175) summed the position up as follows: "Taxes cannot, of course, make poor people rich... If the principal aim of redistributive policy is to level up – make poor people better off – the main role the tax system has to play is thus the limited and essentially negative one of not making them poorer." Consequently, more emphasis is placed on public expenditure policies as instruments of redistribution.

Concerted efforts have been made to **broaden the base** of the tax system. Tax systems in LDCs are known to be allocatively non-neutral, that is, they cause distortions in the goods and factor markets. To reduce the excess burden of taxation in these countries, various reforms have been introduced. The general direction has been towards a broadening of the tax base accompanied by simultaneous reductions in tax rates. The concern with base broadening stems from the following: the narrower the base, the higher the rate required to generate a given income; the higher the rate, the greater the incentive for avoiding/evading the tax; resources used for evading taxes are socially unproductive;

---

4 For a more comprehensive discussion of international tax reform see Boskin (1996), World Bank (1991) and Khalilzadeh-Shirazi & Shah (1991).

and high tax rates cause changes in relative prices which may lead to a reallocation of resources away from taxed activity. The objective, therefore, should be lower rates on a broader base. The base broadening policy debate focuses on the merits of a broad-based value-added tax, a flat tax on consumption and the reduction or removal of tax expenditures (e.g. tax incentives to promote economic activity).

Major efforts are being made to **improve tax administration**. Tax simplification is one of the mainstays of better administration. Tax simplification requires a rationalisation of the number of taxes. Taxes that provide little revenue and have high administrative costs should be done away with. Tax rates should also be streamlined (e.g. fewer personal income tax brackets). There is growing recognition that less complex taxes are easier to administer and will improve tax compliance. In addition, steps are taken to improve information systems and to limit political interference in tax administration.

Lower tax rates and a movement to more uniform tax rates (e.g. less differentiation in VAT rates) have been a worldwide phenomenon in the last decade. Lower tax rates are aimed at reducing the disincentive effects of taxation. Examples include lower import tax rates, lower marginal rates of personal income tax and lower effective company tax rates. Lower tax rates and the transnational convergence of tax bases and rates are also the result of the increased tax competition that accompanies economic globalisation and the regional integration of countries in geographic proximity.

10.5.3 Globalisation and tax reform

Economic globalisation may be defined as the integration of economies throughout the world through trade, financial flows, the exchange of technology and information and the movement of people (Ouattara, 1997: 107). It is a process whereby economic interdependence among nations has increased since World War II and which gained particular momentum since the fall of the command economies in Eastern Europe towards the end of the 1980's.[5] This increasing interdependence has led to increasing competition and is reflected in cross-border economic integration between politically sovereign countries. In a globalised economy the policy measures of one country spill over into other countries. When the tax systems of the world came into being it was at a time when economies were by and large closed economies. Much of economic activity was highly regulated and controlled and the tax policies of other countries could be disregarded.

Globalisation has altered the behaviour of economic actors in ways that required tax redesign. Firstly, **cross-border shopping** has increased as borders between countries were removed. This enables some countries to lower their excise taxes on high-value and easily transportable commodities to attract foreign consumers. In this manner the tax base is extended to other countries and tax revenue is generated. Secondly, transfer pricing has resulted from the expansion of the multinational firm. Through transfer pricing, profits can be repatriated from high tax jurisdictions to low tax jurisdictions by over-invoicing imports and under-invoicing exports. Multinational enterprises are in the advantageous position of being able to minimise their global tax liability by shifting profits (through transfer pricing) from high tax jurisdictions to low tax jurisdictions. To entice multinational and other firms to locate in their countries, tax authorities compete by offering lower tax rates and other tax incentives. Thirdly, tax evasion and tax avoidance by individuals become possible

---

5 The remarks made in this section are attributed to Tanzi (1996). For a more comprehensive discussion of the effects of globalisation on tax policy see Tanzi (1995).

on a global scale as personal savings become more mobile. The proliferation of tax-haven areas or even countries and new financial market instruments have made it extremely difficult for tax authorities to monitor the non-reporting of personal income from savings invested.

How would globalisation impact on the future of tax systems? In his analysis of the globalisation phenomenon Tanzi (1996) identified a number of possible trends. As far as taxes on consumption are concerned, it is expected that as borders are removed, countries, which have high initial tax rates, would be under pressure to reduce their rates in the face of competition. Such reductions would in particular affect excises on luxury products. In as much as taxation is a locational factor, tax competition will tend to drive down effective company tax rates. In an environment where multinational enterprises dominate it is even conceivable that income tax on profits may be replaced by another tax base such as a tax on net assets or gross assets. Because of the mobility of incomes from capital sources (e.g. interest and dividends), these sources could become taxed separately from wage income. This would enable tax authorities to either exempt these forms of income entirely or tax it using a separate schedule. Lastly, taxes on property will probably increase because the tax base is reasonably immobile.

10.6 Tax reform in South Africa

Since the late 1960s South Africa has witnessed three government-appointed commissions of inquiry reporting on aspects of the tax structure: the Franzsen Commission (1968), Margo Commission (1987) and the Katz Commission (1994 to 1999). The work of these commissions resulted in comprehensive reforms of the South African tax system. In addition to these comprehensive tax reforms, several major *ad hoc* tax reforms have also been introduced. Instrumental in

these initiatives were the Standing Commission of Inquiry with regard to Taxation Policy of the Republic (Standing Tax Commission) and its successor, the Tax Advisory Committee (TAC), which is a permanent advisory body to the Minister of Finance. A detailed discussion of their terms of references, findings, recommendations and government's response is not possible here. Only the main tax recommendations and reforms are indicated.

The Franzsen Commission (1968), which reported in 1968, concluded that the tax structure at that time was increasingly inhibiting economic growth. The focus of taxation was shifting from indirect to direct taxes and from direct taxes on companies to direct taxes on individuals. The Commission therefore believed that structural changes were required in the form of: (a) reduced progression in direct taxes; (b) a shift towards indirect taxes by broadening the base; and (c) a broadening of the fiscal concept of income by including capital gains. In its first report the Commission consequently recommended that the maximum marginal income tax rate on individuals be reduced from 66 per cent to 60 per cent; that selective sales duties on a number of items (to be collected from manufacturers and importers) be introduced; and that capital gains tax of 20 per cent on net realised gains be introduced. With the exception of the recommendation in respect of capital gains tax, all the other proposals were accepted by government and duly implemented.

The next major tax reform occurred in 1978 when the sales duties were replaced by a **general sales tax** (GST) at a rate of 4 per cent. The sales duties had inherent disadvantages (e.g. narrow base and high rates) and the major aim was to broaden the tax base and eliminate tax non-neutralities by introducing GST. GST was followed by the introduction of **regional services councils levies** in 1985. These levies, one on remuneration paid to employees (0,25%) and the other on turnover of enterprises (0,1%), commenced in 1987.

The report of the **Margo Commission** (1987) was released in 1987. The Commission reported at a time when inflation was rampant, the business cycle was in an upswing and foreign disinvestment was a threatening factor. The Commission took the view that tax reform should not be driven by short-term economic problems but rather by aspects of the existing tax structure that could hinder economic development. The Commission's general approach (1987: par 1.28) was founded in a base-broadening philosophy: "The ideal, both for direct and indirect imposts, is a broad-base, widely distributed, low-rate, high-yield tax, conforming to these other requirements (equity, neutrality, simplicity, certainty etc.) as far as possible." Such a tax system would reduce the "brain drain", encourage immigration, improve standards of tax morality and compliance, promote entrepreneurship and capital formation and job creation. The following are some of the major recommendations of the Commission which were accepted by government:

- The taxation of fringe benefits.
- Lower personal income tax rates with fewer brackets.
- Accepting the individual as the unit of taxation and phasing-in marriage neutrality and the equal treatment of men and women.
- The rejection of capital gains tax.
- The scrapping of certain tax expenditures and allowances.
- The modification of GST and the reduction of the rate, but if the recommendation was not accepted, GST should be replaced by an invoice VAT system.
- The imposition of a capital transfer tax to replace estate duty and donations tax.

Between 1987 and 1994 two of the most important tax reforms have been the introduction of value-added tax (VAT) and the lowering of the company tax rate (along with the introduction of the **secondary tax on companies** (STC)). Value-added tax (VAT) was introduced in 1991 to eliminate the distorting effects of tax cascading inherent in GST and to reduce tax evasion. Initially the VAT rate was to be 12 per cent with very few exemptions and zero-rates. After much political lobbying by the trade union movement in particular, VAT was eventually introduced at 10 per cent with allowance for a number of zero-rated items. Secondary tax on companies (STC) was introduced in 1993 and is a tax on distributed profits, levied on firms. The aim was to encourage firms to reinvest their profits and thereby promote economic development. In a sense STC was also an astute way of reintroducing tax on dividends, since in 1990 government had exempted the taxation of dividends.[6]

In 1994 the first interim report of the Katz Commission (1994) was released. It was supplemented by another eight reports between 1994 and 1999. The Commission conducted its investigations at a time when South Africa had just entered a new political and constitutional era. The major thrust of the first and third interim reports was to improve tax administration and collection and to reappraise equity aspects of certain taxes. Some of the more important tax reforms introduced between 1994 and 2002 were:

- The status and independence of the revenue authorities was enhanced by the establishment of SARS as a separate department.
- A general tax amnesty was introduced with a view to attract people into the tax system such as the previously disenfran-

---

6 Some argue that since dividends are paid out of after-tax income, it was previously double-taxed.

chised who challenged the equity of the tax system.

- A single rate structure with six brackets for personal income tax was introduced.
- All gambling and fee-based financial services were subjected to VAT.
- Interest, rental and other trading income of the retirement fund industry became taxable.
- Capital gains became taxable.
- The source of income base was replaced by a residence-based income tax.

In the following chapters specific taxes will be studied. Tax reforms that are particular to these taxes will then receive further attention.

Important concepts
base broadening
compliance costs
excess burden
inverse elasticity rule
lump-sum tax
selective tax
specific tax
tax avoidance tax evasion
tax morality
tax neutrality

Self-assessment exercises

10.1 Explain why a lump-sum tax is used for comparing the excess burden of different taxes.

10.2 "A tax on cigarettes is inefficient since it is non-neutral." Do you agree? Explain your answer by using indifference curves.

10.3 Assuming that government needs to raise a certain amount of tax revenue from two goods with different price elasticities of demand. What would your advice be to government if the excess burden had to be minimised? How would your answer differ if other tax criteria are had to be considered as well?

10.4 Briefly discuss administrative efficiency as a property of a good tax.

10.5 Use examples to explain what tax flexibility means.

10.6 Evaluate tax reform in South Africa since the late 1960s in the light of the patterns and directions of international tax reform.

Chapter eleven

Tjaart Steenekamp

Income taxation

In Chapters 9 and 10 the properties of a "good tax" were identified and explained. We are now ready to apply these criteria to the analysis of specific taxes. In this chapter we focus on income taxation, which includes personal income tax and company income tax. In the first section to the chapter the income tax base is defined. We include in this section the international taxation of income. In the next three sections personal income tax is considered. We begin this discussion by defining concepts such as exclusions, exemptions, deductions and rebates (Section 11.2). In Section 11.3 the important feature of progressiveness in personal income taxation is considered together with the topical issue of the flat rate tax. This is followed (in Section 11.4) by an analysis of the economic effects of personal income tax using the tax criteria we identified in Chapters 9 and 10. Section 11.5 attempts to find answers to the question of why companies should be taxed. The structure and calculation of company tax receive attention in Section 11.6 and in Section 11.7 the economic effects of company tax are analysed. We conclude this chapter with a Section (11.8) on capital gains taxation.

The aim of this chapter is to describe and analyse personal income tax and company tax in terms of the tax criteria developed in Chapters 9 and 10.

Once you have studied this chapter, you should be able to
- define the comprehensive income tax base;
- discuss the international principles of taxing income;
- discuss why the personal income tax base differs from the comprehensive income tax base;
- explain what a progressive personal income tax is and how progressiveness is achieved;
- discuss the economic effects of personal income tax;
- explain why companies are taxed separately;
- define the company tax base;
- describe the classical and fully integrated company tax systems;
- describe company tax in South Africa;
- explain the efficiency of company tax;
- discuss the importance of company tax in the investment decision;
- discuss the merits of tax incentives for investment;
- explain the equity implications of company tax;
- discuss the arguments for and against capital gains taxation.

11.1 The comprehensive income tax base

When we introduced the tax base in Chapter 9, we distinguished between three bases: income, wealth and consumption. In this chapter the focus is on income. We first need to know what income is.

We are all familiar with a budget (e.g. our own personal budget), which has an expenditure (or uses) side and a revenue (or sources) side. **Income** can be defined from both the sources side and the **uses side** of the budget. From the uses side, income is the monetary value of consumption plus any change in the net worth over a year. Net worth (or the net value of assets) is obtained by subtracting liabilities from assets (see Chapter 12). Put differently, income is the net increase in the power to consume in a particular period (e.g. a year). It can be expressed as

$$Y = C + S$$

where Y is income, C is consumption and S is saving (or the change in net worth).

From the **sources side** of the budget anything that makes consumption possible (i.e. anything that is available to finance consumption) is considered as income. Income thus includes salaries, wages, interest, capital gains, rent, profits, royalties, dividends, gifts, employer contributions to pension funds, unemployment benefits and income in kind. This **comprehensive** definition of income is referred to as the Haig-Simons definition, named after two early twentieth-century economists who advocated its use. Haig and Simons believed that such a definition of income most accurately reflect ability to pay (one of the criteria of fairness), or purchasing power.

For administrative and other reasons governments tax some of the sources of income separately. In South Africa and most other countries income received by individuals is subject to **personal income tax**. The income of incorporated businesses (i.e. profits) is subject to **company** tax and in some countries net capital gains from increases in the value of assets are subject to capital gains tax. These three income tax bases are discussed separately in this chapter. Gifts, which can also be treated as additions to wealth, are discussed in Chapter 12.

Another dimension of the comprehensive definition of income is that income is recorded as it **accrues** and not only when it is **realised**. For example, if an asset increases in value during the course of the year, the capital gain is an addition to net worth. The asset need not be sold (i.e. realised) for the increased value to be regarded as income. The reason is that an increase in the value of an asset represents an increase in the owner's purchasing power (i.e. ability to pay). In practice the accrual principle causes considerable administrative complications (e.g. valuation problems) and it may also result in cash flow problems for those who have to pay tax on accrued amounts not actually received in cash.

11.1.1 International taxation of income: the residence principle versus source principle

Income is generated within countries but also across national borders. In recent years, the economies of countries have become increasingly internationalised which impacts on a tax jurisdiction's ability to tax individuals and companies. In an integrated and open economy, the returns of factors of production (eg salaries, dividends, profits, royalties, interest) flow much more freely within a country and across national borders. When rates of return differ between countries because of taxation, these tax-induced differentials can be exploited by capital and highly skilled individuals causing distortions within countries and across countries. Over the years, tax authorities have dealt with the international taxation of income using two general principles: the residence of taxpayer principle and the source of income principle.

The **residence principle** (or world-wide basis) is based on the view that it is the country of residence of the person or business that receives the income which determines the tax liability and collects the tax. Thus a person residing in South Africa would be liable for taxes on his or her total (world-wide) income in South Africa if a residence system was applied. For example, if the person earns R300 000 from a source in South Africa and R120 000 from a source in Zimbabwe, the combined income of R420 000 is taxable in South Africa. For a legal person (eg a company), residence is determined where the business is registered or has a permanent presence. Only income that can be allocated to the activities (at home and abroad) of the business would be taxable.

According to the **source of income principle**, income is taxed by the country where the income is generated. Using the example above, only the R300 000 which originated in South Africa would be taxable in South Africa if the source principle was applied.

In practice most countries apply a mix of both systems. This hybrid form of taxing cross-border flows of income could result in double taxation of such income. If South Africa applies the residence principle and Zimbabwe the source principle, then, in our example above, a person residing in South Africa would be taxed on his or her world-wide income of R420 000 in South Africa. In addition, the Zimbabwean tax authorities would tax the person on the R120 000 generated in Zimbabwe. To eliminate or reduce the extent of double taxation, countries using the world-wide basis unilaterally grant tax relief in the form of an income deduction for the income earned in the source country or a tax credit for the tax paid in the source country. Alternatively, countries enter into bilateral tax treaties or attempt to harmonise the tax treatment of cross-border income.

On a multilateral basis, however, it is dif-

ficult to harmonise tax systems because countries perceive the net benefits of each system differently. The debate on the merits of each system is extensive and not clear-cut at all (see Faria 1995: 216-221; Tanzi 1995: chapter 6; and Katz Commission 1997b). The issues which developing countries have to consider include:

- The source basis resembles the benefit principle of taxation. The entity generating the income benefits from public expenditures, for example, uses public roads and schools, should therefore be taxable. This is not a very convincing argument since a resident who earns foreign sourced income also benefits to some extent from public roads and schools. The residence basis, on the other hand, approximates the ability-to-pay principle and enables countries to tax the world-wide income of residents on a progressive scale. Countries with low levels of foreign income (eg dividends, interest and royalties) would have to consider using the source basis on grounds of administrative expediency. On the other hand, where income from investments abroad is considerable, the residence basis has to be considered on revenue grounds.
- From a tax neutrality point of view, a tax system (eg tax rates) should not influence locational decisions of businesses. From the perspective of a capital importing country, a source-based system would have the advantage of being neutral with regard to capital imports, since it does not discriminate between domestic investment and foreign investment, regardless of where the capital originates. Developing countries tend to be capital importers. On the other hand, from a capital-exporting perspective, a residence-based system would be neutral with regard to capital exports. The only concern to an investor would be the tax rate in his or her country of residence.

In South Africa the taxation of income was based on the source principle of international taxation. Due to the increasing globalisation of the economy and the relaxation of exchange controls, a residence-based income tax system was introduced from 1 January 2001. It was argued that the South African income tax base would be broadened, opportunities for tax arbitrage would be limited and the tax system would be brought in line with accepted norms for taxing international transactions (Department of Finance 2000: 84).

This move was contrary to the recommendations of the Katz Commission (1997b). In its Fifth Interim Report, the Katz Commission (1997b) distinguishes between active income (income derived from operational activities, such as manufacturing and rendering services) and passive income (income derived from investment, such as interest and royalties). The Commission recommended that active income should be taxed on the source basis and passive income on the word-wide basis. It argued that taxing active income on a world-wide basis and at the relatively high domestic effective tax rates, would encourage South African multi-national companies to relocate to low tax jurisdictions. Changing the tax system to a world-wide basis would also be administratively complex. The Commission argued that taxing passive income on a world-wide basis would be necessary to protect the tax base. Passive capital is very mobile when exchange controls are limited.

It is still too soon to evaluate the relative merits of the change to a world-wide basis in South Africa. The application of the residence principle may enhance equity by taxing the off-shore income of South African residents. After all, these amounts increase taxpayers' ability-to-pay and allow for progressive rates of taxation. On revenue grounds it is also sound to protect the system from undue losses as exchange controls are relaxed. However, converting to the world-wide basis involves many administrative problems, including problems of def-

inition (eg when is an establishment resident) and requires the (re-)negotiation of various double tax agreements. The possible impact on net foreign investment is unpredictable at this early stage.

11.2 The personal income tax base

Gross income is the starting point in calculating personal income tax. In South Africa **gross income** consists of all receipts and accruals (e.g. wages and salaries, rents, royalties, dividends, capital gains and interest) of South African residents irrespective of where in the world it was earned. From gross income is deducted exempt income (e.g. dividends) and the resulting amount constitutes **net income**. After deducting from net income all the amounts allowed as deductions (e.g. medical expenses) **taxable income** is obtained. Normal tax is calculated at the applicable rate on taxable income.

The comprehensive definition of income is much broader than the definition of taxable income in South African tax law. The reason is that government provides tax expenditures, sometimes referred to as tax loopholes. Tax expenditures include exclusions, exemptions, deductions and tax rebates (or credits) which all affect the size of the tax base. The calculation of personal income tax liable is shown in Box 11.1.

11.2.1 Exclusions

Income tax is generally levied on cash income. Some forms of non-cash income, such as in-kind receipts, are **excluded** from the tax base. For example, if a person were employed as a cook or child minder, the salary of such a person would be taxable. But if a housewife or mother performs the same functions, the value (or opportunity cost) of her services is not taxed. Another source of income that is excluded in South Africa is imputed rent (i.e. the opportunity cost of owner-occupied housing). If a homeowner lets his or her house, the rent received

---

Box 11.1
Calculating personal income tax liability

TOTAL (COMPREHENSIVE) INCOME

minus Exclusions (e.g. imputed rent and unrealised capital gains)

GROSS (CASH) INCOME

minus Exemptions (e.g. dividends and tax-free portion of interest)

NET INCOME

minus Deductions (e.g. contributions to medical scheme)

TAXABLE INCOME

minus Tax according to tables

GROSS TAX LIABILITY

minus Rebates (e.g. primary rebate and rebate for age 65 and over)

NET TAX LIABILITY

---

is taxable. If, on the other hand, the owner lives in the house, the rent forgone is an opportunity cost (and therefore income) that ought to be taxable in terms of the comprehensive definition of income.

In the past, companies could also offer generous fringe benefits (e.g. motorcars, subsidised meals, low-interest loans and housing subsidies) to employees that were not taxed. Nowadays most fringe benefits are taxable, but the real value of such benefits is not always taxed in full. For example, in the case of contributions to medical aid funds, only the amount by which the employer's contribution exceeds two-thirds of the total contribution, is taxed as a fringe benefit. The taxation of fringe benefits is sometimes also difficult to administer. For example, it is often difficult to distinguish between personal use and business use (e.g. the use of a company cellular phone or company stationery for private use). Finally, non-cash transactions such as barter arrangements are also difficult to detect and therefore frequently go untaxed (e.g. a dentist filling a plumber's tooth in exchange for the plumber clearing a drain at the dentist's residence).

11.2.2 Exemptions

A second category of tax expenditures is exempt income (or exemptions). As a method of providing tax relief to the poor and the aged, an amount of income is tax exempt. In 2002/03 the exempt amount for persons below the age of 65 was R27 000 and for those over the age of 65 the exempt amount was R42 640. In practice the exempt amount is determined by tax rebates allowed on the amount of tax, which is due (see the discussion on rebates below). All dividends received as well as the first R6 000 of interest income received by a natural person from a South African source are also currently exempt from income tax in South Africa.

11.2.3 Deductions

In addition to the exempt categories of income, certain expenditures may be deducted from income for tax purposes. There are a variety of deductions (or allowances) which serve different purposes. Some deductions, such as those in respect of pension fund contributions and contributions to retirement annuity funds, are intended to serve as incentives for taxpayers to provide for their old age. This is particularly important in a country like South Africa, which does not have a comprehensive social security network. Deductions are also allowed (within limits) for contributions to medical aid funds and medical expenditures. These are expenses over which the individual sometimes has no discretion and which can significantly affect his or her ability to pay (e.g. in the case of major heart surgery). Another category of deductions is in respect of expenditures incurred with the purpose of producing income (e.g. entertainment, travelling and motoring expenses or allowances).

11.2.4 Rebates

A further tax expenditure, which affects revenue from income tax, is tax rebates. Tax rebates involve the subtraction of a specified amount from the amount of tax to be paid (i.e. taxable income). These rebates are primarily aimed at providing tax relief to the poor and to provide for differences in taxpayers' personal circumstances. In 2002/03, our personal income tax system provided for a primary rebate of R4 860, while persons aged 65 and over are allowed an additional R3 000 to be deducted from their tax liability. What does this mean? The primary rebate determines the *de facto* tax-exempt income (see exemptions above). When the primary rebate of R4 860 is deducted from the gross tax liability of a person earning a taxable income of R27 000, the net liability is zero. The income level at which the effective tax rate is zero is referred to as the minimum tax threshold. Any taxable income above this amount would incur a tax liability. It should be obvious that rebates benefit the poor more than the rich. For example, a rebate of R4 860 is worth more to a person with taxable income of R30 000 than to a person with taxable income of R100 000. Without the rebate, a person earning R30 000 would have had to pay R5 400. With the rebate, the tax liability falls to R540. The benefit is thus 90,0 per cent of the unadjusted tax liability. For the person earning a taxable income of R100 000, the benefit (calculated in the same way) is only 21,0 per cent.

11.3 The personal income tax rate structure

11.3.1 Progressiveness in personal income taxation

In the case of personal income tax most observers agree that the ability-to-pay principle should apply. Ability to pay generally takes taxpayers' income as yardstick, but it is not so simple to determine taxable income and to combine it with the tax rate in such a way that fairness is achieved. For example, one of the most prominent features of personal income tax is that the structure can be adapted to the **personal circumstances** of the taxpayer, but such adaptations complicate the rate structure.

Ability to pay (and thus the rate structure) is affected by the filing status (or **unit of taxation**) of the taxpayer, that is, whether he or she is single, married, or has children. If two people live together, their living costs (per person) should be lower than when they live apart (e.g. because they share certain things). Their combined ability to pay should therefore be greater than it would have been if they had lived apart and they could, therefore, be taxed at a higher rate (on their combined income). But the issue is not quite so simple. For example, a married couple, both working, can be at a disadvantage compared to a couple where there is only one breadwinner: where both spouses work, families have to purchase a number of services which would normally be rendered at no additional cost by a non-working spouse (e.g. cleaning services and child-caring). If imputed income is not taxed, the two-breadwinner couple should be taxed at a lower rate.

There is a further complication when **children** are included in the relationship. Having children involves costs and affects the disposable income of the parents. Some would argue that these costs are non-discretionary (e.g. where contraception is ruled out due to religious beliefs) and that tax deductions or rebates for children should be allowed. Others argue that children are a matter of choice and that there is no reason why special provision should be made for expenses involving children and not for other expenses, which are incurred by choice such as private overseas trips. The particular view taken on these issues also depends on the values of society in respect of the family. Should mothers be encouraged to return to work, or should the income tax system discriminate against **women** to promote a stable family life? Whether or not the personal income tax structure should be used for social engineering purposes is a much-debated issue. It should be obvious that all kinds of cultural, religious and moral factors can enter the picture. This brief discussion shows that an individual's tax rate and tax liability do not necessarily depend solely on his or her income.

Until quite recently, the tax unit in South Africa was the **married couple**. Married and single people were taxed using different schedules. The choice of unit was scrutinised carefully by the Margo Commission. It was argued that joint taxation of spouses amounted to a marriage penalty for income earning wives. Such taxation discouraged people from marrying, discouraged married women from entering the labour market and affected the status of married women as persons. The Margo Commission (1987: 151) recommended that the individual replace the couple as the unit. The Katz Commission also considered the issues of discrimination on the basis of marital status, gender, age, ethnic or social origin, religion, and so on. Their perspective was mainly a constitutional one. The Katz Commission (1994: 73) recommended that all provisions in the Income Tax Act based on gender and marital discrimination violated the Constitution and should therefore be eliminated. The Katz Commission (1994: 73) also recommended that child rebates no longer be granted, but

that discrimination on the basis of age remain for the time being. These recommendations were introduced in 1995 and in the current personal income tax system in South Africa the **individual** is indeed the unit of taxation.

Whether the unit of taxation is the family, a married couple or the individual, the principle that people should pay according to their ability to pay, still holds. In Chapter 9 it was said that a tax system based on ability to pay requires consensus on how ability is to be measured as well as on the rate structure. In the case of vertical equity the question is what the respective tax liabilities of rich and poor taxpayers should be? For this purpose each taxpayer's sacrifice of utility due to taxation has to be evaluated. Most countries apply the equal marginal sacrifice principle. According to this principle the income tax rate should increase **progressively** as taxable income increases (i.e. the richer the person, the higher his or her tax rate should be). The aim is to achieve a more equitable distribution of after-tax income.

What is meant by progressivity and how can it be achieved? In Chapter 9 it was explained that the progressivity of the rate structure could be determined by looking at the average tax rate. When the **average tax rate** (i.e. the total amount of taxes payable divided by the value of the taxable base) increases as taxable income increases, the tax is **progressive**. Progressivity can be obtained by a combination of income exemptions (or tax rebates) and taxing blocks or **brackets** of income at different rates. A higher tax rate is specified for each higher income bracket, but the higher rate is applicable to only that part of the taxable amount that falls into the relevant bracket. These graduated rates are called marginal tax rates since they represent the change in taxes (i.e. the marginal or extra tax amount) paid with respect to a change in income (i.e. the marginal or extra income).

Table 11.1 shows the tax rates for individuals for 2002/03. The first column shows the

Table 11.1 Personal income tax rates in South Africa, 2002/03

Taxable income bracket (R)	Basic amount (R)	Marginal rate (R)	Lowest average rate in each bracket (%)
0 – 40 000		18	–
40 001 – 80 000	7 200	25	6
80 001 – 110 000	17 200	30	15
110 001 – 170 000	26 200	35	19
170 001 – 240 000	47 200	38	25
240 001 and above	73 800	40	29

Source: National Treasury (2002a)

brackets. The second column shows the basic amount of tax paid for each bracket. The basic amount in the schedule is simply the sum of the marginal tax amounts of the preceding brackets and is specified to simplify tax calculations. Thus a person with taxable income of R46 000 pays R7 200 on the "marginal" income in the first bracket (R40 000 × 18%) plus R1 500 on the "marginal" income in the second bracket [(R46 000 – R40 000) = R6 000 × 25%] which is equal to R8 700. Note that this amount is not the effective tax liability. The primary rebate of R4 860 has to be subtracted from this amount, which leaves a tax liability of R3 840. This converts to an average tax rate (or **effective** tax rate) of 8,4 per cent ($\frac{R3\,840}{R16\,000} \times 100$) on taxable income. If we repeat this exercise for an income of R240 001, an average tax rate of approximately 29 per cent of taxable income is obtained. Since the average tax rate increases as income increases, the tax structure is progressive. The importance of the distinction between marginal and average rates will again be emphasised when the economic impact of personal income taxes is discussed in the next section.

11.3.2 The flat rate tax

In recent years there has been renewed interest (in the USA in particular) in taxation of the income tax base at a single flat rate. Such a flat rate tax is a **proportional tax** on income. Remember that a tax is proportional when the average tax rate (the total amount of tax payable divided by the amount of taxable income) remains constant when taxable income changes. The major advantage of such a tax lies in its lower rate. To get some perspective on what is at stake it should be considered that in 2001 current (personal) taxes of R105 560 million were raised in South Africa with average tax rates ranging from zero per cent to in excess of 29 per cent (taxpayers with taxable income of R240 001 – see Table 11.1). If current income (or personal income) as defined in the national accounts is used as the tax base, the same amount of tax could have been obtained by levying a tax of approximately 15 per cent on all income.

Supporters of the flat tax rate base their arguments on the following advantages (see Browning & Browning, 1994: 378-379 and Boskin, 1996):

- High marginal tax rates reduce productivity and the incentive to work.
- A flat rate tax is simple to administer – tax liability is determined on a single page tax return where all forms of income are entered and then multiplied by the tax rate (e.g. 16%).
- Horizontal equity is promoted since different special provisions are not available to people with the same taxable income.
- Bracket creep during inflation is eliminated (see Section 11.4.4 below).

On the negative side a flat rate tax has the following disadvantages:

- Tax preferences based on equity grounds are eliminated.
- The tax burden will be redistributed – the burden of the high-income group will be reduced while the burden of the low-income group will increase (although some adjustments may be possible to counteract these effects).

The most important shortcoming of the flat rate tax proposal, and probably its nemesis, lies in its redistributional impact. Its impact on the tax burden of the low-income and even the middle-income group can, however, be curtailed by applying the tax rate to all income above a minimum income. It would also introduce a degree of progressivity in the tax structure. Even so, this would place a bigger burden on fiscal distribution via the expenditure side of the budget.

Another serious equity problem with the flat rate tax is the treatment of taxpayers with income around the threshold. For example, if a flat rate of 15 per cent were levied on incomes equal to or in excess of R30 000, a taxpayer with an income of R30 000 would be taxed at an inordinately high rate – of 15 per cent – whereas a person with an income of R29 999 would have no tax liability.

11.4 Economic effects of personal income tax

In Chapters 9 and 10 we laid the foundations for analysing different taxes. Recall that we identified four properties of a "good tax": economic efficiency, equity, administrative efficiency and flexibility. These properties or criteria will now be applied to the personal income tax.

11.4.1 Economic efficiency

From Chapter 10 we know that, when the economic efficiency of any tax is considered, economists try to establish whether or not the tax has an **excess burden**. Recall that the excess burden is a burden in addition to the normal burden of a tax that reduces the taxpayer's welfare (i.e. leaves the taxpayer on a lower indifference curve). To determine whether an income tax has an excess burden, we first consider a general tax on income and then a selective tax on income.

General tax on income

The impact of a general tax (a tax which is levied on the entire tax base) was analysed in Chapter 10. We concluded that such a tax has no excess burden since relative prices are not distorted. An example of such a tax is a head tax. If the entire income base (personal income and company income) is taxed and leisure is ignored (or it is assumed that leisure can be taxed at the same rate as income), an income tax is also a general tax. The effect of such a tax was illustrated using Figure 10.1. The tax on income will simply shift the after-tax budget line (*CD*) parallel and downwards to the origin. Relative prices remain unchanged and there is **no excess burden**. The tax has a normal burden only, which is illustrated by consumption occurring on a lower indifference curve (U_1) than before. An income tax that taxes the entire tax base (including leisure) is therefore an efficient tax. Unfortunately, leisure cannot be ignored and neither can leisure be taxed that easily.

Selective tax on income

Once we include leisure in our analysis, it can be shown that a personal income tax does have an excess burden. Workers have a choice between income and leisure. Since leisure cannot be easily taxed, a tax on income only is a **selective tax**. If income (or the goods that can be purchased with that income) and leisure are viewed as two commodities, we can argue that an income tax distorts the relative prices of income and leisure. People may decide to work more or less as a result of the tax (i.e. the **supply of labour** is affected).[1] The net result will depend on the relative strengths of the income and substitution effects of the price change. We focus on these two effects below and show that it is the substitution effect that has an adverse impact on the incentive to work. We also show that the substitution effect is determined by the marginal income tax rate. We start by examining how the supply of labour is determined using budget lines and indifference curves.

Assume that a person, say, Peter, has 18 hours a day (his time endowment), which can be used for two activities: work and leisure. In Figure 11.1 the daily time endowment is measured on the horizontal axis as the distance $0L$. Carefully observe that on this axis we measure two things. From left to right (i.e. from point 0 to point L) we measure the number of hours spent on leisure activities. From right to left (i.e. from point L to point 0) we measure the number of hours worked. For example, if LQ_1 hours are worked, it means that $0Q_1$ hours are available for leisure.

Suppose Peter earns a wage of R10 per hour. If he uses his entire daily time endowment (18 hours) to work, he can earn an income of R180 per day. Peter's income (or

Figure 11.1 The excess burden of a proportional tax on personal income

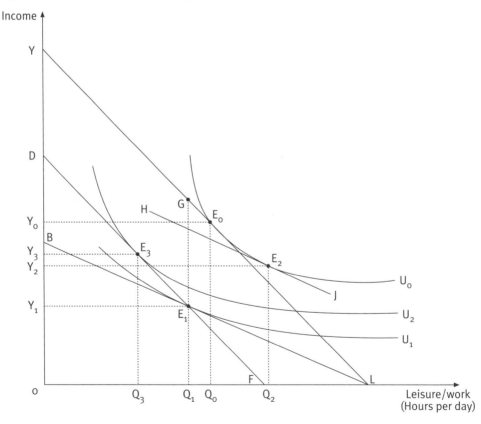

[1] Income taxation also affects saving behaviour in a similar manner to work effort. For those interested in this topic see Rosen (2002: 383-392). Since income tax causes an income effect (which increases saving) and a substitution effect (which lowers saving) the net outcome is unpredictable. Not even empirical estimates provide a clear-cut result. The most reasonable/sensible conclusion is that the two effects tend to cancel each other.

the goods that can be purchased with that income) is plotted on the vertical axis. If the full time endowment is used to earn income, one combination of income and leisure/work is obtained (i.e. point Y). If, instead, he spends all his time playing with his toes, zero income is earned and we have another combination of income and leisure/work, which we can plot (i.e. point L). We can continue in this manner and trace out the different combinations of income and leisure/work for each number of hours worked. This is shown as line YL that is Peter's budget line. The two "goods" in this case are income and leisure. By adding indifference curves (which indicate Peter's preferences or tastes), we can determine the combination of income and leisure/work most preferred by Peter. Suppose that the highest indifference curve that Peter can attain is U_0. He is then in equilibrium at E_0 where $0Q_0$ hours are spent on leisure and LQ_0 hours are used or supplied for work.

Suppose a **proportional tax** or **flat rate tax** (e.g. 30%) is now levied on income only. A proportional tax lowers the after-tax wage. This means that Peter's income (his after-tax wage multiplied by the number of hours worked) is now less at each number of hours worked. The after-tax budget line **pivots** (or swivels) from YL to BL. The after-tax equilibrium is at E_1 where indifference curve U_1 is tangent to the new budget line BL. Peter's welfare has declined as indicated by the fact that he finds himself on a lower indifference curve. At the new equilibrium Peter has a tax liability of E_1G (i.e. the difference between his before-tax and after-tax income earned by working LQ_1 hours). The quantity of labour supplied has increased from LQ_0 to LQ_1 hours per day. This, however, need not always be the case. The movement from E_0 to E_1 is due to the combined effect of the income and substitution effects of the tax change. Whether the number of labour

hours supplied increases or decreases will depend on which effect is the stronger.[2] (The budget line DF and indifference curve U_2 will be discussed later in this section.)

What is the **income effect**? The tax reduces Peter's after-tax income. Peter is worse off as a result of the tax and will tend to work more to partly offset this loss in income. Put differently, Peter has a lower after-tax income and can therefore not afford the same amount of leisure than before – less leisure means more hours of work. The income effect will thus cause the quantity of labour supplied to increase. What about the **substitution effect**? To understand the substitution effect it is important to note that leisure has a price. The price of one hour of leisure is the hourly wage sacrificed by not working. Thus the opportunity cost of leisure is the wage. Since the introduction of an income tax reduces the after-tax wage, the opportunity cost of leisure therefore decreases – leisure becomes cheaper. In other words, consuming leisure involves a smaller sacrifice in income than before the introduction of the tax. Because leisure is now relatively cheaper, it is substituted for work. The substitution effect increases leisure, which means that it reduces the quantity of labour supplied.

The income and substitution effects can also be explained using Figure 11.1. After the introduction of the proportional tax, equilibrium changes from E_0 to the new equilibrium at E_1. The movement from E_0 to E_1 can be decomposed into the income and substitution effects. By hypothetically compensating the individual with an amount just enough to make him as well off as before the tax, the budget line BL shifts parallel outwards to HJ which is tangent to indifference curve U_0 at E_2. The movement from E_2 to E_1 is, therefore, the income effect of the tax. The income effect shows that the individual increases work effort in response to the imposition of the

---

2 The decision to work less or more is also affected by non-economic factors (e.g. the status of work in a society and the need to avoid boredom and to get out of the home environment). We concentrate only on the economic effects.

proportional tax. The movement from E_0 to E_2 is a consequence of the change in the relative price of labour alone. The movement shows how the individual substitutes more leisure for less work if a proportional tax on labour is imposed or increased.

As stated earlier, the income and substitution effects combine to determine whether a person will work more or less. If the income effect dominates, the after-tax quantity of labour supplied will increase. In contrast, if the substitution effect dominates, the number of hours worked will decrease and the quantity of leisure will increase. On the basis of this analysis alone it is impossible to say what the outcome will be. **Empirical evidence**, however, shows that the labour supply elasticities for prime-age men (from about 20 to 60 years of age) are generally close to zero. This means that the supply curve is almost vertical or, put differently, that the quantity of labour supplied is very insensitive to changes in the net (after-tax) wage. For married women on the other hand, the estimated elasticities are generally positive and high. In their case the quantity of labour supplied is thus quite sensitive to changes in the net (after-tax) wage.

The analysis used for a proportional tax can be repeated for a progressive tax on income. One difference would be the shape of the after-tax budget line. In the case of a progressive tax the budget line will be kinked or curved (see Rosen 2002: 377). This does not fundamentally change the conclusion with regard to the impact of the tax on the supply of labour, but there is one important difference between progressive and proportional taxes. For a proportional tax the average tax rate is equal to the marginal tax rate, but for a progressive income tax the marginal tax rate is greater than the average tax rate. This means that the adverse incentive effects due to the substitution effect are likely to be more important for a progressive tax than for a proportional tax (see Box 11.2).

Box 11.2

Marginal tax rates and the substitution effect

In the case of the proportional tax, every taxpayer faces the same marginal tax rate, but in the case of the progressive tax the **marginal tax rate** varies with income (see for example Table 11.1 – for each income tax bracket the marginal tax rate exceeds the average rate). What does this mean?

The size of the income effect is determined by the average tax rate, whereas the size of the substitution effect is determined by the **marginal tax rate**. The average tax rate indicates how much of his or her income the taxpayer sacrifices to the revenue authorities for his or her **total work effort**. To recover some of the lost income due to the tax, the taxpayer will work more. You will recall that this is the income effect of the tax change. The income effect is thus related to how much tax is paid and, for a given income, this is determined by the average tax rate. The marginal tax rate, on the other hand, indicates the additional income individual sacrifices to the revenue authorities for **additional work effort** (i.e. changes in work effort) and is therefore related to the substitution effect. The higher the marginal tax rate, the more of the additional income a taxpayer must sacrifice. As the marginal tax rate increases the incentive to substitute leisure for income becomes greater. So it is the **size of the marginal tax rate** that determines the incentive to work (the substitution effect).

What we know so far is that a tax which selectively taxes income (and not leisure as well) has income and substitution effects which together may cause the quantity of labour supplied to increase or decrease. We also know that the taxpayer's welfare is reduced by the tax (as illustrated by the movement to a lower indifference curve).

However, we still have to determine the economic efficiency of the tax, that is, whether or not it has an excess burden. To arrive at an answer, we have to **compare** the results of the proportional tax to a lump-sum tax of equal revenue. Remember that a lump-sum tax does not distort relative prices and therefore has no excess burden.

If a lump-sum tax (e.g. head tax) is introduced to raise the same tax revenue as the proportional tax in Figure 11.1 (i.e. E_1G at Q_1 hours), the after-tax budget line shifts parallel to the original budget line (YL) to DF, which intersects BL at E_1. Peter will now be in equilibrium at E_3 where the highest indifference curve U_2 is tangent to the budget line. Peter is working LQ_3 hours a day that are more than the LQ_1 hours worked under the proportional tax. Peter's welfare is also higher under the lump-sum tax than under the equal-yield proportional income tax as illustrated by the attainment of a higher indifference curve (U_2) than before (U_1). The difference between U_2 and U_1 can be ascribed to the excess burden of a proportional income tax that selectively taxes income. Note that even though selective income taxes may lead to increased work effort (labour supply increases from LQ_0 without any tax to LQ_1 with the tax) they lower the incentive to work compared to lump-sum taxes. A lump sum tax of equal revenue yield thus results in an even greater quantity of labour being supplied (the quantity of labour supplied increases from LQ_0 to LQ_3). We therefore conclude that income taxes are economically inefficient, the reason being that relative prices are distorted by the tax.

From the analysis above it follows that taxing women at lower marginal tax rates than men may for example, increase the supply of labour. This would induce more women to enter the labour market. This option is not available, however, since the South African Constitution does not permit discrimination on the basis of gender or marriage.

Based in part on the theoretical arguments that lower marginal tax rates will increase work effort and improve tax compliance (the incentive to cheat is lower if tax rates are lower), there has been a worldwide trend towards lower marginal tax rates (see Section 10.5.3 in Chapter 10). South Africa has followed suit. In the early 1970s the maximum marginal tax rate was 72 per cent compared to the present 40 per cent.

11.4.2 Equity

As mentioned earlier, personal income taxation lends itself to the application of the ability-to-pay principle. Through a system of exemptions, deductions, tax rebates and marginal tax rates, the rate structure can be made to conform to society's notion of fairness. However, before we can make final conclusions in respect of tax equity, we need to know who ultimately bears the burden of the tax. If the tax can be shifted quite easily, the achievement of equity objectives could be compromised.

Even though the statutory burden of the tax is on the individual, it may be possible for individuals to shift the burden. The critical issue is how sensitive the supply of labour is to price and tax changes. As noted above, the net effect on work effort will be determined by the relative strengths of the income and substitution effects. Empirical evidence points to an insensitive or inelastic supply of labour for men (i.e. the supply curve is almost vertical). If the supply curve is relatively inelastic, the burden is on the supplier, that is, the employee in this case (see Figure 9.5 in Chapter 9). If the supply curve is less inelastic, the employer and the employee will share the burden. This scenario is possible in the case of married women and high-income professionals who are internationally mobile. Thus government should take due cognisance of tax shifting possibilities when personal income taxes are levied with the purpose of affecting income distribution. Intentions and actual policy outcomes do not necessarily point in the same direction.

In 1998 just over 5,8 million taxpayers were liable for income tax in South Africa. Those with taxable incomes of less than R40 000 constituted approximately 50 per cent of this number and together they contributed only 8 per cent to total taxes paid. In contrast, those taxpayers with taxable incomes of R100 001 and higher, represented approximately 10 per cent of the total number of individuals liable for income tax, but their combined contribution to total taxes paid was approximately 46 per cent. Personal income is distributed very unequally in South Africa and the much higher tax burden of the relatively high-income group therefore conforms to the ability-to-pay principle.

11.4.3 Administrative efficiency and tax revenue

In the discussion of administrative efficiency in Chapter 10 a number of references were made to income tax (see Section 10.3). We recap some of the issues here. Income taxes are complex and administrative efficiency requires relatively sophisticated taxpayers and administrators. In countries where these requirements are generally lacking, the income tax code should be as simple as possible. To simplify tax administration and ease the compliance burden for taxpayers, South Africa has implemented the Standard Income Tax on Employees (SITE). The SITE system makes it unnecessary for persons with taxable income of less than R60 000 to submit tax returns. In addition, the simplification of the South African Income Tax Act is presently the topic of a special project of SARS.

Personal income tax is a major source of government revenue. In 2000/01, taxes on persons and individuals raised R86 478 million, which contributed about 39 per cent to total tax revenue. It must be recognised that the tax base is rather small – 6,6 million tax-payers in 1999 compared to a labour force of about 16,0 million (in 2000). Of the total number of taxpayers 2,3 million were not liable for income tax because of tax preferences (tax rebates). The tax base can be increased by lowering tax rebates (i.e. raising the minimum tax threshold). This would cause hardship for the poorer taxpayers and increase tax administration. Alternatively, efforts could be made to capture those outside the tax net such as those in the informal sector and other difficult-to-tax groups. These groups can be taxed using **presumptive taxes**. Presumptive taxation involves the use of certain indicators (e.g. ownership of certain assets, personal servants, average profit margins or average gross turnover) to determine tax liability.

Another method that has been proposed to increase tax revenue (or maintain the same level of tax revenue) is to **reduce tax rates**. This recommendation is based on the alleged tax rate – tax revenue relationship that has become known as the **Laffer curve**, after the economist Arthur Laffer who popularised the idea. The logic of his argument is that higher tax rates will not necessary produce more tax revenue, since the tax base will shrink as taxpayers reduce their work effort in response to the higher rates. Fundamentally, the debate is again about how sensitive labour supply is to tax changes. Without going into this issue again it should be recognised that the higher the tax rate, the more likely it is that the substitution effect will dominate. For example, if income is taxed at increasingly higher **marginal** rates and ultimately at 100 per cent, work effort will not only decline but a person will eventually not be prepared to do any additional work whatsoever. Tax revenue is the product of the tax rate and the tax base, where the latter depends on work effort (the number of hours worked). At low tax rates, an increase in the tax rate will tend to increase tax revenues (at low rates people will still work more, i.e. the income effect dominates). However, this will only continue up to a point beyond which further tax rate increases will reduce tax revenues (people will eventually reduce their work effort, i.e. the substitution effect will dominate).

The Laffer curve is illustrated in Figure 11.2. Total tax revenue is plotted on the vertical axis and the tax rate on the horizontal axis. If the tax rate is at A, government can still increase tax revenue by raising the rate. Once the tax rate is at B, however, a further increase in the rate will cause tax revenue to decline (e.g. from R_3 to R_2). The supporters of the Laffer hypothesis use the mechanism to show that if the tax rate is at C, the authorities should lower the rate since this will result in higher tax revenue as illustrated by a movement from R_2 to R_3. The critical question, of course, is to determine where we are on the curve. The proponents argue that

some countries may well be beyond point B. The debate can only be settled empirically but it does appear that labour supply elasticities are such that it is unlikely that rate reductions would be fully counteracted by increased work effort.

11.4.4 Flexibility

In Section 10.4 it was pointed out that one of the "good" characteristics of a personal income tax is its built-in flexibility to counter cyclical economic behaviour. Personal income tax is thus considered to be an **automatic stabiliser**. On the negative side, inflation has serious implications for a progressive personal income tax to the extent that it has rendered the automatic stabilising effect meaningless (see Chapter 17). Inflation erodes the value of tax thresholds and deductions and leads to **bracket creep**,

Figure 11.2 The Laffer curve

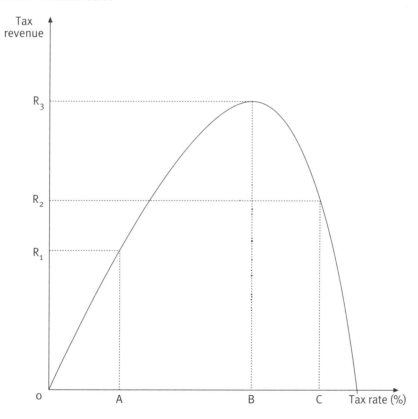

which is a process whereby a person is pushed into a higher income tax bracket as his or her nominal income increases (irrespective of what happens to the person's real income). For government this could be beneficial (it raises more and more revenue without the legislative process to increase tax rates), but if tax brackets and the value of tax preferences are left uncorrected, all taxpayers could end up paying the maximum marginal tax rate. Sometimes the phenomenon of bracket creep is erroneously referred to as "fiscal drag". The latter concept really refers to the dampening effect on the economy of the higher tax revenues (caused by bracket creep), that is, rising tax revenues automatically push the government's budget into a surplus creating a restrictive fiscal policy. This could have very adverse implications in recessionary times (when a deficit on the budget would be more appropriate in Keynesian terms) unless tax brackets are adjusted for inflation.

To understand the bracket creep phenomenon it is essential to distinguish between nominal income and **real income**. Remember that real income refers to the purchasing power of income (i.e. income after adjustment for inflation) whereas **nominal income** is the actual monetary value or rand value of income.

The personal income tax schedule taxes a person on his or her **nominal** income. In inflationary times employers often compensate workers for the decline in purchasing power by increasing their wages or salaries. If the rate of increase is equal to the inflation rate, worker's nominal income increases, but their real income stays the same. However, if the personal income tax schedule is not corrected for inflation, individuals are pushed into higher tax brackets with higher marginal tax rates because their nominal incomes have increased. Consider the following numerical example using the tax schedule in Table 11.1.

Suppose that Ms Shope received a salary of R105 000 in 2001/02. Assume now that the general price level increases by 10 per cent in 2002/03 and that Ms Shope's employer raises her salary by 10 per cent. In real terms her income thus stays the same, but in nominal terms her income increases to R115 500. We now calculate Ms Shope's tax liability in 2001/02 and 2002/03, assuming that the tax schedule in Table 11.1 is unchanged between 2001/02 and 2002/03. In 2001/02 her tax liability (based on her income of R105 000) was R19 840 (remember to take the primary rebate of R4 860 into account). In 2002/03 her nominal income of R115 500 pushes her into the higher (R110 001 and more) tax bracket and the last R5 500 of her income is taxed at a marginal tax rate of 35 per cent. Her tax liability in 2002/03 is R23 265. Ms Shope therefore pays R3 425 more tax, even though her real income has not increased! Her average tax rate increased from 18,9 per cent (= $\frac{19\ 840}{105\ 000} \times 100$) to 20,2 per cent ($\frac{23\ 265}{115\ 500} \times 100$). This increase in her average tax rate (while her real income remains unchanged) is what bracket creep is all about. If left unchecked, bracket creep undermines vertical equity. Even poor taxpayers will be drawn into the tax net and eventually taxed at high marginal tax rates.

The tax authorities can temper or eliminate the effects of bracket creep by linking the rate structure to a price index (i.e. raise each income bracket each year in line with the increase in the general price level). Alternatively, government can adjust the brackets and rebates on an *ad hoc* basis. This has been the preferred method of the South African tax authorities. Following the recommendation of the Margo Commission (1987: 81), government also reduced the number of tax brackets to slow down the inflationary creep to higher and higher marginal rates. For example, in 1991/92 the income tax schedule for married couples provided for 15 brackets compared to the six brackets in 2002/03.

11.5 Company taxation

Due to certain unique properties of company income, most countries tax this source of income separately. The following are the main reasons for taxing companies:

- From a legal point of view companies are separate entities (**legal persons**). They function as institutions with their own identity, independent from their shareholders who are taxed in their own right.
- Companies receive **benefits** from government and should be taxed for these privileges according to the benefit principle. The benefits include companies' limited legal liability to shareholders, the creation of an orderly environment by government, which is necessary for conducting business, the use of infrastructure, etc.
- If companies are not taxed, it is possible for shareholders to limit their personal income tax liability by retaining profits in the company. This increases the capital value of the shareholders' investment in the company. If capital gains are also not taxed, the integrity of the whole system of income taxation is jeopardised. **Tax avoidance** by individuals is therefore limited by taxing company profits. Since it is generally the higher-income group who are shareholders in companies, taxing this income is fair from an **ability-to-pay** perspective.
- By taxing the excess profits of imperfectly competitive firms (e.g. monopolies and oligopolies) **market failures** are addressed. Government can also achieve other economic **policy objectives** such as promoting foreign and local investment and achieving regional development aims by manipulating company tax rates and providing tax incentives (e.g. liberal depreciation allowances, training allowances and tax credits).
- Company taxation is **administratively simple** and generates significant **revenue** as a separate tax, particularly in LDCs (see

the discussion of tax reform in Section 10.5 of Chapter 10).

- By taxing companies, revenue is derived which would otherwise accrue to foreign investors and their home governments. Foreign investors are usually taxed on their investment income at company tax rates in their home countries. For example, when South Africa (the host country) levies company tax, the profits repatriated to the home country (e.g. the USA) will also be taxed at prevailing USA company tax rates. To avoid double taxation, countries usually enter into double tax agreements whereby the home country credits taxpayers with taxes paid in the host country. In other words, only the difference between the home country tax liability and host country liability is payable in the home country.

Company tax is a significant but declining source of **tax revenue**. In 1975/76 income tax on companies amounted to R1 969 million, or about 41 per cent of total tax revenue (net collections) in South Africa. In 2001/02 company tax came to R44 000 million, or about 18 per cent of total tax revenue. There are various reasons for this decline. One reason has to do with the nature of economic development. As a country develops economically, the consumption tax base broadens and the personal income tax base also becomes more important. Another set of possible reasons are factors that reduce company profit margins, such as rising wage costs, import costs and debt finance charges. Tax exemptions, tax evasion and tax avoidance are further possible causes, since they lead to effective tax rates that turn out to be much lower than the nominal or statutory rates.

One of the most important explanations for the declining contribution of company tax to total tax revenue in South Africa is the decline in tax revenue from income tax on mines, particularly gold mines. Tax revenue from gold mining declined from approximately 10 per cent of total tax revenue in 1975/76 to less than 0,5 per cent in 2001/02. This is indicative of the decline in the gold mining industry as well as of structural change as South Africa moved from a mining economy to an industrial economy. The decline in the gold mining industry can also be attributed to the relatively low international gold price, rising wage costs and lower ore grades.

11.6 The company tax structure

11.6.1 The company tax base

Businesses can be classified as incorporated or unincorporated. **Incorporated** businesses or companies include private and public companies and close corporations. **Unincorporated** businesses include sole proprietorships and partnerships. In South Africa mining companies are also distinguished from non-mining companies. The nature of business differs so much between these two categories that they are taxed differently. In the rest of this chapter we concentrate on the taxation of non-mining companies only.

Taxable income is defined as total receipts (or revenue) of the company minus certain allowable expenses (or costs). The latter comprise costs incurred to run the business. The definition seems simple enough, but a number of issues in respect of expenses complicate company taxation. The following are two of the most important complications:

- Interest payments are sometimes deductible from taxable income but **dividends** are not. This has implications for company finance. Companies have three basic sources of finance: share capital, borrowing (debt financing) and retained earnings. In the case of borrowing, the company can write off the cost of the loans (interest) against income for tax purposes. When share capital is used in South Africa, the cost of shares (dividends) cannot be written off against income. There is therefore a built-in bias against the use of share capital as a source of financing. In other words, the tax system encourages the use of loan finance but excessive use of loans increases indebtedness and may lead to bankruptcy.

- Companies are allowed to deduct **depreciation** on assets when taxable income is calculated. Assets wear out over their lifetime. The rationale for a depreciation allowance is that assets (e.g. machinery) lose part of their value each year, which constitutes a cost of production. But it is difficult to precisely determine the true rate of depreciation (i.e. economic depreciation). Sometimes the allowance exceeds economic depreciation. From time to time governments also allow companies to depreciate assets at an accelerated rate. This is sometimes used, for example, as an incentive to attract foreign investors. Such practices have the effect of reducing the effective company tax rate below the statutory tax rate. Assets are also classified into different categories and depreciation allowances differ accordingly. For example, 5 per cent per annum is allowed on buildings but 33,3 per cent per annum on books. Cash registers, main-frame computers and workshop equipment may be written off over five years (i.e. at a rate of 20% per year). Depreciation rates for machinery and plant vary between 10 and 25 per cent.

The problem with differentiated depreciation rates is that this practice tends to open up tax arbitrage opportunities. Investors, for example, will invest in assets, which they can write off quickly or immediately for tax purposes, but which actually depreciate much slower or even appreciate over time. The tax authorities usually become aware of such shelters only after a while and it then takes some time to close the loopholes. In

South Africa investments in forests, ships, motion pictures and aircraft were examples of such tax shelters. Needless to say, such tax-driven schemes are not models of efficient resource allocation.

11.6.2 Type of company tax

There are two extreme **types** of company tax. At the one extreme, companies are regarded as entities separate from their shareholders, and both are taxed on the same income source (referred to as the **classical system** or **partnership approach**). Company income is thus taxed twice, first as company tax and then also as personal income when distributed as dividends. This is commonly known as double taxation of dividends. At the other extreme, the company is simply seen as a conduit for all company income to the shareholders. All company income (retained as well as distributed) is taxed in full in the hands of the shareholders at their marginal income tax rates. The company tax then only serves as a withholding tax, which is credited in full at shareholder level. This type of company taxation is referred to as the **full integration system**.

Prior to 1990, South Africa had a modified classical company tax system incorporating a tax on company income and a tax on dividends, with a certain portion of dividends being excluded from taxation in the hands of the shareholders. On recommendation of the Margo Commission (1987: 204) the double taxation of dividends was discontinued in 1990 when dividends became tax-exempt in the hands of resident individuals and close corporations.

The company tax system was modified again in 1993 in an effort to (a) reduce the company tax rate without undue revenue loss, and (b) encourage companies to finance themselves. A dual tax rate was introduced, that is a basic and secondary rate. Non-mining companies are taxed at a fixed percentage on their taxable income. This is the **basic tax on companies**. Company tax is therefore

a **proportional tax**. The basic company tax rate was lowered from 48 per cent to 40 per cent in 1993 and to 30 per cent in 1999. The basic rate applies to all **retained profits**, that is, profits that are used to finance company investment or build company reserves and therefore not paid out as dividends to shareholders. In addition to the basic rate a **secondary tax on companies (STC)** was introduced in 1993. STC is levied on all profits distributed to the company's shareholders (i.e. dividends). STC is levied at company level and paid by companies. The rate was originally set at 15 per cent in 1993 but it was raised to 25 per cent in 1994 and reduced to 12,5 per cent in 1996. To determine the company tax rate, both rates have to be considered. For example, if a company retains all its profits the rate is only 30 per cent, but if it distributes all its profits to shareholders the maximum rate of 37,8 per cent applies (see Box 11.3 for the calculation of the maximum tax liability).

Box 11.3

Calculating company tax

The maximum tax burden of a company can be calculated as follows: suppose profit before tax is R100. The basic rate of 30 per cent must now be applied first. This causes a liability of R30 (30 per cent of R100) leaving R70. This amount can be retained for financing investment or can be distributed to shareholders as dividends. If the company decides to declare the full amount as dividends, the company is liable for STC of 12,5 per cent on the **net** distribution (i.e. after STC). The STC on R70 is R7.78 (= $\frac{12,5}{112,5} \times$ R70 or 12,5 per cent of R62,22). The total company tax liability is R37,78 (R30 plus R7,78) or 37,8 per cent of gross (before-tax) profit. This means that the maximum amount it can distribute is R62,22 calculated as R100 (profit) minus R30 (basic tax) minus R7,78 (STC).

The Katz Commission (1994: 175-177 and 226-227) thoroughly investigated the advantages and shortcomings of STC. The Commission concluded that STC has served its purpose and that "it has become desirable to consider better ways to achieve its objectives". The Commission suggested that "it could, for example, be eliminated and replaced by an imputation tax". The Commission did not favour the alternative of reverting to a variant of the classical system. The argument was that a return to the pre-STC system would require an increase in the company tax rate to compensate for the loss of STC revenue, which amounted to R6 700 million in 2001/02. In its Third Interim Report the Commission investigated the implementation of an imputation system but argued that such a complex system could only be considered once a restructured tax administration was functioning effectively.

11.6.3 Taxation of small and medium-sized enterprises

It is generally recognised that small and medium-sized enterprises are important for creating job opportunities in the economy. It is also recognised, however, that the tax system severely affects these types of businesses in so far as tax compliance is concerned. In addition, small businesses are highly dependent on working capital provided by the owners. When their profits are taxed owners often have to use short-term debt that increases their risk exposure. To assist small enterprises through the tax system various options can be pursued including taxing enterprises at differentiated rates (e.g. a progressive corporate rate structure), tax incentives (e.g. tax holidays) and taxing these businesses on their cash flow (see Steenekamp, 1996).

The real and financial cash-flow tax (RF-CFT) is closest to current tax base configurations and appears to be the most promising variant. The RF-CFT base = (sales + borrow-ing + interest received) − (real purchases + interest payments + debt repayment). The main advantages of a RF-CFT are:

- The definition of the tax base is simple because the tax does away with problems of defining depreciation, measuring capital gains, costing inventories and accounting for inflation.
- The tax is neutral with respect to the use of capital. Immediate expensing implies that the tax does not discriminate between debt and equity. (Mintz & Seade, 1991: 177-190; Shome & Shutte, 1993; and Sunley, 1989.)

The cash-flow tax has a number of shortcomings:

- During the transition from an accrual to a cash-flow system, the tax creates windfall tax revenue gains or losses, depending on whether government allows or denies companies depreciation on earlier investment.
- Full and immediate expensing seems to reduce the tax base compared to the accrual income tax base. However, this conclusion is disputed by some, who argue that it has to be considered that the corporate income tax base is also eroded through all kinds of tax expenditures.
- The incentive for base shifting is high (the tax base can be shifted from a high-tax entity to a low-tax entity). This could be done by purchasing inputs from the low-tax entity at inflated prices, by low-rate leasing and expensing by a high-tax party to a low-tax party, and by the sale of expensed assets at understated prices to the low-tax entity. Monitoring these practices is difficult and increases the administrative burden.
- The cash flow tax raises serious problems in international taxation, as it may not be creditable in home countries.
- Since no country has so far implemented the tax, administrative problems are difficult to predict.

The Katz Commission (1994: 157-158) also considered cash flow accounting and recommended that it be introduced as an option for small enterprises. Government accepted this recommendation in principle but had not implemented it at the time of writing.

The theoretical case for a cash-flow tax system is quite strong. One serious problem is the international consequences. South Africa, however, intends implementing cash-flow taxation in a particular sub-sector of the economy, namely the micro and small business sector, which functions mainly in a closed economic environment. The international consequences of such a tax are therefore less acute. Limiting cash-flow taxation to this sub-sector has the added advantage of improving its cash flow and capital requirements. On the negative side, cash-flow taxation increases the incentive for tax evasion and avoidance, as described above. The application of this form of taxation to a sub-sector of the economy will probably add to opportunities for tax arbitrage.

In 2000 government opted for a graduated tax rate structure for small business corporations. Tax on such businesses is levied at a rate of 15 per cent on the first R150 000 of taxable income and 30 per cent on the taxable income exceeding R150 000. Small businesses may write off investment in manufacturing assets in full in the tax year in which the assets are brought into use. At the time of writing these benefits were limited to businesses with an annual turnover of less than R3,0 million. Businesses where more than 20 per cent of gross income consists collectively of investment income and income from personal services are excluded. These tax reliefs are thus mainly intended for manufacturing businesses and are aimed at promoting job creation and improving the cash flow of small businesses.

11.7 The economic effects of company tax

11.7.1 Economic efficiency

In analysing the economic efficiency of company tax we again have to consider the excess burden of the tax. Does company tax cause an excess burden, that is, are relative prices (or returns) distorted, resulting in resources not being optimally allocated? The answer depends on whether company tax is seen as a tax on excess profits (or economic profits) or as a selective tax on capital.

If company tax is regarded as a tax on **economic profits** only, then company tax has no excess burden. The economic profits of firms are simply reduced by the tax and firms still maximise profits. The tax does not cause any other changes in behaviour (i.e. marginal cost are unchanged) and prices are not affected. But companies are taxed on their **accounting profits** (i.e. economic profit plus normal profit). In the short run normal profits is a fixed cost. Therefore marginal costs, which change only when variable costs change, are not altered by the tax. However in the long run there are no fixed inputs (all become variable) and taxing normal profits as part of accounting profits may then affect marginal cost. Thus in the long run a tax on accounting profits may cause a change in the behaviour of owners and prices, which could result in an excess burden.

The return on capital of shareholders invested in companies (i.e. dividends) is a non-deductible expense. Company tax can therefore be regarded as a **tax on capital**. However, all forms of capital are not taxed at the same effective rate. In South Africa, incorporated businesses (e.g. public companies) are taxed at a rate which varies between 30 and 37,8 per cent (the actual rate being determined by the amount of dividend payments). Non-incorporated businesses (e.g. sole proprietorships) are taxed at marginal personal income tax rates, which vary between 18 and 40 per cent.

The important point about **differential taxes on capital** is that if companies are taxed at different rates, the net (after-tax) returns differ from sector to sector. Capital will then move from the sectors with lower net (after-tax) returns to sectors where a higher net (after-tax) return can be obtained. This process will continue until net returns are equal in all the sectors. This migration of capital is purely in response to tax-induced differences in returns, and not because capital can be used more productively elsewhere. Resources are therefore misallocated and an **excess burden** results. In the United States this loss in welfare has been estimated at about 0,5 per cent of GNP (or about 12% of total tax revenue).

11.7.2 Company taxation and investment

The decision to invest

Another issue concerning the economic efficiency of company taxation is its impact on local and foreign fixed investment. The company tax structure can lower or raise the **user cost of capital**. The user cost of capital includes, firstly, the **opportunity cost** of holding an asset in a company. By investing capital in a company instead of, for example, saving it, an opportunity cost is incurred (i.e. the interest forgone). Secondly, the user cost of capital includes d**epreciation cost**. Capital invested in, for example, machines decreases in value. Finally, the user cost of capital is affected by **company tax**. The returns on share capital (realised profits and dividends) are taxed and constitute a cost to the investor. By lowering nominal company tax rates, providing depreciation allowances, or giving tax incentives (e.g. tax holidays and tax rebates) the user cost of capital can thus be lowered, and vice versa.

Non-tax factors

One should guard against overemphasising the impact of the company tax structure and rates on the decision to invest. Non-tax factors also influence the investment decision and are often more important. The following **non-tax factors** are important to investors:

- **Business opportunities**. Investors look for market opportunities to maximise profits, for example, by increasing market size or vertically integrating their production processes across national borders. Portfolio investors look for speculative profits (such as offered by exchange rate differentials) or are interested in spreading risk.
- **Political stability**. Political instability disrupts investors' calculations of the expected rate of return on their investment.
- **Economic stability**. This includes price and exchange rate stability as well as fiscal stability (i.e. a sustainable fiscal deficit).
- **Labour stability**. The work ethic is important for certain types of investors. For a businessperson interested in manufacturing goods that use labour-intensive technology (e.g. clothing) a reliable workforce is essential.
- **Security and respect for property rights**. Investors are sensitive to policy in respect of nationalisation and privatisation and to the honouring of international commitments, such as double taxation agreements and debt repayment obligations.
- **Transportation costs**. In principle it is always desirable to manufacture goods as close as possible to the market(s) they serve.

Although tax considerations are important, they are only one among a variety of factors to be taken into account. Based on the evidence brought before it, the Katz Commission (1994: 213) observed that "while tax is an important investment consideration, it ranks well down the list of priorities unless it poses a specific and actual inhibition". However, corporate taxation might be a **major policy issue** for the following reasons:

- A punitive corporate tax regime constrains investment, while a liberal regime could result in an unnecessary loss of revenue to the treasury, thus allowing foreign treasuries to capture bonus revenue.
- An unfavourable corporate tax regime might lead to other forms of profit taking (e.g. repatriation of profits through transfer pricing and setting up branches instead of subsidiaries). The willingness of multinational corporations and others to lower their effective tax rates through transfer pricing indicates their sensitivity to tax rates.
- When non-tax factors are approximately the same in countries competing for investment, taxation becomes all-important, as is evident from the intense tax competition in the East Asian region.

Tax incentives

Tax incentives (e.g. capital allowances, incentives for research and development, deductions for training expenses) are used in most developing countries in an effort to attract investment to particular regions, sectors, and industries. They are also used for specific purposes such as export promotion, employment creation, local participation, local sourcing of materials, improved infrastructure and the promotion of technological transfers, skills development, and the development of geographical regions. There is no clear pattern in respect of the direction of reform with regard to the use of incentives. Countries such as Mexico, Colombia, Jamaica, Chile, Brazil, Argentina, Zimbabwe and Indonesia have moved away from tax incentives in an effort to broaden the tax base. At the same time, tax rates were lowered. In contrast, the intense tax competition in the East Asian region between Singapore, Malaysia, Thailand, and the Philippines has resulted in an extensive range of tax incentives, although tax rates are also being lowered in these countries.

The reasons for and arguments in favour of the use of tax incentives are (see Boadway & Shah, 1995; and Chia & Whalley, 1995):

- Incentives are regarded as a means of offsetting the effects of regulations and controls in developing countries, such as exchange control and licensing restrictions. Incentives compensate for these distortions.
- Likewise, labour market distortions may be corrected by using investment incentives as a second-best policy and in this manner employment can be created.
- Capital markets are often imperfect in respect of small firms. By targeting these firms selectively incentives can be used to overcome these constraints.
- Temporary investment incentives may be effective devices for assisting infant industries.
- To the extent that they are effective in encouraging investment, incentives generate external benefits for the economy over and above those accruing to the investor, for example, innovation and training.
- Tax incentives can be used to signal to investors that a country is open for business. They announce to investors that government has certain priorities and that investors will be compensated for their commitment. Niche markets can also be promoted through income tax incentives.

Various analysts have questioned the use of incentives to promote investment and other objectives. The arguments raised against incentives include the following (see Easson 1992: 387-439; Shah 1995; and World Bank 1991):

- Incentives complicate tax administration.
- Tax concessions erode the revenue base and necessitate higher tax rates.
- Incentive schemes are often the result of pressure group action rather than an analysis of the economy as a whole; thus favouring certain sectors over others.

- Tax incentives result in an uneven tax burden among taxpayers.
- Tax incentives are less likely to succeed in attracting foreign investment than a general reduction in corporate income tax.
- Investment incentives often lead to windfall gains in respect of investments that would have taken place anyway – they have little impact on new investment.
- If there are obstacles to investment (e.g. untrained labour) it is better to address these problems directly instead of using tax incentives, since such incentives simply add further distortions to the economy.

In spite of these apprehensions, tax incentives are widely used by developing countries to attract investment and promote certain objectives. The Katz Commission (1994: 204) thoroughly reviewed tax incentives in South Africa and concluded that "... the range of incentives should be narrowed as far as possible and that those which exist should all be justified in terms of the objectives in the Reconstruction and Development Programme." This, however, is a very vague guideline. The Commission also endorsed the principle that tax incentives be subject to thorough cost-benefit analysis.

South Africa has for some years been moving away from tax incentives to broaden the tax base and has at the same time lowered the corporate tax rate. Since 2000, however, a number of industrial incentives to facilitate investment in South Africa have been introduced. These include a 100% initial investment allowance for companies undertaking strategic projects and an accelerated depreciation allowance for manufacturing businesses. It is hoped that these measures will encourage investment and compensate for the impact of the depreciation of the rand on new investment. In addition, to encourage job creation and lower the cost of hiring new workers and offering learnerships, a tax allowance to employers that offers approved learnership programmes was proposed in 2002.

11.7.3 Fairness

When we considered tax incidence in Chapter 9 it was explicitly stated that only **people** could bear the burden of a tax. In the case of companies, the people in question are shareholders, workers and consumers. We now analyse the incidence of company tax on each of these groups.

In Section 11.7.1 we noted that when companies are taxed at different rates, capital will move from high-taxed sectors to low-taxed sectors so that a higher net return can be obtained. Theoretically this process will continue until net (after-tax) returns are equal in all the sectors. **All owners of capital** therefore bear the burden of the tax, not only the capital owners in the taxed sector. The real controversy regarding the incidence of company tax is whether capital owners bear the full tax burden. Empirical studies indicate that capital bears almost the entire burden, but it is still worth examining how the tax can theoretically be shifted to other groups.

When the net (after-tax) return of taxed businesses declines, firms will attempt to recover the tax by increasing their prices to **consumers**. The extent to which the taxed businesses can shift the tax will, of course, depend on the price elasticities of demand and supply of goods and service produced by these businesses (see Chapter 9).

How can the company tax be shifted to **workers**? Just like firms may attempt to pass on the tax burden to consumers in the form of higher prices, so they may try to shift the burden to workers in the form of lower wages or lower employment. Some observers argue, for example, that company tax affects savings and investment over time. Since capital is internationally mobile, a tax on capital will cause capital to move to lower tax jurisdictions. This lowers the amount of capital available per worker in the country where capital is taxed and causes the marginal physical product of labour (MPP or labour productivity) to fall. A decline in labour productivity may lead to a fall in wages or lower employment. Thus labour may bear a part of the company tax burden. Details about how company tax can be shifted to labour fall beyond the scope of this chapter. Suffice it to say that the incidence of company tax on consumers and labour remains controversial.

Ultimately equity (or fairness) depends on who the owners of capital are. Capital is usually owned by the higher-income group. If the burden of company tax falls mainly on capital owners, vertical equity is thus achieved.[3] Horizontal equity depends on the type of company tax system in operation and is not discussed here. The fully integrated income tax system (see introductory remarks in Section 11.6.2) appears to serve both horizontal and vertical equity objectives best but this type of tax system is unfortunately administratively complex.

11.8 Capital gains tax

Capital gains can be defined as increases in the net value of assets over a period (eg an accounting period or fiscal year). According to the Haig-Simons definition of comprehensive income, anything that makes consumption possible without diminishing wealth at the beginning of a fiscal year is considered to be income. Capital gains are, accordingly, often classified as a form of income and are taxed as such. Capital gains can be taxed as they accrue (an unrealised gain) or when they are realised. An unrealised capital gain occurs when an asset increases in value in a given fiscal year and the asset is not sold, for example, an increase in the rand value of a Krugerrand when the rand depreciates against the dollar. A capital gain is realised when an asset has increased in value and is sold for cash.

Capital gains tax is currently levied in a number of developed countries, such as Canada, the USA, the UK, Australia and Japan, as well as in some developing countries, including Argentina, Brazil, India, Nigeria and Zimbabwe. In South Africa, capital gains were generally not taxable. Where assets were kept as an investment and then sold, the yield on realisation of the asset was regarded as a receipt of a capital nature: one asset (capital) was simply converted into another (cash), and the yield was therefore not taxable. But where assets were sold in the course of normal business, that is, to make a profit, such profit was regarded as income and taxed as such. In many cases the courts had to rule on the application of this principle, which caused a great deal of uncertainty about the taxability or otherwise of capital gains. On 1 October 2001 South Africa implemented a capital gains tax (CGT).

Capital gains tax comes into play when there is a change in the ownership of an asset, i.e. when it is sold, given away, scrapped, swapped, lost or destroyed. It is thus a "realisation" or transaction-based tax and when capital gains are realised or deemed to be realised, such gains form part of the income tax base. The capital gain (or loss) is determined as the difference between the realised proceeds from the sale of the asset and the total base cost of the asset. The **base cost** of an affected capital asset includes the original acquisition costs and related transaction costs (e.g. legal fees and brokerage), the costs of any improvements, and VAT.

Capital losses may only be deducted against capital gains _ there is no such thing as a negative CGT! Capital losses incurred on assets not used for business purposes cannot be subtracted from realised gains for tax purposes. These include assets used for

---

3 It should, however, be recognised that there are people with low-incomes (e.g. pensioners) who derive their income mainly from capital. This could affect our equity conclusion with regard to company taxation.

personal consumption, such as sailboats, second vehicles and aircraft.

The first R10 000 of net capital gains of a natural person during a tax year is excluded from CGT. Although capital gains in excess of R10 000 are included in taxable income, some relief is granted to individuals and other legal persons. In the case of an individual, only 25% of the net capital gain is included in taxable income. A company has to include 50% of its net capital gain. This meant that the effective capital gains tax rate in respect of individuals varies between 0 per cent and 10 per cent, depending on the marginal tax rate, and for companies it was 15 per cent. The effective capital gains tax rate for small businesses ranged from 7,5 per cent to 15 per cent.

Any individual or legal person (e.g. a company, close corporation or trust) resident in South Africa is liable for CGT in respect of the disposal or deemed disposal of capital assets held both inside and outside the country. Where an individual or legal person is not resident, a liability will only arise in the event of the disposal of immovable property inside South Africa, or the sale of the assets of a local branch, permanent establishment, fixed base or agency, through which a trade, profession or vocation is being carried out.

Capital assets liable for CGT are property of any kind, whether movable or immovable or tangible or intangible, and include land, mineral rights, office blocks, plant and machinery, motor vehicles, boats, caravans, trademarks, goodwill, shares, bonds and Krugerrands. Some assets are exempted from CGT, such as trading stock and mining assets qualifying for income tax deductions as capital expenditure; and in the case of individuals, principal owner-occupied residences, private motor vehicles and personal belongings (e.g. clothing, stamps, works of art, antiques, medallions, foreign exchange and coins not minted in gold or silver). Small business assets (businesses with a market value of assets of less than R5,0 mil-

lion) realised by individuals over 55 who use the proceeds for retirement purposes are also exempted from CGT, provided the assets had been held for at least five years. The latter provision is limited to a one-off exemption of R500 000 per taxpayer.

In order to safeguard the reinvestment of profits, a capital gains tax liability may in certain cases be deferred until a subsequent CGT event. Deferral (rollover) relief applies to asset disposals, such as certain transfers of property to establish or reorganise a business, transfers of property from a deceased estate, donations of property, and transfers between spouses.

The Franzsen Commission (1968) recommended the introduction of a separate capital gains tax. This Commission regarded profits arising from the sale of shares and fixed property (with the exception of property that the person liable for tax uses for residential purposes) as the principal components of the capital gains tax base. The Margo Commission (1987) opposed a capital gains tax primarily because of the administrative problems involved. The Katz Commission, in its Third Interim Report (1995: 49), also recommended that "... by reason of the lack of capacity on the part of the tax administration, there should not be capital gains tax in South Africa at this stage". The low revenue potential of such a tax reinforced the Katz Commission's conclusion.

Capital gains are not really taxed for the sake of the revenue they yield, but rather for other reasons. It is estimated that CGT could raise about R1 to R2 billion a year directly (i.e. around 1% of total tax revenue). The following are the most important **reasons for** capital gains taxation:

- To protect the integrity of the **personal income tax base**. If capital gains are not taxed, taxpayers have an incentive to convert income into capital gains in order to avoid taxation. Take the example of a sole proprietor who reinvests his/her profit instead of taking it as a salary (which is taxed at marginal income tax rates). The reinvested income increases the value of the business. When the business is sold one day the benefits are reaped in the form of long-term capital gains (regarded as non-taxable capital income in the absence of capital gains taxation).

- To ensure **horizontal equity**. A capital gain represents an increase in economic power and increases the individual's ability to earn income and to be taxed. Consider two persons with the same net additions to wealth (income plus net assets): person A's net additions consist of salary income and capital gains; person B's net additions consist of only salary income. Both have the same horizontal ability to pay in terms of the comprehensive definition of income (i.e. the Haig-Simons definition). If capital gains are not taxed, person B is unfairly taxed on his or her income.
- To ensure **vertical equity**. Capital gains accrue mostly to higher-income tax-payers. If they are not taxed on these gains, the vertical ability to pay principle is jeopardised.
- **To improve economic efficiency**. If investments are chosen on the basis of tax considerations, the allocation of investment funds is distorted and an excess burden results.

There are also a number of **arguments against** capital gains tax of which the following are the most important:

- Capital gains taxation is subject to numerous **administrative problems**. Assets have to be **valued** and there is a need for accurate and up-to-date deeds registers in the case of, for example, works of art and real property. The valuation problem is more acute in the case where an accrual base is used (i.e. where unrealised capital gains are also taxed). The problem of valuation is less severe when a realisation base is used – in other words, when the selling price is compared to the purchase price

when the asset is sold and tax payment is only due when the asset is sold.

- If nominal profits (instead of real profits) are taxed, **equity** is at risk. Inflation causes imaginary capital gains (i.e. increases the nominal value of assets) and it may be unfair to tax someone just because inflation has increased the nominal value of an asset. Nominal capital gains should therefore be deflated by an appropriate price index. The choice of a suitable index is a further complication.
- Capital gains are usually one-off events, and to avoid the tax, taxpayers tend to lock in rather than realise investments. This **lock-in effect** can affect investment negatively. Concessions are therefore usually made either in the form of lower personal income tax rates on capital gains or by not taxing capital gains once a certain period has elapsed. To compensate for the effects of inflation and the lock-in effect, the South African tax authorities opted for low effective capital gains rates.

Important concepts

basic tax on companies
bracket creep
capital gain
classical system
comprehensive income tax base
flat-rate tax
full integration
gross income
income effect
Laffer curve
marginal tax rate
nominal income
real income
residence principle
secondary tax on companies
source of income principle
substitution effect
tax exclusions
tax exemptions
tax expenditures

tax rebates
tax threshold
unit of taxation
user cost of capital

Self-assessment exercises

11.1 Define and explain the "comprehensive income-tax base".

11.2 Critically evaluate the introduction of a worldwide basis of taxation in South Africa.

11.3 Differentiate between the following concepts:
- gross, net and taxable income
- nominal and real income
- accrued and realised income
- average tax rate and marginal tax rate
- tax exclusions, tax deductions and tax credits

11.4 Explain the rationale behind the progressive nature of individual income tax structures.

11.5 What is a flat rate tax, and what are the reasons for the renewed interest in this type of tax?

11.6 With the aid of a graph, explain the likely effects of an increase in individual income tax on the supply of labour.

11.7 Discuss the economic effects of personal income tax by referring to economic efficiency, equity, administrative efficiency and flexibility.

11.8 Why are policy makers so concerned about the impact of inflation on personal income tax?

11.9 Discuss the relevance of the so-called Laffer effect.

11.10 Why is company income taxed separately from other forms of income? Explain.

11.11 Why are the economic consequences of company tax regarded as controversial?

11.12 The combined effect of income tax on companies and individuals implies the double taxation of dividends. Explain the efficiency and equity aspects of this interaction.

11.13 Explain the arguments for the integration of the individual and the company income taxes.

11.14 If special provision is made in income tax law for small business or the agricultural sector, it means that the tax is not neutral. What is your opinion on this issue?

11.15 How will income tax on companies affect the decision of an entrepreneur to invest?

11.16 "Tax incentives are not effective instruments for attracting investment." Do you agree? Discuss.

11.17 Analyse the following statement: "Capital-gains tax is an inappropriate form of taxation for South Africa."

Chapter twelve

Tjaart Steenekamp

Taxation of wealth

In Chapter 10 we noted that taxes could be imposed on three bases: income, wealth and consumption. In this chapter we consider the wealth base. Wealth is the product of accumulated savings, assets that gained in value and the free gifts of nature. Richard Bird (1992: 134) argues that the existing distribution of wealth in a country is "... largely the outcome of historical accident, as condoned by the state and frozen in law. The result of this pattern of distribution of initial wealth is that many of those successful in life stand not on their own feet but on the shoulders of their fathers." Wealth holdings thus contain an element of personal effort (self-accumulated wealth) and an element of luck (inherited wealth). Particularly in countries with vast inequalities of wealth, these characteristics make wealth taxation a much-debated topic and also an emotive one.

We begin this chapter by distinguishing between different types of wealth (Section 12.1). In Section 12.2 we investigate the reasons why wealth is taxed. The taxation of real property, which is an important type of wealth, is studied in Section 12.3. The chapter concludes with a discussion of capital transfer taxes such as estate duty and gift taxes.

The aim of this chapter is to analyse the economic impact of the personal net wealth tax, property taxes and capital transfer taxes.

Once you have studied this chapter, you should be able to
- define the wealth tax base;
- explain the merits and shortcomings of taxing personal net wealth;
- define the property tax base;
- describe property tax rating and assessment;
- explain the effect of property tax on equity using the benefit principle;
- analyse property tax incidence using partial and general equilibrium analysis;
- discuss the efficiency effects of a property tax;
- define a capital transfer tax;
- discuss the economic effects of capital transfer taxes.

12.1 Wealth and types of wealth taxes

Income and consumption are **flow concepts** since both are measured over a period. Income consists of wages, rental income from property, interest on savings, dividends on shares and so on. In contrast to income, wealth is a **stock concept** which is measured at a particular point in time.

Wealth is the value of accumulated savings, investment, gifts and inheritances. If a person does not save or receive inheritances or gifts, the person will never accumulate wealth. A **person's wealth** consists of the net monetary value of assets owned. Another and technically more correct definition is that personal wealth is the present value of a person's expected real income. Personal wealth includes tangible things such as houses, durable goods (e.g. motorcars, jewellery, valuable paintings) and land. In addition, individuals hold financial assets such as cash, deposits in bank accounts, shares in businesses and government bonds. These are all **assets** that can be traded in the market. We can also identify other items such as insurance policies and pension rights, though these types of assets are difficult to trade in the market and thus to value. Human capital acquired through investment in education and training should also be included as (intangible) forms of personal wealth, although valuing human capital is obviously difficult. A person's wealth must also take account of any **liabilities**, since assets are often acquired through incurring debt. By subtracting liabilities from assets we obtain the **net value of assets** (i.e. personal wealth), which is also called **net personal worth**.

The wealth tax base is not restricted to personal wealth. Company wealth should also be considered. **Company wealth** includes different forms of capital such as fixed capital (premises, plant and machinery), floating capital (raw materials and inventories) and financial capital (stocks and shares, cash and bank deposits). It is not difficult to see why the term capital is often used synonymously with company wealth. To these assets we should, in principle at least, add intangibles such as goodwill, brand name and market power. As in the case of human capital, it is difficult to value these assets. To arrive at **net company wealth** we must subtract liabilities from the gross value of assets.

The taxation of the wealth base has a long history dating back to a form of property tax introduced in ancient Rome. The most important **types of wealth taxes** today include:

- annual wealth taxes (e.g. on persons and/or companies);
- property tax (e.g. tax on land and improvements);
- capital transfer tax (e.g. tax on estates and gifts).

12.2 Why tax wealth?

The case for a wealth tax is best presented by considering the arguments in favour of an **annual wealth tax on individuals** (also called a personal **net wealth tax** or net worth tax).[1] The arguments for a net or gross assets tax on businesses are somewhat different and will not be addressed here.[2]

12.2.1 Equity considerations

When we discussed fairness as a criterion of a "good" tax in Chapter 10, two principles emerged: the benefit principle and the ability-to-pay principle. A wealth tax is often justified in terms of the **benefit principle**. Governments provide public services, which increase the value of real assets (e.g. property). Governments also provide protection for property (e.g. law enforcement and legislation). Consequently, owners of assets should pay for the benefits (expenditures) of the protection they receive. It may, however, be difficult to determine the extent of the benefits received – some properties, for example, need more protection than others.

Next we consider the **ability-to-pay** principle. Money income is normally subject to income tax, which may include income arising from realised or unrealised capital gains (see Chapter 11). But from the **horizontal**

---

1 The personal net wealth tax as implemented in a number of developed countries is discussed in detail in Organisation for Economic Co-operation and Development (OECD) (1988: Chapter 1).

2 For a discussion of a gross assets tax on businesses, see Sadka & Tanzi (1993: 66-73).

equity perspective, wealth confers additional ability to pay (over and above the money income derived from wealth itself and from work) to the owners of wealth. Take the example of a poor person with almost no income and a wealthy person who keeps his or her wealth in the form of Kruger Rands and Persian carpets. Surely, even if the wealthy person has no income, he or she is bound to have greater taxable capacity than the poor person on account of the potential income-generating capacity of the assets. Besides, because wealth owners have the ability to realise assets, they have economic security, which enables them to exercise purchasing power (e.g. by obtaining loans). Wealth also provides them with the power to exploit economic opportunities.

From a **vertical equity** point of view, people with different taxable capacities should be taxed differently. Wealth is generally distributed very unevenly and it is argued that wealth taxes could reduce this concentration. The distribution of personal wealth in South Africa is also very uneven. The Gini coefficient in respect of the distribution of **wealth** in the former Transvaal province[3] in 1985 has been estimated at 0,67 (Van Heerden, 1996). This distribution, however, was not more skew than in other countries (e.g. 0,81 for the USA in 1983, 0,68 for the UK in 1968 and 0,52 for Australia in 1968). What makes South Africa's distribution different, though, is its racial dimension. In 1985 whites comprised approximately 36 per cent of the population of the Transvaal, but owned approximately 91 per cent of the wealth.

According to the equity principles it seems fair to tax wealth. But we need to consider the **incidence** of a wealth tax as well. Remember that wealth is mostly accumulated savings. A tax on wealth is therefore largely a tax on savings. The incidence of a wealth tax will thus depend on the price

elasticity of the supply and demand for savings. If the supply is perfectly inelastic, the tax is borne by the owners of capital (wealth), and since wealth is concentrated in the hands of the middle- and upper-income groups, the tax is progressive. If, however, the supply of savings is not perfectly inelastic, the incidence becomes complex but it is probable that wealth owners would then be able to pass on some of the tax to consumers and workers.

12.2.2 Efficiency considerations

Wealth taxes may affect economic efficiency positively or negatively. On the **positive side**, a net wealth tax has less of a disincentive effect on work effort than an income tax. A tax on wealth is levied on past effort whereas income tax is levied on current effort. Furthermore, in the absence of a wealth tax a person may invest in assets that do not yield income to avoid paying income tax. A wealth tax would counteract such tax avoidance to some extent. A wealth tax might therefore serve as an incentive to wealth holders to put their assets to productive use. We will address this point again when land taxation is considered in Section 12.3.5.

On the **negative side**, wealth taxes may affect saving because the tax base (wealth) is mainly accumulated savings. A tax on saving will also translate into a tax on labour, that is, insofar as the purpose of work is to save (for future consumption). When the tax becomes a disincentive to work, efficiency is lost. In addition, although wealth taxes may encourage a more productive use of assets, it may also have the opposite effect. High yield and efficiency are not necessarily the same. Assets are sometimes invested in ventures that yield little or no profit over the short run (e.g. investments in plantations). A wealth tax on these assets would cause an undue liability on its owners, and also ulti-

3 The land area largely corresponds with the present-day provinces of Gauteng, Mpumalanga, Limpopo and North West Province.

mately on the community/economy, especially if taxes have to be paid when wealth increases even though there is no cash flow.

A discussion of the efficiency of wealth taxes will be incomplete without reference to the **excess burden** of such taxes. Wealth taxes reduce the net return on saving (i.e. the after-tax interest rate). Since wealth taxes distort the relative prices of goods that can be consumed presently and goods that can be consumed in the future, an excess burden results. The size of the excess burden will depend on how sensitive saving is to changes in interest rates.

12.2.3 Revenue and administrative considerations

Like all taxes, wealth taxes can be introduced to generate **revenue**, but this is not a particularly important consideration. In fact, in most countries where such a tax is in force, the net wealth tax revenue rarely exceeds one per cent of total tax revenue.

Wealth taxes do have **administrative advantages**. The database for these taxes can be used to crosscheck income tax returns. Since the income tax base is often eroded by tax avoidance and evasion schemes, wealth taxes may thus complement income tax systems by curtailing these schemes. On the other hand, wealth taxes also have **administrative shortcomings**. In the past, wealth was relatively easy to tax since it was held in very visible forms (e.g. immovable property). Nowadays, wealth holdings and their valuation have become very complex (e.g. derivatives such as options and swaps) and are often held in foreign countries. This calls for a sophisticated and costly tax administration, which deters many countries from introducing such taxes.

It appears as if there is a trend away from taxes on wealth. In France a wealth tax was introduced in 1982 and scrapped in 1986. Other developed countries such as Japan and Ireland also abandoned the net wealth tax for reasons of equity, complex adminis-

tration and impeding economic growth. Colombia introduced a net wealth tax in 1935 but repealed it recently. In South Africa the Margo Commission (1987: Chapter 20) and the Katz Commission (1995: Chapter 7) both considered an annual wealth tax but concluded that such a tax (including an inheritance tax) should be avoided because of the administrative and compliance burdens involved. The Katz Commission (1995: 50) argued that redistribution is better achieved by other means, particularly through the expenditure side of the budget.

12.3 Property taxation

The property tax base can be defined very broadly to include real property (realty) and **personal property** (e.g. furniture, motor vehicles, shares, bonds and bank deposits). We focus exclusively on real property partly because it is the most common one. Such a tax is an **impersonal** (*in rem*) tax.

Although central governments also levy property taxes, property tax in South Africa is collected mainly by urban local authorities. The introduction of a land tax as a revenue source for rural local government has also been investigated by the Katz Commission (1995) and a final recommendation in this respect is awaited. National government taxes on property are primarily in the form of transfer duties (payable by the person who acquires a property), marketable securities tax and tax on donations and estates. In the latter cases, the tax is levied when immovable property is alienated or acquired in terms of a donation or an inheritance. However, the property taxes levied by local authorities are by far the most important form of property tax in South Africa.

Property tax is a major source of revenue for local authorities. When sales of bulk services (e.g. electricity and water) are excluded from budget figures, local authorities generated property tax revenue in 2001/02 to the tune of R11,5 billion, which represented approximately 47 per cent of the consolidated operating income of municipalities. Important as this source may be for local governments, its relative insignificance as a national revenue source is illustrated by the fact that it would contribute only about 4 per cent to total tax revenue of the general government.

12.3.1 The tax base

The **real property tax base** includes land (farm, residential, commercial and forest land) and capital invested in improvements (farm buildings, homes, business buildings, fences and so on). The importance of the distinction between the two tax bases will become clear once we analyse the incidence effects of a property tax.

In South Africa all land and improvements in urban areas (from metropolitan local councils to small local councils) are rateable. A property tax (collected by local authorities) is currently not levied on rural land. This topic, however, was the subject of an investigation by the Katz Commission, which was scheduled to report on it during 1999. In its Third Interim Report the Katz Commission (1995:29) considered the possibility of a national tax on agricultural land, but found that such a tax is not a viable option for South Africa. Regarding the urban property tax, municipalities have the option of choosing at least two of the following:

- **site value rating** (i.e. rating the value of the land only);
- **flat rating** (i.e. rating the value of improvements);
- **composite** (differential) **rating** (i.e. rating both land and improvements, but at different tax rates).

In four provinces the majority of municipalities use the site value rating system. In four other provinces many councils use flat rating, while KwaZulu-Natal opted for composite rating (Franzsen, 1997).

12.3.2 Tax rates

Property tax is usually levied as a percentage of the taxable assessed value of the property. The assessed value for tax purposes is often less than the market value of the property. Because of this difference between the assessed value and the market value, the nominal tax rate differs from the effective rate (the latter being the tax liability expressed as a percentage of the estimated market value). Tax rates generally differ between jurisdictions because of the selectivity of the property tax. Since the property tax is considered burdensome to certain categories of taxpayers (e.g. elderly homeowners), these taxpayers usually receive some kind of tax relief.

Flat (uniform) rates are levied in South Africa but differ between provinces and between municipalities within provinces. The taxes are levied annually but are generally collected in monthly instalments. A maximum rate is prescribed in some provinces. Before 1994 a number of categories of properties were **exempted** from paying property tax (e.g. properties used for religious and educational purposes, hospitals and national theatres). Since 1994, however, almost all exemptions have been repealed and replaced by a system of **grants-in-aid**, which may not exceed the equivalent rateable amount. **Rebates** are granted for certain classes of properties (e.g. residential properties) and categories of ratepayers (e.g. the handicapped, pensioners and other ratepayers with annual incomes below a specified minimum).

12.3.3 Assessment

Probably the most controversial part of property taxation is the valuation of property. There are a number of different approaches to assessing the value of property, such as the capital value of land and improvements, the site value system and the rental value of premises and the comparable sales method (see Bahl, 1998). The **capital value system** attempts to determine the full market value of land and improvements (as a bundle) on a willing buyer and willing seller basis (i.e. the value they would agree to in an open market). In practice the capital value is determined by assessing land independent of improvements. Land is valued using data based on a judgmental approach. The expert opinions of professional appraisers and real estate agents are enlisted. Improvements are valued with the aid of schedules of value per square meter (based on building costs).

The **site value system** assesses the value of land only. The value of land can be based on sales of vacant land or estimated by a residual method (e.g. by determining the bundled value of the property and then deducting the value of improvements).

The British tradition is to assess the value of property on the basis of some estimate of the **rental value** of the property or the rental income derived from the asset. The sales value of a property tax and the rental value are supposed to yield equal results.[4] However, in developing countries, property is often under-utilised and an assessment based on the rental value would thus understate the value of the property. Idle land also generates no net income and rental value will therefore have to be imputed in such a case.

In South Africa property taxes (or rates) are levied only in urban areas and the practices have varied between different provinces. In a White Paper on Local Government (1998) national government indicated that a number of issues with regard to property tax had to be addressed. The issues identified included the uniform application of property rates in newly amalgamated urban municipalities, the assessment of properties at market value using various valuation systems, regular assessments of property values, and clear procedures regarding the full or partial relief to those who are genuinely too poor to pay for rates. In the Draft Local Government: Property Rates Bill (2000) provision is made for a rate based on the improved value of the property. The improved value of property may be composed of separate amounts on the site value of the property and the value of improvements. The Minister of Finance may set a limit on the amount of the rate that municipalities may levy or the percentage by which the rate may be increased annually. These measures should simplify property rating in South Africa and bring greater uniformity. The role of central government in rate setting ought also to ensure that government's macroeconomic objectives (eg a lower overall tax burden) are not jeopardised.

12.3.4 Equity effects

Benefit principle of taxation

According to the benefit principle of taxation, people should pay tax in relation to the benefits (or cost of expenditure) of public services received. At the level of local authorities this rule suggests that owners should pay for services which raise the value of their properties, such as pavements, tarred roads and street lighting. A property tax on site value can then be viewed as a **comprehensive benefit tax** and may be regarded as a fair tax from this perspective.

Although the link between benefits received and the tax paid is not always clear, empirical studies indicate that property taxes and the value of local public services are capitalised into housing prices (see Box 12.1 for the meaning of capitalisation).

> **Box 12.1**
> **The capitalisation of a property tax**
> The capitalisation principle can be illustrated by means of a simple example. Suppose that a piece of land in Cape

---

4 In theory the discounted stream of net rent payments is equivalent to the capital value of the property.

Town has an expected yield of R10 000 per annum and that the current interest rate (the opportunity cost of capital) is 20 per cent per annum. The capitalisation value is determined by answering the following question: what amount needs to be invested to earn this return? This amount can be determined by using the formula for capitalised value. The capitalised value (CV) is income from the property (R), divided by the interest rate (i): $CV=R/i$. Thus the capitalised value of the land will be R50 000 (=R10 000/0, 20).

Let a property tax of R1 000 now be levied. This would be equivalent to a tax on the income from the land at a rate of 10 per cent (R1 000 as a percentage of R10 000 = 10 per cent). The capitalised value of the land changes to

$$CV = \frac{(1-t)\,R}{i}$$

where t is the tax rate (equal 10%)
or

$$CV = \frac{(1-0,10)10\,000}{(0,20)} = R45\,000$$

The value of the Cape Town property has been reduced by R5 000. When the owner wants to sell the property he or she will have to absorb the loss since the new buyer will want to obtain a net return (after the R1 000 property tax) of 20 per cent on the investment (= R9 000).

The implication is that we can expect property taxes to depress property values but that this effect will be countered by the positive effect of public services financed by these taxes.[5] Property taxes based on land values have so far not been considered as benefit taxes (or user charges) because benefit taxes are usually linked to specific services (e.g. access to a public park or bus fees for public transport). Furthermore, there are taxpayers who are eligible for but do not use these services. Take the example of a childless couple. Although an activity centre in a public park may affect the value of their property, they derive no further benefit from it. Taxing them at the same (uniform) rate as other property owners would be unfair. Thus, only if the revenue from property tax is spent on infrastructure and activities that genuinely benefit property owners as a group (individually and collectively), can it be said that the property tax is a benefit tax.

Incidence of a property tax

By now we know that information on the statutory (or direct) burden of a tax is insufficient to arrive at conclusions on the fairness and distributional implications of that tax. We also need to identify the economic incidence of the tax. The incidence of property tax can be studied using partial equilibrium analysis and general equilibrium analysis.

Partial equilibrium analysis

When property tax is analysed within a partial equilibrium framework, it is regarded as an excise tax which falls on land and on the capital invested in improvements. We consider the incidence of each in turn.

Property tax on land. Since the quantity of land in a country is fixed, the supply of land is in effect perfectly inelastic. This means that landowners cannot increase the quantity of land if prices increase. All they can do is to change the use of land and, to a very limited extent, to reclaim parcels of land (e.g. swamp land). In Figure 12.1 the supply curve (S_0) is vertical and the demand curve is D_0. The equilibrium rental before tax is P_0 and the equilibrium quantity is Q_0. Suppose that an *ad valorem* property tax (t) is now introduced. The before-tax demand curve D_0 swivels downwards to D_1 which is the new effective (after-tax) demand curve (the

---

5 See Rosen (2002 : 492-493) for references to empirical studies which support this conclusion.

Figure 12.1 Incidence of an *ad valorem* property tax on land

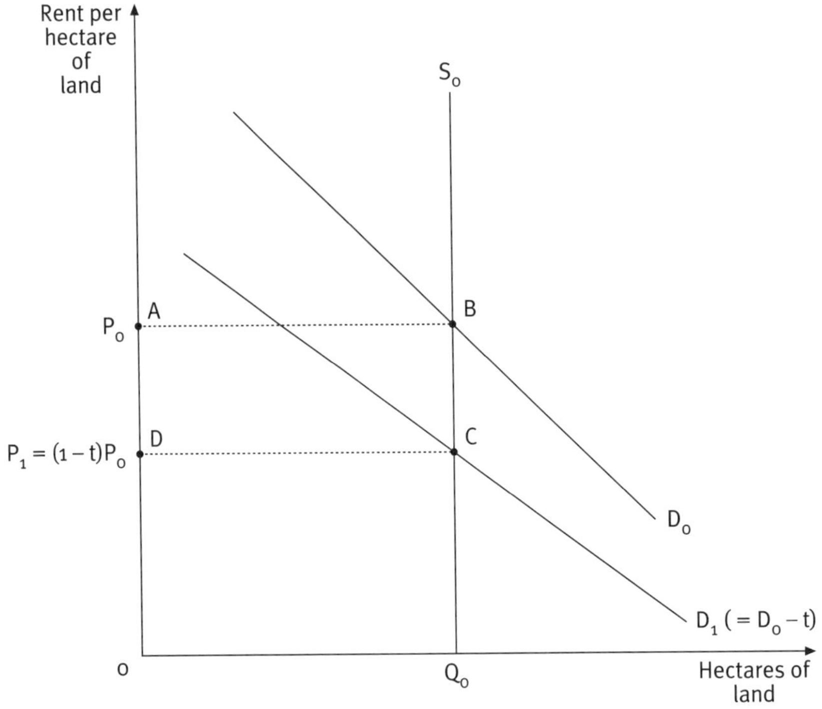

demand curve as perceived by landowners). The rent paid by the users of land remains unchanged at P_0. However, the rent received by the owners of land is reduced by the tax to P_1. The total tax revenue is equal to the area $ABCD$ and is borne entirely by the owners of land. Thus the incidence of a tax on land is on the landowner. Since income from land ownership increases as income increases, the tax falls relatively more on taxpayers with higher incomes. This makes a land tax progressive and from the ability-to-pay point of view the tax is therefore fair.

The lower rent on the land will cause the price of land to fall to account for the future tax burden – taxes are capitalised into the value of land (see Box 12.1). When subsequent buyers make property tax payments, these payments should not be seen as a burden in the true sense of the word, since the payments have already been capitalised into a lower purchase price. In other words, the incidence of the property tax is only on the initial owner of the land (i.e. the owner at the time when the tax was imposed). Should property taxes be increased, the increase would again be capitalised. The extra tax burden would fall on whoever owns the property at that time. The determination of the incidence thus becomes quite complicated since the identities of the owners at the time when the tax was imposed or increased must be known.

Property tax on improvements. In contrast to land, which is fixed in supply, the capital invested in improvements is elastic in the long run. The argument is that in the long run investors can find all the capital they require at the market price. When market rents are taxed, it is possible for property owners to shift the burden to the users of property (tenants and, indirectly, consumers and workers). This is illustrated in Figure 12.2. The supply of capital for improvements

Figure 12.2 Incidence of an *ad valorem* property tax on improvements

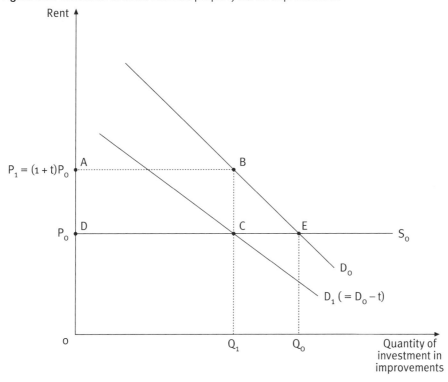

is the perfectly elastic curve S_0. The before-tax equilibrium is at Q_0 and P_0. If an *ad valorem* property tax is now levied on property, the effective (after-tax) demand curve becomes D_1. This is the demand curve as perceived by property owners. At the after-tax equilibrium property owners still receive P_0 but the users (e.g. tenants) have to pay P_1, which includes the property tax. Note that the after-tax equilibrium quantity of property supplied is lower. Property owners are thus able to shift the full **tax burden** (= *ABCD*) of a tax on improvements to **users**. The distributional implications depend on who the users are. If the users are lower- to middle-income tenants or owner-occupiers of residential property, the distribution tends to be **regressive**. The reason is that housing expenditures decrease with increases in income, that is, low-income taxpayers spend relatively more on housing than high-income taxpayers. If the users are tenants of commercial property, the higher after-tax rents will be reflected in higher prices for goods and services. Since consumption as a whole decreases as income increases, the regressive effect of a tax on the improvements part of property is again emphasised. However, since these effects disregard dynamic general equilibrium effects, the question of who bears the burden of the property tax is not fully resolved.

General equilibrium analysis
In a general equilibrium framework the full effect of the tax is traced throughout the economy. Viewed from this perspective, a property tax levied at different rates is equivalent to a selective tax on capital. In the **short run** the tax will be capitalised and the value of property lowered. Since land and the capital invested in improvements are immobile in the short run, the incidence of the tax is on the initial owners of the assets.

The burden is distributed **progressively** because property is not only heavily concentrated in the hands of the well to do (particularly in developing countries), but income from ownership of property tends to be an increasing proportion of income.

In the **long run** the capital invested in improvements is more mobile. Capital then migrates from high tax rate areas to low tax rate areas. The stock of capital is reduced in the high tax rate area (increasing the net return on capital in this area) while the stock of capital in the low tax rate area increases (thereby reducing the net return of capital in this area). This process continues until net (i.e. after-tax) rates of return are equal throughout the economy or region. Thus even though the tax was imposed on capital in one area, the burden is shared by capital owners in other tax jurisdictions. The process does not stop here. When capital moves out of one area in which labour is immobile (often the case of unskilled labour), the labour in that area must now be combined with the reduced stock of capital in production. The capital-labour ratio thus falls and this adversely affects the productivity of labour, with the result that real wages fall. Thus labour also bears part of the burden of the property tax, which adds a regressive element to the equity equation.

12.3.5 Efficiency effects

At the outset it should be noted that the property tax is a **selective tax** on wealth. Elements of selectivity include the following:

- Only immovable property is taxed.
- The tax base can include land or improvements.
- Tax bases and rates can differ between tax jurisdictions (e.g. between urban and rural areas and between different urban areas).

Selective taxes have non-neutral allocation effects. As discussed in Chapter 10, tax non-neutralities can have positive or negative influences on resource allocation. Some of the effects of selective property taxation are now discussed.

- The industrial and residential locational decisions of entrepreneurs and individuals are influenced by tax differentials. These differentials cause a reallocation of resources away from jurisdictions with high property tax rates to those with low property tax rates. This kind of regional competition based on tax differentials can promote efficiency if, for example, agglomeration benefits[6] are created. But it can also be very disruptive in areas where labour is not very mobile. A lower capital-labour ratio could depress already low wages even further or could result in unemployment.

- High property tax rates on improvements may discourage investment in the taxed property and lead to speculative purchases of low-taxed unimproved land. Large pockets of unimproved land in developed urban areas are inefficient since infrastructure (e.g. roads, telephone lines) has to be provided for the greater area.

- High property tax rates on land may encourage more efficient use of land. A tax on land, for example, could serve as an incentive to develop the land to its most profitable use. Badly managed land or idle land which is taxed, may generate no net (after-tax) income. The owner will have to improve the productivity of the land or sell the land to someone able to do so. Otherwise the owner may go bankrupt.

- Property taxes on improvements may have perverse effects. In 1696 a window tax was introduced in England, based on the number of windows in a home. Each household paid a basic two shillings and those with between 10 and 20 windows a

---

6 As firms concentrate (or agglomerate) in an area, benefits such as better access to a larger market and larger pools of managerial talent result.

further eight shillings. The tax proved to be very unpopular and many householders simply bricked up their windows to avoid payment. In 1825 all houses with fewer than eight windows were exempted from the tax and the tax was finally abolished in 1851 (Richardson, 1986).

12.3.6 The unpopularity of property taxation

Property taxation is known to be particularly unpopular. Why? (See Rosen, 2002: 494-495; and Skinner, 1991.)

- Property taxation is a tax on unrealised capital income, which may cause **solvency and liquidity problems** for some taxpayers.
- The burden of the land part of a property tax is on the owner of the property at the time of taxation. Since land ownership is mostly concentrated in the hands of a few property owners and ownership is often coupled with political power, the tax is fiercely resisted.
- A land tax increases the **riskiness** of farming which is already subject to external risks and seasonal fluctuations in income.
- The **administration** of property taxes has shortcomings. Properties and the liable taxpayers must be accurately identified. The taxation of, for example, communal land is problematic. Each parcel of land must be valued, which is difficult and sometimes judgmental. Since valuation is not done regularly, there is often outrage when values are updated. Property taxes are generally viewed as regressive and unfair. In addition, property taxes are highly visible forms of taxation and relatively easy targets for political action.

12.4 Capital transfer taxes

Capital transfer taxes are taxes on inheritances, estates and gifts. Inheritance tax and estate duties are called death duties. The **estate duty** is donor based, in other words, it is imposed on the estate out of which the legacy has been made. The liability is determined on the basis of the size of the total estate. **Inheritance tax** is donee based (i.e. it is levied on the receiver of the legacy). The tax liability is determined by the size of the wealth transfer. **Donations (gift) tax** is levied on gifts. The reason for this tax is that estate duties can be avoided if such a tax does not exist. Individuals would simply transfer wealth before their deaths. The donations tax is levied on the donor. Usually certain exemptions are allowed.

12.4.1 Economic effects of capital transfer taxes

Equity issues

Capital transfer taxes are viewed as important tax instruments to reduce wealth inequalities, particularly vertical inequalities. Inheritances tend to perpetuate wealth inequalities and in this respect the inheritance tax has an advantage over estate duties – it targets the source of inequality. Inheritance tax is also fair to the extent that it is levied according to the donee's ability to pay. Taxing the donee may also serve as an incentive to the donor to spread his or her wealth in order to minimise the tax burden of donees.

To fully comprehend the impact of death duties on wealth distribution, it must be realised that the act of leaving inheritances in itself can reduce wealth inequalities. Take the example of the father leaving his worldly possessions to four low-income earning children with no accumulated wealth. Intergenerational inequality is reduced in this manner. By taxing each child on his or her inheritance, the promotion of inter-generational equality of wealth is thwarted.

Efficiency issues

Capital transfer taxes affect people's choice between current consumption and saving. If bequests (accumulated savings) are taxed, the individual must give up more current consumption (i.e. save more) to maintain a given estate size. This is the familiar income effect of a price change. But in addition to the income effect there is also a substitution effect. Capital transfer taxes increase the opportunity cost of accumulated wealth (i.e. savings) causing an increase in current consumption (i.e. lower saving). The final impact of capital transfer taxes therefore depends on the relative strengths of the two effects, making the outcome uncertain.

Administrative issues

Capital transfer taxes are probably easier to administer than an annual wealth tax – the estate is valued only once. By the same token estate duties are easier to administer than an inheritance tax. In the case of estate duties there is only one tax identity, whereas under an inheritance tax there could be a number. Possibly the gravest problem associated with death taxes is the ability of taxpayers to minimise tax liability through various forms of generation-skipping devices, such as trusts and interest-free loans. Not only does this erode the tax base but is also utilised mainly by wealthy individuals, thereby perpetuating wealth inequalities. Tax avoidance activities are also unproductive (no new wealth is created). Other problems with death taxes relate to the hardships they may cause surviving spouses and children. Special provision has to be made for these categories of donees, which often complicates tax administration. Many forms of wealth (e.g. jewellery) are easy to hide and lend themselves to evasion under death duties. Transfers made in kind are also difficult to tax under a donations tax. It is no coincidence, therefore, that capital transfer taxes in the form of death and gift taxes are an insignificant source of revenue in developing countries (comprising less than one per cent of total tax revenue).

12.4.2 Capital transfer taxation in South Africa

Capital transfer taxation in South Africa includes taxes on estates and gifts. A flat rate of 20 per cent is applied in both cases. There is relief on a sliding scale where the same asset is taxable by reason of a second death occurring within 10 years of a preceding death. A rebate of R30 000 is applicable to donations and a R1 500 000 rebate in respect of an estate. The assets bequeathed to the surviving spouse of the deceased are not subject to estate duty.

Estate duty is not only decreasing in importance but is also an insignificant source of total tax revenue. From 1984/85 to 2001/02 estate duty as a percentage of total tax revenue declined from 0,42 per cent to 0,18 per cent. In 2001/02 approximately R440,0 million was raised in donations tax and estate duty.

Both the Margo Commission (1987) and Katz Commission investigated transfer taxes. In its Fourth Interim Report, the Katz Commission (1997a) confirmed the viewpoint that a donations tax and a system of estate duty should be retained rather than be replaced by an inheritance tax. It is argued that

- an inheritance tax is more complicated;
- the estate duty has been in place over many years and is well documented;
- estate duty has been the subject matter of numerous judicial decisions;
- the administrative systems are geared to an estate duty.

The Katz Commission (1997a) recognised that the transfer tax system has deficiencies. It recommended that there should be provisions to deal with generation-skipping trusts which would tax capital transfers in a trust. It was suggested that net assets of a trust be valued at intervals of 25 to 30 years (more or less reflecting a single generation).

Important concepts

capital value system
capital transfer tax
capitalised value
composite rating
donations (*gift*) tax
estate duty
flat rating
impersonal (*in rem*) tax
inheritance tax
net wealth tax
personal property
real property
site value rating
site value system
wealth

Self-assessment exercises

12.1 Distinguish between innate wealth tax, property tax and capital transfer tax.

12.2 "Wealth taxes tend to generate limited revenues for government and should therefore be eliminated." Discuss this statement.

12.3 "Municipal rates boycotts in South Africa confirm the notion that a property tax is a benefit tax." Discuss.

12.4 "Property taxes on land are not only efficient but are also equitable." Do you agree? Discuss.

12.5 Who really pays the property tax on improvements? Explain, using partial and general equilibrium analysis.

12.6 Discuss the possibility that high property rates in Sandton can be shifted to other forms of capital and even to low-income earners in Soweto.

12.7 A factory located in Epping, an industrial area near Cape Town, is valued at R1,2 million. The opportunity cost of capital (or current interest rate) is 14 per cent. Because of the high incidence of crime, the Cape Town Metropolitan Council introduces a once-off "protection levy" of R1 200 payable by all local property owners. Assuming full capitalisation, what will the impact be on the value of the property in Epping?

12.8 Discuss the economic effects of capital transfer taxes in South Africa.

Chapter thirteen

Tjaart Steenekamp

Taxes on goods and services

In Chapter 9 we identified three major tax bases: income, wealth and consumption. So far we have studied taxes on income (Chapter 11) and wealth (Chapter 12). In this chapter we examine taxes on goods and services (i.e. the consumption base). When we introduced tax equity and efficiency in Chapters 9 and 10, we explained most of these concepts using excise taxes as examples. Excise duties have thus largely been dealt with.

In this chapter we first identify the types of indirect taxes in Section 13.1. The debate on the relative importance of indirect taxes versus direct taxes is an ongoing one. In Section 13.2 the advantages and disadvantages of indirect taxes are discussed. Value-added taxes have increased in importance worldwide. This type of indirect tax is described and its economic effects are analysed in Section 13.3. In Section 13.4 we conclude with a discussion of the personal consumption tax, which has so far only received theoretical attention by tax analysts.

Once you have studied this chapter, you should be able to
- distinguish between different indirect taxes and indicate their relative importance as sources of revenue;
- discuss the merits of indirect taxation;
- describe the consumption type VAT applicable in South Africa;
- explain the economic effects of VAT;
- describe the personal consumption tax base;
- discuss the rationale for a personal consumption tax;
- discuss the shortcomings of a personal consumption tax.

13.1 Types of indirect taxes

Indirect taxes are taxes that are imposed on commodities or market transactions (see Section 9.2.4). The burden of an indirect tax is likely to be **shifted**. Consider, for example, an excise tax on locally produced washing machines. Although the statutory burden is on the supplier, the consumer usually indirectly bears the burden. Indirect taxes can be imposed at different **stages** of the production process: the resource (mining or farming) stage, the manufacturing stage, the wholesale stage or the retail stage. If collected at only one stage it is called a **single-stage commodity tax**. If collected at more than one stage it is called a **multi-stage commodity tax**. VAT is an example of such a multi-stage tax.

We distinguish between **selective** (narrow-based) taxes (e.g. specific excise duties) and **general** (broad-based) indirect taxes (e.g. turnover tax, general sales tax, value-added tax) (see Section 9.2.2). **Excise duties** are selective taxes levied on certain goods or transactions.

Table 13.1 Main domestic taxes on goods and services

Source of revenue	Rate of duty (2002/03)	R'ooo (% of total domestic tax on goods and services) (revised estimates for 2001/02)
1 Value-added tax (VAT	14%	58 600 000 (70,0%)
2 Excise duties		25 349 000 (30,0%)
2.1 Specific excises		9 561 000 (11,3%)
Beer	R25,63/litre of absolute alcohol or 13% of VAT inclusive price of R3,33 per 340 ml can	2 751 000 (3,3%)
Cigarettes and cigarette tobacco	350,8c/20 cigarettes or 35% of VAT inclusive price of R10,00 per packet of 20	3 900 000 (4,6%)
2.2 Ad valorem duties		800 000 (1,0%)
Beauty make-up preparation	5%	
Computers, printers, modems	5%	
Cellular phones	7%	
Dishwashers (domestic)	7%	
Perfumes	7%	
Binoculars	7%	
2.3 Fuel levy	118,5c/litre or 30% of retail price of R4,00/litre (leaded)	14 988 000 (17,8%)
Domestic taxes of goods and services		84 342 491 (100%)

Source: Calculated from National Treasury (2002a)

Excise duties can be **specific** (unit) taxes or *ad valorem* (percentage of value) taxes (see Section 9.2.3). Excise taxes are collected on both domestically produced and imported goods. When levied on imported goods, they are generally known as customs duties or tariffs. The **personal consumption** tax (see Section 13.5) is also included under indirect taxes.

From Table 13.1 it is clear that VAT is by far the most important indirect tax source in South Africa (contributing more than two-thirds of the revenue from domestic taxes on goods and services), followed by the fuel levy (17,8%) which is an excise tax. Specific excise duties are levied mainly on alcoholic beverages and cigarettes (the so-called sin taxes), whereas *ad valorem* excise duties are levied on a number of luxury goods. Excises imposed to reduce consumption of certain goods are known as **sumptuary taxes**. Specific excise duties (11,3%) generate much more revenue than *ad valorem* duties (1,0%).

13.2 The merits of indirect taxes

Indirect taxes have a number of **advantages**. Indirect taxation is a practical way of raising **revenue** from those who have small incomes and those who are not captured by the income tax net. This advantage hinges on the proposition that all citizens should contribute to some extent to the upkeep of government (i.e. it is based on the benefit principle).

Taxes on goods and services are often **invisible**. Consumers hardly know that they are paying excise taxes, while the inclusion of VAT in prices is mostly noted only after the goods and services have been paid for. The advantage of fiscal illusion makes these taxes less susceptible to tax resistance.

The **tax liability** is largely determined by how much is purchased of the taxed good. In the case of consumption goods (excluding certain necessities), consumers sometimes have a choice between different goods and services (i.e. substitution possibilities exist). For example, if an excise tax is imposed on golf equipment (e.g. golf balls), individuals may decide to rather take up cycling (an untaxed leisure activity). Within certain limits taxpayers themselves can thus determine their tax liability. In respect of direct taxes (income and company tax) the liability cannot be avoided that easily and the substitution possibilities are also fewer (e.g. in the case of income tax, breadwinners have to earn an income). Government enforces the tax liability much more strongly in the case of income tax.

Consumption taxes can be used to achieve **multiple objectives**. Excise taxes can be used to correct market failures such as externalities. By levying a lower tax on unleaded petrol, environmental objectives are promoted. High sumptuary taxes on liquor and cigarettes are in part aimed at reducing alcohol abuse and smoking, and in so doing improving general health levels. It could be argued that best tax practice in developing countries may well be to levy the highest excises on luxury goods produced with capital-intensive technology and the lowest on necessities produced by labour-intensive means.

Taxes on goods and services are often levied on the value of the commodity, that is, on an *ad valorem* basis (e.g. *ad valorem* excises and VAT). Tax revenue from this source automatically increases, as the price of the commodity increases, and is therefore effectively **indexed for inflation**.

Indirect taxes are relatively **simple to administer**. Consumers also have limited scope for evading taxes on goods and services and compliance is accordingly easier to enforce.

Analysts have also pointed to a number of **disadvantages** of indirect taxes.

According to the ability-to-pay principle broad-based taxes on goods and services tend to be **regressive**. The reason is that consumption declines as a percentage of income as income increases. This conclusion has led to the exemption or zero-rating of certain basic consumption goods and services from indirect taxation, in particular where a broad-based VAT applies (see Section 13.4). Even excise taxes, which are generally levied on sumptuary goods, can be **regressive**. It has been calculated that in 1993 the poor in South Africa spent approximately 2,7 per cent of their income on cigarettes in comparison to the 1,8 per cent spent by rich people. Even if it is assumed that cigarette prices are the same for both income groups (the poor often pay higher prices since they buy cigarettes at inflated prices in rural areas or townships and in units, e.g. a single cigarette), the tax is regressive. The same conclusion applies to excise taxes on beer and "luxuries" such as skin care, hair and shaving preparations (see Steenekamp, 1994 and Katz Commission 1994: 124).

Indirect excise taxes are selective and lead to **inefficiencies**. For example, in developing countries the opportunity to purchase luxury goods may act as an incentive to work harder and save more, but if high rates of indirect taxation are levied this may result in a substitution effect in favour of leisure, thereby adversely affecting work effort (see Cnossen, 1990). In addition, high indirect tax rates may lead to smuggling and black market activities. To counter smuggling, the Swedish government lowered taxes on cigarettes and tobacco in 1998.

Since indirect taxes can be levied for various purposes there is often a **policy conflict** (too many goals and only one instrument). When we considered economic efficiency as one of the properties of a "good tax" in Chapter 10, we concluded that to minimise the excess burden, commodity taxes should be high on goods and services with an inelastic demand and low on goods and services with high demand and supply elasticities. This tax rule is referred to as the inverse elasticity rule. In practice, excise taxes are imposed on luxuries for equity reasons. The demand for luxury goods, however, tends to be both price and income elastic. Taxes on these commodities will therefore decrease the quantity demanded significantly. Application of the inverse elasticity rule means that, from an efficiency point of view, such goods should bear low tax rates, which is contradictory to the equity requirement. There is thus a policy conflict that requires a trade-off between equity and efficiency objectives.

Indirect taxes may have an **inflationary effect** if wages are raised in response to tax increases. Some multistage commodity taxes also have a cascading effect on prices. If the tax at each stage of production is based on the gross price up to that stage, including tax levied at earlier stages, tax is in effect levied on tax. This may encourage vertical integration of production processes and thereby reduce the degree of competition in the markets concerned.

13.3 Value-added tax

Value-added tax is a multistage sales tax levied on the **value added** at the different stages of production. Roughly speaking, value added is the difference between sales and purchases of intermediate goods and services over a certain period (normally a month). If a retailer purchased goods to the value of R150 000 from suppliers in a month and had sales worth R300 000 in that month, the value added by the retailer would be R150 000 – to which the tax will be applied. The value added consists of wages, rent, interest, depreciation and profit. The calculation of value-added tax is illustrated in Box 13.1.

VAT comes in many **forms**. A tax authority wishing to introduce VAT therefore faces a number of choices. We now discuss these choices and the South African practice in respect of each.[1]

There are three broad types of VAT: a consumption type VAT, an income type VAT and a VAT on gross product. When South Africa introduced VAT in 1991, the universal practice of a **consumption type** VAT was chosen. In a closed economy $GNP = C + I = W + P + D$ where GNP is gross national product, C is consumption, I is gross investment, W is wages, P is net profit after depreciation, and D is depreciation. The consumption VAT base is then $C = W + P + D - I$.

The regime for international trade can be based on the origin principle (exports taxable, imports zero-rated) or the destination principle (exports zero-rated, imports taxable). Again South Africa decided to follow the popular route of applying the **destination principle**. This is perceived to be a fair practice (domestic and imported goods are treated the same) and one which does not affect the competitiveness of exports.

Tax liability can be computed using three methods: subtraction, tax credit (or "invoice")

---

1 For a comprehensive discussion of VAT see Gillis, Shoup & Sicat (eds) (1990: Chapters 1 and 19); and Katz Commission (1994: Chapter 9).

Box 13.1
Value-added tax: an illustrative example

Consider the transactions of three firms for the month of September. Agent A is an importer of bicycle components who, for argument's sake, is assumed to add no further value to the value of imports. Firm B is an assembler of bicycles and firm C is a bicycle shop. Agent A imports bicycle components to the amount of R100 000, sells them for R100 000 to firm B who, after assembling the bicycles, sells them for R150 000 to firm C. Firm C sells the bicycles for R300 000 to the cycling public (consumers). The tax trail would be as follows:

Production stage	Goods, wages, profit etc.	VAT (14%)	Total on invoice
Agent A: Imports (value added is found in wages, rents, interest, profit, etc. in country of origin)	100 000	14 000	114 000
VAT payable		14 000	
Firm B: Purchases of inputs from Agent A	100 000	(14 000)	114 000
Value added (wages, rents, interest, profit, etc.)	50 000		
Selling price	150 000	21 000	171 000
VAT payable		7 000	
Firm C: Purchases of inputs from Firm B	150 000	(21 000)	171 000
Value added (wages, rents, interest, profit, etc.)	150 000		
Selling price	300 000	42 000	342 000
VAT payable		21 000	

VAT is collected at different stages of the production process and at the end of the distribution channel the tax is passed on to the consumer. Thus the incidence (the burden) of the tax is on consumers, but the sellers make the tax payments to the SARS. VAT is collected by the seller at the point of sale (this is referred to as the **output tax**). The seller may now deduct taxes paid on intermediate products (this is referred to as the **input tax**). For example, firm B purchases components from agent A. Included in the price is input tax of R14 000 (this amount is collected by Agent A and paid over to the SARS). Firm B may deduct the input tax from the VAT of R21 000 (the output tax) payable on his or her selling price. At the end of the month the total tax liability of firm B is R7 000 (or R21 000 minus R14 000 on inputs). Firm C's tax liability is R21 000 (R42 000 on the selling price less input tax of R21 000). The total VAT collected is R42 000 (R14 000 from agent A; R7 000 from firm B; R21 000 from firm C). Note that the same result can be obtained by levying 14 per cent VAT on the value added at each stage of the production process (remember to include the value added included in imports).

or addition. The **tax credit** (invoice) method is generally used, also in South Africa. This is the type of VAT illustrated in Box 13.1.

Two techniques can be used to free goods and sectors from VAT: outright **exemption** (the firm need not file a VAT return and does not, therefore, levy VAT, but it also cannot claim refunds for any VAT included in the price of purchased goods and services) and **zero-rating** (the firm files a return but pays zero tax on sales and gets a refund in respect of VAT payments made at earlier stages in the production and distribution chain). South Africa uses both techniques. Education and health services and the services of various non-governmental organisations are exempt. In addition to goods and services destined for export, a list of basic foodstuffs is zero-rated. This list includes brown bread, maize meal, samp, mealie rice, dried beans, lentils, pilchards, milk powder, dairy powder blend, rice, vegetables, fruit, vegetable oil, milk, cultured milk, brown wheat, eggs and edible legumes.

VAT can be levied at a single rate or **multiple rates** (rates in addition to the zero rate). South Africa has a **single-rate** VAT.

13.3.1 The economic effects of VAT

Revenue

Value-added tax (VAT) has a worldwide reputation of being a "money machine" and in developing countries this has indeed proved to be the case. In South Africa VAT was introduced in October 1991 at a rate of 10 per cent, but the rate was increased to 14 per cent in April 1993. The **revenue importance** of VAT cannot be contested. In 1992/93 collections amounted to R17,5 billion, or approximately 21,7 per cent of total net tax revenue. In 2001/02 the revised budgetary estimate amounted to R58,6 billion or 23,2 per cent of total net tax revenue.

Efficiency and the tax rate

In our discussion of the efficiency effects of general taxes in Chapter 10 we concluded

that taxes imposed on a broad base and at a **uniform rate** resemble lump-sum taxes and are efficient. In arriving at this conclusion we ignored equity considerations. Whether efficiency requires uniform rates is a much-debated issue. The theory of optimal taxation (see Section 10.1.3) provides convincing arguments on efficiency and equity grounds, which refute the notion of uniformity (see Newbery & Stern, 1987). The inverse elasticity rule is one of the examples of this line of thinking (see Section 10.2.2).

You will recall that the inverse elasticity rule states that the excess burden of selective taxes can be minimised by taxing price-inelastic goods and services at higher rates. Put more eloquently, the rule states that excess burden will be minimised if the proportional reduction in compensated demand that results when a set of selective taxes is imposed are the same for all goods. When we move away from the one-person assumption of the model and also include equity considerations, the rule calls for higher taxes on goods with low distributional characteristics and lower taxes on goods with high distributional characteristics (goods where the share of the poor in its total consumption is high). The important conclusion from optimal tax theory is that uniform taxation is not desirable. In other words, to minimise inefficiency, different tax rates should be applied to different commodities. A case for uniform rates can only be made under certain strict conditions. One condition is that governments should make optimal lump-sum transfers to households. In other words, when taxes are designed one has to consider what government does with the tax revenue.

Using optimal tax theory in formulating policy is, however, severely restricted by data limitations. For example, to design separate rates for each commodity requires information on elasticities and patterns of complements and substitutes that are difficult to come by. It is also doubtful whether the efficiency gain from designing a great variety of tax rates would outstrip the costs involved in administering such a system. One solution could be to lump together large categories of commodities and to subject them to uniform *ad valorem* taxes. Another option is to achieve the desired equity objectives with a combination of differentiated or uniform excises on luxuries and a uniform VAT rate. The lumping-together process is however still analytically and empirically problematic. In the end there appears to be some agreement that the loss of economic efficiency due to VAT is likely to be minimised when uniform rates or a few rates (three or four) are applied to the broadest possible base. Moreover, if a system of income and expenditure supports for the poor are in place (see Chapter 15), the case for uniformity in rates is strengthened.

Equity

There is no question that a broad-based (comprehensive) VAT with no exemptions or zero-rating, is **regressive**. To reduce the regressive impact of VAT, tax relief could be given to the poor, or transfer payments could be directed at them. **Tax relief** includes exemption from VAT and zero-rating. **Exemption** of a good or service from VAT means that the firm or supplier need not levy VAT on sales, but at the same time such a firm may not claim refunds of the VAT already collected at earlier stages of the production process. The buyer of the service thus pays VAT levied on all but the final stage in the production chain. **Zero-rating** of a good or service means that the firm charges a zero rate of tax on sales of the commodity and is also allowed to deduct VAT collected at earlier stages. The buyer of a zero-rated product does not pay any VAT. None of the stages of production is thus subject to VAT.

A major shortcoming of zero-rating is that the tax **base is eroded**, perhaps necessitating a higher VAT rate, given the total revenue which the government requires. For example, the estimated revenue loss due to zero-rating

in South Africa in 1994/95 was R2 600 million. It was calculated that by abolishing zero rating on foodstuffs the standard rate could have been reduced by about 1,25 percentage point without affecting the yield from VAT. Furthermore, since zero-rated goods and services are consumed by the rich as well, they also benefit from the zero rate and affluent households spend substantially more in absolute terms on zero-rated goods than less-affluent households. It is estimated that of the above-mentioned R2 600 million loss in VAT revenue, more than two-thirds of the benefit accrued to households in the top half of the income distribution (Katz Commission 1994: 113). Zero-rating may also lead to over-taxation of suppliers who cannot credit VAT collected at earlier stages. In South Africa this is of particular concern to unregistered vendors who operate in the informal sector.

Another method of reducing the regressivity of VAT is to levy multiple rates (e.g. higher rates on luxuries). This is similar to the earlier mentioned option of combining uniform VAT rates with differentiated excises on luxuries. This option, however, is subject to various administrative and efficiency complications.

In its first Interim Report the Katz Commission (1994: 133) recommended that the further erosion of the VAT base through zero rating or exemptions should not be considered and that targeted poverty relief and development programmes should receive priority. In addition, the Katz Commission (1994: 133) recommended against higher VAT rates on luxury goods or a multiple VAT rate system. The Commission argued that such a system would not make much of a contribution to reducing regressivity, would have high administration and compliance costs and would not have much additional revenue potential. Government accepted these recommendations.

Administration

The credit-type VAT system has the reputation that it is **effective against tax evasion**. The anti-evasion features are its self-policing attributes, the possibilities for the crosschecking of invoices and the fact that a large portion of tax revenue is collected before the retail stage. The **self-policing** feature shows itself in the lack of incentives for sellers and buyers to collude to make underpayments of VAT. Sellers would prefer to understate the output tax but all buyers who are not final consumers would like to overstate the input tax since they can reclaim it. Therefore, if the seller does not pay the full VAT, it increases the VAT liability of the buyer who will certainly complain about it. Since VAT requires the maintenance of records of both purchases and sales, the revenue authorities have a basis for **cross-checking** returns. The benefit from **collecting** VAT at the **different stages** of the production process can be seen from our example in Box 13.1. If the retailer (firm C) is not a registered VAT vendor and therefore does not charge VAT on sales or claim an input tax credit, SARS will still collect R21 000 from firms A and B.

Opportunities for fake claims increase when goods are zero-rated, exempt or taxed at different rates. A retailer can, for example, understate output tax by understating sales of higher-rated goods. Multiple rates not only open up avenues for tax evasion but also complicate administration for the tax authorities and taxpayers alike.

13.4 Personal consumption tax

In Section 13.3.1 we saw that one of the disadvantages of a VAT is its regressivity. An alternative tax on consumption that can address this shortcoming is the **personal consumption tax** (also known as the expenditure tax). The base of the personal consumption tax is **income** less **net saving** (saving minus dissaving). This tax is collected directly from the consumer, like the personal income tax, and can be made progressive by applying a rate schedule and allowing for exemptions on certain consumption items (e.g. medical expenditures). Although it looks simple enough, it is more complicated to determine than income tax or VAT. Nonetheless, there is a large body of support among economists for such a tax.

13.4.1 The rationale for a personal consumption tax

The proponents of a consumption tax argue that it is more **equitable** to tax what an individual takes out of the economic system (as reflected in consumption) than what an individual contributes to society (as measured by income). From this perspective it would be considered fair that a millionaire who lives like a miser ends up with a low current tax liability. This conflicts with the ability-to-pay principle, which views potential consumption (the power to consume) as the yardstick. The counter-argument is that the millionaire is simply postponing the tax until he or she consumes the funds accumulated. The tax liability of the individual must thus be viewed over a longer period, that is, a lifetime equity perspective is required.

It is further argued that a personal consumption tax is more **efficient** than an income tax. This conclusion rests on two assumptions: (1) that income tax affects saving; and (2) that the supply of labour is fixed. A tax on saving (e.g. an income tax) distorts the choice between present and future consumption. An income tax therefore causes an excess burden. In contrast, a tax on consumption does not create an excess burden since saving is not taxed. If the supply of labour (or work effort) is not affected by a tax on personal consumption, it has no excess burden. If, however, a tax on consumption induces a consumer to work less (i.e. enjoy more leisure time), it entails an excess burden. Nevertheless, there is some empirical evidence that a consumption tax is on balance more efficient than an income tax.

If consumption is taxed (leisure is too difficult to tax anyhow), the price of consumption goods increases relative to leisure. It means that one hour of leisure (or labour sacrificed) is now equivalent to less consumption than before, that is, the opportunity cost (or relative price) of leisure has decreased. Put differently, a tax on consumption decreases the return to work effort. Leisure hours will increase and work effort decreases. Thus, a tax on consumption does cause an excess burden. Since the consumption tax base is smaller than the income tax base, to yield the same tax revenue, the tax rate on consumption would have to be higher. Because the excess burden of a tax increases with the square of the tax rate, the excess burden of the consumption tax is higher than the equal-yield income tax. This efficiency loss must be subtracted from the efficiency gain derived from not taxing savings. The net effect must then be compared to the excess burden caused by an income tax. Whether the excess burden of a personal consumption tax is less than that of an income tax, ultimately depends on empirical evidence. Some studies show that a consumption tax creates a smaller excess burden than an income tax and this has advanced the case of the proponents of the personal consumption tax (see Rosen, 2002: 452).

It is also argued that a consumption tax would be beneficial to developing countries. These countries have a critical shortage of saving. Since the personal consumption tax is neutral in respect of the choice between present and future consumption (saving), consumption would be a good tax base. Furthermore, consumption (like income) tends to be distributed highly unequally in these countries. A progressive expenditure tax could tap this base effectively and equitably.

The personal consumption tax is usually considered too complex to **administer**. It is argued, for example, that to arrive at the taxpayer's annual consumption, a list of expenditures would have to be made and then added up. This, together with the required

record keeping, would be a mammoth task. Proponents argue, however, that these problems can be overcome by observing the individual's cash flow in qualified bank accounts. In addition, certain problems normally associated with income tax, such as valuing unrealised capital gains and depreciation, are also avoided when consumption is taxed. Under a consumption tax, capital gains are taxed when they are realised. Capital purchases are immediately expensed (written-off when purchased), thus making allowances for depreciation unnecessary.

13.4.2 The disadvantages of a consumption tax

The personal consumption tax has not been successfully implemented anywhere in the world. India and Sri Lanka experimented with such a tax but abandoned it. The problem areas in designing a personal consumption tax are administration, treatment of bequests and gifts, and the problems of transition.

Critics are concerned about the risks of implementing such a tax because we know too little about the practical **administration** problems to be encountered. In contrast, the problems with the current income tax system are known and can be addressed. Furthermore, proponents of a consumption tax tend to compare an ideal consumption tax to the current income tax with all its impurities introduced over years. This is not really a fair comparison since there is no guarantee that a personal consumption tax will not follow the same route and become progressively more impure and complicated.

A personal consumption tax creates a host of specific administration problems. For example, under an income tax system taxes are withheld at source for administrative and compliance purposes (e.g. the PAYE and SITE systems mentioned in Chapter 11). This would be difficult under a consumption tax. How would an employer estimate the consumption and saving of each employee? A presumptive consumption-to-income ratio may have to be applied. As mentioned earlier, extensive record keeping would also be required in respect of bank balances, expenditures and assets.

It will be necessary (and difficult) to **distinguish** between consumption **and** investment. Consider expenditures such as housing and education. The purchase of a house, for example, should be regarded as investment and subtracted from consumption to determine the tax base. Owner-occupied housing, however, generates a service, which should be classified as consumption. An imputed rent value would have to be determined for this purpose. An alternative would be to exclude housing altogether from the tax base, but this would erode the tax base. Education also has both an investment and a consumption component. Another source of base erosion is the consumption of goods and services in kind. The consumption tax system is not necessarily superior to the income tax system in detecting such consumption. Under the cash flow system consumption is calculated as a residual (income minus saving). Thus the definitional problems related to income all still apply and are compounded by problems relating to the definition of saving. Would it therefore not be simpler to use an income tax system where only income needs to be determined?

Another major problem is the treatment of **bequests and gifts**. Should bequests and gifts be considered as consumption by the donor or as income of the donee (i.e. the recipient of the donation)? According to one view a gift (e.g. cash) by a parent to a child is no different to any other form of expenditure and should be treated as consumption. From another angle it is argued that consumption only occurs when the child spends the cash. Exempting bequests and gifts would solve the administrative problems but could lead to large concentrations of wealth. Some form of wealth taxation, however, could address the

latter. Introducing a personal consumption tax will cause **transition problems**. One dilemma is the treatment of savings once the new system comes into effect. Under the income tax system, saving comes from after-tax income. If an existing asset is now realised or previous saving is spent on consumption goods, the same base will be taxed again under a consumption tax, which appears to be unfair.

Important concepts

customs duties

excise duties

input tax

multi-stage commodity tax

multiple rates

output tax

personal consumption tax

single-stage commodity tax

sumptuary taxes

uniform rate

value added tax

zero-rating

Self-assessment exercises

13.1 Distinguish between the following indirect taxes:
   (a) single-stage and multi-stage sales taxes
   (b) excise tax and customs duty
   (c) VAT and personal consumption tax

13.2 Explain why the government should levy indirect taxes.

13.3 "Indirect taxes are not transparent enough and inhibit informed choices by taxpayers. The direct tax base should therefore be the major basis of government tax revenue." Discuss this statement.

13.4 What are the characteristics of value-added tax in South Africa? Why is it said that VAT is inequitable and what can be done to correct the inequity?

13.5 In designing VAT and other indirect taxes there is always a conflict between equity and efficiency. Do you agree? Explain your answer.

13.6 A uniform VAT rate is preferable to multiple rates. Discuss.

13.7 Personal consumption is a better tax base than income. Discuss.

13.8 Do you think a personal consumption tax has not yet been successfully introduced elsewhere in the world?

Chapter fourteen

Jack Heyns

The benefit principle of taxation, user charges and tax earmarking

This chapter focuses on three related issues which have received considerable attention in the scholarly literature and are of practical significance for tax policy and the public budgets in South Africa. These issues are the benefit principle of taxation as well as so-called user charges and tax earmarking or dedication. Both user charges and tax earmarking represent specific attempts to apply the benefit principle of taxation in the public finances.

We begin this chapter by revisiting the benefit principle of taxation introduced in Chapter 9. This principle is central to an understanding of the issues of user charging and tax earmarking. For purposes of coherence some repetition in Section 14.1 is therefore considered functional. In Section 14.2 the benefit principle is applied to the case of user charges. This is followed by a section on taxes in lieu of charges (e.g. fuel levies) (Section 14.3). When taxes are assigned to special funds we refer to these as earmarked taxes and this topic is discussed in Section 14.4. In the final section to this chapter (Section 14.5) we focus on the practice of user charging and tax earmarking in South Africa.

Once you have studied this chapter, you should be able to
- define the "benefit principle" of taxation;

- contrast the benefit principle with the ability-to-pay principle;
- argue the merits and shortcomings of dividing tax shares in accordance with the benefit principle;
- define a user charge/fee;
- identify the principles of user charging;
- define tax earmarking;
- identify various forms of tax earmarking;
- argue the advantages and disadvantages of tax earmarking;
- assess the scope of benefit taxation, user charges and tax earmarking in South Africa.

14.1 The benefit principle of taxation

14.1.1 Equity rules revisited

A discussion of the benefit principle of taxation must necessarily begin with the concept of tax equity. As already mentioned in Chapter 9, equity is a basic criterion of a "good" tax structure. It was the first of four canons of taxation espoused by Adam Smith in 1776. Tax equity requires that each taxpayer should contribute his or her fair share of the cost of government services. There is no agreement in either theory or practice about how the concept of fairness or equity in taxation should be defined. In some ways equity is in the eyes of the beholder. However, there are several useful principles of tax equity that could serve as a guide for the design of tax policy. These principles were dealt with in Chapter 9 and are therefore merely summarised below as an introduction to a fuller discussion of the benefit approach.

The first set of equity principles is that of horizontal and vertical equity. **Horizontal equity** relates to the appropriate tax treatment of persons in similar circumstances. It is generally accepted that persons in like circumstances should be taxed alike. **Vertical equity** relates to the tax treatment of persons in unlike circumstances. A traditional statement in this regard is that if equals are taxed equally, persons who are not equals should be taxed differently.

The second set of principles relates to what the basis of taxation should be. Under the **benefit approach**[1] each taxpayer should contribute to the support of government in line with the benefits that he or she enjoys from public services. Taxpayers who enjoy the same amount of benefit from government services will pay the same amount of taxes, and those who enjoy greater benefits than others will pay more taxes.[2]

Under the **ability-to-pay approach**, individuals should contribute towards the cost of government in accordance with their respective abilities to pay, as measured by some indicator of ability to pay such as income, spending or wealth. Those who possess the same ability to pay would contribute the same amount, and those who have a greater ability to pay would contribute more to the cost of government. Both these approaches thus rest upon a value judgement about income distribution.

In practice, the concepts of horizontal and vertical equity are most commonly associated with ability to pay and progressive taxation, even though there is much controversy about the appropriate measure of ability to pay and the desirable degree of progression in the tax system. However, the rationale for or against progressive taxation may also be discussed in terms of benefit taxation.

14.1.2 Benefits received

Under the benefit principle of taxation, taxes are set in a way analogous to setting prices in a private market economy. In other words, taxes are regarded as the "prices" that individuals voluntarily pay for the goods and services they "buy" through their government. The benefit principle therefore represents an attempt to extend the principle of consumer sovereignty to the conduct of government.

The benefit principle of taxation is therefore firmly rooted in the public goods literature. In Chapter 3 we showed that if individuals were willing and able to reveal their respective preferences, they would derive different marginal benefits from a given supply of a public good, and thus be prepared to pay different prices for it. If the price of a public good is thought of as a tax, then the partial equilibrium analysis introduced in Chapter 3 assumes the use of benefit taxation for the financing of pure **public goods**. Since the benefit taxes would play the role of prices they will in principle ensure that resources are allocated efficiently.

An aspect of the benefit principle that appeals to the economist's mind is its emphasis on the essential two-sided nature of budgetary decisions in the public sector. The benefit criterion of taxation is therefore not one of tax policy alone, but of expenditure policy as well. That is to say, equity in taxation on the basis of benefits received requires that account be taken of the entire

---

1 For a review of the historical evolution of the benefit approach, see Musgrave (1959: 61- 89).
2 Benefits in this context refer to marginal benefits rather than total benefits. Benefit taxation thus conceived will leave the taxpayer with a tax surplus analogous to the consumer surplus encountered in price theory.

public budget inclusive of the expenditure structure. This comprehensive approach contrasts sharply with the ability-to-pay approach, under which the tax problem is viewed by itself, independent of expenditure determination.

It might also be mentioned in defence of the benefit approach that in a very general sense the benefit principle underlies the determination of tax and expenditure policy in a democratic process. After all, taxpayers as a group or some majority of taxpayers will not tolerate fiscal programmes – including a tax system based on ability to pay – which do not ultimately benefit them. Hence it is not uncommon for tax revolts to occur in particular circumstances when taxpayers perceive a tax to be unfair, that is, not related to expected benefits (witness the recent rates boycotts in some parts of South Africa). However, is the benefit principle practicable? Can it be applied as a guide to actual tax structure design?

14.1.3 Shortcomings of the benefit approach

The concept of benefit pricing of public goods as an analogue to the market mechanism suffers from at least two major shortcomings. Firstly, for the benefit principle to be operational, the benefits accruing to particular taxpayers should be known. However, it is very difficult if not impossible, to obtain such information in many cases since it depends on taxpayers' personal evaluations of benefits received. A problem with obtaining credible estimates of personal evaluations is the breakdown of the market mechanism in the case of public goods. As discussed in Chapter 3, public goods are goods in respect of which consumption is non-rival and **exclusion** is not possible. Examples of goods and services that possess both these qualities in a high degree are national defence, in a national geographical sense, and street lighting, in a local geographical sense. The problem is,

how does one, in the absence of a market mechanism, apportion the relative benefits that individuals derive from the government's provision of public or social goods such as national defence, the administration of justice, the provision of clean air, street lighting, and so on?

In the case of private goods such as hamburgers, sporting equipment or personal computers, this is done quite automatically when consumers reveal their preferences in the market by purchasing different quantities at given market prices. However, when consumption is non-rival and exclusion impossible, individuals will not be willing to reveal their preferences. This is after all why the link between producers and consumers is broken and the market system breaks down in the case of public goods. Because a public good can be obtained by the **free rider** at no cost, there is no incentive to pay his/her contribution voluntarily. If taxpayers know that tax shares will be based on personal evaluations, there will be a temptation on their part to understate the true value that they place on government services. In others words, the benefit principle of taxation suffers from the strategic behaviour of the free rider.

Even if exclusion is possible, in the case of **non-rival consumption** (e.g. an underutilised bridge), direct charging and exclusion should not be enforced as a method of determining preferences. The reason is that no marginal cost is incurred from admitting additional consumers, therefore no one should be excluded from consuming public goods on efficiency grounds. To do so would lead to an inefficient allocation of resources. This maxim will be particularly true in respect of goods of the pure public goods variety, such as national defence. However, to the extent that the consumption of publicly provided goods and services is rival (e.g. water, electricity, a crowded public swimming pool or library) the rationale for direct charging is stronger (see Sections 14.2

and 14.4). But for many categories of budgetary expenditure the assessment of individual benefits is essentially impossible and benefit pricing inappropriate on efficiency grounds.

A second major shortcoming of the benefit approach is that it restricts a government in the exercise of its redistributive function. An allocation of the cost of public services strictly in accordance with benefits received from the services will be distributionally neutral because the structure of benefits and tax prices will be a mere reflection of the prevailing distribution of income. For benefit taxation to be considered equitable it must therefore be assumed that a "proper" state of distribution exists to begin with. However, in view of the tendency of market systems to produce unacceptable income and wealth inequalities, as discussed in Chapter 5, redistribution via taxes and spending remains a major on-going obligation of government.

The benefit approach can ideally only handle a tax-expenditure process that has no redistributive objectives (i.e. where redistribution is not a significant justification for the service being provided). It cannot handle a tax-expenditure programme designed for redistributive purposes; for example, taxes levied to finance transfer payments or expenditure programmes designed to benefit the poor part of the community more than the rich part, or where it is administratively not feasible to exempt poor people from paying for the benefits of a particular service (e.g. a toll road). Indeed, benefit taxation implies that the recipients of redistributed income support or health care should pay for the cost of the programmes, or that poor or disadvantaged local or regional communities who are in receipt of grants from the central government should reimburse the government. In other words, a strict application of the concept of benefit taxation will rule out these kinds of programmes that have redistribution as their goal.

Of course, an absence of benefit taxation may create its own kind of inequities. For example, it may result in forced carrying. Whilst free riding refers to someone failing to carry a "proper" tax burden, **forced carrying** refers to someone being made to carry a heavier than "proper" burden. General-fund financing may have the latter effect, for example if a bridge is financed out of general revenues, those who do not use the bridge are made worse off. It may seem unfair to them that they should subsidise those who use the bridge.

14.1.4 Benefit taxation and the tax structure

What kind of tax structure would an application of the benefit principle of taxation produce? This question relates to an important issue around tax equity, which has occupied the minds of economists over the ages. Do the benefits of public services in some way vary systematically with income? More specifically, how do the different income classes benefit from government services? For example, do the rich or the poor benefit most from public protection? If the rich enjoy more benefit from protection because they have more to lose than the poor, they would need to pay a higher tax than the poor to finance protection services. However, if the poor receive more benefit because they are in greater need of protection, they would have to pay a higher tax than the rich. The question is essentially whether a **general benefit tax** (each person taxed in accordance with his/her own evaluation of the marginal benefit derived from government services or demand for public services) would give rise to regressive, proportional or progressive taxation. Musgrave and Musgrave (1989: 220-221) show that this depends on the price and income elasticities of the demand for public services. Since the magnitudes of these elasticities are not known, the outcome is inconclusive. But this type of analysis does highlight the point already made above that the case for or against progressive taxation may be discussed in terms of the benefit principle as well as the ability-to-pay principle.

14.1.5 Conclusion

In the light of the shortcomings of the benefit principle of taxation it has limited usefulness in respect of the financing of the provision of public goods and redistribution. However, the benefits to individuals of services provided by governments are more or less measurable and in such cases it is often possible to exclude those who do not pay. To many people it would seem reasonable that, if the beneficiaries are clearly identifiable and the benefits measurable, those who enjoy the benefits should pay the cost of such goods and services on equity grounds. Some economists argue that the joint consideration of tax and expenditure decisions also promote efficiency in public sector decision-making. Therefore, most tax systems do contain an element of the benefit principle, as indicated in the discussion below.

14.2 User charges

As noted by Musgrave and Musgrave (1989: 221), the concept of a **general benefit tax** is of interest mainly as a theoretical concept. However, practical applications of benefit taxation may be found in specific instances where particular services are provided on a benefit basis. Three sets of instances may be cited. Firstly, the benefit principle forms the basis of so-called user charges. Secondly, in some instances certain taxes may be applied in lieu of charges. Thirdly, the widespread practice of tax earmarking may be regarded as an indirect form of user charging when there is a benefit connection.

In many countries there is a growing interest by governments in user charges and earmarked taxes. For example, Anderson (1991) mentions that user fees are an important contributor to government revenue in the United States, and McCleary (1991) notes

the significant role played by the earmarking of taxes in many developing countries. The trend seems to represent a reaffirmation of the benefit principle as a guide to public finance. In principle it represents an attempt to expand the scope of the area over which contractual relationships rather than compulsion guide governmental conduct. A similar trend is observable in South Africa (see Katz Commission 1994: Chapter 17; Heyns, 1996; and Katz Commission, 1995: Chapter 3).

However, a cautionary note is in order. Whilst user charges and earmarked taxes are usually justified as a means of making those who use government services pay for the cost involved, there is no guarantee that this ideal will be achieved in practice. On the one hand, true **marginal cost pricing** of publicly provided goods and services is seldom achieved. Indeed, often the user charges imposed by governments bear little or no relation to the actual cost of providing the service. On the other, the instruments in question might be used simply as a means by which politically dominant groups of people place costs on others, that is, use the proceeds elsewhere. Instances may be cited where user charging and tax earmarking deviate from the benefit principle by acting as mere redistributive devices.

14.2.1 What is a user charge?

User charges, which are essentially a public sector phenomenon, are usually perceived to be voluntary payments in exchange for particular government services. User charges can take several forms: direct prices associated with the consumption of particular goods and services; fees for the use of certain facilities or services; general or special assessments on private property; and fares or tolls. In South Africa many sources of government revenue at the national and sub-national levels of government represent direct charging for specific goods and services. Examples of user charges are entrance fees to public parks, libraries, museums and swimming pools, tariffs for water, electricity, sewerage and refuse removal, fees and prices for postal services, compulsory school fees, fares for municipal transport, charges for the provision of airport facilities, road and bridge tolls, ambulance transport fares, rents on public housing, fees for the issuing of passports and driver's licenses, parking fees, hospital and health fees and charges. All of these, as well as the sale of government enterprises, represent an effort to place government more directly and immediately on a contractual footing with the people than might characterise general-fund financing. How does a user charge differ from a tax?

14.2.2 User charges and taxes compared

User charges may be contrasted with taxes, which are defined as compulsory payments to government without any direct *quid pro quo*. However, the distinction between taxes and charges on the basis of the degree of compulsion involved is not a categorical one. On the one hand, the amount of taxes that people pay is to some extent also voluntary. For example, individuals can change the amount of excise taxes (on the sale of specific commodities such as cigarettes, wine, motor tyres, etc.), or VAT (on consumption generally) which they pay by varying the amounts of these products or services that they purchase. Even the liability for personal income taxation can be affected by varying the amount of labour supplied. On the other hand, there is often little or no practical alternative to paying user charges for an essential commodity or service that is prescribed by law, such as an identity document, driver's licence or passport. Whilst the entrance fee to a public swimming pool may be avoided relatively easily by choosing alternative forms of leisure such as jogging or surfing in the sea, avoiding a fee for a driver's licence or passport is not a practical option for many people. It might thus well be easier to avoid paying excise taxes or income taxes than to avoid fees for driver's licences and, say, the issuing of a passport.

The distinction between user charges and taxes might thus seem rather to rest on the point that charges involve a direct connection between making a payment and receiving a service from the government while taxes do not. An entrance fee to a public swimming pool would be one illustration, as is a levy on wool sales imposed on sheep farmers to finance the marketing of wool, or a levy on the sale of fuel with the proceeds earmarked for the financing of the construction and maintenance of the national road network. In all such cases, those who pay the levies are the same people who receive the service financed by the revenues generated by the "charge". In sharp contrast to this, there is no direct connection between tax payments and government services received in return. That is to say, tax revenues (be they income tax, VAT or excise duties) mostly go into a general fund and appropriations to expenditure programmes are made according to a process which makes no effort to connect the two sides of the budgetary process.

It should be mentioned that this latter distinction between taxes and user charges expands considerably the potential domain of user charges. Some excise taxes may thus assume the character of user charges. For example, excise taxes on tobacco products or alcoholic beverages (the so-called "sin taxes") might be described as indirect user fees imposed on smokers and alcohol consumers, who are defined as "users" of government-subsidised health care services. Excise taxes on the sale of motor cars and trucks, which lead to more traffic accidents, might be described as charges to generate funds to cope with the effects of congestion and traffic accidents. Indeed, some economists argue that all excise taxes are essentially user charges. The problem is that if excise taxes are user charges, why not also other sales taxes such as VAT. For example, VAT on fast foods and restaurant meals, which are often unhealthy and therefore lead to more expensive public health care, might be described as user fees imposed on the consumers of expensive government health care. These links between tax payment and alleged benefits are too weak and opportunistic to meet the efficiency conditions of benefit taxation, however. Furthermore, it is worth bearing in mind that governments intent on raising additional revenue without increasing taxes are likely to exploit this vagueness of the distinction between taxes and user charges.

14.2.3 The case for user charging

The case for levying direct charges on the users of a service provided by government as an alternative to tax financing is most clear-cut where the goods or services are in the nature of **private goods**, that is, when there is **rivalry** in consumption of the goods or services. Benefits can then be allocated or imputed to particular users who can be asked to pay a price equal to marginal cost. That is to say, where benefits are internalised, the government may act in a capacity similar to that of a private firm by charging on the basis of marginal cost. (As already mentioned, when consumption is wholly non-rival, marginal cost pricing would not be appropriate.) Placing qualifying public services on this basis will achieve a more efficient determination of the appropriate level of supply because users of the good or service will be confronted directly with the cost of providing the good or service in question, thus forcing them to compare costs and benefits.

The most frequently cited example of a rationale for government to sell private goods is that of a natural monopoly. Recall from Chapter 4 that a **natural monopoly** occurs when the production of some good or

service is subject to continually decreasing average costs so that marginal cost lies below average cost over all relevant outputs. Under such circumstances it is unlikely that the market for the good or service will be competitive because a single firm can take advantage of economies of scale and supply the entire output. Examples of natural monopolies are freeways, electricity, water supply and sewerage systems. In some cases the government produces such commodities. In others they are produced by the private sector but regulated by government. A problem is that a natural monopoly which adopts a policy of marginal cost pricing will run losses, thus requiring government subsidisation from tax revenue. The alternative of average cost pricing will not require government subsidies but will generate a less than optimal combination of prices and output. Other solutions, for example, marginal cost pricing plus lump-sum taxes and two-part tariffs have been suggested (see Rosen 2002: 313-316).

User charges may also be applied to mixed goods and services, which generate both internal and external benefits (e.g. education, housing and health services). A system of user charges may be implemented to get the users to pay at least part of the cost of provision in accordance with the internal benefits enjoyed (see Chapter 3, Section 3.5 on mixed and merit goods). A system of compulsory school fees to cover a part of the cost of providing public education will fall in this category as we illustrate below.[3]

Figure 14.1 shows the marginal social cost and marginal social benefit of public schooling (measured in terms of the number of pupils attending school per year). The marginal social benefit has two components: marginal private benefit (MPB) from public education, which accrues to the individuals undergoing the education, and a marginal external benefit (MEB) which, accrues indi-

---

3 The discussion of Figure 14.1 and Figure 14.2 relies substantially on Hyman (1999: 393).

visibly to all in the community. The external benefits are the various intangible benefits that flow from having a more educated society, including a more enlightened and responsible attitude towards justice, democracy, public policy and education itself. These are public benefits enjoyed by all residents of the local community, province or country as a whole. For ease of exposition, the *MEB* is assumed to be a fixed amount irrespective of the number of users. The *MSB* curve is thus parallel to the *MPB* curve.

If education were to be financed privately, the entrance fee would be F_0 and N_0 number of students will attend school. This is below the socially efficient number of pupils attending school per year, N_e, corresponds to point E_e at which $MSC = MSB$. The efficient rate of attendance N_e could be attained by charging pupils a user fee of F_u per year. At that price, N_e pupils would attend school

every year. However, a user fee of F_0 per year falls short of the marginal social cost of providing schooling to N_e pupils every year. The difference must be made up by a subsidy to the education department of s rand per pupil. Taxpayers thus pay a subsidy of s rand per pupil per year, whilst the pupils who attend school pay school fees of F_u rand per year.

In the case of congestible public goods such as public roads, bridges, parks, swimming pools and parking space in central business districts, user charges such as tolls, entrance fees and parking fees may enhance efficiency and serve as a rationing device. Figure 14.2 illustrates the case of an entrance fee imposed to ration the use of municipal swimming pools over weekends. If a pool is subject to congestion on weekends, additional users after the point of congestion diminish the benefits that all pool users

Figure 14.1 User charges and efficiency

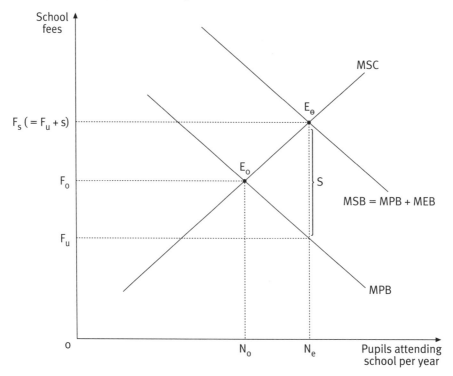

obtain. To attain the efficient level of usage of the pool, an entrance fee should be priced according to the marginal social cost imposed at any given level of usage. A zero entrance fee is desirable only when the level of patronage is below the point of congestion. In Figure 14.2 the MSC of accommodating additional users in the given pool becomes positive only after the point of congestion, which we assume to begin once the usage is 170 persons per hour.

In Figure 14.2 the demand curve (D_0) for pool usage is defined for usage up to 120 persons per hour. A zero user charge (entrance fee) would be efficient, because at a zero charge, equilibrium usage would be at E_0 where $MSC = MSB_0 = 0$. This follows because the MSC is zero at level of usage E_0 is 120 persons per hour, which is below the point of congestion at 170. If, however, the demand for the pool were to increase to D_1,

a zero entrance fee would no longer lead to efficiency. At a zero entrance fee, the equilibrium would be at point E_1, at which 250 persons per hour would be using the pool. Because the MSC (i.e. R3,80) at that level of patronage exceeds the MSB, which is zero ($MSC > MSB_1$), more than the efficient number of persons would be using the pool. The efficient level of usage corresponds to point E_e for which $MSB_2 = MSC$. This corresponds to 210 persons per hour. To attain that level of usage, the municipal authority would impose an entrance fee of R2,00 per person. Thus an entrance fee of R2,00 per person (per hour) would ration the pool's use. The positive charge of R2,00 will decrease usage to its efficient level while producing some revenue to the government.

By reducing the range of government services and its financing over which compulsion is practised, user charges also assist the

Figure 14.2 User charging as a rationing device

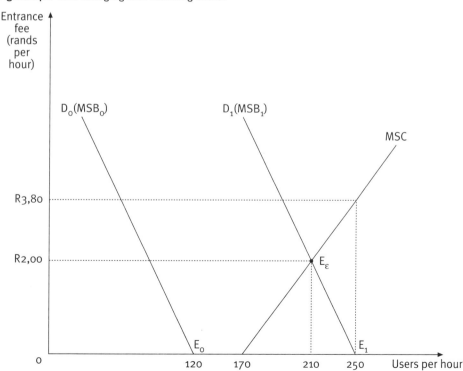

process of rolling back the frontiers of the public sector. Finally, user charging could ease the pressure on general revenue. Politicians often view user charges as a means to avoid reneging on promises to reduce taxes or not to increase them. Often people who might be opposed to raising taxes would support the imposition of user charges instead.

14.2.4 User charges and equity

As noted above, the benefit approach may be rationalised on equity grounds. However, a frequent criticism against user charges is that they may contradict the equity objective by preventing the poor from using government-supplied services. For example, it is argued that education and publicly supplied cultural and recreational facilities such as art galleries, museums and parks, often referred to as merit goods, should be made available free of charge to all people, so as not to prevent those who are unable to pay from enjoying these services. A problem with this approach is that the implicit subsidy that is involved when general financing is applied accrues to both the rich and the poor. If the services are heavily used by the rich, the subsidy to the rich may be substantial. To the extent that the poor contribute to general revenue, a part of the cost of the subsidy is borne by the poor. In certain circumstances general-fund financing could even redistribute income from the poor to the rich. This dilemma may be resolved by imposing a charge for the use of facilities but offering special reductions to targeted groups such as children, the elderly and so on.

14.3 Taxes in lieu of charges

Where the imposition of direct charges is desirable on efficiency grounds, but too costly or impracticable, a tax on a complementary product may be imposed in lieu of charges. Several South African examples of taxes **in lieu of charges** may be quoted.

Taxes on the sale of fuel (fuel levies) are imposed in lieu of direct charges in the form of tolls to help finance the construction and maintenance of national roads. It should be noted, however, that the collection of tolls on existing roads to finance the construction of new roads elsewhere would probably be largely redistributive and therefore violate the benefit principle. Social security taxes (employer and employee contributions to benefit funds), are another instance of taxes in lieu of direct charges to finance a public service, in this case the social security system, comprising the three social security funds in South Africa, that is, the Unemployment Insurance Fund, the Workmen's Compensation Fund and the Mines and Works Compensation Fund. Employee contributions to these funds and related benefit payouts represent an application of the benefit principle. This would also apply to employer contributions to the social security funds, provided these contributions are shifted to the employees who are the ultimate beneficiaries of the subsequent benefit payouts.

At the local and provincial level the revenue obtained from motor vehicle and truck licences are used in lieu of tolls to finance the construction and maintenance of roads in cities and towns. At the local authority level, property taxes (rates and taxes) have traditionally been viewed as a charge for the rendering of local services such as sewerage, refuse removal, cleansing, lighting, traffic control and so on.

Finally, as noted above, the various so-called "sin taxes" on the sale of tobacco products and alcoholic beverages, whether earmarked or not, may also be viewed as indirect charges for government services related to the adverse effects of smoking and the excessive consumption of alcohol.

The proceeds of user charges and taxes in lieu of charges are often earmarked for the purposes for which they are collected. Tax earmarking is discussed below.

14.4 Tax earmarking

14.4.1 What is tax earmarking?

Formally, tax earmarking may be defined as "the designation of funds – either from a single tax base or from a wider pool of revenues – to a particular end-use" (Teja, 1991). Tax earmarking may be contrasted with general-fund financing of expenditures from a common pool. Earmarking is frequently associated with the creation of special funds or segregated budgets. Tax earmarking is, therefore, often related in practice to the existence of a so-called off-budget or extra-budgetary sector. Expenditures from **extra-budgetary funds** and **accounts** are frequently financed by designated taxes or levies, which method of financing provides the rationale for the creation of the special funds and accounts in the first place. Döckel and Calitz (1988) treat extra-budgetary funds and accounts as virtually synonymous with tax earmarking, and show that in South Africa a considerable number of levies, fees and taxes in lieu of charges are dedicated to the financing of off-budget spending. In principle, tax earmarking is also related to so-called tax expenditures (Bracewell-Milnes, 1991) and the undistributed profits of government business enterprises (Bird, 1992).

14.4.2 Categories of earmarked taxes

Earmarked taxes may be classified in a variety of ways. Two forms of classification are mentioned here. Firstly, the concept of tax earmarking may be divided into (1) strong or substantive earmarking, and (2) formal, weak or nominal earmarking. Strong or substantive earmarking refers to cases where a specific source of revenue is dedicated to a specific type of expenditure, and the level of such expenditures is influenced or strictly determined by the proceeds of the taxes so designated. An example of this type of earmarking is the dedication of employee and employer contributions (from payroll taxes) to the financing of the aforementioned social security funds, which do not have significant other sources of revenue apart from interest on investments. In contrast, formal, weak or nominal earmarking refers to instances where the designated revenues go towards the financing of a specific service, but the level of expenditure is not necessarily linked to the revenue source, that is, expenditure on the designated activities may receive funds from other sources, perhaps from a general fund. A case in point is the proceeds of the sale of TV licences, which go towards the partial financing of public broadcasting.

Secondly, earmarking practices may be distinguished on the basis of whether or not there is any direct or indirect benefit connection between the earmarked tax and the activity financed by the tax. A distinction may, therefore, be drawn between earmarked taxes, which serve as a substitute for, or an approximation of, a user charge, and instances where there is no obvious connection between the tax base and the benefits financed from the proceeds of the tax. By imposing a tax on a good or service that is complementary in consumption with the service provided, and earmarking the revenue to financing the supply of that service, a type of quasi-pricing of the service results. An example of tax earmarking in this latter sense of the term would be the levying of an excise tax on the sale of a complementary product such as fuel in order to finance the construction and maintenance of a national roads network. As mentioned above, excise taxes on tobacco products and alcoholic beverages may be considered a quasi-user charge if there is presumed to be a positive correlation between a person's smoking and drinking habits and his/her demand for medical care from the state. A further example of a direct connection is the use of a part of the proceeds of the fuel levy for the financing of the Multilateral Motor Vehicle Accident Fund.

If, by contrast, a predetermined percentage of, say, VAT or personal income tax was to be earmarked for the financing of a national health scheme, there would be no obvious connection between the base of the tax and the benefits received. In that case the tax would violate the benefit principle because it would be purely redistributive, i.e. from those who pay the tax to those who benefit from the service. The rationale for this type of earmarking is weak.

14.4.3 An evaluation of tax earmarking

The advantages and disadvantages of tax earmarking have recently received considerable attention in the scholarly literature. Deran (1965) provides the following list of traditional public financial criticisms of earmarking, which are a combination of economic, political and administrative issues: tax earmarking hampers effective budgetary controls; leads to a misallocation of funds, giving excess revenues to some functions while others might be under-funded; imparts inflexibility to the revenue structure, making it difficult to make suitable adjustments when conditions change; tax earmarking provisions often remain in force long after the need for which they were established has disappeared; and by removing a portion of fiscal action from periodic review and control, tax earmarking infringes on the policy-making powers of state executives and legislatures.

However, many arguments have been presented in favour of tax earmarking. One is that it represents an approximation of the benefit principle in taxation, which may in principle be rationalised on both efficiency and equity grounds. Another argument is that earmarking is politically attractive in a developing country because it may serve as a means to expand government revenues. Taxpayers will be more willing to pay taxes if they know how their taxes will be spent. A third argument is that tax earmarking advances democracy by devolving economic power to the taxpayers, thus promoting transparency and accountability. A fourth is that it may protect the integrity and permanence of high-profile programmes, such as environmental protection, skills development, road maintenance and healthcare. On the whole, the case for or against tax earmarking cannot be established *a priori*.

14.5 User charges and tax earmarking in South Africa

As already mentioned, user charges and tax earmarking (this distinction is not always drawn in practice) have become popular with governments as means to enhance non-tax revenue. How prominent are they in South Africa? The financing of off-budget accounts by earmarked levies, fees and taxes has been mentioned. Recently a number of additional high-profile user charges have been proposed. One is the proposal to convert certain freeways in the Gauteng Province into toll-roads to finance the construction of new roads. Another is the Skills Development Levy introduced in 2000 at the rate of 1 per cent of payrolls to finance the acquisition of sectoral skills and a social plan to deal with the social and economic effects of job losses. A variety of other levies have been proposed, for example, a wheat levy. The proceeds of most of these levies will be earmarked for designated purposes.

However, quantitatively, user charges and earmarked taxes do not as yet constitute a major portion of government revenues at either national or sub-national level of government. The latter conclusion is borne out by data compiled by the Katz Commission (1995: 26-27). In 1993/94 user charges, fees and sales amounted to R6,33 billion. This latter sum represented less than 10 per cent of total tax and non-tax revenues of the general government in that year. Likewise, the earmarked taxes and levies identified equalled R6,4 billion or approximately 6 per cent of general government revenues. However, given the current orientation of the South African Government, the role of user charges, with or without earmarking, is likely to increase in importance in South Africa's public finances.

Important concepts

extra-budgetary funds and accounts

forced carrying

general benefit tax

marginal cost pricing

tax earmarking

taxes in lieu of charges

user charges

Self-assessment questions

14.1 Critically discuss the most important advantages and disadvantages of the benefit principle of taxation.

14.2 Distinguish between a user charge and a tax.

14.3 Argue the case for user charges.

14.4 List four advantages of user charges.

14.5 Define tax earmarking.

14.6 Distinguish between strong and weak tax earmarking.

14.7 Discuss the strengths and weaknesses of the practice of tax earmarking.

14.8 Briefly review the incidence of user charges and tax earmarking in South Africa.

PART FOUR

Fiscal and social policy

Chapter fifteen

Servaas van der Berg

Poverty, socioeconomic development and the distribution of income in South Africa: Fiscal and social policy issues

In Chapter 5 we explained why an efficient allocation of resources need not correspond with society's equity preferences. We also explored the various methods of social choice, pointing out the trade-offs between equity and efficiency.

The aim of this chapter is to analyse in more practical terms the role of government in addressing problems of inequity, with special reference to the South African experience. We first consider the distributional context in South Africa, which includes a brief overview of the nature of poverty and inequality in South Africa. Next we explain the role of public finance in redistribution, both in theory and with reference to international experience. This is followed by an historical perspective on fiscal redistribution and a discussion of changing patterns of fiscal incidence in South Africa. We conclude with an analysis of selected policy issues in which we concentrate on social security, welfare services and the subsidisation of housing.

Once you have studied this chapter, you should be able to:
- distinguish primary from secondary income distribution and understand the redistributive impact of the budget on the latter;

- explain the calculation of a Gini coefficient;
- identify the excess burden of a subsidy;
- show how a subsidy could be welfare-enhancing if there are positive externalities associated with consumption of certain goods (e.g. food for the poor);
- distinguish between the impact of a cash transfer and a subsidy in kind;
- show how social transfers may create a disincentive to work;
- identify major trends in racial fiscal incidence in South Africa, particularly with regard to social spending;
- understand the redistributive impact of some major social policy interventions in South Africa.

15.1 The distributional context in South Africa

Through its effect on resource allocation, the national budget is the most important redistributive mechanism available to any government to change the distribution of private earnings in the medium term. In the longer term, even earnings itself are strongly influenced by the current allocation of fiscal resources through its impact on human capital and economic growth in general. The budget therefore has a pivotal role in determining distributive outcomes. In South Africa, where poverty, socio-economic development and income distribution are such important issues, the role of fiscal policy in this regard is particularly pertinent. At the same time one should guard against unrealistic expectations about the redistributive power of the fiscus. In the words of De Wulf (1975:95):

"While an agnostic attitude may be extreme, at the very least a critical attitude with respect to any assertion concerning the extent of income redistribution through the budget seems warranted."

This chapter addresses the issue of the budget as redistributive device, focusing on the taxation and spending patterns that impact on distribution. Although there is a brief discussion of some social spending programmes and the problems encountered, these are big issues, which warrant separate treatment. The approach here is rather to show how the budget affects redistribution, painting a picture with a broad brush and focusing on the analytical considerations underlying redistributive actions in general.

15.1.1 Poverty and inequality in South Africa

South African society is characterised by extreme poverty and inequality in the distribution of income and earnings opportunities. Almost a quarter of the total population lives below the international poverty line of $1 a day, an extremely high proportion for an upper middle-income developing country (Klasen, 1996:10).

The **Gini coefficient** is often used to measure inequality and is usually linked to the Lorenz curve. The Lorenz curve is calculated after arranging the population from poorest to richest. It shows the cumulative percentage of the population (horizontal axis) against the cumulative percentage of income

(vertical axis), as in Figure 15.1 for South Africa in 1995. If there were perfect inequality, the poorest 20 per cent of the population, for instance, would have earned 20 per cent of the income, as reflected in the diagonal line of absolute equality. The actual deviation from this line as a proportion of the maximum possible deviation, that is, the area between the line of absolute equality and the Lorenz curve as a proportion of the area under the diagonal, is then a measure of the inequality of income. Countries with extreme inequality of income, such as South Africa and Brazil, have Gini coefficients ranging between 0,60 and 0,70, while countries with relatively equal income distributions generally have ratios of between 0,20 and 0,35. The South African Gini coefficient has remained at an extremely high 0,68 from 1975 to 1991 – the highest figure recorded anywhere in the world (Whiteford and McGrath, 1994:16), although studies using different data have shown slightly lower Gini coefficients of around 0,60 (Klasen, 1996; Central Statistical Service, 1996).

The perseverance of poverty and inequality despite substantial interracial redistribution in the past two decades may be attributed to widening inequalities within groups, especially amongst black South Africans. Since the mid-seventies the combination of rapid black wage increases and rising unemployment has had mixed outcomes for black households. While incomes among the top black income earners have increased greatly, the poorest have experienced a sharp deterioration in their incomes (see Whiteford & McGrath, 1994: 11 & 17). The racial divide in respect of poverty and affluence has been eroded ever since: poorer whites have experienced similar income declines as poor blacks during the past two decades (Whiteford & McGrath, 1994: 11). Yet recent national household surveys show that poverty in post-apartheid South Africa still remains concentrated among black, particularly rural, households (World Bank, 1995; Klasen, 1996).

Figure 15.1 The Lorenz Curve for South Africa, 1995

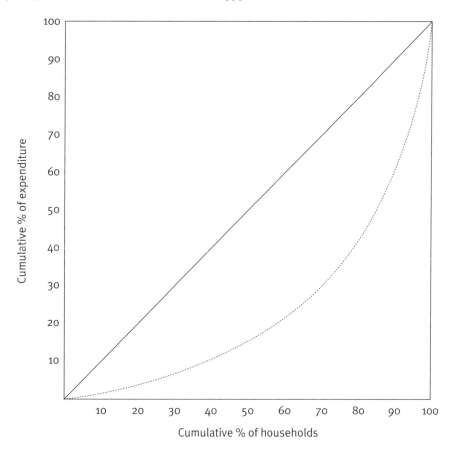

Table 15.1 presents one recent estimate of per capita incomes and unemployment by race. Access to employment has become a major dividing line between **insiders** sharing in the privileged situation formerly reserved for whites, and unemployed **outsiders** who, through lack of skills, geographic location and marginalisation in the wider society, became further impoverished. Patterns of access to social services accentuate this cleavage, even in the post-apartheid period. The Government thus faces a major challenge to effectively bring services to the poor, both as a means of alleviating immediate acute poverty and of establishing a socio-economic environment conducive to self-advancement.

15.1.2 Primary versus secondary income

In order to determine the impact of the budget on distributive outcomes, note that a household's disposal over goods and services depends upon both the personal incomes of members and upon the taxation and spending of government. **Primary income** or personal income of any group is the actual value of income received in cash or in kind by individuals and households, including the value of subsistence production activities such as subsistence agriculture. **Secondary income** consists of primary income minus direct taxation (which leaves disposable income), to which is added the

Table 15.1 Per capita income and unemployment by race

Race	Personal income per capita, 1993 (R)	Rate of unemployment[a] (%)
Blacks	2 520	44,0
Coloureds	5 316	23,6
Indians	11 112	20,2
Whites	25 344	6,8
Total	5 616	36,2

Notes: [a] Expanded definition of unemployment

Source: Saldru, 1994:322; World Bank, 1995:14; Statistics South Africa, 1999:table 5.1

value of government services consumed (Bromberger, 1982), that is

$$Y_s = Y_p - Td + G \qquad [15.1]$$

where Y_s = secondary income
where Y_p = primary income
where T_d = direct taxes, and
where G = government spending.[1]

Social spending is the only category of government spending that can be assigned to beneficiary households with any degree of certainty. If other public expenditures are ignored, equation (15.1) above becomes

$$Y_s = Y_p - T_d + G_s \qquad [15.2]$$

where G_s = social expenditure.

Considering the high degree of racial inequality of primary incomes in South Africa, it is indeed pertinent to ask what the role of the budget is in accentuating or reducing this inequality through its impact on **secondary** income. This goes beyond investigating only the fairness of the budget itself, and also asks how much inequality remains once the budget has had its effect.

15.2 The role of public finance in redistribution

Conceptually the factor $(G_s - T_d)$ in equation (15.2) combines the notions of tax and expenditure incidence (as discussed in previous chapters) into what is called **fiscal incidence**, that is, the net result of the incidence of tax burdens and expenditure benefits in society.

One approach to determining fiscal incidence is linked to the normative questions of fairness of the burdens and the benefits of public expenditure and taxation and focuses only on the budget, that is the factor $(G_s - T)$. This kind of fiscal incidence study often contrasts government expenditure benefits with **all** taxes paid by certain groups or households to determine whether, presuming no tax shifting, they benefit in net terms and how the political process allocates fiscal benefits and burdens. The usual point of departure is the **balanced budget incidence**, which entails calculation of the combined effect of government spending and the taxes levied to finance it, assuming no budget deficit or surplus. In this context, the distributional impact of a tax depends not only on the incidence of the tax itself, but also on

---

1 Strictly speaking, social transfers should not be included in government spending, as they already form part of personal incomes.

how the government spends the proceeds from the tax. An example is the very different redistributive impact of using tax revenue to finance either defence spending or social old age pensions for the poor.

However, balanced budget incidence ignores the distributional impact of fiscal policies on primary incomes and hence fails to take into account the overall distributional context within which the budget is but one element. In other words, it ignores the fact that primary income has already been influenced by the impact of fiscal policies on market prices. For example, company tax has already influenced personal income by reducing the after-tax company income for distribution to shareholders, while value-added and sales taxes enter into the price level and are reflected in the reduced purchasing power of consumers. At any point in time, therefore, the primary income distribution already incorporates an element of fiscal incidence. To avoid "double counting", balanced budget incidence studies should adjust for this. Since fiscal incidence studies in South Africa are mostly of the balanced budget incidence type, we therefore have to keep the above qualification in mind when we discuss the results of these studies later on.

15.2.1 Government's distributive role

Fiscal redistribution addresses an enormously complex issue. As stated by Bromberger (1982: 167):

"(The distribution of income is determined) by immensely complex processes in which government activity interacts with relatively autonomous initiatives and adjustments by 'the myriad forces of the market'. There does not exist a well-tested, widely endorsed body of theory to model all of these processes. But it is clear that governments cannot readily control all of them, and there are limits to what governments may be able to do to change distributions. We must avoid assuming that if

there is a change, or no change, government policy is responsible. Nor should we assume that government policies are either coherent or necessarily successful."

The government budget embodies the fiscal measures of redistribution. It influences income distribution by determining which services are provided to whom (government expenditure) and how these expenditures are to be financed (taxes and loans), including their impact on the long-term distribution of human capital that fundamentally determines the distribution of earnings (primary incomes). But the budget is only one part of the distributive role played by government.

From a broad economic perspective it is possible to identify a number of ways in which the government can affect distribution (see Bromberger, 1982: 168):

- As a rule-maker – in particular the rules of competition in markets, or phrased differently, rules of access to various levels of market opportunity.
- As a controller of prices and wages in markets.
- As a market operator – in particular as a major employer of labour and through the size and nature of its purchasing activities.
- As an influence on the long-term pattern of activities, for example industrial decentralisation measures that affect location decisions of employers, or the impact of taxes on the capital intensity of production.
- As taxer, supplier of public goods and welfare services, and payer of transfer incomes.
- As (potential) redistributor of assets which carry claims to current and future income.

Whereas the first four mainly affect primary incomes in the market and are only indirectly related to public economics, the last two activities influence secondary income through the budget. It is this role of government, as fiscal redistributor, that mainly concerns us in this chapter. Note that we discuss the distributional impact of public debt (government loans) in the next chapter.

15.2.2 Government taxation

The distinction between the statutory and the economic incidence of a tax is well known in the public finance literature and has been discussed in Chapter 9 (Section 9.5). The extent to which taxes can be shifted of course differs, as does the progressivity of different forms of taxes. Just as the perceived equity of a tax system is very important for the legitimacy of taxes and for tax morality, so the perceived (statutory) incidence, in contrast to the economic incidence, is often quite crucial.

In terms of the statutory incidence, the most progressive taxes are usually income taxes. In its extreme form, an income tax may even be extended to include a negative income tax (i.e. a transfer) for low levels of income, thus strengthening its progressive distributional effect. This may be seen as an alternative to means-tested social transfers, discussed in some detail in Section 15.5.1 below. Wealth taxes, where they apply, are also progressive, and appropriately selected excise duties too can have a progressive impact. By contrast, most other indirect taxes are usually relatively regressive. This regressivity can in some instances be reduced through certain exclusions, for example zero-rating certain food items from value-added tax, but this has to be weighed against the increased complexity of administration and the erosion of the tax base that this entails.

15.2.3 Government spending, subsidies, externalities and income transfers

The distributive stance of a government can furthermore be determined from its spending priorities and in particular its social spending. Social spending includes impor-

tant income transfers as part of social security, as well as publicly provided or subsidised goods and services such as education, health and housing.

In analysing social spending, one should take note that subsidisation or the public provision of goods or services gives rise to economic inefficiencies in the form of the excess burden of a subsidy. The concept of consumer surplus as developed by Marshall and Hicks may be used to show that the costs of a subsidy are larger than its benefits, thus leaving an **excess burden** (Rosenthal, 1983: 88). This is illustrated in Figure 15.2. Assuming constant production costs, if the full benefit of a subsidy were passed on to consumers, it would result in a lowering of the price charged from P_0 to P_1 and an increase in quantity demanded from Q_0 to Q_1. This would increase consumer surplus (the difference between what the consumer is willing to pay and the actual price) from the area aP_0E_0 to the area aP_1E_1. Thus, the subsidy results in a benefit for consumers measured as area $P_0E_0E_1P_1$ consisting of area $P_0E_0cP_1$ due to the lower price for the original quantity demanded, and area E_0E_1c, originating from the extra quantity purchased due to the lower price.

However, the cost of the subsidy to the state, that is, area $P_1P_0bE_1$ (the subsidy per unit multiplied by the Q_1 units consumed) still has to be accounted for. This cost exceeds the consumer benefit by area E_0bE_1. This is known as the excess burden, or deadweight or welfare loss, of the subsidy system (Rosenthal, 1983: 88-9).

As subsidies interfere with consumer choice and therefore lead to a socially suboptimal outcome, it seems that public subsidies should in principle be avoided, perhaps by rather providing income transfers if the intention is to redistribute resources.

The case for subsidies, however, is stronger where there are **externalities**, that is, where the marginal private benefit a consumer derives from a public good or service

Figure 15.2 The excess burden of a subsidy

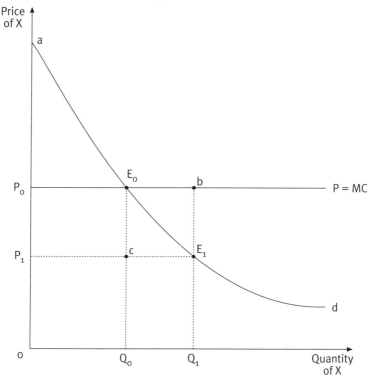

deviates from the marginal social benefit because of an external benefit to a non-user. Consider the case where society attaches value to improving the nutrition of the poor.[2] The private benefit of food consumption to the poor individual is thus lower than the social benefit of such consumption due to the positive externality. Figure 15.3 shows the marginal private benefit to a consumer MPB, the marginal external benefit MEB, and the marginal social benefit MSB (the vertical summation of MPB and MEB). The marginal cost MC is assumed to be constant and equal to the competitive market price (P_0).

The socially optimal consumption Q_1 by the individual consumer is where marginal

social benefit MSB equals the marginal cost MC. But the consumer will not consider the external benefit of his or her increased consumption and will thus only consume an amount Q_0 where $MPB = MC = P_0$. This is not socially optimal. An in-kind subsidy that reduces the cost to the consumer from P_0 to P_1 would, however, encourage socially optimal consumption. The size of the subsidy is indicated by the area $P_0E_1E_2P_1$.

Can a cash transfer achieve the same results as an in-kind subsidy? Note that a cash transfer is not targeted at increasing only the consumption of those goods which society attaches value to. Thus, a cash transfer to a poor individual could increase his/her consumption of food, but also of

2 This explanation is derived from Rosenthal (1983: 100-101).

Figure 15.3 Externalities and subsidies for public goods or services

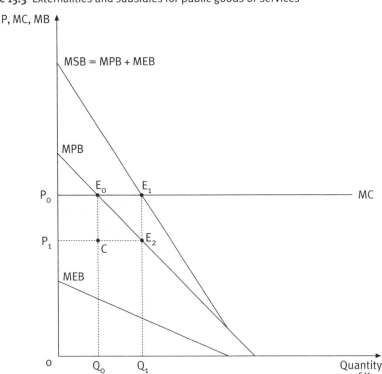

other goods (e.g. alcohol and luxury items). A cash transfer is therefore less certain of improving the consumption of those goods to which a positive externality is attached. In Figure 15.3, a cash transfer could shift the *MPB* and the *MSB* curve to the right,[3] thus increasing the social optimum level of consumption. Cash transfers will only lead to socially optimum consumption where the private benefit curve (*MPB*) is shifted enough to eliminate the marginal external benefit, consequently equating private with social benefit. In this case the *MPB* curve shifts to the right to intersect *MC* at E_1 and *MEB* becomes zero. The external benefit has been fully internalised to the advantage of the consumers who caused it.

Thus, a subsidy for a specific good could, via its effect on price, encourage socially optimal consumption in the presence of goods-specific externalities. A social optimum will be reached where the marginal social benefit equals marginal cost and hence the market price. In contrast, a cash transfer will only encourage more socially optimal consumption (Rosenthal, 1983: 100-101) if the *MPB* curve shifts as described above. Save for this exceptional circumstance, subsidies are socially more efficient than cash transfers.

In practice, though, it is difficult to determine external benefits. Some also criticise the paternalism and the negation of consumer sovereignty inherent in the provision of public goods. Subsidies on specific goods furthermore entail high implementation costs, including enforcement costs to prevent the conversion of subsidised goods into

3 It is assumed that *MEB* is not affected by the cash transfer.

cash equivalents. If in-kind subsidies can be readily converted into cash, such subsidies become very similar to cash subsidies. Costs and effects of subsidies are more complex to administer, understand and analyse than income transfers. But public support for specific subsidies or merit goods is usually stronger than for income transfers, thus these are more likely to be provided.

15.2.4 Asset redistribution

Asset redistribution usually takes place over a considerable period of time through the interaction of market and fiscal processes. Direct interventions to force rapid changes in asset distribution usually require a large degree of coercion and are therefore only common in post-revolution situations, for example nationalisation or land redistribution without compensation. Where compensation does take place, such asset redistribution is usually much slower and has a high opportunity cost in terms of opportunities foregone for redistributive social spending. Thus, land reform in South Africa has to compete with other services such as education for public funds. For that reason, asset redistribution through direct measures has limited application in market-based economies and will not receive more attention here. Our focus is on redistributive fiscal measures that operate directly on flow rather than stock variables. Of course, given positive saving propensities on the part of recipients, income redistribution could result in wealth accumulation.

15.2.5 International experience and practice

The rise of the modern welfare state has been the major force behind the secular rise in public expenditure ratios in industrial countries. Since the nineteenth century, the state's role has gradually shifted from an earlier emphasis on the indirect satisfaction of needs (e.g. infrastructure, defence and administration) to a greater emphasis on the more direct satisfaction of needs (e.g. education, health and social security) (see Chapter 7, Section 7.2). There was a particularly strong rise in income transfers in the form of social security spending. Increased expenditures also necessitated increased taxation, which later caused growing tax resistance.

Social spending in developing countries is more constrained by limited fiscal resources. Nevertheless, the period after the Second World War saw social spending ratios rising to levels far above those that had prevailed in today's industrial countries at a similar stage in their economic development. However, in trying to meet the demands of strong urban pressure groups, many governments embarked on social policies that were biased towards the urban population. Thus the major beneficiaries were often the non-poor. Moreover, spending often favoured higher-level services (e.g. tertiary rather than primary education, hospitals rather than primary health care facilities), which again benefited the relatively privileged. In most developing countries, social security has been relatively neglected, with education usually dominating social spending.

15.3 Historical perspective on fiscal redistribution

As in other countries, the South African budget has always been used as a distributive device and, given our history, race and ethnicity have always played a big role. In this country, the social expenditure dilemma of rising expectations that cannot be satisfied within current budgetary constraints, which is common to most developing countries, is complicated by the fact that apartheid allowed white standards to be set at a level far exceeding the ability of the country to extend them to all, thereby raising expectations of all groups. Political democratisation further raised expectations.

We now briefly consider the fiscal and distributive issues in three time-periods.

15.3.1 Fiscal policy in support of apartheid: 1948-1974

The period shortly after the introduction of political apartheid saw retrogression in the government's distributive stance, with the benefits of spending becoming more concentrated on whites. Gaps in social spending between the different race groups remained large or even widened, despite favourable economic circumstances. Defence spending remained relatively low, despite some expansion in the early 1960s after the Sharpeville incident and South Africa becoming a republic. Sustained economic growth provided ample scope for social spending on whites to rise strongly with only limited upward drift of the public spending ratio, especially during the 1960s. The attempts at creating independent homelands for blacks – a fiscally very ambitious undertaking – may never have been undertaken in a fiscally less optimistic climate.

15.3.2 Fiscal shifts since the mid-1970s: reform and repression

After the retrogression in distributive policies since 1948, a reversal in such policies only started occurring from the mid-1970s (Bromberger 1982). It is perhaps appropriate to date this shift in distributive stance from 1975, when South Africa entered the Angolan conflict, the Soweto riots erupted and a major economic downswing started in South Africa (a gold boom had at first protected South Africa against the effects of the world recession induced by the first oil-shock).

Since 1975, fiscal policy has been characterised by a combination of high military and security outlays and rising social spending to reduce racial gaps. The period can indeed be described as one of reform and repression, for the attempts at social reforms (including the three-chamber parliament and a rapid expansion of black education) were too limited to ensure social peace, thus high security outlays continued. Consequently, expenditure ratios rose very rapidly, tax resistance increased, public deficits grew, and expenditure overruns on the budget became quite common.

Indeed racial spending gaps did narrow considerably. For instance, the racial gap in the value of individual social pensions closed from two sides until parity was reached in 1994: black benefits increased, but in order to free resources and achieve parity within overall budget constraints, white benefits also had to be reduced in real terms. But in many areas the government was still hesitant about fully-fledged reforms, perhaps because of the fiscal consequences. In 1986, for example, social spending would have had to increase from less than 10 per cent to between 25 and 31 per cent of GDP to extend white levels (standards) of social spending to all (Van der Berg, 1992). Not even sharp cutbacks in other expenditures could have made this feasible, particularly in education, by far the most expensive social spending programme. Thus, achieving equality across racial lines would have necessitated a sharp cutback in white benefit levels.

15.3.3 After 1994: redirecting public resources under full democracy

When the South African redistributive debate escalated a few years before the unbanning of the ANC, it soon became the conventional wisdom that the major redistributive role of the budget lies on the expenditure side, as there are limits to how progressive or how high taxes could be. This particularly applied after the election, as investors were wary of a new government with no track record and unproven policies. To gain the confidence of the business community, which was crucial for economic growth, the new government had to show that it was not intent on punitive levels of taxation. Thus it committed itself to reducing the tax ratio and the budget deficit, thereby implicitly also limiting public expenditure.

To effect the redistribution of resources within these constraints, spending had to be redirected towards the social sectors where the major redistributive thrust was to take place; and within social spending, racially discriminatory spending had to give way to patterns that better reflected the population's needs. Most of the major redistributive opportunities on the expenditure side of the budget had been exhausted by the end of the 20th century, so that economic growth remained the only major potential source of significant increases in public spending. Given the limited scope for increasing social spending, it is crucial also to improve its efficiency, especially since the bulk of social expenditure cannot be avoided: social pensions, teacher salaries, medical personnel and equipment, et cetera.

Redirecting spending was complicated by the fact that most social spending takes place at provincial level and that the formula-driven nature of fiscal transfers to the provinces left less control of resource allocation to the national departments than they desired (see Chapter 18).

15.4 Changing patterns of fiscal incidence

We have seen in Section 15.2.3 that, just as the burden of taxation is often shifted, so are public expenditure benefits. This may have all kinds of unintended consequences. The means test for social grants may, for example, affect labour force participation or saving for retirement. Most incidence studies reflect only the static effects of spending, without considering the dynamic effects or the effects of previous rounds of taxation or public spending on distributive outcomes. De Wulf (1975: 75), in an important

overview of the incidence literature in developing countries, was highly sceptical of attempts at full net fiscal incidence estimates:

"(I)t should be emphasized that the impression of preciseness left by the studies surveyed here is definitely questionable; the estimates obtained in these studies are at best approximations. In any study, the overall effective tax rate or the effective tax rates of those income classes that, from a political point of view, deserve more attention – the wealthy and the poor – can be changed considerably by altering the shifting assumptions or by using different consumption and income data."

Fiscal incidence studies in South Africa naturally focused on the racial incidence of taxation and public spending. Until recently blacks contributed only a small share of taxation, thus taxation was not often considered in these studies, but more has been done to study the inequality of public expenditure. Such studies go back as far as 1932, when the Native Economics Commission (1932) concluded that expenditures (both directly assignable to individuals such as social services, and an imputed value for non-assignable expenditures) of R8,3m to the benefit of blacks in 1929/30 well exceeded the R6,6m they paid in taxes. (Native Economics Commission, 1932: 170-178). A number of subsequent studies[4] confirmed this trend and pointed to a significant shift in social spending towards blacks since the 1970s, leaving the net fiscal incidence considerably more favourable to blacks by the early 1980s. But throughout this period, disposable income and indeed secondary income (primary income plus the net effect of the budget on command over resources) remained highly skew. Leistner's estimates, summarised in Table 15.2, show that black

4 See Social Security Committee (1944); Social and Economic Planning Council (1944); Tomlinson Commission (1955); Spandau (1971); Leistner (1968); Theron Commission (1976); Terreblanche (1978); McGrath (1983); Van der Berg (1989, 1991 & 1992); Lachman & Bercuson (1992); and Janisch (1996).

Table 15.2 Fiscal incidence for the black population, various years, R million

Financial item	1929/30	1946/47	1956/57	1964/65
Direct taxes	3,0	4,5	7,6	9,5
Indirect taxes	3,5	8,9	14,9	28,5
Total taxes	**6,5**	**13,4**	**22,5**	**38,0**
Admin expenditure[1]	1,4	6,4	24,4	39,9
Social expenditure	2,5	22,6	78,6	146,2
Capital expenditure	0,4	1,4	22,2	29,1
Total expenditure	**4,3**	**30,4**	**125,2**	**215,2**

Notes: [1] This presumably refers only to "black administration", i.e. of the former homelands and townships and of the departments dealing with the black population

Source: Leistner (1986–1975)

social expenditure benefits had over a long period far exceeded their contribution to taxes, even when including an estimate of indirect taxes. Note, however, that this had not always been the case, and that social spending benefiting blacks had increased more than the other fiscal magnitudes shown.

McGrath (1983) utilised survey data and census results for his income distribution estimates, but his estimates on racial fiscal incidence were based on data obtained from the tax and expenditure authorities. "Apartheid bookkeeping" allowed social expenditure on education, health, housing and welfare, and to a lesser extent also on subsidies on certain foods to be assigned by race. His conclusions for the period 1949 to 1975 were that blacks gained under all sets of assumptions, that redistribution from whites probably increased, but that a vast post-redistribution gap in racial (secondary) incomes remained.

Van der Berg (1989) identified two competing norms underlying views about appropriate and socially just public expenditure. The first norm, based on the apartheid paradigm, saw groups as in principle fiscally autonomous units, that is, it presupposed

that the taxation paid by members of a particular group should also be used to fund public expenditures benefiting that group. Even under apartheid, this norm was not fully applied, as whites, paying some 77 per cent of taxes in 1975, effectively received only 56 per cent of the benefits of total public expenditure.[5] From an apartheid perspective, this could be regarded as unfair – or at best as a form of "development aid" to poorer groups.

The alternative norm for allocating public expenditure departs from the view that need, rather than the origin of taxes, should determine public expenditure. But need, approximated by population shares, clearly had not been the norm determining past public expenditure either. The white population – only 17 per cent of the total – obtained a far larger share of the benefits of public expenditure. From the perspective of this unitary society paradigm, then, expenditure patterns in apartheid South Africa could not be justified.

Later work (Lachmann & Bercuson, 1992) showed that even under conservative assumptions, it would have been fiscally impossible to extend white expenditure

---

5 These figures are at best indicative, because they necessarily require highly contentious assumptions about the shifting of tax burdens and who benefits from non-assignable expenditures, yet the broad picture they sketch is undoubtedly true.

levels to the whole population. The conclusion was clearly that white expenditure levels would have had to decrease quite substantially and further emphasised the need for accelerated economic growth to enhance fiscal resources, as available resources could not meet expectations in a simple static redistributive exercise.

Fiscal incidence studies usually cannot distinguish between differences in the costs and the quality of providing a service to different households or in different areas. In apartheid South Africa, however, racial differentials in the costs of services provided were more readily determinable, and as this was a major source of discrimination, expenditure incidence analysis tried to incorporate these differences. For instance, Janisch (1996) determined the extent to which social services were used, as shown in the 1993 *Living Standards and Development Survey*, and

then applied cost patterns by race and/or region from public expenditure data to these. Table 15.3 shows that before the redistributive effect of the budget is considered, per capita income of blacks (excluding social pensions, which are part of social spending) was only 10,3 per cent of white levels in 1993. After incorporating the impact of the budget, black secondary income per capita was 15,6 per cent of white levels, due to a net gain from fiscal incidence of R895 per black person and a net loss of R3 421 per white person – more than black per capita income before the budget. But even though the budget redistributed considerably, the racial post-budget gap remained extremely large.

The scope for further redistribution through the budget is rather limited, however. The government's *Macroeconomic strategy on growth, employment and redistribution* (GEAR) (Department of Finance, 1996)

Table 15.3 Racial distribution through the Budget, 1993, and limits to such redistribution

	1960	1960-69	1970-79	1980-89	1990-99
Income per capita (excl. social pension) (R)	26 850	2 758	5 088	10 921	6 305
% of white level	100,0	10,3	18,9	40,7	23,5
Less income tax per capita (R)	5 546	187	500	1 320	941
Disposable income per capita (R)	21 304	2 571	4 588	9 601	5 364
Plus social spending pc (R)	2 125	1 082	1 473	2 144	1 278
Secondary income per capita: Actual 1993	23 429	3 653	6 061	11 745	6 642
% of white level	100,0	15,6	25,9	50,1	28,3
Assuming equal social spending of R1 278 pc (R)	22 582	3 849	5 866	10 879	6 642
% of white level	100,0	17,0	26,0	48,2	29,4
Per capita effect of budget Actual 1993 (R)	−3 421	895	973	824	337
Assuming equal social spending of R1 278 pc (R)	−4 268	1 091	778	−42	337
Scope for distribution	−847	+196	−195	−966	0

Source: Own recalculations based on Janisch (1996)

acknowledges that taxation is already too high. If anything, taxes on the middle-income group, including most whites, may be reduced to eliminate the effect of past fiscal drag in an inflationary environment. Political resistance by the more affluent, limited capacity to deliver especially rural services by government, and the fact that access to education is likely to remain differentiated for a considerable time, make parity in social spending per capita at best a distant goal. But even this would have a limited effect, as Table 15.3 shows: Black post-budget command over goods and services, that is, secondary incomes, would then still be only 17 per cent of white levels. The latter conclusion emphasises the limits to the budget as an instrument of redistribution and points to the importance of the distribution of pre-budgetary or primary income.

The budget has for a long time redistributed across race groups. Due to much higher incomes, whites always paid by far the largest share of taxes, and even under

apartheid part of these taxes were used to finance certain services to blacks. The secondary distribution of income by race has therefore been more equitable than the primary distribution, even though public expenditure as such has been highly inequitable and clearly conflicted with the demands of social justice (based on a needs approach).

It also appears from the available data that racial redistribution through the budget actually accelerated over time, even under apartheid. Fiscal redistribution across races before the 1930s may have been negligible or even regressive, but rising social spending for blacks led to substantial redistribution through the budget. Figure 15.4 shows not only a narrowing gap between white and black, but also a real reduction in white benefit levels after 1975 that far predates political democratisation. The combination of the strong rise in the general government expenditure ratio as a percentage of GDP, reprioritisation towards social spending, and the

Figure 15.4 The estimated racial incidence of social spending for selected years

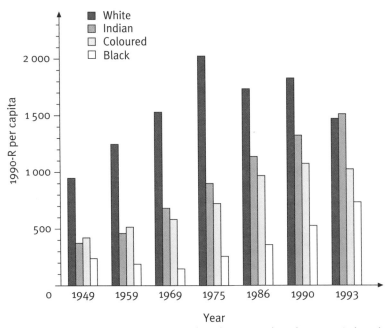

Source: Own calculations based on De Villiers (1996), Janisch (1996), McGrath (1983) & Van der Berg (1989, 1991 & 1992).

shift within social spending programmes towards blacks meant that real social spending for blacks grew at 6,5 per cent per annum from 1975 to 1991, in a period of sluggish economic growth and before apartheid had been officially abandoned. The largest part of the remaining gap arises not from differentials in expenditure levels for specific services, but from differential service provision or utilisation.

The inherited racial spending inequalities from the apartheid era were translated into provincial spending gaps after the political transition. The new provinces were given the function of controlling most social spending and are funded predominantly from transfers from central government. The horizontal division of revenue between provinces is based on formulae, which allow only five years for fiscal equalisation between provinces (see Chapter 18, Section 18.7.2). Consequently, there has been a sharp cutback in fiscal resources in the richer provinces, which have historically had a relatively smaller black population. At the same time, in all provinces racial expenditure gaps had to be eliminated.

Expenditure cutbacks in some provinces may have resulted in a poorer utilisation of national fiscal resources. For example, the retrenchment of teachers in the Western Cape and Gauteng could not be matched by new appointments of skilled teachers in Northern Province or Mpumalanga. The net result of such redistribution patterns across provinces may therefore well have been a reduction in the marginal efficiency of public resource use. That is, a million rand spent on additional teachers in the Northern Province, for example, contributes less to educational output than the million rand saved in Gauteng.

Expenditure data provide little information on the efficiency of social spending or on how well they match consumer preferences. The presumption in fiscal incidence studies that "a rand is a rand is a rand" (the accounting approach), is palpably untrue. One billion rand spent on pensions, for instance, may make a greater difference to people's welfare than another billion rand spent on teachers. If teacher salaries were to double, would pupils and parents experience a commensurate increase in welfare? These questions relate to who the presumed beneficiaries are (teachers or students), how well the increase in spending translates into command over real goods and services, and how spending reflects the preferences of consumers – or match the utility function of the consumers of public goods and services (see also Musgrave, 1987:1057)

In the absence of data broken down by race, it is impossible to even crudely estimate the fiscal incidence of the budget by race directly from the budget. The only source that offers some possibility for doing so is socio-economic surveys, which show the distribution of access to various resources. However, that still does not enable one to determine how spending is distributed, given continued differentials in social spending between and within the provinces. What is clear from the data on access to social services, however, is that racial disparities in some fields are still large, particularly in higher education.

15.5 Selected policy issues

With full democratisation in 1994, the trend towards reduced racial disparities in social expenditure was already well established. In education for instance, starting from a low base, spending benefiting blacks increased remarkably from the late 1960s as more blacks entered schools; those in school remained there longer and expenditure per pupil rose. As recently as 1982 total spending on black education was still less than half that on whites; five years later it had surpassed that on whites for the first time. Yet even today, differential access to higher levels of education leave blacks worse off than their white counterparts, especially in rural areas.

We now turn to a brief discussion of three social programmes that illustrate the types of difficulties faced in social policy in the South African context. The three areas are:

- Social security, where a crucial issue is the incentives that flow from the means test for social assistance and that inhibit the evolution of the system of occupational insurance.
- Social welfare services, where the restructuring of services is intended to ensure greater equity across both race groups and provinces, and greater responsiveness to the needs of the poor.
- Housing, where accelerated provision is sought to reduce the accumulated backlog by combining state and private funding and provision.

Other areas, such as public job creation programmes (public works), water and infrastructure provision, and health are not discussed here.

15.5.1 Social security

The embryonic welfare state erected for whites in apartheid South Africa was later expanded to other groups, leaving the country with a relatively advanced social security system for a semi-industrialised country. **Social security** protects people against various contingencies, such as income loss from unemployment, disability, injuries sustained at work, illness or old age. The South African social security system has two major components:

- **Occupational insurance** is based on contributory insurance to protect those in formal employment and includes the following: **retirement benefits** for a large part of those in formal employment; a somewhat inadequate system of **workers compensation**; a system of **unemployment insurance** which cannot address the major unemployment risks associated with

structural rather than cyclical unemployment; and **health/medical insurance** for some of the employed and their dependants.
- **Social assistance** (also called social grants or social transfers) has three main pillars, namely **social old age pensions, disability grants** and **child support grants**. All are means-tested to ensure targeting at the poor. It is funded from the national budget and is means-tested.

The interaction between occupational insurance and social assistance, particularly in the field of retirement provision, poses the greatest challenge to policy, for in this interaction – largely regulated by the means test – lies many incentive problems that perversely affect the behaviour of potential or actual recipients.

Occupational insurance

Occupational retirement insurance has expanded its coverage to most industries. Assets of private retirement funds alone amounted to 73 per cent of GDP in 1993 (Smith Committee, 1995: D2.16). In 1992 occupational retirement funds paid out retirement benefits of R13,9 billion, compared to only R4,8 billion paid by the state in the form of social old-age pensions. (Smith Committee, 1995: D2.1, 2.2 & 2.6)

Insofar as convention and agreements between employers and employees have made occupational insurance for retirement the norm in the formal sector, occupational insurance can be regarded as social insurance, despite the absence of legal compulsion. It is mandatory for employees in most industries or firms to join their pension fund or provident fund. However, as the "taxes" imposed on employers and employees do not flow through state coffers, fiscal comparisons understate social security provision in South Africa. Coverage is still low in agriculture, trade/catering/accommodation, and domestic service, and is probably much lower among women, who are disproportionately employed in some of these industries.

Insurance against certain types of risk is unlikely to be offered by the private sector because of the problem of **adverse selection**. This means that people most likely to face certain risks (e.g. of unemployment) and collect benefits from insurance, will have an especially high demand for and are thus more likely to buy such insurance (Rosen, 2002: 179). However, the high premiums needed to compensate for these high-risk clients could lower the demand to such an extent that it is unprofitable for a private insurance firm to offer such coverage. This problem is exacerbated by that of **moral hazard**, which is said to exist when economic behaviour adjusts to incentives in such a manner as to increase the likelihood that the event insured against will actually take place. For instance, the presence of lucrative unemployment insurance may make continued employment less attractive and therefore lead to greater unemployment than would have been the case in the absence of such insurance. This phenomenon ties in with the question of asymmetric information: the insurer's insufficient knowledge about the insured persons' circumstances makes such an insurer more susceptible to such moral hazard. Thus, adverse selection and moral hazard generally result in market failure and an inefficient allocation of resources: there is a lack of insurance against risks for which a sufficient demand does exist (see Rosen, 2002: 201).

Occupational retirement insurance is vital for many South Africans, but cannot reach those outside paid employment, nor those parts of the employed population presently uncovered. Although coverage of the formally employed by occupational pension schemes for retirement (even after allowing for some double counting) is high

at about 73 per cent (Mouton Committee, 1992: 490; Smith Committee, 1995: D2.11), large-scale unemployment means that only about 40 per cent of the labour force is covered (Kruger, 1992: 215; Smith Committee, 1995: D.2.11). According to the Smith Committee (1995: D2.8), retirement fund benefits were paid to only 44,5 per cent of the elderly in 1993, as against 78,7 per cent receiving social old-age pensions.[6] Of particular concern is that the interaction with the means test for social old-age pensions may discourage private retirement provision for many low-income workers, an issue we return to below.

Unemployment insurance applies only to certain workers covered by the Unemployment Insurance Fund (UIF) against short-term unemployment. Workers and employers each contribute 1 per cent of the wage to the UIF, which is publicly administered and to which the government also commits funds from time to time. Recognising the financial pressures inherent in the present functioning of the fund, a task team was asked to investigate alternatives (Meth, Naidoo & Shipman, 1996). Its recommendations are still under review. **Workers' compensation** requires employers to make risk-related contributions to the accident funds (Kruger, 1992: 198), and is paid to employed workers below a threshold income who are temporarily or permanently disabled as a result of injuries or industrial diseases sustained at work.

Social assistance

Figure 15.5 explains the effect of a cash transfer or the free provision of public goods and services on work effort of an economically active individual who is therefore also subject to income tax. We measure available hours per time unit (e.g. a week or a month) on the horizontal axis and the corresponding unit income on the vertical axis. *OA* hours

6 Due to double counting these percentages add up to more than 100.

Figure 15.5 The effect of an income transfer on work effort

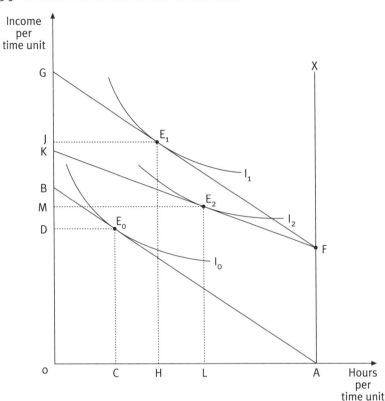

are available to the worker to allocate between work and leisure. This distance is referred to as the **time endowment**. The vertical line AX signifies that time endowment is fixed at all income levels. The line AB shows his/her combined budget and time constraint, where sacrificing leisure would allow him/her to earn a bigger wage income and therefore to increase his/her consumption of goods. Initially the worker is in equilibrium at E_0 on the price line AB, given his/her indifference curve (I_0) between goods (income) and leisure, sacrificing CA hours of leisure (or alternatively, works AC hours) in order to consume OD of goods. OD is the value of goods which can be purchased with the revenue earned by working AC hours and thus, assuming no saving, is equal to total income earned.

If the government now provides an income transfer irrespective of its effect on individual work effort, the budget constraint shifts parallel to the right to FG. Note that this parallel upward shift is similar to the downward movement of the budget constraint when a lump sum tax is levied (see Chapter 11, Section 11.4.1), that is, the relative prices of the items of choice remain unaffected. The worker is now at point E_1 on the new budget line and on the higher indifference curve I_1. Thus, consumption of both leisure and goods is increased (from OC to OH and from OD to OJ, respectively). The individual now has a higher level of welfare but works fewer hours (AH as opposed to AC), due to the income effect arising from the cash transfer.

If an income tax is now imposed to finance the cash transfer, this would reduce the opportunity cost of leisure, thus swivelling the budget line from *FG* to *FK*. The individual moves to E_2 (where *FK* is tangent to indifference curve I_2) and work effort is further reduced to *AL*. This is even lower than the work effort arising from the cash transfer alone (*AH*). The combined effect of the cash transfer and taxation to finance is thus to reduce work incentives in two ways, namely the negative (income) effect *CH* of the cash transfer plus the negative net (income and substitution) effect *HL* of the income tax. Thus the government needs to be as careful in the design of its cash transfer programmes as in its taxes to ensure that, in combination, they lead to as little reduction in work effort as possible. Social old age pensions are an example where the cash transfer would not provide a disincentive to work as the beneficiaries are not part of the labour force.

In South Africa social old-age pensions are the most important social assistance grants, covering almost three-fifths of the 3 million recipients of social grants, followed by disability grants (another fifth) and child and family maintenance grants. Although grants and pensions to the old and the disabled effectively target many of the poor (Ardington & Lund, 1995; Case & Deaton, forthcoming), not all the poor can be reached in this way. In 1999/00, about R17 billion will be spent on social assistance. This income largely ends up in the pockets of the poor, thus contributing substantially to their secondary income.

The absence of adequate occupational retirement insurance in the past has left most people of pensionable age with few other income sources than social old-age pensions to fall back on. **Social old-age pensions** are paid to men from 65 years of age and to women from age 60, subject to a means test. Applicants whose private incomes fall below the lower threshold (30 per cent of the value of the annual social benefit) qualify for the full pension. Above this level, every R2 increase in private income reduces the benefit by R1. This marginal "tax" rate or claw-

back of 50 per cent creates a typical poverty trap (see below) and has severe implications for the behaviour of low-income workers.

Disability grants are the second most important form of social assistance and are paid to the disabled (including the blind) from age 16 up to retirement age, subject to medical eligibility criteria and the same means test as for old-age pensions.

For many years child and family maintenance benefits consisted of **child allowances and parent allowances**, and were paid mainly to single mothers and their children without other means of support. In the past blacks were largely excluded. When the social assistance system was deracialised, it became apparent that the cost of these grants could become astronomical, that there were potentially perverse incentive effects associated with them (e.g. the requirement that mothers had to be single to remain eligible for these grants), and that other equally poor children in intact families were not eligible for such support. Thus, following the Lund Committee's (1996) recommendations, the Cabinet approved the phasing out of the former child and parent allowances and the institution of a new flat rate **child support grant** of R100 per month to caregivers of the poorest children under seven years of age, identified through a simple means test.

The means test for social pensions

A crucial area of concern is the interaction between social assistance and the tax system, especially with regard to retirement provision. This hinges particularly around the so-called **poverty trap** associated with most means tests. A poverty trap exists when certain regulations or tax systems make it unattractive for people to increase their private income beyond a certain point (earnings level), as this leads to a reduction in the resources obtained from the state. A poverty trap is then said to exist at that level of income. For instance, if a person receives a cash benefit of R100 from the state as long as his/her private earnings are below R500, it is not in his/her interest to expend any effort to increase private earnings marginally above R499. Someone with private earnings between R500 and R599 may actually be worse off than someone whose private earnings of R499 are supplemented by transfer payments from the state. The means test may thus be a disincentive to work for a low-income worker. Moreover, when income from pension or provident funds are also taken into account when the means-test is applied, it could be a deterrent for making provision for retirement or for supplementing his/her retirement pension through such provision. Besides encouraging dishonesty and the withholding of information on some income sources, the means test is also difficult to administer. This was not such a great problem in the past, when many low-income black workers were not covered by occupational insurance, but now that many of them belong to pension or provident funds, the perverse incentives are coming into play more.

For these reasons the National Consultative Retirement Forum in 1997 expressed some support for a universal grant for the elderly. Removing the means test would remove the perverse incentives that favour premature withdrawal of retirement benefits, would encourage the institution of private retirement insurance for informal sector participants and domestic servants, and would affect the choice between lump sum retirement benefits and pensions as well as the form in which assets are held. Although the fiscal costs of a universal old-age grant could be partly reduced by removing the old-age tax rebate and raising income taxes payable by more affluent old people, the ageing of the population may lead to the growth of the elderly population outstripping the growth of fiscal resources.

The limits to social security

The challenge for the state is to offer a safety net for the poor, who are often outside of remunerated employment, while insuring those in employment against major contingencies (loss of employment, old-age, ill health, disability), in the process avoiding schemes that discourage the private provision of security. The poorly educated rural black population is worst affected by the major contingency against which no proper protection is given, namely unemployment. Occupational insurance can reach at best only half the labour force, leaving the most vulnerable dependent upon various forms of social assistance. But such social assistance is in turn almost exclusively tied to the presence of elderly or disabled members in households, thus leaving uncovered the major social security need. This may not change easily, for the resources devoted from state general revenue to social security (as opposed to enforced social security contributions) are already generous and competing demands on fiscal resources leave little scope for additional social security spending to fill the current gaps in coverage.

15.5.2 Welfare services

Welfare spending covers both social security, discussed above, and **welfare services**, that take up less than 10 per cent of the combined national and provincial welfare budgets. Publicly funded social welfare services are provided either directly by government or through subsidising private welfare organisations. Although there is a vibrant network of such private providers of welfare services, they are less active in rural areas (where the greatest unmet needs are) and many are currently experiencing financial pressures. Welfare spending takes place mainly at the provincial level. Almost four out of every five rand spent by the state in various fields of social welfare services – both for services provided by government and for financial support of private welfare institutions – goes to child and family care or care of the elderly. The only other major field of service is care of the disabled.

The White Paper for Social Welfare (Department of Welfare, 1997) advocated a major overhaul of the system of welfare payments in South Africa. In the past welfare services were highly discriminatory, inequitably distributed across provinces, contributing to social disintegration by being poorly directed at communities and families, mainly rehabilitative rather than preventive, and often based on a fiscally inappropriate model of institutional-based care.

Discrimination in the provision of welfare services occurred on a massive scale under apartheid. In 1993, spending per member of the elderly population was seven times as much for whites as for blacks. Racial disparities were also translated into unequal provincial expenditure allocations when the new constitution was implemented: provinces with a large white and coloured population share (Western Cape, Northern Cape and Gauteng) were far better served with welfare services than other provinces. By 1995 the Western Cape still spent more than four times as much as Mpumalanga, the worst served province. Inter-provincial redistribution of fiscal resources through the provincial funding formula (see Chapter 18) has placed strong downward pressure on welfare service spending in the historically better-served provinces and considerably narrowed the spending gaps. In poorer provinces, the lack of institutional capacity in terms of both private and public welfare institutions and personnel remains an even more binding constraint than finance, and increased financial resources might only conceal this problem and lead to cost escalation without improved service provision. In contrast, spending cuts in richer provinces have placed severe strain on service provision and on the financial health and service provision of well-established welfare organisations in metropolitan areas. The government believes that more affordable welfare services are required to serve the whole population equitably. Thus it attempts to move away from expensive models of institutional care of the elderly that are fiscally difficult to afford for a country with limited resources and many unmet welfare needs. The focus is to shift to rehabilitation and preventive government intervention, with special attention to developmental needs. Preventive programmes are to focus on high-risk groups who are vulnerable to particular social problems, such as children and youth at risk.

15.5.3 Subsidisation of housing

The fact that poor consumers spend a large part of their income on housing, and that many others cannot afford or get access to housing, provides a rationale for the emphasis governments place on subsidies in both private and public housing sectors (Rosenthal, 1983:108-118). The case for government intervention in housing rests on the basic needs argument and the alleged existence of externalities (e.g. investment in housing enhances the return on non-residential physical and social investment (such as education), especially in a development context) (Calitz, 1986: 340-341). South Africa's huge housing backlog in urban areas has accumulated through the combined effects of influx control, which long kept most of the poor out of the cities, and limited housing construction.

The impact of a housing subsidy depends on the price-elasticity of housing supply and demand. This may be analysed on the basis of a shift in the supply curve of housing (which implies a producer subsidy), or in terms of a shift in the demand curve (a consumer subsidy). As in the case of an indirect tax (see Chapter 9, Section 9.5), the result in terms of the shifting of the subsidy benefit is the same. We illustrate the impact of the subsidy by means of a shift in the market demand curve for housing, as shown in Figure 15.6. Assume first a perfectly price-elastic supply of housing S_0 (i.e. $P = MC$, which is constant). The initial equilibrium is at E_0, with P_0 and Q_0 the corresponding equilibrium price and quantity. A housing consumer subsidy will increase the purchasing power of prospective homeowners and thus shift the demand curve upwards and to the right, that is, from D_0 to D_1. (For simplicity we assume a fixed subsidy amount, which entails a parallel shift in Figure 15.6). The new equilibrium is at E_1. Since the price of houses has not been affected, buyers enjoy the full benefit of the subsidy. No shifting of the benefit occurs.

At the other extreme, however, where there is a fixed housing supply (a perfectly price-inelastic supply curve such as S_1 in Figure 15.6), a housing subsidy will only result in an increase in house prices (from P_0 to P_1) to the benefit (increased capital gains) of existing homeowners, thus completely cancelling the benefit which the subsidy was supposed to have for potential buyers. In practice, neither of these extremes is likely, and the net impact is likely to be that some benefit will accrue to existing homeowners through an increased demand for housing and higher prices, and some benefit to the intended beneficiaries through an increase in their purchasing power (or a reduction in their costs) and an acceleration of housing supply. To the extent that the price of new houses is increased by the subsidy, some of the benefit is shifted to home-builders (the construction industry) as well or, in a general equilibrium context, to the owners of the factors of production (mainly labour and capital).

The major problem with housing provision in South Africa is that the incomes of a large part of the urban population are too low to allow them to afford even a relatively small house with rudimentary services.

Figure 15.6 The impact of a housing subsidy

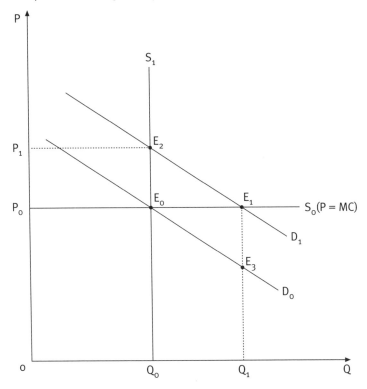

Early ambitions about providing a "proper" house for every household have given way to an acceptance that this is simply not affordable. Now the policy is one of incremental housing provision, to try and reach as many households as possible within a reasonable time frame, and to supplement their own incomes where necessary to allow them to afford at least a minimal level of housing.

At the time of writing the housing subsidy scheme, considered a "cornerstone of the government's approach to the housing challenge" (Department of Housing, 1995: 8), provided various forms of assistance to eligible households earning less than R3 500 per month. **Individual ownership subsidies** assist recipients to own fixed residential properties (housing opportunities) for the first time, with the lowest income-bracket – households earning less than R1 500 per month – being subsidised by R15 920 (after a 1998 inflation adjustment) (Department of Housing 1996: 8; Department of Finance 1999b: 139). These subsidies can either be allocated to individual beneficiaries for housing units in **projects** approved by provincial housing boards, or enable an **individual** to acquire ownership of an existing property or a property not in an approved housing project. Part of these funds may even be paid directly to developers when certain conditions are met, in order to smooth the payment procedure. The **individual subsidy** can also be linked to further credit provision, that is, a home loan to buy a property is obtained in addition to the subsidy amount, and a household can engage in a savings plan with the mortgage lender to save the required money for the deposit and remaining fees. **Consolidation subsidies** provide further housing assistance to beneficiaries who had already previously owned serviced sites for the provision or upgrading of a top structure on such a site. Institutions that give eligible people access to affordable subsidised residential properties based on

secure tenure receive **institutional subsidies** from the state.

Despite the provision of public assistance to boost home ownership, progress has been painfully slow with the Government failing to meet its initial ambitious goals. The problem often revolved around coordinating the financing, the provision of serviced land, and the selection and involvement of communities and households who qualify. Only by 1997 could a marked acceleration of housing output be seen and the annual target of 300 000 units a year was reached.

15.6 Conclusion

The South African fiscal dilemma – an example of the economic problem of allocating scarce resources in a situation of unlimited wants – is the result of the conflict between the rising expectations of a mobilised urban workforce and the resource constraints of an economically stagnant middle-income developing country. This is the economic problem of scarcity, which requires a reprioritisation of needs as satisfied via the political system (see the opening paragraph of Chapter 1).

In Chapter 17, we provide an outline of the overall fiscal policy approach necessitated by this fiscal dilemma. Suffice it to say at this stage that there is considerable scope for addressing the expectations of the poor. Only in respect of education is the problem especially severe. Yet, even there the financial resources that could be freed to address the needs of the black school-going population could have a considerable impact.

In this chapter we have seen that there is ample scope for a redistribution of resources *via* the expenditure side of the budget. This entails a reallocation of resources towards social expenditure but also a restructuring of the social budget towards services benefiting the really needy. Moreover, if the restructuring of social services could also ensure greater effectiveness in their delivery to the poor, these resources could be put to even better use without over-straining the capacity of the budget. Success in this regard would substantially lighten the burden of a government faced with the demands of a newly enfranchised and expectant constituency, and increase the likelihood of social stability and therefore economic growth. Economic growth, the big prize to aim for, is in turn a prerequisite for ensuring that the benefits of social expenditure can continue to keep up with a rapidly expanding need, especially in education. If it does not, budgetary redistribution would have accomplished very little.

But there are limits to redistribution through the budget, and unless economic growth improves substantially to draw more people into remunerative employment, the large inequalities in South African society, and the widespread poverty, will remain. The limits to budgetary redistribution again emphasise the need for job-creating economic growth to address South Africa's major need for redistribution. Thus fiscal policy has to balance the short- to medium-term need for budgetary redistribution against the long run need for growth to ensure a more substantial redistribution of both primary and secondary incomes. We return to this balancing act when we analyse fiscal policy and the national budget in Chapter 17.

Important concepts

adverse selection
balanced budget incidence
fiscal incidence
Gini coefficient

---

moral hazard
occupational insurance
poverty trap
primary income
secondary income
social assistance

Self-assessment exercises

15.1 Distinguish primary from secondary income.

15.2 Explain the role of public finance in redistribution.

15.3 Is it possible for the budget to redistribute resources yet still to discriminate? Discuss, with reference to racial fiscal incidence in South Africa.

15.4 Do you think racial fiscal incidence has become less discriminatory since the mid-1970s?

15.5 Under what conditions would a subsidy be welfare-enhancing? Do you think this is the case for social old age pensions in South Africa? Would it equally be the case for grants to single mothers?

15.6 Why is it so difficult for the private sector to provide insurance against unemployment?

15.7 Poverty traps can also exist for other social programmes and social security. Do the conditions for housing subsidies and South Africa also create a poverty trap?

15.8 Explain, by means of a graph, the incidence of a housing subsidy when both the demand and supply curves are moderately elastic.

Chapter sixteen

Estian Calitz

Public debt and budget deficits

The aim of this chapter is to study the essence of and rationale for public debt and its impact on the economy.

Public debt arises from the borrowings of government – as reflected primarily in the annual budget. A systematic study of public debt provides important insights into both the relationship between the various components of public finance and the interaction between fiscal and monetary policy in their impact on the economy.

Our study of public debt and budget deficits begins with a discussion of the concept of public debt, followed by an overview of the size and composition of public debt in South Africa. Next we examine various ways of measuring public debt and identify the different components of the cost of public debt. This is followed by a discussion of various theories on the rationale for public debt, before we conclude with an investigation of the question: should government tax or borrow?

Once you have studied this chapter, you should be able to
- define public debt;
- discuss different measurements of the size of the public debt;
- describe salient characteristics of the size and composition of public debt in South Africa;

- identify and describe the different types of public debt cost;
- explain and compare different theories of public debt and evaluate them critically.

16.1 The concept of public debt

Public debt may be defined as the sum of all the outstanding financial liabilities of the public sector in respect of which there is a primary legal responsibility to repay the original amount borrowed (sometimes called the **principal**) and to pay interest (sometimes called **debt servicing**). Most of the time, especially when considering the macroeconomic implications, the term public debt is used to refer to the debt of the national government only. We use this narrower definition in this chapter.

Public debt arises primarily from the government's annual budget deficits.

The government borrows mainly by issuing bonds or treasury bills. The **treasury bill** is a short-term debt obligation of the national government, representing a charge on the revenues and assets of the Republic of South Africa (see Fourie, Falkena & Kok, 1999: 166-167). A treasury bill is normally issued for a 91-day period. Treasury bills form part of the liquid asset base of the private banking sector.

The majority of public debt is incurred through the sale of **government bonds** (also called stock or securities) with a maturity of more than three years. These are fixed-interest bearing securities issued by the national government and also represent a charge on the revenues and assets of the Republic (see Fourie, Falkena & Kok, 1999: 170). All government bonds, irrespective of their maturities, are regarded as liquid assets in the hands of banks.

Occasionally debt is incurred outside the budget (off-budget debt) and not reflected in the budget deficit. For example, in the early 1990s the Government transferred bonds directly to the public employees' pension funds to improve their funding levels, instead of budgeting for the expense in the normal fashion.

The debt of the national government is published in the *Quarterly Bulletin* of the South African Reserve Bank. This excludes the debt of extra-budgetary institutions (such as universities), provincial and local governments and the non-financial public enterprises (such as Eskom and Transnet). Of course, if the national government were to take over the debt of any of these institutions, the legal responsibility to service and repay the debt is transferred to the national government. From that moment the debt will be counted as part of the public (i.e. national government) debt.

Our definition of public debt also excludes **contingent liabilities**, that is, the outstanding financial liabilities of public entities (such as public enterprises) and private entities whose debt carries an explicit guarantee by the national government. Only when such a guarantee is called up, will the payment obligation be transferred to the national government (as guarantor) and the amount involved be added to the national debt. Some authors (e.g. Abedian & Biggs, 1998: 251) regard guarantees by government to the debt of third parties as part of public debt. We differ from this approach because

such debt is not the primary legal responsibility of the government.

16.2 Size and composition of the public debt

On 31 December 2001, the total debt of the South African Government (public debt for short) amounted to R462 billion, which was 50,7 per cent of the GDP, or roughly R10 400 per head of the population. This tells us that, if all the public debt were to be repaid immediately, the Government would on average have to impose a tax of R10 400 on each citizen. Those citizens that are government bondholders as well will, of course, also be on the receiving side when the debt is repaid.

The size of public debt as a percentage of GDP rose substantially during the first half of the 1990s (see Table 16.1), after which it stabilised in the 48–51 per cent range. The surge led various economists to warn against the dangers of a debt trap, a term used to signify an inability of a government to repay and service its debt. We shall return to this issue when discussing fiscal sustainability in Chapter 17.

Table 16.1 Public debt-GDP ratio in South Africa by sub period, 1969-2001

Period	Average public debt as percentage of GDP
1969–1972	44,3
1973–1979	38,3
1980–1988	31,9
1989–1993	38,5
1994–1999	49,3
2000–2001	46,8

Source: South African Reserve Bank, *Quarterly Bulletin* (various issues)

The South African Government has traditionally made relatively little use of foreign financing, so that most of the public debt is **domestic** debt. During the period 1970 to

2000 **foreign** public debt as a percentage of total public debt fluctuated between 10,9 per cent (1976) and 1,6 per cent (1992). Over this period, foreign debt never exceeded 4,3 per cent of GDP. In 1985, 1986 and 1987 foreign loans were used to counter private capital outflows, but access to the international financial markets subsequently became increasingly difficult due to international financial sanctions. Access to international financial markets was normalised in 1994. Although this has, together with the gradual phasing out of exchange control, provided the fiscal authorities with an increased array of foreign financing options, the rise in the share of foreign debt in recent years has remained modest. A sharp rise occurred in 2001.

An analysis of the **ownership distribution** of public debt shows that the majority of public debt is in the form of long-term bonds held by pension funds (including the Public Investment Commissioners (PIC)) and long-term insurers. In 2001 the PIC alone owned almost 37 per cent of the long-term government stock. The biggest investor remains the Government Employees' Pension Fund. This Fund's investment in government bonds is channelled, along with investable funds of other government pensions funds and other public bodies, via the PIC. At the end of 2001 government bonds constituted 47,0 per cent of the PIC's assets.

Until 1989 insurance companies and private pension funds were compelled by law to hold 53 per cent of their untaxed liabilities and 33 per cent of their tax liabilities in fixed-interest bearing public sector securities (Abedian & Biggs, 1998:261). This provided the Government with a captive loans market. To the extent that the interest on such bonds was lower than would have applied if government had to compete for these funds in a competitive market, these prescribed investments constituted a hidden tax on the relevant institutions. For the Government, the cost of debt was therefore lower. This implicit tax, which impacted negatively on savings, was criticised for its unfairness and adverse influence on investment performance and abolished in 1989.

For some time the PIC continued to be subject to strict investment requirements, but this has also changed and during the 1990s the PIC was increasingly allowed to make market-related investment decisions. One reason for this was that the PIC, as the investment arm of the government's pension funds, was responsible for the investment yield of these funds. The public employees were entitled to a defined pension benefit. It meant that the weaker the investment performance of the PIC, the higher the Government's future obligation was going to be to improve the solvability of these funds. This was the reason why the Government transferred stock to the pension funds at various occasions in the early 1990s, thus reducing its contingent liability (to ensure future solvability) and increasing its actual debt.

An intriguing question, which we will address during the course of this chapter (see Section 16.5), is whether, and on what basis, public debt is justified. When attempting to understand the nature and causes of public debt, an important issue is the purpose for which debt is incurred. For example, are the borrowed funds to be used to finance current or capital expenditure? Spending on goods and services that are used up within a specified, usually short, period is called **current expenditure** or consumption expenditure (see Bannock, Baxter & Rees, 1971:82). In fiscal terms these goods and services are normally associated with tax rather than debt financing. **Capital expenditure** refers to expenditure on durable items that yield services over a long period, such as roads, irrigation dams and electricity networks (Bannock, Baxter & Rees, 1971:82). This kind of expenditure is normally financed through loans (public debt).

The inverse of the question about the justification for debt is whether public debt is something that should be paid off. Most people would argue that a government is not like a business, the health of which is determined by factors such as the value of its shares, its profit, its debt-equity ratio and various measures of liquidity and solvency. These criteria are important determinants of whether a business is bankrupt or thriving. If the business is to be sold, one needs to know its value or net worth to determine the price. **Net worth** may be defined as the difference between the value of all assets and liabilities, that is the "shareholders' (or, in the case of government, the taxpayers') interest". In the case of government, the mirror image is the **net indebtedness**,[1] which is the difference between the value of all liabilities and assets. Many would argue that this kind of information is irrelevant when analysing the financial state of a government, because a government allegedly cannot go bankrupt or is unlikely to be put up for sale.

In recent times these ideas have been challenged. The government is not only the supplier of public goods and services. It is also the custodian of public assets owned collectively by the citizens (taxpayers) of the country. Informed and enquiring citizens have tended to become interested in the way in which the government is managing their (public) assets and liabilities. The net worth of government has become important, not as an indication of the potential selling price of the government, but as a measure of the quality of fiscal management. Attention to the balance sheet of government is becoming a feature of public economics. Privatisation, for example, has raised questions like: is society getting poorer if public assets are sold and should the revenue from privatisation be used to pay off public debt or to acquire new assets?

Balance sheet accounting, incidentally, is also required to answer many of the questions raised by public auditors who have over the past two decades been advocating the importance of value for money in a number of countries, for example, Canada and New Zealand. In South Africa we increasingly focus on commercially oriented questions such as the value of public assets, the (opportunity) cost of non-earning or badly managed assets, and the cost of excessive stockpiling – such as occurred in the defence force in the past.

No systematic information on the South African Government's assets and liabilities was published before 1992/93. Since then the Auditor-General's annual reports started including such information and nowadays a statement of the Government's assets and liabilities is published annually. The Government's annual *Budget Review* now also contains a separate section on asset and liability management.

There are many conceptual and measurement difficulties associated with the compilation of a balance sheet for the government. For example, how does one determine the value of national monuments? Does one value public debt at historical cost or current market value, in nominal or real terms? The quality and coverage of the data are improving every year and should a complete balance sheet for the Government one day become available, it would be possible to determine the **net worth** of government.

For purposes of our later study of budget deficits and the financing of such deficits, a closer inspection of the difference between the above-mentioned types of valuation of public debt is warranted. Note that in each of the cases that we discuss the same considerations will also apply to the concept of the net indebtedness of the state.

---

1 Sometimes "net indebtedness" is only used in respect of the difference between the financial assets and liabilities of government.

16.3 Measuring public debt

In this section we consider various methods of measuring public debt. It will help our understanding if we note at the outset that government borrowing is similar to any other form of borrowing in the sense that whoever lends to the government does so to earn a return on his/her investment. In a market-based economy, therefore, the effective return on government stock has to be market-related. In other words, it has to allow for inflation and offer investors a real return comparable to those offered elsewhere in the economy.

16.3.1 Nominal versus real debt

The conventional method of valuing public debt is to express it at book value or historical cost, that is at the issue price of the stock. If the government borrows R100 on 1 January, repayable on 31 December, then the outstanding debt on 31 December will be R100. This will then be the size of the public debt in nominal terms. On that day the government will require R100 of taxpayers' money to redeem its debt.

In an inflationary environment the value of the public debt in real terms is reduced over time. In the above example, suppose the inflation rate is 10 per cent per annum. At the end of the year the government owes R100 in nominal terms, but in real terms the value of the debt will be 10 per cent less. Like with all debtors, inflation favours the government as debtor. If the full loan is to be redeemed after one year, the purchasing power of the R100 used in the repayment is less than the purchasing power of the R100 received when the loan was made. It is as though inflation has repaid a portion of the debt in real terms. This kind of borrowing is tantamount to a tax on lenders. It is therefore also called an **inflation tax**, that is, an uncompensated reduction in the real value of a government bond due to inflation (see Chapter 9, Section 9.1 on inflation as a source of government income).

If the government does not want to levy an inflation tax – explicitly or implicitly – the long-term nominal interest rate should be equal to the time value of money. In efficient financial markets the interest earned on the bond should thus be high enough to compensate for the loss of capital value in real terms from the perspective of the lender *and* to earn a real return on the investment. Put differently, if inflation is 10 per cent and the government were to issue a bond for R100 and repay (say) R115 at the end of the year, R10 of the R15 would merely be to preserve the real value of the asset. The real interest earned on the bond will be 4,5 per cent (and not 15 per cent).[2] Unless the owner of the bond suffers from money illusion, he/she will invest the R10 and only regard the R5 as an increase in wealth and spending power. For the economy as a whole, real aggregate demand should therefore only be affected by the real-interest component, that is, assuming rational investors in government bonds.

At any point in time, however, there are many government bonds, which were issued at different points in the past, at different interest rates and under inflationary conditions that might have differed from the present. The interest rates applicable to these bonds cannot be altered when the inflation rate changes. When inflation is on the increase, therefore, public debt in real terms is reduced at an increasing rate. The opposite is also true: during times of declining inflation, the rate at which public debt is reduced in real terms, slows down.

Some high inflation countries introduced the practice of indexing public debt to the inflation rate. This can take various forms, but basically it means that the value of the investment (from the point of view of the lender) is regularly adjusted to maintain its

2 The real rate of interest is calculated as $100\{(1{,}15 \div 1{,}10) - 1\} = 4{,}5\%$.

real value. Brazil is an example of a country that has issued index-linked bonds. If the reason for resorting to indexed debt lies in unstable inflation and lax (inflationary) fiscal policy, then rising debt service cost and an increasing tax burden will result. Also, index-linked bonds may be the symptom of, rather than the cure for, the underlying inflationary problem. We are reminded (Dornbusch & Draghi, 1990:8) that by early 1990 Brazil's index-linked bonds had lost so much credibility that the average maturity had shrunk to less than a day! However, if inflationary expectations are higher than the actual inflation to which new bonds are linked, such bonds are a method of saving on debt servicing cost.

16.3.2 Valuation at historical cost or market value

Recall that the price of a bond (P) is inversely related to its yield (i). If the coupon (the fixed amount of earnings) on a consul (a perpetual bond) is denoted as E, we can write:

$$P = E/i$$

Assuming efficient markets so that the long-term interest rate is equal to the yield rate on all bonds, higher interest rates imply lower bonds prices (value) and *vice versa*.

Although the government cannot change the interest payments applicable to debt issued previously when changing inflation rates affect the real value of the debt, the owner of such bonds can be protected against capital losses and realise capital gains if the bonds are sufficiently marketable. The government, on the other hand, may for example be able to realise the benefits by buying back unexpired bonds during periods of rising inflation.

When interest rates are volatile, the market value of bonds (and the government's net worth or net indebtedness) changes all the time. By valuing the government's outstanding liabilities at market prices (so-called mark to market), a truer picture of the state of the fiscus is obtained. If the financial assets and liabilities of government were to be managed by a profit-driven treasury, such valuation will be a continuous routine as a means of maximising profits and minimising losses as a going concern. However, public debt management has macroeconomic stability as one of its objectives and is therefore not solely driven by the profit-and-loss bottom line.

16.4 The cost of public debt

16.4.1 Interest on public debt

How much does it cost the government to borrow? The immediate response would be that the answer depends on the interest rate. The **interest cost** is indeed the main cost factor. If the government wants to borrow R100 and the interest rate is 10 per cent, the interest cost will be R10 per annum. If the interest rate rises, so will the interest bill, and *vice versa*. Note that, because (or to the extent that) government stock is issued at a fixed rate of interest or coupon, a rising interest rate affects only the interest cost pertaining to new debt or debt incurred to replace maturing debt. In 1998/99, the interest cost on government debt amounted to R42,7 billion, which was 20,9 per cent of total government expenditure or 5,7 per cent of GDP[3] Interest cost was 85,8 per cent of total debt cost.

16.4.2 Discount on public debt

The interest cost is not the only cost. In modern capital markets bonds are often issued at a **discount**, which means that the government receives less money than what it will be obliged to repay. The reason for the discount is that, because of time differences

---

3 Based on the GDP estimate of R613 billion used by the Department of Finance (1998: 2.28).

inter alia, the market rate of interest may be higher than the specified interest rate (or coupon rate) on the bond when the bond is issued. Instead of having to raise the coupon every time a bond is issued, the amount of cash received is adjusted. The discount, together with the coupon rate, therefore gives a better indication of the effective interest rate (also called the **yield**) applicable to the bond.

Assume that a bond of R100 (the **nominal value**) is issued at a discount of 5 per cent. This means that the bond will sell at R100 − $(0,05 \times 100) = $ R100 − 5 = R95. The investor thus pays R95 for an asset with a nominal (book) value of R100. The amount received when a bond is issued at a discount (i.e. the yield value) differs from the nominal value. In this example the government incurs an extra cost of R5 (in addition, that is, to the coupon or interest payment applicable to the bond). Suppose this bond has to be repaid after five years. The government will then have to repay R100, that is the R95 received plus the R5 discount cost. The discount on a bond is thus defined as the difference between the nominal value and the yield value of the bond.

The figures in our example may appear insignificant, but the amounts involved can be quite large. In 1998/99 for instance, the discount on public debt in South Africa amounted to R6,4 billion, which represented 12,8 per cent of the total debt cost in that year.

The budget deficit, which the Minister of Finance announces in the annual Budget Speech, does not account for discount on public debt on an accrual basis. Had this been done, the result in any particular financial year would have been higher budget deficits and state debt cost and lower amounts of government debt, as shown in Table 16.2.

A bond may, of course, also be issued at a **premium**. If the market interest rate were to be below the coupon rate on the day of issue, the bond would be sold at a premium

Table 16.2 Adjustment to state debt cost and total government debt to account for discount on an accrual basis, 1992/3-2001/02.

Fiscal year[a]	Adjustment to state debt cost and budget deficit (% of GDP)[b]	Total debt at year end (%of GDP)	Adjusted total debt at year-end (%of GDP)
1992/93	0,3	36,9	33,3
1993/94	0,3	42,7	38,9
1994/95	0,4	46,9	41,8
1995/96	0,5	48,0	42,1
1996/97	0,5	48,1	42,0
1997/98	0,5	47,4	41,3
1998/99	0,5	47,5	41,3
1999/00	0,5	45,6	40,0
2000/01	0,4	43,6	38,6
2001/02	0,5	42,9	38,8

Notes: [a] Years ending 31 March.

         [b] To calculate the discount-adjusted deficit and state debt cost as a percentage of GDP, these figures have to be added to the standard budget figures.

Source: National Treasury (2002: 113)

because the effective interest rate would be lower than the coupon rate. The premium will close this gap.

16.4.3 Foreign exchange cost

When foreign borrowing is undertaken, a **foreign exchange cost** may be incurred in the event of subsequent exchange rate depreciation. Assume that South Africa issues a one-year bond of US$100 on 1 January. To simplify the explanation, we initially assume an exchange rate of R10 = $1 on 1 January, a zero interest rate, no discount on bonds and a 20 per cent depreciation of the rand against the US dollar during the year. On 1 January the Government receives R1 000 as the proceeds of the loan. On 31 December the Government has to repay $100. In order to do this, rands have to be converted into dollars. After the depreciation of the rand the new exchange rate is R12 = $1. The Government will therefore require R1 200 to repay the loan. The depreciation of the rand has caused an extra cost of R200. An exchange rate depreciation can therefore substantially increase the cost of foreign borrowing. The opposite happens in the case of an appreciation of the rand against the dollar.

One must be careful, though, not to conclude that the cost associated with an exchange rate depreciation is such that foreign loans are out of the question. In a country with a depreciating currency nominal interest rates are usually much higher than in countries with stable or appreciating exchange rates. The latter countries are normally also the sources of foreign financing. If, in the above example, the bond rate was 5 per cent in the USA and 20 per cent in South Africa, the total cost of the foreign loan after one year would be R200 (the exchange rate depreciation cost) + (0,05 × R1 000) = R200 + 50 = R250. The cost of a local bond (ignoring discount cost) would be 0,20 × R1 000 = R200. Had the South African bond rate been 25 per cent (i.e. the margin between the domestic and foreign interest rates been 20 percentage points), there would have been no difference between the cost of domestic and foreign borrowing. Because the South African rand generally depreciates against the currencies of countries in which foreign borrowing is undertaken, the fiscal authorities revalue (in rand terms) the value of maturing foreign loans in the year of repayment.

16.4.4 Other costs

There are various other costs associated with debt, such as conversion costs, which are incurred when bonds are redeemed before maturity and converted into other bonds, and the cost of raising loans. These costs are relatively small.

16.5 Theory of public debt

16.5.1 Introduction

In Section 16.2 it was stated that loan finance (debt) is an acceptable method to finance capital expenditure, while current expenditure may be a better candidate for tax finance. Is this necessarily true? We have already seen that the distinction between current and capital expenditure can be ambiguous. What is the rationale for debt finance and what are the criteria for choosing between tax and debt finance of government expenditure? These are some of the oldest questions in economics and there are a number of divergent views on the issue. The answer depends in part on who actually pays the public debt, which is a question about the nature of the distribution or incidence of the public debt burden.

We begin our analysis of the rationale for debt finance by introducing the concept of the **inter-temporal burden**. This refers to the shifting of the burden of the public debt over time from one generation to the next. The burden of the debt refers to the responsibility for the actual payment of the principal and interest.

The American President Herbert Hoover once remarked: "Blessed are our children, for they shall inherit the public debt". Is this necessarily true? There are different views on this.[4] Before investigating them, a few preliminary observations are necessary. When debt is incurred, benefits accrue to the present generation since the proceeds of the loan are used to supply public goods and services. If capital goods such as infrastructure are provided, the future generation also stands to benefit. The debt furthermore establishes a responsibility to pay interest and to repay the loan or to refinance it. In both of the latter instances a statutory burden will be conferred on the next generation. The next generation will pay interest to bondholders until the bonds expire. In the case of bonds that expire and are not replaced by the issuance of new bonds (refinancing), the next generation will transfer income to bond holders. In the case of the refinancing of maturing bonds – a common practice in public finance – the next generation will pay interest to the new bondholders.

In our study of tax incidence (see Chapter 9, Section 9.4.2) we saw that there may be a marked difference between statutory and effective (or economic) tax incidence. The same applies to public debt. The chain of events set in motion by government borrowing may lead to an economic incidence that may differ substantially from the statutory or legal incidence. The actual incidence depends on the assumptions about economic behaviour and the concomitant relationships between economic agents. The answer obviously also depends on the balance of the fiscal benefit and burden, that is, the net fiscal burden.

Two kinds of public debt have to be distinguished. **Domestic** or **internal debt** is the debt incurred by government when borrowing from domestic residents or institutions.

The value of the debt is expressed in rand. The sale of the bond does not involve an inflow of foreign capital and the payment of principal and interest does not cause an outflow of funds from the country. The balance of payments is therefore unaffected by transactions in such bonds. **Foreign** or **external debt** is the debt incurred by government when borrowing from foreign residents or institutions. The value of the debt is normally expressed in a foreign currency but can also be denominated in rand. The sale, repayment and servicing of the bond all affect the balance of payments. There is an impact on the balance of payments when:

• bonds are sold to foreigners, thus causing an inflow of foreign capital (affecting the financial account);
• foreigners sell the bonds to South Africans before the expiry date (i.e. before maturity), resulting in an outflow of capital (financial account);
• bonds are repaid in the hands of foreign investors, also amounting to a capital outflow (financial account);
• interest is paid to foreign bondholders, a payment for a foreign service affecting the current account.

Since South Africa started to liberalise its financial markets, foreign investors increasingly started buying government bonds in the secondary capital market (i.e. the Bond Exchange of South Africa on which government bonds are traded after the issue date). This means that the bond may often change hands so that the debt associated with a bond may, during the "lifetime" of the bond, at different times be counted as foreign or domestic debt, depending on the nationality of the registered bondholder. In financially integrated markets the distinction between domestic and foreign debt becomes blurred, since a foreigner can also purchase bonds issued domestically, just as a South African

4 The discussion of these views relies substantially on Rosen (2002: 429-434).

may buy foreign issued bonds of the South African Government. It is thus more appropriate to distinguish between bonds issued in the domestic money and capital markets (domestically issued bonds) and bonds issued in foreign money and capital markets. The distinction between domestic and foreign becomes one of source rather than residence.

16.5.2 Internal versus external debt and the burden on future generations

A view that characterised economic thinking in the 1940s and 1950s was that internal debt does not create a burden for the future generation. This view is attributed, inter alia, to the American economist, Abba Lerner. The argument is that certain members of the future generation will inherit a debt repayment or debt-servicing obligation, but other members of the same generation will be the recipients of these payments. In other words, members of the future generation owe the debt to themselves. On repayment of the debt, income is transferred from one group of citizens (those who do not hold bonds) to another group of citizens (the bondholders). As a whole the future generation is therefore no worse off since it is capable of the same aggregate level of consumption would otherwise have been the case. The repayment of the debt results in an intra-generational transfer or redistribution of resources (i.e. a transfer within the same generation) rather than an inter-generational transfer (i.e. a transfer between two generations). In terms of this line of thinking, therefore, internal debt is neutral with regard to inter-generational equity.

The situation is different when external debt is used. Then the distribution of the burden depends on the way in which the funds are used, the fact that interest payments constitute a net transfer of funds to the rest of the world and the fact that bondholders are now external to the economy. If the borrowed money is used to finance current consumption expenditure, the future generation has to repay the loan without enjoying the benefits. In fact, their income will be reduced by the amount of the loan and/or the accrued interest that needs to be paid to the foreign lender. Aggregate consumption will be lower than in the case of domestic debt repayment. Should the money be used to finance capital accumulation, for example a railway line, the project's productivity is crucial. If it is a long-term asset with a real investment return in excess of the marginal cost of funds obtained abroad (i.e. the real interest rate on the loan), the combination of the debt and the performing asset actually makes the next generation better off. The opposite applies when the investment return is less than the marginal cost of funds.

Today it is realised that the incidence of the burden of public debt is a more complicated matter. Generations overlap and the inter-generational incidence of the debt burden may differ according to the income distribution, tax burdens and inflation rates experienced by future generations, information which is unknown at the time of the decision to borrow.

It should be noted that, apart from the equity considerations, external debt could alleviate pressures on the domestic financial markets (i.e. on the domestic supply of saving) during an economic upswing. Should the government decide to borrow abroad during such times, external debt may therefore also fulfil a macroeconomic stabilisation role.

16.5.3 Inter-temporal burden

Lerner regarded a generation as consisting of everyone who is alive at a given time. If, however, we define a generation as everyone who was born at the same time, several generations exist at any particular point in time and the burden of the debt may in fact be transferred across generations. An inter-temporal burden is said to exist.

Suppose the government introduces a new programme that benefits everyone alive at a specific point in time. Debt finance is used. Suppose further that a special tax has to be instituted once the debt repayment commences. It may well be that older citizens, who benefited from the programme, are no longer around. This implies that they escape the burden of the tax, which has to be carried by members of younger generations.

The burden of the debt can thus be transferred to future generations. The distinction between external and internal debt is of no relevance in this case. Even if the debt is all internal, a burden is created for the future generation. It is of course possible for the next generation to shift the burden forward once again!

From the point of view of inter-generational income distribution, it is very difficult to anticipate whether the next generation will be richer than the present generation. It is not inconceivable, of course, that if this is to be known or suspected, the present generation may deliberately vote for an **inter**-generational redistributive fiscal policy such as using debt finance, much the same as they may vote for **intra**-generational redistribution from the rich to the poor. The wealth of the next generation can of course not be known, but it could be that the present generation's actions add to the wealth of the future generation. If, for example, there is a legacy of high quality public infrastructure to the next generation, the present generation may judge that the next generation will have a much better prospect of generating wealth than they had. In the eyes of the present generation debt financing would then be an appropriate policy instrument of inter-generational redistribution.

The inter-generational debt burden is a more complicated issue in a country experiencing a major change (discontinuity) in its political dispensation, such as experienced by countries in Eastern Europe and South Africa, and countries in Africa, Asia and South America which converted from autocracy to democracy. Often there are strong populist pressures on the new government to renege on debt payment or on foreign countries (or institutions) for debt exoneration. The argument is that the present generation cannot be held ransom by creditors of the rejected previous regime. The discontinuity in the political system does not imply, however, a discontinuity in debt commitments, which are a legal obligation. Moreover, you cannot claim debt forgiveness while enjoying the benefit of the assets, which were accumulated in the process.

The inter-temporal fiscal burden reminds us that the distribution of fiscal benefits and burdens between generations cannot be measured in terms of what happens in a particular fiscal year. A lifetime perspective is required. In generational accounting the present value of lifetime taxes to be paid by a representative person of each generation is compared to the present value of lifetime benefits to be enjoyed from government services. The difference is the "net tax" (at present value). A comparison of the "net tax" of different generations gives a sense of how fiscal policy distributes income across generations (see Rosen 2002: 432).

16.5.4 Fiscal neutrality and Ricardian equivalence

We now consider the question whether the burden of debt financing is any different from that of tax financing. This introduces the oldest view on debt financing, associated with the British classical economist of the early nineteenth century, David Ricardo. This view, of which Robert Barro is probably the most important modern exponent, states that it is immaterial or irrelevant whether government uses tax or debt finance. The behaviour of individuals will be the same in both cases.

The argument is as follows. When government borrows (sells bonds) instead of levying taxes to finance public expenditure, the current generation is "under-taxed". They are rational, however, and realise that the loan will have to be repaid from tax income at some future date. Debt finance is therefore a postponement of the tax burden, which will fall on the next generation. The current generation will not want their heirs to be worse off (i.e. enjoy a lower level of consumption) on account of the "under-funded" benefit which they are enjoying and will therefore increase their bequests by an amount equal to the increase in the tax burden of the next generation. This constitutes a voluntary reduction in private spending, cancelling the impact on domestic demand of the debt-financed government expenditure. The result is that the government's choice of debt financing is neutralised in terms of its effect on aggregate demand, and the effect on the well being of successive generations is nullified by the rational behaviour of taxpayers and bondholders (i.e. investors in government bonds). Tax finance is therefore equivalent to debt finance (the so-called **Ricardian equivalence**) and activist fiscal policy (i.e. increasing the budget deficit to stimulate the economy – see Section 16.5.5) becomes ineffective.

This argument has been the subject of much debate and empirical testing. A number of qualifications need to be noted. Firstly, the type of public expenditure is important. It may be equally rational to argue that capital expenditure benefits future generations as well and that they should in fact co-finance the expenditure. Tax finance will place the full burden on the current generation, whilst debt finance will spread the burden over both generations, provided the maturity of the debt is long enough. In this case debt finance will be justified in that it will avoid an excessive burden on the present generation. Debt finance will, in other words, ensure inter-generational equity.

Secondly, the neat theoretical separation of two generations has been criticised. Heirs are not universal to all families and genera-

tions overlap as well, as we have already seen in Section 16.5.3. Thirdly, information about the implications of debt finance for future generations will not be easy to determine. Finally, empirical results are an important test of the existence of Ricardian equivalence. If it were to apply, one would expect the current generation to increase private savings in the event of an increase in government debt. However, the opposite tends to occur. In South Africa, for instance, a drop in private savings as a percentage of GDP accompanied an increase in public debt as a percentage of GDP during the 1980s and 1990s.

Ricardian equivalence thus suggests that it is immaterial whether tax or debt finance is used. We have not, however, exhausted all the arguments in our search for the rationale for debt finance. We now come to a very powerful argument for debt finance that dominated economic policy thinking from the Great Depression to the first half of the 1970s.

16.5.5 Fiscal activism and Keynesian demand management

According to the famous British economist, John Maynard Keynes, aggregate demand determines total production and income in the economy. Due to the working of the income multiplier (see Chapter 7, Section 7.6) the government is able to increase or decrease the national income by changing aggregate demand. During recessionary economic conditions the appropriate fiscal policy may be either a reduction in taxes or an increase in government expenditure, both of which would increase the budget deficit (or reduce the surplus). The converse applies during an economic boom.

Keynesian demand management dominated fiscal and monetary policy thinking for more than 40 years. The government was not expected to present balanced budgets as advocated by classical economists (a view to which we will return in the next section), but to stimulate domestic demand as long as there was unemployment. Budget deficits (or deficit spending) were regarded as an effective way of reducing unemployment in a non-inflationary manner. In Keynesian thinking, deficit spending can be the result of either an increase in government expenditure or a decrease in taxes. Rising public debt in periods of recession and falling public debt in boom periods were associated, conceptually at least, with macroeconomic stabilisation. The Keynesian approach entailed efforts to fine-tune the economy and ensure the correct level of domestic demand commensurate with full employment and price stability.

Gradually economists and politicians began to lose faith in attempts to manage domestic demand in this manner. Two reasons for this scepticism may be highlighted. The first is that it became much easier to increase budget deficits and the public debt in periods of economic downswing than to reverse the trend during upswings. In fact, increasingly higher deficit-GDP and public debt-GDP ratios were observed. It was problematic to justify further increases in budget deficits to increase employment in a non-inflationary manner if the existing high deficits were already fuelling inflationary expectations.

Secondly, during the 1970s and 1980s a growing body of economists and economic policy-makers in various countries came to realise that the economic problems of both industrial and developing countries were structural rather than cyclical in nature. Core or structural unemployment and inflation persisted to such an extent that short-term demand management was increasingly regarded as an ineffective way of trying to deal with unemployment and inflation. This resulted in a switch to the so-called supply-side approach in which debt financing had much less, if any, justification from a macroeconomic stabilisation point of view. The emphasis shifted to small(er) budget deficits, balanced budgets and even budget surpluses. Neo-classical thinking and public choice theorists are the driving forces behind these views, which, incidentally, date back to the eighteenth and the nineteenth centuries. It would therefore be more correct to talk of the revival of old ideas rather than of new insights, although some modern variations have been added.

16.5.6 The crowding-out phenomenon

Suppose an initial equilibrium in the goods and money markets is disturbed by a budget deficit incurred through an increase in government spending. What will the effect be on the economy? The increase in government expenditure means that aggregate demand increases, setting the multiplier process in motion. The resultant increase in income leads to an increase in the demand for money. If the supply of money remains constant in real terms, the excess demand for money causes interest rates to increase. Higher interest rates dampen private investment and thus aggregate expenditure. This reduction in aggregate demand dampens the initial multiplier effect, resulting in a lower new equilibrium level of income than would have applied if interest rates had remained unchanged. Such a fiscal policy therefore dampens the rate of private capital formation (i.e. private investment) in the economy. This phenomenon is called **crowding out** and may formally be defined as the dampening of private investment on account of increases in interest rates associated with an increase in debt financed public expenditure.[5] This happens when government, through its borrowing, competes with the private sector for funds. This line of argument is associated with the neo-classical school of thought.

---

5 More generally, crowding out may occur whenever there is fiscal expansion that increases interest rates, implying its occurrence under tax financing as well. See Dornbusch, Fischer, Mohr & Rodgers (1994: 171).

16.5.7 The public choice view

In Chapter 6 we studied the properties of the various social choice rules and the extent to and conditions under which an optimal allocation of resources would be possible. We also encountered the public choice argument that democratic institutions (politicians, bureaucrats, voters and interest groups) exhibit inherent biases towards an "over-expansion" of the public sector, that is, the democratic process tends to lead to higher than optimal levels of government expenditure.

Public choice economists argue that there are two causes of this bias. Firstly, it is attributed to the alleged co-existence of concentrated benefits and a diffused or widely spread distribution of costs in respect of the government's expenditure programmes. Put differently, small groups tend to benefit from certain public expenditure programmes but the cost is spread over all (or a larger group) of taxpayers. A programme or set of programmes with clearly defined benefits will have a better chance of being approved if the advocating groups are well organised and the cost of financing is obscure or hidden.

Salary increases for highly unionised public officials are an example of the above-mentioned kind of expenditure programme. Debt finance, especially inflationary financing through money creation, is an example of a very diffuse financing mechanism. In the case of loan finance only a part of the burden of the cost is incurred in the year in which the expenditure has to be voted. It may actually be a deliberate political strategy to sell debt-financed programmes to voters because it enables politicians to be vague about the cost. This form of strategic behaviour may be particularly prevalent at the sub-national level in cases where the

particular tier of government is highly dependent on transfer income from a higher tier of government. It is so much more tempting (and even easier) to sell expenditure programs to your voters if another politician is accountable to a different constituency for the financing. Provincial politicians, for example, may use these tactics to force larger transfer payments from the national government to the provinces with the result that the tax or debt burden at the national level is increased.[6] These practices rest on the assumed existence of **fiscal illusion** among the electorate which may be defined as the belief that taxes are lower than they actually are or are going to be.[7]

The second cause of the bias towards high levels of government expenditure is the separation of benefits and costs in the budgetary process. This actually reinforces the first cause. Expenditure and revenue budgets are designed and voted on separately by parliaments. The one-year nature of budgeting is a further cause, because annual budgeting allows for the approval of expenditure programs without information on the concomitant long-term expenditure commitments and the long-term tax or debt implications of the total of all expenditure programs. The future gap between expenditure and revenue, which by definition amounts to future debt financing, may increase without anyone being aware of it. This separation of revenue and expenditure decisions is linked to the ability-to-pay approach to taxation, in other words, financing on basis of equity rather than efficiency considerations. Public choice economists therefore tend to argue strongly for the increased application of the benefit principle of taxation (instead of the ability-to-pay principle). An additional method of correcting for the above-mentioned problems is to apply medium-term

---

6 Incidentally, taxation through inflation as a result of bracket creep, which was discussed in Chapter 11 (Section 11.5.4), falls in the same category.

7 More than 90 years ago an Italian fiscal economist by the name of Puviani recognised that the existence of a fiscal illusion or the potential for its establishment would enable or ensure the continued tax financing of growing demands for public goods.

fiscal planning (see Chapter 17, Section 17.7).

Public choice economists also argue that the alleged bias towards "over-expansion" of the public sector has been fed by the Keynesian legacy of budget deficits explained in Section 16.5.5. In many countries the size of the public debt and the budget reached such proportions that their concomitant fine-tuning properties were lost.

The public choice view on how to improve efficiency in the allocation of public resources has important implications for debt financing. Public choice economists argue that **constitutional fiscal limits** are required to correct for the over expansion bias, that is, they favour more rules and less discretion in fiscal policy. **A balanced budget** – in other words, no debt financing – is an extreme version of this prognosis. In the United States the idea of a balanced government budget has become very popular. This can be attributed to the fact that there is a strong correspondence in this regard between public choice and neoclassical thinking which gained the upper hand in macroeconomic policy thinking in the United States in recent years. There are many practical problems associated with statutory fiscal limits, such as the difficulty of enforcing a balanced budget rule when the margin of error in government revenue projections is substantial.

16.5.8 Summary of views on the impact of debt

The time has come to summarise our findings. Table 16.3 consists of a matrix of possibilities associated with the various viewpoints discussed above (the rows) and the basic economic considerations of efficiency, equity and macroeconomic stability (the columns). Where possible, the name of the major exponent or school of thought is also indicated.

Table 16.3 Summary of views on the impact of public debt

Viewpoint	Efficiency	Equity	Macroeconomic stability
Internal-external debt argument (Lerner)		External debt creates a burden for the future generation; internal debt is an intra-generational transfer	External debt can relieve pressures on domestic saving during economic upswings
Inter-temporal burden		All (external and internal) debt can impose a burden on the future generation	
Ricardian equivalence (Ricardo)		Individuals behave in such a way that the impact of tax and loan finance on the future generation is equated	Individuals increase saving (reduce consumption), thus rendering activist fiscal policy ineffective
Fiscal activism (Keynes)			Debt financed fiscal expansion increases aggregate demand to equate aggregate supply at full employment and price stability

Crowding out of private investment (neoclassical)		Debt may accompany transfer of earning assests (e.g. infra-structure) to future generation	Debt financed fiscal expansion reduces private investment rate and economic growth, or increases inflation
Public choice	Bias towards overexpansion of public sector (non-efficient expenditure levels) to be neutralised by balanced budget rule (no debt financing) (some correspondence with neo-classical thinking)		Excessive government spending is fed by deficit budgeting without achieving macro-economic stability

16.6 Should the government tax or borrow?

On the basis of the foregoing discussion of the rationale for public debt and our earlier analysis of taxation, we consider the question as to which of taxation or loans (debt) is best as financing instrument for public expenditure. Remember that debt is nothing but postponed taxation, so that in a sense our question is one of **when** to tax, rather than **whether or not** to tax. We look at the question by referring to the allocation (efficiency) and distribution (equity) of resources, and by considering the implications for macroeconomic stability.

16.6.1 Allocation (efficiency)

Is taxation more efficient than debt? The answer lies in its impact on technical efficiency, that is, the amount of excess burden created. In the previous paragraph we noted that the difference between tax and debt is one of timing. In order to compare efficiency, therefore, we must inquire as to the impact of the time difference on efficiency. Consider a particular project which is completed in one year and which may be financed either through tax or debt. If tax finance is used, the full cost of the

project is financed by levying a one-off tax. If loan finance is chosen, the loan will have to be repaid over a number of years, for purposes of which an amount of tax will have to be levied every year. If lump-sum taxes are used in each case, there is no excess burden, efficiency is ensured and there is thus no difference between tax and debt on efficiency grounds.

Not all taxes are efficient, however. In Chapter 10 (Section 10.2.3) we saw that, in the case of an *ad valorem* tax on a commodity, the amount of excess burden increases exponentially with the size of the tax rate. When a specific tax is collected by levying a one-off, relatively high, tax rate, it will therefore be less efficient than if the same amount of tax is obtained by levying a succession of low tax rates. The latter is precisely what happens in the case of debt financing. The debt servicing cost is spread over a number of years and requires a series of tax revenues. In this case debt financing will be **more** efficient than a one-off tax to finance the entire project up front. The choice between tax and debt on efficiency grounds, therefore, depends on the type of tax used.

The efficiency issue goes further, though. It extends also to the source of the funds. Generally speaking, taxation reduces private consumption and savings. Debt finance represents a direct use of savings, reducing the amount of savings available to finance private investment. To the extent that debt finance represents a larger reduction in the country's savings than tax, it will be less efficient than tax from the point of view of investment decisions. This is the crowding-out argument discussed in Section 16.5.6.

In combination, it is impossible to know *a priori* which of the above efficiency effects will dominate, that is, which of tax or debt finance is the more efficient. The net effect can only be established empirically.

16.6.2 Distribution (equity)

Intuitively debt finance constitutes the one method whereby more than one generation could contribute to the financing cost of activities that confer an inter-generational benefit, something that tax finance cannot effect. All debt imposes a burden on the future generation. The difficult part is knowing in advance what the concomitant benefit to the future generation will be. If we were to know, for example, that the future generation would be poorer than the present one, it would make sense to transfer income from the present to the future generation, for example by tax financing an infrastructural project with long-term benefits. The opposite would of course apply in the case of a richer future generation.

Ricardian equivalence theory suggests that the government need not concern itself with inter-generational equity, since society will voluntarily effect such equity as is preferred. By increasing their bequests in the face of debt finance, individuals will ensure that the impact of tax and loan finance on the next generation is equated. From an inter-generational equity point of view it is thus immaterial whether tax or debt finance is used.

The final equity consideration is linked to the benefit approach to taxation (see Chapter 14). According to this approach, if a particular programme benefits a particular group, it is fair (and efficient) for that group to pay for it.

There is thus no reason why the future generation should not pay for programmes that benefit them. To the extent that a programme benefits a future generation, they should carry part of the financing burden. Debt finance will ensure that.

16.6.3 Macroeconomic stability

From a macroeconomic perspective the choice between tax and debt arises at the margin, that is, should **additional** expenditure be financed by taxes or by loans, thus incurring a deficit or increasing the size of an existing deficit? No one has suggested that the full budget be loan financed. Keynesian economists argue that when unemployment is high, for example, debt-financed fiscal expansion is warranted in order to stimulate aggregate demand until it equals aggregate supply at the full employment level of income. Such a fiscal expansion may occur with or without a reduction in tax. The choice is therefore in favour of new debt rather than tax and may also entail substituting new debt for existing tax. On the other hand, when unemployment is low in the Keynesian world, deficit financing may be inflationary and tax increases (a lower budget deficit or a higher budget surplus) will be needed to constrain private spending.

In Section 16.5.5 we saw that the Keynesian consensus started to break down (in the early 1970s) when periods of high unemployment and high inflation were experienced and when it was no longer possible to increase employment in a non-inflationary manner. Lower budget deficits, preferably by keeping government expenditure in check, became the consensus view of Keynesians and monetarists (Dornbusch, Fischer, Mohr & Rogers, 1994: 397), albeit for quite different reasons. The monetarist argument is the crowding-out one already encountered (see Section 16.5.6): debt finance has to be reduced to "crowd in" private investment. The positive impact on investor confidence of reduced budget deficits may outstrip the depressing effect on income in the short term and may on balance be "good for growth". In addition, lower budget deficits reduce the risk of inflationary financing. The Keynesian argument is that a reduction in the budget deficit should be effected by curtailing government expenditure in order to avoid the cost-push effects of higher taxation – in other words, to avoid the cost of using tax rather than debt.

In the present era of globalisation, countries' freedom of choice to independently change budget deficits by large margins in order to pursue macroeconomic stability has been reduced substantially. In a world of competitive tax rates and increasing convergence of countries' budget deficit-GDP ratios at low levels, the choice in especially developing countries has become one of how much and how fast to reduce budget deficits, rather than of how high the budget deficit should be (i.e. how much debt instead of tax).

Important concepts
capital expenditure
contingent liabilities
crowding out
current expenditure
discount on a bond
domestic or internal debt
foreign exchange cost
foreign or external debt
government bond
gross borrowing requirement
inflation tax
inter-temporal burden
maturity or term structure
net worth of government
public debt
Ricardian equivalence
treasury bill

Self-assessment exercises

16.1 Distinguish between:
- Nominal and real debt
- Interest and discount on public debt
- Internal and external debt

16.2 Explain the nature of the different public debt costs.

16.3 Assume that the South African government borrows £100 in Britain on 1 January. The exchange rate is R16 = £1. How much will have to be repaid in rand after two years if the rand depreciates by 10 per cent per annum against the British pound over the period? How much will the loan cost the South African government if the British interest rate is five per cent per year? (Assume that interest is calculated and paid in advance on the first day of each year.)

16.4 If the government issues a bond with a nominal value of R100 at a discount of 10 per cent, what will be the return on investment for the bondholder?

16.5 Compare the different theories of public debt in terms of efficiency, equity and macro-economic stabilisation considerations.

16.6 Explain the contradictions (if any) between Ricardian equivalence, fiscal activism and crowding out as theories of public debt.

16.7 Are the following statements true (T) or false (F)? Explain your answer.
(a) Contingent liabilities form part of the public debt.
(b) The net worth of government is the difference between the value of all assets and the liabilities of government.
(c) If the government borrows in another country and the relative value of the respective currencies do not change over the period of the loan, there will be no foreign exchange rate cost.
(d) Ricardian equivalence means that it makes no difference to the level of aggregate demand whether the government uses tax or debt finance.
(e) There is no need to be concerned about a rising public debt-GDP ratio because public debt is something which a country owes to itself.

Chapter seventeen

Estian Calitz

Fiscal policy and the national budget

Fiscal policy-making and national budgeting are very complex tasks. Gerald Browne, Secretary of Finance from 1960 to 1977, aptly describes the experience of the fiscal policy-maker as follows:

"Those who have not personally taken part in such an exercise (of budgeting)[1] may find it difficult to appreciate the tremendous pressures for higher expenditure to which the Treasury is exposed – pressures applied, for the most part, with the best of motives and for expenditure on services of unquestioned merit. The Minister of Finance and his aides are condemned to fight a lonely and thankless battle for a cause that is seldom adequately understood." (Browne, 1983: 64)

The aim of this chapter is to study the nature of fiscal policy and its application in South Africa, with reference to theory and empirical observations discussed in earlier chapters.

Once you have studied this chapter, you should be able to
- define fiscal policy, and describe fiscal goals and instruments at macro, sectoral and micro level;
- describe the role and functions of the different fiscal authorities in South Africa and explain the need for policy coordination;
- discuss the effectiveness of fiscal policy with reference to different schools of thought, lags and uncertainty, and rules and discretion;
- describe salient features of fiscal policy in South Africa with reference to theory, and against the backdrop of international experience and aspects of the performance of the South African economy;
- distinguish between the various definitions of budget balance and explain the significance of each in economic analysis.

17.1 Introduction

The decisions of government about the allocation and distribution of resources is embodied in its fiscal policy and reflected in its budget. The term **fiscal policy** is normally used in relation to macroeconomic policy. Our focus, however, is broader and encompasses the micro aspects of the economy as well. This chapter affords us the opportunity to integrate, with reference to government decisions and decision-making processes, many of the theoretical and practical insights encountered in the previous chapters.

1 Part in parenthesis added.

Fiscal policy is conducted with a view to satisfying a range of macroeconomic objectives, but when it does not consider or map out the implications for resource allocation at the sectoral and micro level, it is seldom sustainable. For example, if aggregate government expenditure has to be reduced to combat inflation and all spending programmes are simply cut in equal measure, the efficiency and equity consequences at the programme and project level of government can be profound. On the other hand, if the government yields to pressures for more government expenditure at the programme and project level without proper cognisance of the macroeconomic consequences, it can have serious implications for inflation, balance of payments stability and even long-term economic growth, thus also jeopardising fiscal sustainability. Fiscal policy and budgeting is therefore a juggling act of balancing "unlimited" demands with limited resources. After all, that is what economics is all about.

In this chapter we first explore the nature of fiscal policy, with special reference to the South African experience. Then we discuss key features of fiscal policy in South Africa since 1970. In conclusion, various aspects of the national budget and the budgetary process are considered.

17.2 The nature of fiscal policy

17.2.1 Definition

Fiscal policy may be defined as national government decisions regarding the nature, level and composition of government expenditure, taxation and borrowing, aimed at pursuing particular goals. Fiscal policy, like any other form of economic policy, has both an **active** element (when a deliberate step is implemented to do **something**, e.g. to increase the budget deficit) and a **passive** element (when there is a deliberate decision to **do nothing** or to refrain from doing some-

thing, e.g. when no tax increases are announced in a particular budget).

17.2.2 Goals of fiscal policy

We can distinguish between the following **macro goals** of fiscal policy:
- Economic growth
- Job creation
- Price stability
- Balance of payments stability
- A socially acceptable distribution of income
- Poverty alleviation

Note that none of the government functions, programmes and taxes, which constitute the annual budget of the government, appears in this list, the reason being that these are the **instruments**, which the government uses to pursue the above goals.

The **sectoral goals** of fiscal policy include the following:
- Development of particular economic sectors, such as agriculture, tourism, mining, manufacturing or the financial markets.
- The pursuance of social goals pertaining to sectors such as housing, education, health and welfare.

It is also possible to specify **micro goals** of fiscal policy. Such goals will arise when fiscal action is aimed at a single economic participant or group of participants. Normally they can be seen as subdivisions of sectoral goals. The following are examples of micro goals:
- Improving efficiency by addressing negative externalities in respect of a particular **product** (e.g. tobacco) or **activity** (e.g. toxic waste disposal of a chemical plant).
- Combating poverty (the equity consideration) by intervening in the **market** for a particular product (e.g. a bread subsidy).
- Pursuing goals with regard to a particular **geographical** (suburban or rural) **area**, for example where government financed infrastructure and housing subsidies for

low-income earners are incorporated in a residential development project.

The goals in these different categories are not pursued by applying fiscal policy only. Monetary policy, trade and industrial policy, competition policy and labour policy are important allies in the endeavour to achieve these goals. Sometimes the goals are in conflict and it is necessary to prioritise them. For example, it may not always be advisable to increase economic growth further because of the inflationary dangers associated with striving for higher growth. The government must then decide which of economic growth or price stability should receive the highest priority. In such circumstances we say there is a **trade-off** between economic growth and inflation. If the growth objective is accorded the highest priority, fiscal policy is bound to be different than when price stability receives the highest priority.

Certain policies or policy instruments are more effective in pursuing some goals than others. An increase in interest rates (monetary policy) may, for example, achieve quicker results than tax increases (fiscal policy) if private spending is to be reduced to combat inflation. The policy authorities must therefore not only decide on the priority of policy goals, but also choose the most effective policy instrument for the job at hand.

What, might be asked, happened to **efficiency** and **equity**? Are they not the ultimate goals? Have we not on numerous occasions emphasised these as the two eminent measures for assessing any fiscal action? In previous chapters we extensively studied various theories regarding public goods, government expenditure, taxation and debt. In all these theories efficiency and equity were recurrent themes. We paid particular attention to the following:

- The conditions for Pareto efficiency in the allocation of resources between the supply of public and private goods and the equity implications (Chapters 2, 3 & 5).

- The extent to which different voting rules produce efficient outcomes (Chapter 6).
- Identifying those taxes that maximise efficiency (or minimise inefficiency) in the allocation of resources in the private sector and assessing the equity implications of different taxes (Chapters 9 & 10).
- The trade-offs that have to be considered between efficiency and equity when dealing with the issues of poverty and income distribution (Chapter 15).
- The choice between taxes and debt on the basis of efficiency criteria, while considering the inter- and intra-generational distributional consequences of debt financing (Chapter 16).

Efficiency and equity, however, do not readily lend themselves to the specification of quantifiable targets at the macro level. Instead of equity, we therefore use more specific goals such as a socially acceptable distribution of income or poverty alleviation, for which we can develop quantified goals. The government may, for instance, decide on a programme to reduce the Gini coefficient (see Chapter 15, Section 15.1.1). Under certain conditions the promotion of economic growth and job creation will also serve the equity goal. Efficiency goals can be developed at the level of government programmes while the tax system can be designed with efficiency in mind, but at the macro level it is not that easy. In general terms higher economic growth may be seen as a reflection of improved efficiency, but this is by no means obvious. Inflation may also be a barometer of efficiency, or the lack of it. The "ultimate" goals of efficiency and equity are thus included (or subsumed) in the list of macro goals of fiscal policy.

17.2.3 Instruments of fiscal policy

As in the case of goals, we also distinguish between **macro** and **micro instruments** of fiscal policy. In **macro** terms the instruments include total government expenditure; the economic categories of consumption and capital expenditure; the total tax amount; the budget deficit; and the way in which the deficit is financed. In **sectoral** or **micro** terms the instruments are the various expenditure functions (e.g. education, health and defence); votes and programmes; the different kinds of taxes and their rates; and the different dimensions of the public debt (such as maturity, ownership structure, etc.).

To form an idea of the many government activities that affect the allocation of resources in the economy, note that in 2002/03 no fewer than 121 government programmes (excluding administration and auxiliary and associated services) were specified in the 33 votes in terms of which budgetary allocations were made. These programmes cover a wide and divergent set of activities, ranging from surveys and mapping to air defence; from legal aid to pollution control; from higher education to the promotion of mine safety and health; and from social security to land reform (National Treasury 2002b). In the *Budget Review 2002* (National Treasury 2002a: 196-198), a total of 31 taxes or groups of taxes were identified (i.e. counting all the different excise duties as one tax). The economic impact of some of them is largely limited to a particular sector or a limited number of sectors of the economy (e.g. in the case of the excise tax on tobacco). Others, such as value-added tax, the fuel tax and income tax on individuals and companies, exert their influence throughout the economy and changes in these taxes may therefore affect the macroeconomic performance of the country.

17.2.4 Classifying fiscal policy goals and instruments

On the basis of the above discussion we can classify the fiscal policy goals and instruments as shown in Table 17.1.

Table 17.1 Classification of fiscal policy goals and instruments

Instrument category	Goals	
	Macro	**Sectoral/micro**
Expenditure	Changes in total level of expenditure Changes in total level of consumption expenditure Changes in total level of capital expenditure (investment)	Changes in functional composition of expenditure and in underlying policies Changes in votes, programmes, projects, etc. (expenditure amounts and underlying policies) Introdution of new votes, programmes, projects etc.
Revenue	Changes in total level of tax	Changes in individual taxes (tax bases and rates) Introduction of new taxes
Borrowing and public debt management	Changes in total budget deficit	Changes in the composition of public debt (maturity, ownership structure, etc.)

17.3 The fiscal authorities

17.3.1 Parliament

The executive organs of the state are accountable to the National Assembly in terms of the Constitution. As far as the budget is concerned, Parliament has the power to accept or reject it as a whole. This limited legislative power is regarded as an obstacle to more extensive parliamentary involvement in the budgetary process.

Parliamentary committees play an important role in assisting the National Assembly to fulfil its obligations to the budget. The **Standing Committee on Public Accounts** deals with the monitoring and control of government expenditure. It fulfils this task by publicly debating the findings of reports of the Auditor-General and reporting to Parliament. In addition there are a number of **Portfolio Committees**, responsible for, *inter alia*, the monitoring of the activities of individual government departments and for making recommendations relating to their budgets.

17.3.2 The Minister of Finance

The key figure in fiscal policy is the **Minister of Finance** who is given certain statutory powers by acts of parliament. He/she has the authority to levy taxes, allocate state income (tax and non-tax revenue) and borrow funds domestically and internationally. No state guarantees can be given to borrow money without the approval of the Minister of Finance. He/she is also responsible for the protection of the country's gold and foreign exchange reserves. In some cases the Minister has immediate decision-making authority, such as increasing the rate of value-added tax,[2] excise duties or the fuel levy during the course of the government's financial year, or giving guarantees for foreign borrowing by parastatals such as Eskom. In other cases, such as changing income tax rates or implementing the appropriation of state monies in the annual budget, parliamentary approval in the form of specific acts of parliament is required before any changes can be made. The Minister of Finance does not take important decisions without the approval of, or after consultation with, Cabinet. He/she is accountable to Parliament for all decisions taken.

17.3.3 The need for policy coordination

The Minister's statutory functions translate into a responsibility for macroeconomic policy, even though this is not specifically spelled out as such in any act of parliament. His/her statutory powers include all the fiscal policy instruments of government expenditure, taxation and borrowing. The Constitution furthermore requires consultation between the South African Reserve Bank and the Minister of Finance regarding the implementation of monetary policy, the Bank's generic policy function. In practice, therefore, the Finance Minister is responsible for macroeconomic policy formulation and coordination, lays down the basic framework for monetary and exchange rate policy, and manages fiscal policy.

The two key institutions in support of macroeconomic policy are the **South African Reserve Bank** (monetary and exchange rate policy) and the **National Treasury** (macroeconomic and fiscal policy, expenditure allocation and control). Another very important fiscal institution is the **South African Revenue Service** (SARS), which is responsible, *inter alia*, for tax collection and tax law enforcement. SARS also plays an important supportive and advisory role in the determination of tax policy. Close coordination between these institutions is necessary for effective economic policy making.

There is an old saying that monetary

---

2 Section 77 of the Value-added Tax Act (Act 89 of 1991) authorises the Minister to make such adjustments, with the proviso that Parliament has to legislate this within six months after notification.

policy begins in the **Treasury**. This signifies much more than the fact that public debt is financed by issuing government bonds, the main instrument of open-market policies by the central bank. It is a statement about the close links between monetary and fiscal policy in the pursuit of macroeconomic goals. The economic impact of fiscal and monetary policies are such that each of the fiscal and monetary authorities has to systematically study and regularly monitor the combined impact of these measures on economic behaviour. The fiscal policy menu that a particular country chooses has to be framed in the context of a coherent macroeconomic policy strategy including monetary policy and a number of other policies (e.g. trade and competition policy). The implementation of such a strategy requires regular consultation and active coordination between the Minister of Finance and the Governor of the Reserve Bank and their respective staff.

Another important form of coordination pertains to the formulation of tax policy, where close cooperation between the Department of Finance and SARS is essential. The main functions of the above-mentioned fiscal institutions are summarised below.

17.3.4 National Treasury

The National Treasury supports the Minister of Finance in conducting macroeconomic policy. It has the following operational tasks relating to macroeconomic and fiscal policy:
- To pursue monetary and fiscal policies in support of macroeconomic stability and economic policy goals of a longer-term nature.
- To manage the public debt.
- To promote a fair and efficient system of taxation and a cost-effective funding strategy.
- To introduce budget reforms to facilitate

expenditure planning and reprioritisation of government expenditure.

In addition, the following functions pertain to government expenditure:
- Control of government expenditure.
- Planning, coordination and determination of budget allocations.
- Cash flow management.

17.3.5 South African Revenue Service (SARS)

Following years of experimentation on how to structure the organisation of revenue collection in South Africa so as to ensure maximum efficiency, SARS was established as a separate government department on 1 April 1996. It gained administrative autonomy as a public body outside of the public service as of 1 October 1997 (Department of Finance 1998: 9.2). The South African Revenue Service Act (Act 34 of 1997) mandates it, *inter alia*, to collect all national taxes, duties and levies, and advise the Minister of Finance on revenue-related matters.

17.4 The effectiveness of fiscal policy[3]

How effective is fiscal policy in achieving particular economic goals? Throughout this book we encountered various schools of thought on the possible influence of fiscal policies on economic behaviour. These influences depend on the particular **view** of the **role of government** (or of **fiscal policy**) and on some **realities about policy-making**.

17.4.1 Different views of the role of government (fiscal policy)

After World War II **Keynesian activism** elevated fiscal policy to the macroeconomic level. Government was given the responsibility to actively manage (increase or decrease) aggregate demand so that it equals

---

3 This section relies substantially on Dornbusch, Fischer, Mohr & Rogers (1994: 394-397).

aggregate supply at the full employment level of income. In recessionary conditions policy-makers should increase government expenditure or reduce taxes (which could increase the budget deficit or change a budget surplus into a balanced budget or a budget deficit). Should the economy become overheated during an economic boom, thus experiencing (rising) inflation, the opposite measures are warranted, that is, a decrease in government expenditure or an increase in taxes.

The stabilising impact of fiscal policy was seen to be strengthened further by income taxes and unemployment benefits. These were regarded as automatic (or built-in) stabilisers, in the sense that changes in income would automatically trigger changes in tax revenue and transfer payments, thus stabilising aggregate demand, income and output. An **automatic** (or **built-in**) **stabiliser** can be defined as any mechanism in the economy that reduces the income multiplier effects of changes in autonomous demand. As income rises in an economy with a progressive individual income tax system, for example, taxpayers move into higher income tax categories, causing their tax liabilities to rise faster than their income. The result is a slower rise in their disposable income and, therefore, in their capacity to spend. However, inflation and the apparent propensity of governments to spend all additional tax revenue, have rendered the concept of automatic stabilisers practically irrelevant.

Keynesian economics dominated fiscal policy until the early 1970s. The conventional Keynesian wisdom began to crumble in the wake of the joint appearance of unemployment and inflation after the oil price shocks of 1973 and the realisation that the popular version of Keynesian economics, namely short-term demand management, did not present a solution for structural unemployment. The contemporary view is that the appropriate combina-

tion of policy measures to pursue goals of higher economic growth, job creation and price stability is of an eclectic nature. It incorporates prescriptions derived from more than one economic theory, but is firmly based in neoclassical thinking (Calitz, 1997: 328).

Neoclassical economists view excessive government intervention in the economy as a source of instability or as an action, which crowds out private investment. They prescribe a smaller budget deficit to promote price stability and increase economic growth. **Monetarists**, in particular, do not see any anti-cyclical or anti-inflationary role for fiscal policy. They are only interested in the financing of whatever budget deficit arises, and particularly in the extent to which government expenditure is financed by money creation (with its possible inflationary consequences).

The inability of Keynesian policies to face up to the challenges of cost-push inflation, supply shocks and stagflation, forced Keynesians to re-examine their earlier views on fiscal policy. Apart from the direct effects of increases in indirect taxes on costs and prices, it also became apparent in many countries that a rising personal income tax burden could be a major source of increased wage claims.

Three major implications emerged from this Keynesian re-think on fiscal policy.
- Given the nature of the inflation process, tax increases could no longer be regarded as an instrument of anti-inflationary policy.
- The notion of the income tax as an automatic or built-in stabiliser was no longer valid – in fact, it could operate as a built-in **destabiliser**, *via* its effect on the determination of wage levels.
- Government spending had to be kept in check, since the increasing tax burden associated with increased government spending could give further impetus to inflation.

Besides Keynesianism and monetarism, there is a third approach to fiscal policy, namely that of the **supply-side** economists. This line of thinking became very popular in the United States in the 1970s and 1980s. Supply-siders advocate a particular brand of fiscal policy as a cure for stagflation. Recall, from our discussion of the **Laffer curve** in Chapter 11, that supply-siders base their argument for reducing the relative size of government in the economy on microeconomic incentives. They recommend a reduction in marginal tax rates (to increase the incentive to work, save and invest) and a concomitant reduction in government spending (to create more scope for private sector activity).

One common denominator in the different views on fiscal policy that emerged during the 1970s was that **government spending had to be kept in check** for the following reasons: to avoid crowding out and/or inflationary financing (the monetarist argument); to avoid the cost-push effects of higher taxation (the Keynesian argument); and to create the necessary scope for tax cuts to increase the incentive to work, save and invest (the supply-side argument). The emphasis on government expenditure restraint also corresponds with the public choice view of an over-expansionary bias in social choices regarding the size of government (see Chapter 7, Section 7.2.7).

Government expenditure restraint remained an important ingredient of the fiscal strategies, which came to characterise the conventional wisdom regarding economic restructuring during the 1980s and 1990s. Fiscal discipline, entailing smaller budget deficits and, in some cases, even budget surpluses, became a feature of the Washington consensus[4] – the name given to the growing international consensus which developed since the early 1980s in industrial, transition-al and developing economies about the appropriate package of economic reform measures to deal with structural unemployment and low economic growth. This market-based reform strategy entails fiscal rectitude, competitive exchange rates, free trade, privatisation, non-distorted market prices and limited government intervention (except in respect of exports, education and infrastructure) (Rodrik, 1996: 1).

Criticism of these reforms emanates mainly from economists working within the **structuralist** tradition of development economics. They argue that social, institutional and economic institutions can exert a powerful influence on the way in which (policy) instruments work, perhaps even undermining the effectiveness of measures that might be regarded as the obvious ones to apply in a developed country context (Weiss, 1995: 5). The implication is that market-based solutions may not always be effective and that direct controls and interventions may be required from time to time. Structuralist models often see a useful role for direct measures, for example credit ceilings, import quotas and wage and price controls (Weiss, 1995: 262). Though these measures may have short-run effects that will reduce allocative efficiency, structuralists argue that such measures will help to overcome macro bottlenecks and thus restore growth.

The international financial crisis of 1997-1998 precipitated further criticism of the Washington consensus. In an attempt to promote a post-Washington consensus, World Bank Chief Economist Joseph Stiglitz (1998: 17) attacked the underlying set of policies of the Washington consensus as "neither necessary nor sufficient for macroeconomic stability or long-term development". Since the Washington consensus emanated from an attempt to deal with rampant inflation in Latin American countries in the 1980s, he

---

4 The Washington consensus owes its name to the similarities between the policy requirements or conditions which the International Monetary Fund, the World Bank and the United States include in their lending agreements with countries.

did not regard it as suitable to deal with the problems of macroeconomic instability, unemployment and poverty which plagued the world economy at the end of the 20th century. The financial crises of the early 1980s occurred in the context of highly regulated financial systems, in which many of the regulations were designed to limit competition. At the time of the 1997-1998 crisis, however, there was a lack, rather than a high degree, of financial regulation and inflation was under control in the countries in which the crisis began. Furthermore, the contention is that the microeconomic underpinnings of macroeconomic stability require much more attention. The post-Washington consensus warns against liberalisation of goods and financial markets as a goal in its own right. Stiglitz (1998:6,14) argues that the key issues are **proper competition**, rather than trade **liberalisation** and injudicious and hasty **privatisation**, and the construction of a **regulatory** framework that ensures an effective financial system, rather than financial liberalisation or deregulation.

In addition to the above differences of view regarding the appropriateness or relevance of fiscal policy, there are some **practical features of fiscal policy** that determine its potential effectiveness, namely the existence of lags in fiscal policy and the degree of discretion which policy-makers have in decision-making. We now consider these issues.

17.4.2 Lags and uncertainty in fiscal policy

Whenever fiscal steps are considered, it has to be noted that the policy-making process goes through various stages, each with its own delays or time lags. Four such lags can be distinguished.

The **recognition lag** is the delay between changes in economic activity and the recognition that the changes have occurred. Economic data are not immediately available. It takes time, for example, to compile the national accounts, which provide information on economic growth and the state of the economy in general. This data is published every three months in the *Quarterly Bulletin* of the South African Reserve Bank. By the time the South African Government's annual budget is presented in February every year, the latest available GDP figures are estimated up to the end of the third quarter of the previous year. If, for example, the Minister of Finance wants to present a budget to stimulate economic growth, a significant margin of error is possible, since information about the performance of the economy is lagging by six months.

The **decision lag** refers to the time that elapses between the recognition of the problem and the decision how to react. Various factors play a role, such as the analysis of various options, the time required for discussion between officials and Ministers and, eventually, the speed with which Cabinet takes a decision. The South African Constitution places a high premium on consultation and various consultative forums exist for this purpose, such as the National Economic Development and Labour Council (Nedlac) and the Budget Council and Budget Forum (bodies of consultation with provinces and local government, respectively). These forums and various consultative processes, such as the public hearings of the Parliamentary Committees, may all contribute to the decision lag. These lags are particularly evident when legislation is required and key role players have to be consulted before a proposal is put to Cabinet.

The **implementation lag** refers to the time it takes before a decision is implemented. This lag arises mostly from **procedures of orderly and accountable government**. The national budget, for example, can only be implemented once it has been enacted by Parliament. In South Africa this normally happens round about June of each year, that is, about three months after the start of the fiscal year. The Government therefore has a standing legislative authority to spend funds provisionally until the budget is approved by Parliament. If an urgent matter turns up after the budget has been legislated, there are provisions enabling the Government to make limited changes during the course of the year. Otherwise it has to stand over until the next year.

The implementation lag, however, is also influenced by **administrative procedures in the private sector**. If the VAT rate is to be changed, for instance, adjustments are required to financial documentation, cash registers and other automated business machines in the private sector before the decision can be implemented.

The **impact lag** refers to the time it takes before a policy measure, having been implemented, begins to affect economic behaviour. An increase in income tax, for instance, can take quite some time before its full impact on private expenditure is realised. Taxpayers may not immediately behave as though their after-tax spending power has been reduced. They may reduce personal savings, for instance, in an attempt to maintain their living standard for some time. Another example of an impact lag arises when businesses delay price increases on account of higher taxes to reap some temporary competitive benefits. On the expenditure side of the budget, certain programmes (e.g. welfare payments) have a much shorter impact lag than others (e.g. capital expenditure). In the latter case the time lag may be quite long, for example when transport or defence equipment are ordered with long delivery lags.

In combination these lags mean that there are definite limits to the ability to use fiscal policy when rapid changes in economic behaviour are required. This is one reason why activist demand management by means of fiscal policy is easier in theory than in practice. Attempts to fine-tune the economy are often thwarted by one or more of these lags, the result frequently being that too much or too little is done too late.

Because of this, intended counter-cyclical fiscal policy may *de facto* be **pro-cyclical**. If, for example, by the time of the budget the economy has already entered a growth phase, an expansionary budget may have the perverse effect of boosting inflation rather than real income. Small wonder that the structure of the public finance in South Africa during the period 1960 to 1986 was found to have had a destabilising rather than a stabilising effect on the economy (Strydom, 1987). Generally, the decision and implementation lags are normally shorter in the case of monetary policy, thus increasing the latter's relative effectiveness regarding macroeconomic stabilisation policy.

17.4.3 Discretion versus rules in fiscal policy

A useful perspective on the fiscal ability to effect rapid changes in economic behaviour is obtained when looking at the extent of discretion that fiscal authorities have in fiscal decision-making. **Rules** are statutory or non-statutory practices, which are implemented automatically, routinely and without significant variation. **Discretion** refers to independent decision-making within or without a set of rules. Two examples illustrate this distinction. The fiscal authorities cannot change personal income tax rates at will. These rates can only be changed by an act of parliament which rules out short-term discretionary changes by the executive. Once a set of income tax rates has been legislated and for as long as these rates apply, the effect of income tax on the spending behaviour of taxpayers is driven by the prevailing tax **rules**. Such tax rates can only have a stabilising effect on domestic demand if the rates are significantly progressive to act as automatic (rule-driven) stabilisers on private expenditure (see Chapter 10, Section 10.4 & Section 17.4.1 above).

The second example pertains to government expenditure. Under our Constitution provinces are entitled to an equitable share of nationally raised revenues. As will be explained in Chapter 18, once the vertical division of revenue between the national and provincial spheres of government are determined on the basis of their respective expenditure responsibilities and revenue capacity, the horizontal distribution of revenue between provinces is determined by certain formulae. These formulae (i.e. **rules**) are based on the economic and demographic profiles of the provinces and take account of the services – primarily health, welfare and school education – for which they are responsible. Transfer payments to provinces constitute about 40 per cent of the national budget. The formulae that govern the aggregate allocations to provinces are the product of intensive analysis and negotiation in which the national fiscal authorities have a say. Once these block allocations have been determined, however, provinces themselves have the discretion to decide how the funds are to be allocated.

This means that the discretionary powers of the national fiscal authorities do not extend to the provincial allocation of unconditional transfers out of the national budget, thereby limiting these powers to only a portion of the national budget. In fact, if interest payments (which constitute a first and statutory claim on state revenues) and other transfer payments to sub-national authorities (so-called ear-marked funds or conditional transfers) are also excluded, we see that the fiscal authorities potentially have short-term discretionary powers over less than 40 per cent of national budgetary expenditure. This figure is reduced further if contractual commitments, including employment contracts and other statutory expenditure obligations such as welfare payments, are taken into account. The ability to effect major expenditure changes in the short run is therefore limited. These limitations were spelled out many years ago by

Gerald Browne (1975: 8), who observed that "the variation of public expenditure has only a limited utility as an instrument of short- and medium-term fiscal policy".

17.5 Fiscal policy in South Africa

In an increasingly integrated world economy, an assessment of a country's fiscal policy has to reckon with the impact of international events. Moreover, much can be learnt from experiences elsewhere. With globalisation, countries have found that their independence or discretion in respect of economic policy has also been reduced. Tax policy, for example, cannot be made without keeping in mind that skilled labour and capital are internationally mobile and that excessive taxes can stimulate emigration. We therefore begin this section with a brief international perspective. We then take a quick glance at features of the South African economy that have an important bearing on fiscal policy, before proceeding with an overview of fiscal policy since 1970.

17.5.1 An international perspective

At different times during the past 20 to 25 years developing countries exhibited a number of similarities in their economic and social performance. A few of these, some of which have been or are still present in South Africa, are as follows:

- High and persistent unemployment
- Persistently low and even negative economic growth
- High inflation
- Balance of payments crises, resulting in or reflective of excessive foreign debt, capital flight, deteriorating terms of trade, overvalued currencies or – at other times – major exchange rate depreciations
- Large budget deficits and high public debt-GDP ratios
- Very skew income distributions
- Widespread and acute poverty
- Low skills levels and low literacy

These problems can obviously not be solved by fiscal measures alone. The challenges facing developing countries require a much wider range of policies.

For many years – at least up to the middle of the 1970s – the **focus** of macroeconomic (including fiscal) policy in industrial and developing countries was pretty much **short term** in nature. The concern was with preserving macroeconomic stability and pursuing the highest possible level of economic growth and employment commensurate with such stability. As noted earlier, during the 1970s industrial countries started experiencing stagflation, that is, high unemployment and persistent inflation during periods of low or negative economic growth. It was realised that in both industrial and developing countries short-term stabilisation measures were no longer sufficient to address the structural economic problems of unemployment, low growth and high inflation.

Gradually the emphasis in economic policy-making shifted from an excessive reliance on stabilisation policy to economic strategies combining stabilisation measures and measures of **structural reform**. The policy measures were aimed at increasing the growth and job creation capacity of the economy. As far as fiscal measures were concerned, the focus changed to:

- Lower budget deficits with a view to reducing government dissaving
- Stricter expenditure discipline, often amounting to reductions in the share of government expenditure in GDP
- Tax reform measures aimed at removing distortions in the economy caused by taxes and tax exemptions
- Tax and regulatory changes aimed at improving the efficiency of the goods, financial and labour markets
- Increased public investment in social and economic infrastructure
- Privatisation (sale of public assets and enterprises)

- Job creation programmes
- Targeted poverty relief programmes

Generally, developing countries that have incorporated these kinds of fiscal measures in their economic reform programmes appeared to have had more success in effecting sustainable economic growth. The international financial crisis of 1997-1998, however, revealed important shortcomings in international financial markets and in the regulatory role of governments (see Stiglitz, 1998), and dampened some of the free-market euphoria of the previous 10-15 years.

17.5.2 Aspects of the performance of the South African economy

There are various aspects of the performance of the South African economy which have been particularly important in shaping fiscal policy.

- During the 1960s South Africa, in common with many industrial and developing countries, experienced high rates of economic growth. Over the period 1960 to 1970 an average real growth rate of 5,8 per cent per annum was recorded. During the next two decades the growth performance deteriorated and an average real growth rate of only 1,5 per cent per annum was achieved during the period 1980 to 1990. Similar patterns were again experienced in comparable developing countries, but in the 1990s the growth performance of developing countries such as Argentina and Chile improved markedly, whereas the South African economy experienced negative growth during the period 1990 to 1993. The South African growth performance subsequently improved to such an extent that, after four consecutive years of decline, real per capita GDP increased each year from 1994 to 1997. In terms of the Government's *Macroeconomic strategy on growth, employment and redistribution* (GEAR) (Department of Finance, 1996) which was announced in June 1996, an economic growth rate of substantially higher than 3 per cent per annum needs to be sustained if the unemployment rate of more than 30 per cent is to be reduced. If the absolute level of unemployment is to be reduced, even higher rates of growth will be required.[5]

- Double-digit inflation characterised the economy for 19 consecutive years from 1974 to 1992. The prospects for low inflation improved steadily after the 10 per cent barrier was passed in 1993. In 2001 the annual consumer price inflation rate was 5,7 per cent.

- In 1985 the country was not able to pay back all its short-term private-sector foreign debt and had to declare a moratorium on the repayment of foreign debt. At the time foreign debt[6] amounted to 51,6 per cent of GDP, a ratio[7] that had been reduced to as low as 20,6 per cent by the end of 1991. After 1993, South Africa's foreign financial relations were normalised, with the result that the ratio increased gradually to 31,4 per cent by the end of 2000. This compares favourably with that of other developing countries.

- As a developing country, the balance of payments represents an important constraint on economic growth. GDP growth of about 3 per cent has usually been associated with a substantial current account deficit. When this rate is approached, it is a signal that fiscal and/or monetary discipline should be applied, especially when foreign reserves are low. During the sanctions era (in the 1980s and early 1990s) the negotiated foreign debt repayment obligations necessitated the generation of foreign exchange through current account

surpluses. This additional ceiling to economic growth was removed after 1993.

- South Africa has a highly unequal distribution of income – the skewest ever measured (see Chapter 15, Section 15.1.1).

- In 1999 South Africa ranked number 94 in the world in terms of its comparative development performance as measured by the Human Development Index. This represented a deterioration from the 80th position held in 1990. This index combines economic indicators (per capita GDP) with social indicators (adult literacy and life expectancy) (United Nations Development Programme, 1997: 147) and shows that economic growth may not be a sufficient condition for human development.

17.5.3 Salient features of South African fiscal policy since 1970

Our discussion of the salient features of South African fiscal policy since 1970 follows the goals of fiscal policy discussed earlier, drawing on conclusions reached in previous chapters. We refer to figures pertaining to the general government, the national government (budget) or the consolidated finances of the national and provincial governments, as the case may be.

Macroeconomic stabilisation and growth

During the period under review the emphasis in fiscal policy shifted from anti-cyclical demand management to structural economic reform. We now focus on a few fiscal episodes to trace this shift.[8]

During the first half of the 1970s – the period of "fiscal expansion" (Browne, 1983: 154-162) – the share of general government expenditure in gross domestic product rose

---

5 When GEAR was released, it was envisaged that the annual real economic growth rate would increase to six per cent by the year 2000 and that the number of new jobs created would reach a level of 409 000 in that year. In his 1998 budget speech the Minister of Finance implicitly reduced the expected growth rate for the year 2000 when he stated: "We remain confident that growth...will be...rising to four per cent and higher as we move into the next century".

6 Included is debt denominated in foreign currency and in rand.

7 For purposes of international comparison the Reserve Bank publishes these ratios in dollar terms. South Africa's rand-denominated foreign debt is also included.

8 For this analysis we rely on Dornbusch, Fischer, Mohr & Rogers (1994: 394-407).

Table 17.2 Trends in general government spending, 1970-2001

Year	Growth in real consumption spending (%)[a]	Growth in real investment spending (%)[b]	Government spending as % of (GDP)[c]
1970	7,9	8,8	20,4
1971	7,9	20,4	22,0
1972	−0,5	14,6	22,8
1973	4,4	−9,6	21,5
1974	7,7	3,3	21,5
1975	12,1	12,7	23,8
1976	5,5	5,0	24,5
1977	3,8	−15,3	23,6
1978	0,7	−12,9	22,1
1979	4,8	0,3	22,0
1980	9,1	0,7	22,0
1981	1,9	12,0	21,9
1982	6,3	1,5	23,0
1983	1,8	−9,7	23,1
1984	6,8	−9,6	22,5
1985	3,4	−0,2	23,4
1986	2,3	−12,4	23,2
1987	3,7	−8,1	23,0
1988	1,7	−2,1	22,3
1989	4,0	3,8	22,6
1990	2,3	−14,8	22,5
1991	2,3	−11,4	22,8
1992	1,9	−15,4	23,2
1993	1,2	−6,2	23,0
1994	0,8	−0,8	22,4
1995	−6,0	6,0	20,7
1996	3,8	14,1	20,9
1997	2,1	7,3	20,9
1998	−1,9	−1,8	20,3
1999	−0,7	−2,0	19,7
2000	0,5	−6,9	19,0
2001	1,4	0,1	18,8

Notes:
[a] Percentage increase in consumption spending by general government at constant prices.
[b] Percentage increase in gross fixed capital formation by general government at constant prices. This does not include investment by public corporations.
[c] Nominal consumption spending by general government plus gross fixed capital formation by general government as percentage of gross domestic product at current prices.

Source: South African Reserve Bank, *Quarterly Bulletin*, Various issues.

sharply, as shown in Table 17.2. The relative-ly rapid expenditure growth in 1971 and 1972, and again in 1975, coincided with downward phases of the business cycle. But, the belief in counter-cyclical fiscal policy began to waver: in spite of the lowest growth rate since the Second World War – the real gross national income had actually **declined** in 1975 – the Minister of Finance introduced a particularly restrictive budget in 1976 and **financial** (or **fiscal**) **discipline** became the slogan. This major policy switch was the result of a number of factors, includ-ing the widely held view that the rapid increase in government spending had been a major cause of the increase in the inflation rate during the first half of the 1970s, and the conditions attached to a loan, which South Africa had obtained from the International Monetary Fund. Note, however, that after some success in curtailing government expenditure, the ratio of general govern-ment expenditure to GDP increased consis-tently and reached 23,4 per cent in 1985. This longer-term upward trend was impervious to the state of the business cycle. After 1986 the ratio, which is indicative of the resource use by government, remained fairly stable, before dropping significantly after 1992. Note, however, that the resource mobilisa-tion by the **public sector** remained high until 1997, after which it started to decline as a percentage of GDP (see Chapter 1, Section 1.2.2).

As far as taxation is concerned, we have already seen that bracket creep has made the automatic stabiliser effect of South Africa's progressive income tax structure virtually impotent (see Chapter 11, Section 11.4.4). Taxation has not been employed as an instrument of stabilisation policy since the early 1970s (Dornbusch, Fischer, Mohr & Rogers, 1994: 406). In fact, the increasing pressure on government spending in the 1980s and the declared policy of keeping the deficit before borrowing within the limits prescribed by the IMF and – towards the end of the 1990s – the Government's macroeco-nomic policy strategy (GEAR), effectively ruled out an anti-cyclical taxation policy. Given that the pressure on government spending remains, and in view of the contin-ued unequal distribution of personal incomes in South Africa (which implies a very narrow income tax base), there does not appear to be much scope in future for an **anti-cyclical** tax policy either. As a result, the debate on taxation policy in South Africa came to be dominated by **structural** issues, such as those mentioned in Section 17.5.1.

The most widely used barometer of the extent of anti-cyclical fiscal policy is the bud-get deficit. Recall that even a balanced bud-get is said to have a multiplier effect on national income (see Chapter 7, Section 7.3) and that increases (decreases) in the budget deficit are regarded as stimulatory (contrac-tionary).

We distinguish between three concepts of the budget balance (a negative balance signi-fying a **deficit** and a positive balance indi-cating a **surplus**). Each has a different use. The **conventional balance** is equal to the dif-ference between total revenue and total expenditure. **Total revenue** consists of tax and non-tax current revenue (the latter including entrepreneurial and property income and administrative fees and charges – see also Chapter 14, Section 14.2), capital revenue (such as the sale of fixed capital assets) and other receipts (such as recoveries of loans and advances). In the conventional balance all *ad hoc* income such as privatisa-tion income is treated as financing sources. This balance is a measure of the total loan finance and other financing that would be required in a particular year.

The **current balance** is the difference between total current revenue (i.e. tax and non-tax revenue) and total current expendi-ture (i.e. including interest payments). Capital revenue and capital expenditure are not considered. This definition is a measure of the extent of saving or dissaving by

Table 17.3 Comparing the calculation of various budget balances in South Africa, 1998/99

Budget item	R billion	% of GDP
(1) Total ordinary revenue	180,0	
(2) Total current revenue	178,9	
(3) Total expenditure	204,3	
(4) Total non-interest expenditure	160,9	
(5) Total current expenditure	194,0	
(6) Conventional balance: (1) – (3)	–24,3	–3,3
(7) Current balance: (2) – (5)	–15,1	–2,0
(8) Primary balance: (1) – (4)	+19,1	+2,6

Notes: All figures are revised budget estimates. The conventional and primary balances differ from those of the South African Reserve Bank in Table 6.4, since the latter excludes extraordinary revenue and expenditure inter alia.

Source: Department of Finance. (1999a)

Government. If there is a current surplus, some current revenue is *de facto* "saved" and applied in the financing of capital expenditure (public investment). In the case of a current deficit, Government is *de facto* **dissaving**, that is, it has insufficient current revenue to cover its current expenditure and has to borrow or sell assets in order to finance some of its current spending. This is an example of what is sometimes described as "selling the family silver to pay for the groceries".

The tendency to finance current expenditure through loans has been a disturbing feature of the South African fiscal scene. From 1982 onwards, current expenditure by general government consistently exceeded current revenue. In effect this meant that government was **dissaving**, with increased public debt as the counterpart. Between 1982 and 1993 public debt increased almost sevenfold. As a percentage of GDP it increased from about 31 per cent to about 44 per cent during this period. The large public debt and high interest rates caused the interest on public debt to become one of the major expenditure items in the budget. By 1998/99 it accounted for about 20 per cent of the total

consolidated budget expenditure of the national and provincial governments.

The **primary balance** is calculated as the difference between total revenue and total non-interest expenditure. The primary balance should immediately be recognised as the conventional balance **plus** interest. This is a measure of the Government's ability to service its debt (pay interest) through ordinary revenue. It measures the impact of the budget on the Government's net indebtedness, that is, its liabilities net of assets. If the primary balance is positive (i.e. there is a primary surplus) and larger than the interest bill, Government's ordinary revenue (which is predominantly tax income) is sufficient to pay all the interest on public debt **and** redeem at least part of its debt or finance some of the public investment. Net indebtedness is reduced. If the primary balance is positive but smaller than the interest bill, a portion of the interest bill is tax-financed. The rest is loan financed (capitalised) and added to the public debt, thus increasing net indebtedness. If the primary balance is negative (i.e. there is a primary deficit), all of the interest and some of the current expenditure are loan financed, thus adding to the public debt. In this case Government is borrowing to finance all its interest payments and some non-interest current expenditure. In so doing net indebtedness is also increased. A negative primary deficit is normally regarded as an unsound fiscal practice, particularly when it increases the risk of runaway public debt. A general rule of thumb is that a negative primary balance can be maintained for some time without an increase in the Government's debt-GDP ratio, provided the real rate of economic growth is higher than the real rate of interest in the economy.

With reference to the revised budget figures for 1998/99 we demonstrate the calculation of these balances in Table 17.3.

Keep the state of the business cycle in mind when interpreting these balances. During an economic downswing, government revenue (notably individual and company income tax) tends to be lower than the longer-term trend line, whilst government expenditure (such as on welfare) tends to rise above it. The budget deficit, therefore, tends to be higher than the trend line. The opposite applies during an economic upswing. In the design of fiscal policy the effect of the business cycle is taken into account by calculating **cyclically adjusted budget balances**. Allegedly the cyclical component of the South African budget deficit has been increasing since 1975, at times constituting as much as 60 per cent of the observed overall deficit (Fourie, 1997: 22).

Always remember that the above concepts refer to the national government. They do not cover the demands on private saving emanating in the public sector at large. For the public sector as a whole we use the term **public sector borrowing requirement** (PSBR), which consists of the net borrowing requirement (i.e. after allowance for the refinancing of maturing debt) of the general government, extra-budgetary institutions, social security funds and non-financial pub-

lic enterprises. The latter exclude institutions such as the Development Bank of Southern Africa (DBSA). Because the DBSA lends to public institutions, we would be counting some borrowing requirements twice if the DBSA's requirements were also included. In South Africa the PSBR rose from 2,0 per cent of GDP in 1989/90 to a recent high of 9,6 per cent in 1993/94, before receding to 1,3 per cent in 2000/01. The decrease in the PSBR echoes the national Government's attempt to reduce the public claim on private savings.

When discussing fiscal policy, however, we focus on the national budget balance. In this respect prominent movements in the budget balance (the conventional balance) have occurred at various times during the period under review. Since no budgeted surpluses were recorded, these movements only amounted to increases and decreases in the budget deficit. We reflect on two periods of marked increase in the budget deficit in recent times. The first increase occurred in the fiscal years 1986/87 and 1987/88. Since these were years of economic upswing, the deficit increase signifies pro- rather than anti-cyclical fiscal policy.

The second increase took place from 1989/90 to 1992/93, during which period the deficit as a percentage of GDP increased from 1,4 per cent to 7,3 per cent. Although this surge occurred during a downward phase of the business cycle, it was not received with much enthusiasm. One of the concerns was the primary balance which went into a deficit and soared to 3,0 per cent of GDP in 1992/93. The rapidly increasing public debt-GDP ratio, which was also due to extra-budgetary debt obligations, added to this concern. The rising budget deficit represented an anti-cyclical policy stance in an economy that experienced a downward phase of the business cycle from March 1989 to May 1993. The growing budget deficit and rising debt-GDP ratio were not, however, welcomed as an attempt to soften the impact of the cyclical downturn. Instead, they resulted in alarming predictions by South African economists that the Government was heading for a debt trap in which it would not be able to service its debt and might even find it increasingly hard to raise loans in the capital market. This reaction once again illustrates the extent to which belief in anti-cyclical demand policies had waned.

The transition from anti-cyclical demand management to structural reform as the guiding consideration in fiscal policy was reconfirmed in the Government's macroeconomic strategy announced in 1996. It entailed a systematic multi-year reduction in the budget deficit, notwithstanding the course of the business cycle. In this manner the Government's economic strategy corresponded with the tenets of the Washington consensus (Calitz, 1997: 322-328).

There is clear evidence that the fiscal authorities see the **contribution of fiscal policy to economic growth** as involving, inter alia, a reduction in government dissaving, a somewhat smaller share of government expenditure in the economy, an increase in public investment, privatisation and increased efficiency of government expenditure (Department of Finance, 1996: 7-9). At the time of writing, however, privatisation was still occurring at a slow pace and the budgeted share of public investment in the consolidated national and provincial government expenditure had been declining up to 1999/00, after which it started to increase.

With regard to **employment**, the GEAR strategy subscribed to the view that a climate had to be created that is conducive to job creation in the private sector. In his 1998 Budget Speech the Minister of Finance reiterated the President's earlier statement that "Government is not an employment agency". On the contrary, fiscal discipline requires a reduction in spending on person-

nel. The preferred approach to employment creation is to promote the creation of jobs in the private sector through various government programmes, such as programmes catering for the needs of emerging and small-scale farmers; tourism promotion; industrial support, trade promotion and small business development programmes; job creation programmes; and the implementation of procurement policies to promote labour-based production activities in the private sector (Department of Finance, 1998:1.7-1.9).

Redistribution and poverty reduction (equity)

From our earlier discussions we can highlight various features of fiscal policy dealing with redistribution and poverty reduction.

Firstly, in recent years **redistribution** has gained **major importance** as an economic policy goal. The fact that redistribution was the last in the sequence of goals in the Government's GEAR strategy (i.e. growth, employment and redistribution) did not necessarily indicate that it is less important than the first two. The sequence should rather be interpreted as an indication that growth and employment creation are regarded as necessary conditions for a sustainable improvement in the distribution of income in South Africa.

As far as **redistribution and poverty alleviation** are concerned, economic growth may be necessary but it is not sufficient. Tax and expenditure measures have always been used in tandem to serve redistribution goals. One of the sub-strategies of GEAR entailed "budget reform to reflect the redistributive thrust of expenditure", of which the reprioritisation of government expenditure is testimony. The tax instrument also continues to fulfil a redistribution role. This explains, for instance, the still rather steep progression in personal income rates – despite the reduction in the maximum marginal rate from 45 per cent in 1999/00 to 40 per cent in 2002/03 – and why a special levy on the free reserves of demutualising life-insurers was introduced in the 1998/99 Budget.

During the second half of the 1990s a two-pronged approach was advocated to alleviate poverty: the stimulation of economic growth and job creation, along with redistributive social and infrastructural expenditure. The latter included: social grants (paid to more than 3 million beneficiaries); developmental welfare services aimed at income-generating projects with a community-based focus; the provision of free health care to pregnant women and children under six years of age; the primary school nutrition programme; programmes focussing on the disabled; housing development; water and sanitation programmes; community-based public works schemes; and the "working for water" programme of clearing alien plants from water catchment areas. Investment in economic and social infrastructure through transformation of the construction industry, the consolidated municipal infrastructure investment programme, special urban renewal projects, hospital rehabilitation, roads construction, spatial development initiatives, the management of water resources and the activities of the Development Bank of Southern Africa were also aimed at improving the quality of life of the poor. On the expenditure side of the budget the emphasis therefore shifted away from defence to internal safety and security and to social services, notably education, health and housing. Within education and health there has also been a reallocation towards primary education and health. This went hand-in-hand with a larger amount of private financing being allocated towards the more sophisticated types of services (e.g. private hospitals and private schools).

Various regulatory measures have supported the redistribution programme, such as the land reform programme (involving land redistribution, land restitution and tenure reform); and legislation regarding employment equity and employment standards.

Efficiency

Earlier we noted that the pursuance of efficiency (be it allocative or technical efficiency) is not easily determined. It is however associated with certain developments with which we now deal briefly.

The effectiveness of **expenditure control** is a key factor in government efficiency. One weakness in the efficiency chain is when the annual budget is exceeded.

When budget limits are easily exceeded, it not only increases the dangers of inflation, but it encourages laxness in planning and expenditure control. Moreover, if cut-backs are required at a later stage and these are done in equal measure across the board, high- and low-priority programmes or efficient and inefficient programmes are treated alike. This does not promote thrift nor judicious planning and prioritisation in resource allocation.

Since the early 1980s there has been an increasing tendency to exceed budget estimates. Dornbusch, Fischer, Mohr and Rogers (1994: 400-401) point out that fiscal discipline was still regularly preached in the annual budget speeches, but it was not practised. Although the overspending was invariably explained *ex post* (often quite plausibly), a serious credibility gap developed which undermined taxpayer morale and the influence of the fiscal authorities. This was particularly serious in 1983 and 1985. In both these years the fight against inflation was accorded the highest priority by the Minister of Finance. Restrictive budgets were introduced in an apparent attempt to dampen inflationary expectations. The fact that this did not have the desired effect can be attributed, in part at least, to considerable scepticism in the private sector that the envisaged fiscal discipline would be achieved. As it turned out, these doubts were well grounded.

Overspending did decline during the latter part of the 1980s. In 1990/91 and 1991/92 the Minister budgeted for contingency reserves of R1 billion and R1,2 billion respectively. Whether or not this should be regarded as (anticipated) overspending is debatable. If it is classified as normal expenditure, then the excess expenditure during 1990/91 and 1991/92 declined to 1,5 per cent and 0,9 per cent, respectively, of budgeted expenditure. To limit overspending even further, a separate Department of State Expenditure was created in 1991. By 1993/94 this step showed clear signs of success. However, in 1994/95 the elections and the transition to a new constitution and new government resulted in renewed overspending which had to be financed by means of a one-off 5 per cent transition levy.

The percentage of excess spending since 1994/95 was generally speaking lower than during the previous 11 years. The reinstatement of the contingency reserve and the introduction of medium-term expenditure planning were contributing factors. There has also been an increasing awareness of the importance of expenditure control among key role players (see Box 17.1) who support the Finance Ministry in balancing the demands on the fiscus with the macroeconomic constraints. No wonder that, in 2000, the Departments of Finance and State Expenditure were reunited into a single body, the National Treasury.

Box 17.1
Role players in the control of public expenditure
The National Treasury is inter alia responsible for expenditure control. There a number of important allies in the determination and enforcement of the resource constraint.

A number of bodies exercise discipline on the overall level of public expenditure in the **period preceding the approval** of the budget. The **Budget Council** and the **Budget Forum** have been established to coordinate intergovernmental financial relations between the national government and provincial governments and between the national government and local governments, respectively. These are important forums for establishing consensus on the macroeconomic constraints within which government finances have to operate. The **Medium Term Expenditure Committee**, chaired by the Director-General of the National Treasury, is responsible for evaluating budgetary proposals, in consultation with the various spending agencies, and reconciling them with the MTEF (or to adjust the latter). This occurs within the overall fiscal constraint as determined by the Government's macroeconomic strategy. The **Parliamentary Portfolio Committee on Finance** debates the budget and makes recommendations to Parliament on its acceptability.

There are also important role players enforcing resource constraints **in the course of the fiscal year**, that is, after the budget is approved by Parliament. An important institution in controlling expenditure demands at the political level is the **Treasury Committee** which is chaired by the Minister of Finance and also includes the Executive Deputy President, the Ministers of Home Affairs, of Labour and of Trade and Industry, and the Deputy Minister of Finance. Its main function is to evaluate all requests for additional funds throughout the year to determine whether such expenditure is unforeseen and unavoidable and to advise the Cabinet accordingly. The **Accountant-General**, who is a senior official in the **National Treasury**, together with departmental chief financial officers, are responsible for cash management and the development and maintenance of systems and practices of cash management. **Accounting officers** (basically the directors-general of government departments) are held accountable for the spending of their departmental allocations according to the fiscal goals and the criteria of efficiency, effectiveness and equity. In recent times there has been a movement towards giving directors-general more managerial authority and, concomitantly, enforcing accountability more strictly. This is a more decentralised system of financial management and control than that traditionally applied in South Africa. It is based on the belief that better control will be exercised if there is more managerial freedom, provided managers have the required capabilities and are adequately trained.

Finally, there is the supervisory function of the Auditor-General whose office conducts **regularity and performance auditing**. The Auditor-General reports directly to Parliament on fraudulent and unauthorised spending and on the standard of financial management of government institutions. The constitutional independence of the Auditor-General has strengthened Parliament in its watchdog function regarding the use of public money. The **Standing Parliamentary Committee on Public Accounts** completes our list. It publicly debates the findings of the Auditor-General and reports to Parliament, the custodian of public money. The accounting officers of the government are publicly held accountable by this Committee.

An important factor in determining allocative efficiency concerns the issue of consultation and consensus seeking. In Chapter 6 we discussed the theory of optimal voting rules, and identified the point where the sum of the internal (or decision-making) costs and the external (opportunity) costs of obtaining consensus are minimised. This illustrated the importance of the processes of consultation and consensus seeking in a democracy. Space does not allow for an in-depth analysis of all the consensus-seeking methods in the budgetary process in South Africa. A few examples, however, will highlight some of the recent developments.

- Since the middle of the 1980s the **budgetary process** in the executive branch of government has become increasingly **transparent**. Before that time, a lot of secrecy surrounded the preparation of the budget, and Cabinet was informed of the contents at a very late stage. This undermined collective Cabinet responsibility for the budget, which is very important to ensure expenditure control.

- One of the important changes in the parliamentary process in recent years has been the more extensive use of **public hearings** on important policy and legislative issues. After such hearings the particular portfolio committee reports to Parliament, which, in turn, refers contentious issues back to the relevant government department. A strong requirement that must be met before legislative approval is recommended, is that all the relevant stakeholders in the particular issue must have been consulted. These stakeholders also have the opportunity to testify before the portfolio committees.

- **Nedlac**, consisting of representatives of government, the business and labour communities and development organisations, was established by law in 1994. One of its functions is to seek consensus on economic policy, including fiscal policy. Deliberations on fiscal matters take place in the Public Finance and Monetary Policy Chamber, one of four chambers which report to the Executive Council. It would appear, however, that Nedlac has had little influence on macroeconomic policy, which includes fiscal policy (Alence, 1998).

- The **Intergovernmental Fiscal Relations Act** (Act 97 of 1997), which took effect on 1 January 1998, established a formal process for considering inter-governmental budgetary issues. The Act was designed to facilitate and regulate a process of consultation to promote a fair budget-making process. Fairness refers to the stipulation in Section 214 of the Constitution that there should be an equitable division of revenue raised nationally among the national, provincial and local spheres of government. Under the above-mentioned Act, the budget process begins ten months before the start of the financial year with the Financial and Fiscal Commission (FFC) (see Chapter 18) making recommendations on this division (see Box 17.3). The Minister of Finance is then required to consult with the provinces, local government and the FFC about these proposals. The Budget Council and the Budget Forum were established by this Act to facilitate the consultation with provinces and local government, respectively.

Openness regarding budgetary matters has much to commend it. There are, however, two important qualifications.

Our first qualification has to do with **whether all interest groups are heard in equal measure** in the budgetary process. Certain interests are hard to mobilise and organise, for example the unemployed or farm workers. If interest groups are not heard, or their case is not represented in equal measure, the likelihood of inefficient and unfair public choices is higher. (See, for example, our discussion in Chapter 6 on the tyranny of the majority.) Allocative efficiency is thus impaired.

The second qualification has to do with the question **whether all budgetary information should be disclosed in advance**. Certain information may benefit the recipi-

ent if it is obtained exclusively and may warrant different treatment. Opportunities to obtain such privileged information arise, for example, in the event of changes in tax policy and in the government's funding programme, changes that may affect share, bond and other asset prices. Expenditure decisions in respect of land transactions and up-coming government contracts fall in the same category.

We have seen during the course of this book that government intervention in the allocation of funds in the private sector can cause inefficiency if the preferences (economic choices) of individuals or companies are distorted. A number of steps have been taken in recent years to reduce or eliminate this kind of distortion, the intention being to increase allocative efficiency. Examples are the phasing out of tax subsidies in respect of training, welfare, health and the General Export Incentive Scheme (GEIS), and the abolition of interest rate subsidies for agriculture and housing. As some go, others appear, however, such as the Section 37E tax deductions in respect of new investment, which were in force for a number of years during the second half of the 1990s, tax incentives to the tune of R3 billion for a strategic investment programme, announ-ced in 2001, and a tax allowance to employers that offer approved learnership programmes, announced in 2002.

The budgetary system is very important from an efficiency point of view. We highlight a few budgetary techniques in this regard. The first is **incremental budgeting**, which means that the previous year's expenditure level and allocations are not evaluated critically and that budget designers are much more concerned with the reasons for **additions** to the budget. The whole idea of zero-based budgeting is partly a reaction to the unyielding nature and automatic growth of budgets characterised by incrementalism. **Zero-based budgeting** is a system of budgetary choice, whereby all programmes –

existing and new – are reviewed systematically and periodically in terms of consistent criteria, and have to be ranked sufficiently high to receive allocations. South Africa implicitly went through the biggest zero-based budgeting exercise in many years after the constitutional change of 1994, when virtually every government programme was questioned and reviewed de novo.

Bottom-up budgeting refers to any kind of budgeting whereby statements of needs are formulated at every level of management, without serious reference to constraints, and these needs are then added up to determine whether the total need can be afforded. If the aggregate need exceeds the available funds, scaling down takes place. These cutbacks are often of an *ad hoc* or across-the-board nature and are not supported by systematic prioritisation. Until the middle of the 1980s the annual budgetary process in South Africa commenced with an invitation to government departments to submit their funding requests without any ceiling being specified. It was only during the latter half of the 1980s that the fiscal authorities introduced the practice of laying down limits at the outset, which served as constraints within which individual government departments had to do their budgeting. (Note from Box 17.3 below that such resource constraints are nowadays laid down early in the budgetary cycle.) Simulated budgetary constraints such as these arguably lead to different and more efficient choices.

Another innovation in the budgetary reform process has been the introduction of medium-term fiscal planning in 1997. This involves an extension of the period for indicative expenditure allocation per function, budget vote and programme from one to three years. Since these allocations are constrained by the overall expenditure limits imposed by macroeconomic considerations and goals, the allocative efficiency of public spending programmes is facilitated in

a multi-year framework. We return to this topic in Section 17.7.

A development which could have a major impact on the delivery of public services in South Africa is the introduction of the Public Finance Management Act (PFMA) of 1999. Its aims are to empower public-sector managers in their managerial responsibilities, while at the same time making them accountable for their actions. The Act emphasises disciplines such as regular financial reporting, sound internal expenditure controls, independent audit and supervision of control systems, improved accounting standards and training of financial managers, and greater emphasis on outputs and performance monitoring. Recent progress with the implementation of the PFMA includes the requirement that by fiscal year 2003 the main divisions of expenditure should be accompanied by "measurable objectives" so that departments can be held accountable and their service delivery performance scrutinised by taxpayers.

17.6 The national budget

17.6.1 Introduction

In the previous section we discussed the nature and features of fiscal policy and examined fiscal policy in South Africa. The presentation of the annual budget of the national government is the major event on the fiscal calendar. It enables the Minister of Finance to present a systematic and comprehensive overview of the state of the public finances in a macroeconomic context and to motivate to the electorate and their political representatives in Parliament the expenditure, revenue (tax) and loan financing proposals of the Government for the next fiscal year. Although it always contains decisions which are announced for the first time, the budget is largely a collection of fiscal decisions taken over a long period. The management of the finances of government is a continuous process of decision-making, culminating once a year in the budget, which provides the opportunity to present all the decisions coherently in a single set of documents.

In South Africa the national budget is normally presented during the second half of February. The Minister of Finance reads the Budget Speech in Parliament and tables a number of documents along with the Speech. They include the Budget Review (which extensively covers macroeconomic and fiscal issues relevant to the Budget and contains a wealth of fiscal information), as well as the proposed expenditure allocations and the revenue estimates for the next fiscal year, which runs from 1 April to 31 March. A full list of the documents tabled in Parliament is presented in Box 17.2.

Box 17.2
List of documents tabled in Parliament by the Minister of Finance on budget day
- Budget Speech by the Minister of Finance
- Budget Review
- Estimate of Revenue
- Estimates of National Expenditure (containing a detailed account of spending and service delivery by national government departments and spending agencies, covering the four years preceding and the two years following the year of the budget)
- Appropriation Bill (setting out the proposed allocations per departmental vote – the eventual approval of this Bill legalises the expenditure proposals)
- Division of Revenue Bill (containing the division of revenue between national, provincial and local government)
- Documents containing tax proposals

In addition all government departments have to table strategic plans in Parliament within 15 working days after the annual budget was submitted.

17.6.2 Brief accounting outline of the budget

We begin with a brief explanation of the budget figures as presented by the Minister of Finance to Parliament. We do this with reference to the 2002/03 Budget, of which a summary appears in Table 17.4, together with the revised figures for 2001/02. Note that this table is divided into four parts: expenditure, revenue, borrowing requirement and financing.

The first part contains the **expenditure** estimates (see heading 1 in Table 17.4). A few weeks before the budget is presented, the document entitled *Estimates of National Expenditure* (see Box 17.2) is printed. The total of the expenditure estimates is the first amount shown in Table 17.4 (item 1.1). It often happens that there are still some unresolved prospective expenditure allocations when this document is printed. Sometimes the Minister of Finance may even deliberately decide to hold back information on a particular programme until budget day. These allocations are then presented as **supplementary** estimates (item 1.2). In 2002/03 there were no such alocations.

The provision for the **contingency reserve** is also stated separately (item 1.3). This is an amount which is not allocated at the time of the budget, but which acts as a cushion to finance unavoidable and unforeseen expenditures that may arise in the course of the year. If such additional allocations can be limited to the amount of the contingency reserve, the Government will be able to meet them without exceeding the budget. The total expenditure amount that has to be financed is shown as item 1.4.

The next section deals with revenue (heading 2). The first entry is an estimate of the revenue to be received by the South African Revenue Services on the basis of the previous year's tax rates (item 2.1). This is thus the revenue that should result if no tax changes are made (i.e. if the previous year's tax rates were applied to the tax base as projected for the budget year). Next the net revenue increase or loss due to new tax proposals is indicated (item 2.2). In other words, this item represents the expected revenue increases on account of increases in tax rates minus the expected revenue losses due to rate reductions. Item 2.3 gives the total budgeted revenue for the financial year.

The third section deals with **borrowing** (heading 3). The difference between expenditure and revenue is the **national budget deficit** (item 3.1), which is also expressed as a percentage of GDP (item 3.2). From the different definitions of the budget balance or deficit explained in Section 17.5.3 it should be obvious that the deficit in Table 17.4 is the conventional budget deficit. By adding extraordinary transfers that occur from time to time (item 3.3) and subtracting proceeds from the sale of state assets (item 3.4) we cal-

Table 17.4 2002/03 National Budget summary

Budget item	2001/02 Revised estimate (Rbn)	2002/03 Budget (Rbn)	Change 01/02–02/03 %
1 EXPENDITURE			
1.1 Printed estimate		284,6	
1.2 *Plus* supplementary expenditure		–	
1.3 *Plus* contingency reserve		3,3	
1.4 Total expenditure	262,6	287,9	9,6
2 REVENUE			
2.1 Estimate of revenue (existing rates)		280,4	
2.2 *Plus* proposals		−15,2	
2.3 Total revenue	248,4	265,2	6,7
3 BORROWING REQUIREMENT			
3.1 National budget deficit	14,2	22,7	
3.2 Budget deficit as % of GDP	(1,4)	(2,1)	
3.3 *Plus* extraordinary transfers	2,1	1,6	
3.4 *Less* proceeds from sale of state assets	−4,7	−12,0	
3.5 Net borrowing requirement	11,5	12,3	
4 FINANCING			
4.1 Domestic short-term loans (net)	−7,6	−4,0	
4.2 Domestic long-term loans (net)	−11,0	−11,0	
4.3 Foreign loans (net)	33,1	16,3	
4.4 Change in cash and other balances[1]	−3,0	3,0	
4.5 Total financing (net)	11,5	12,3	

Note: [1] A negative sign signifies an increase in cash balances.

Source: National Treasury (2002a: 108, 274–275)

culate the net borrowing requirement, which indicates the amount of new loan finance that the government will require during the fiscal year (item 3.5).

The last section contains the **financing plan** (heading 4), which indicates how much of the **total new financing** (i.e. after subtraction of loan redemptions) (item 4.5) will be contributed by **short-term loans** (treasury bills) (item 4.1), **long-term domestic loans** (government stock) (item 4.2), **foreign loans** (item 4.3) and changes in the Government's cash balances (item 4.4). Note that in both years a repayment of domestic loans was budgeted for. Privatisation income and foreign loans made this possible.

17.6.3 The annual budget cycle

The preparation of the annual budget takes almost a full year. The basic components of the annual budget cycle, together with the relevant dates, vary from year to year but are more or less as set out in Box 17.3. Note the early stage at which consultation with provincial and local government takes place and the various interactions between the technical (bureaucratic) and policy-making (political) level. Observe also that the budgetary planning process begins with medium-term guidelines in respect of prospective allocations (**resource constraints**) within which spending agencies must plan their budgetary requests. These guidelines are developed to serve macro and sectoral fiscal goals and are contained in the *Medium Term Budget Policy Statement*, which was first published in 1997 and has become a regular feature of the fiscal agenda.

Box 17.3 only gives an outline of the key moments in the development of the annual budget of the national government. Provinces draw up their own budgets and have their own budget cycles. The budget for a particular year is not completed until the relevant fiscal year is finished. After the end of a fiscal year some minor adjustments can still take place as accounts are settled

and unauthorised expenditures are reviewed by Parliament. The final report on the budget appears in the annual report of the Auditor-General. Information regarding the expenditure outcome of the three years preceding the budget year is published in the *Estimates of National Expenditure* (see Box 17.3).

17.7 Medium-term fiscal planning

In November 1997 South Africa entered a new phase of fiscal planning with the publication of the first *Medium Term Budget Policy Statement* (MTBPS) (Department of Finance 1997), which enables the presentation of the annual budget in the context of a medium-term policy framework.

Multi-year fiscal or expenditure planning has been practised in different forms by various countries over the past 40 years. Various concepts are used, ranging from multi-year budgets to medium-term fiscal plans, strategies or frameworks, expenditure plans, and so on. The essential distinction is between a multi-year budget, which signifies a formal, statutory, multi-year appropriation of funds, and a multi-year plan, a statement of intent, which serves as a reference framework or road map for the annual budget. South Africa's MTBPS falls into the latter category.

Over the years, governments in countries covering the whole range of economic systems have experienced the need for multi-year fiscal practices, albeit for different reasons. In centrally planned economies, multi-year economic plans were key policy instruments but they have all but disappeared during the transformation of the Eastern European economies. In market-oriented economies the need for multi-year fiscal practices arose from macro, sectoral or micro considerations.

Macroeconomically, the need derived from the realisation in developed and developing countries that the problems of low eco-

Box 17.3
Annual budget cycle of the national government

Date	Activity
Mid Apr	National Treasury guidelines issued to national government departments and provincial treasuries to guide the preparation of budget submissions
Mid Apr – end May	Financial and Fiscal Commission (FFC) makes recommendations on equitable sharing of revenues between national, provincial and local government
Mid – end May	Ministers' Committee on the Budget (MCB) holds initial discussions on the medium-term policy priorities and other considerations
End June	Departments present budgetary submissions to National Treasury
End June – mid Aug	National Treasury reviews budget submissions
End Aug – early Sept	MCB considers forthcoming macroeconomic and fiscal framework and the division of revenue (between national, provincial and local government) in relation to government priorities, and submit for consideration to Cabinet
Early Oct	Departments submit three-year corporate plans and budgets of public entities to National Treasury
Mid Oct	MCB considers draft Medium Term Budget Policy Statement
End Oct	Medium Term Budget Policy Statement presented to Parliament
Early Nov	Cabinet considers medium-term expenditure allocations to national votes
Early Feb	Division of Revenue Bill submitted to FFC and Cabinet
Second half of Feb	Budget presented to Parliament

nomic growth and high and persistent unemployment and inflation required structural economic reform. A multi-year fiscal plan was seen as an essential component of a medium-term economic or financial restructuring (reconstruction) and development strategy. Inflationary environments, increasing international mobility of capital and strong expenditure demands in newly democratised countries all added to the risk of fiscal instability. The increasing complexity of the economic and fiscal scene and the multi-year nature of the objectives to be pursued strengthened the case for longer-term fiscal planning. At the same time, however, this complexity ironically tended to limit the usefulness of such planning. Some countries (e.g. Canada and the UK) have therefore reverted back to less ambitious planning exercises. Public investment expenditure, though, still requires proper long-term planning.

Sectorally, in terms of the various government functions (such as education or health) and government's role in certain economic sectors (such as construction or transport), there is also a strong case for a longer-term approach. In countries undergoing rapid change, like South Africa, important social development goals and the concomitant expenditure reprioritisation cannot be achieved systematically and consistently without proper longer-term planning. The costing of policies and trade-offs between key choices often re-quire a multi-year framework. Also, the dominant role of government demand in certain economic sectors, for example construction, is such that proper planning and phasing of expenditure are important requirements for private sector efficiency.

In this regard, a number of actions can be particularly harmful to sound financial management in both government and private business. These include stop-go policies, which may be the result of political indecision, across-the-board-cuts by Treasury in response to looming excess expenditure, or abortive attempts at deliberate anti-cyclical capital expenditure. There is a growing desire for a government to smooth fluctuations in its own expenditure, rather than to try to reduce expenditure peaks or troughs in the economy. For this, a long-term approach is required.

Finally, at the micro (i.e. programme or project) level, efficiency also warrants multi-year financial planning. Proper cash flow planning, cost projection and a measure of certainty about future resource commitments, are important requirements for efficient delivery. (Naturally, a zero-based approach to budgeting also requires sufficient flexibility, constant re-appraisal and cost-awareness to avoid complacency and the concomitant inefficiencies.)

In South Africa the medium-term budgetary budget policy statement consists of three-year rolling expenditure and revenue projections for the national and provincial government, presented against the backdrop of economic and fiscal goals and prospects for the economy. This policy document and the planning processes that generate the information have been described as the cornerstone of government's broader budget reform process. The three-year medium-term expenditure framework is regarded as being particularly important for bringing greater certainty and transparency to the budget process (within and outside government), strengthening the link between policy priorities and the government's longer-term spending plans and improving expenditure control, as reflected in reduced levels of overspending in recent years.

Important concepts
automatic or built-in stabiliser
bottom-up budgeting
budgetary vote
contingency reserve
conventional balance
current balance
cyclically adjusted budget balances
decision lag
discretion
dissaving
fiscal policy
gross borrowing requirement
impact lag
implementation lag
incremental budgeting
macro, sectoral and micro goals of fiscal policy
macro, sectoral and micro instruments of fiscal policy
net borrowing requirement
ordinary revenue
primary balance
public sector borrowing requirement
recognition lag
rules
Treasury
zero-based budgeting

Self-assessment exercises

17.1 Distinguish between macro, sectoral and micro fiscal policy goals and instruments and give an example of each.

17.2 Describe the role and functions of the different fiscal authorities and explain why co-ordination between them is so important.

17.3 "The effectiveness of policy is solely determined by the practical realities of policy-making." Discuss critically.

17.4 "Due to lags, fiscal policy is irrelevant." Do you agree with this statement? Substantiate your answer.

17.5 Is fiscal policy in South Africa driven by rules or discretion? Substantiate your answer.

17.6 "The conventional budget deficit is superior to other definitions of budget deficit as a measure of the stance of fiscal policy." Do you agree? Why (not)?

17.7 Discuss the features of fiscal policy in South Africa since 1970. Specify the similarities between fiscal policy in South Africa and developing countries in general.

17.8 "Fiscal policy in South Africa has been driven by practical reality rather than sound theoretical principles." Discuss critically.

PART FIVE

Intergovernmental fiscal
relations

Chapter eighteen

Tania Ajam

Fiscal federalism

The aim of this chapter is to study the rationale for fiscal federalism and the nature of intergovernmental fiscal relations from an efficiency and equity point of view, with particular reference to the South African situation.

We commence with an inquiry into the economic rationale for fiscal decentralisation, followed by a contraposition with the reasons for fiscal centralisation. This is followed by an explanation of the considerations on which the assignment of tax powers and expenditure functions to sub-national governments are based. Next we discuss tax competition and tax harmonisation as well as the borrowing powers and debt management at sub-national level, before proceeding with an analysis of different kinds of intergovernmental grants. The chapter is concluded with an overview of intergovernmental fiscal issues in South Africa.

Once you have studied this chapter, you should be familiar with the key principles of fiscal federalism. In particular you should be able to
- explain why sub-national governments exist at all and compare the merits of fiscal decentralisation and centralisation;
- describe the Tiebout model;
- describe the assignment of expenditure functions and revenue sources

(tax powers) to the national, provincial and local spheres of government in South Africa;
- distinguish between tax competition and tax harmonisation;
- list the types of intergovernmental grants;
- explain the issues surrounding borrowing powers and debt management at sub-national level;
- explain the reasons for and nature of intergovernmental grants;
- review the role of the Financial and Fiscal Commission (FFC) in sharing revenue across the three spheres of government;
- discuss trends and issues in provincial and local government financing in South Africa.

18.1 The economic rationale for fiscal decentralisation

At the beginning of this book we introduced the concept **general government** (see Chapter 1, Figure 1.1), which signifies that governments typically consist of more than one level, that is, there may be provincial or local tiers of government in addition to central or national government. Budgetary decisions are generally made at different levels of government. **Sub-national government** (i.e. provincial and local government) refers to those levels of government that have smaller jurisdictions than the national government. National government's jurisdiction would of course extend to the whole country, but the jurisdiction of a local government, for instance, would only be within a particular municipality.

The greater the discretion that subnational governments have to make decisions about spending, taxation and borrowing, the more **decentralised** is the fiscal system (see Chapter 17, Section 17.4.3). **Intergovernmental fiscal relations** or **"fiscal federalism"** as it is sometimes known, is concerned with the structure of public finances in a state with more than one level of government: how taxing, spending and regulatory functions are allocated between the different tiers of government, as well as the nature of transfers between national, provincial and local governments. In contrast to approaches followed in political science and constitutional law, the generic meaning of the term "federalism" in economics is decentralisation, and the fiscal federalism literature deals with the fiscal implications of a decentralised system of multilevel government.

The motivation for a decentralised system embodying sub-national decision-making powers tends to be mainly political. From an economic perspective, however, the justification for a fiscally decentralised system is its potential to improve allocative efficiency. As seen in Chapter 2, allocative efficiency in the public sector is concerned with whether the public sector produces the level and mix of public services that citizens demand and which correspond with their preferences. This theme will be explored more fully in the discussion below of the Tiebout model and the allocative role of government.

Why is a centralised unitary state not sufficient for the purpose at hand? Why do sub-national governments exist at all? The answer lies in the phenomenon of **local public goods**. Some public goods are national in scope (like defence). Local public goods, however, confer benefits which are confined to a limited geographic area. For instance, the transmission of a radio programme would benefit only those people within the broadcasting range of the transmitter, or parks would serve the recreational needs of people living close by. Local public goods are therefore specific to a particular location. Consumers, by electing to locate in a particular geographic jurisdiction, can therefore choose the quantity and type of local public goods they receive. As the size of the local population increases, some local public goods may become crowded and congested (e.g. public roads).

Local and provincial governments therefore exist because the spatial incidence of public goods differs. In practice, however, the boundaries of sub-national governments are often historically or politically determined, and therefore may not coincide exactly with the benefit areas of the public goods which sub-national governments produce. As a result, **spatial externalities** may exist, that is, spillovers of costs and benefits at the boundaries between sub-national government jurisdictions.

18.1.1 The Tiebout model

Tiebout (1956) asserted that if there were a large enough number of local government jurisdictions and each of these local governments offered a different mix of local public goods and taxes, then individuals would reveal their true preferences for local public goods by choosing a particular local government jurisdiction in which to live. In this model, citizens (who have different tastes) are mobile and choose to settle in the local government jurisdictions that produce a mix of tax and public good outputs, which correspond most closely to their preferences. Their choice of location thus reveals their preferences for public goods in the same way that their choice of private goods purchased in the market reveals their preferences for private goods:

"Just as the consumer may be visualised as walking to a private market place to buy his goods, we place him in the position of walking to a community where the prices (taxes) of community services are set. Both trips take the consumer to market. There is no way in which the consumer can avoid revealing his preferences in a spatial economy." (Tiebout, 1956: 422)

The greater the number of communities and the greater the variation in taxes and public services offered, the closer consumers will be to satisfying their preferences. Under these conditions, local public goods can be decentralised in a way that is immune to the free-rider problem. Tiebout's notion of "voting with one's feet" permits the revelation of preferences by allowing people to sort themselves into groups of like tastes. Furthermore, the equilibrium that will be achieved by voting with one's feet will be Pareto efficient. The Tiebout model thus describes a theoretical solution for the problem of preference revelation, a phenomenon that inhibits the achievement of allocative efficiency (see Chapters 2, 3 and 6).

It must be noted that the Tiebout model is based on a number of restrictive assumptions, namely:

- All citizens are fully mobile.
- Individuals have full information about the local public goods offered by each jurisdiction.
- There are a large number of jurisdictions to choose from, spanning the full range of public good combinations desired by citizens.
- There are no geographic employment restrictions: people receive income from capital only and are not tied to a particular location through job or family ties.
- There are no spillovers across jurisdictions.

- There are no economies of scale in the production of public goods.

If there are economies of scale in the production of public goods and hence declining average cost (for example the cost of an additional listener to a local radio programme or of an additional road user may be zero), then a local public goods equilibrium may not exist at all. Preference revelation once again becomes a problem.

If there are only a limited number of communities, these may compete with each other to attract outsiders. While this behaviour (analogous to a monopolistically competitive firm) may provide an incentive towards an efficient production of public services, the mix and level of public services provided may not be Pareto efficient. If there are fewer communities than types of individuals, a person might not be able to find a jurisdiction where people's tastes match his/her own.

Finally, there are issues concerning redistribution. Because there is an element of redistribution involved in the provision of local public goods (e.g. health and education) the rich may attempt to avoid this redistribution by segregating themselves from the poor (Atkinson & Stiglitz, 1980).

Although the Tiebout model is based on a number of stringent assumptions, it does clearly demonstrate that a decentralised fiscal system – which can accommodate a diversity of preferences for public goods – can be welfare-increasing in relation to a centralised system which imposes a standardised public good-tax mix on people, no matter what their tastes. Fiscal decentralisation can in principle contribute to a more efficient provision of local public goods by aligning expenditures more closely with local priorities.

18.1.2 Public choice perspective on fiscal federalism

The Leviathan hypothesis, proposed by Brennan and Buchanan (1980), views government as a revenue maximising monopolist which seeks systematically to exploit its citizens by maximising the tax revenue that it extracts from the economy. From this perspective, fiscal decentralisation would serve as a powerful restraint on the government's leviathan tendencies. Devolution of taxing and spending powers to sub-national governments would act as a disciplinary force on the size of government by forging a closer link between where money is spent and where it is raised. For instance, any additional expenditure by a sub-national jurisdiction may have to be funded by increased sub-national taxation. Centralised fiscal systems break this link, encouraging the growth of government. In centralised fiscal systems, local residents have more opportunities to lobby for spending programmes that are financed out of nationally collected revenues or national loans.

18.1.3 Other reasons for fiscal decentralisation

Competition between sub-national jurisdictions may enhance innovation. Successful local government experiments may be replicated elsewhere and the failures discarded. This argument will be examined in greater detail later.

Furthermore, there may be a high cost associated with decision-making if it is completely centralised. Because of the smaller groups involved, the devolution of spending and taxing powers may reduce the cost of decision-making. Fiscal decentralisation could also encourage public participation in decision-making since local and provincial governments may be closer to the communities they serve and may foster fiscal accountability.

18.2 Reasons for fiscal centralisation

Although there are advantages associated with fiscal federalism, there are also factors that favour centralisation.

Firstly, there may be **spatial externalities**, which arise when the benefit or costs of a public service "spill over" onto non-residents of a particular jurisdiction. Goods with external benefits are likely to be under-produced, since each sub-national government is concerned primarily with the welfare of its own residents. Similarly public goods with significant external costs may be over-produced since the residents of a jurisdiction do not bear the full social cost. Under these circumstances centralised provision to "internalise" these costs and benefits may be preferable.

Secondly, centralised provision of public services may be justified by economies of scale, that is, certain services (such as transport systems and water) may require areas bigger than a single sub-national jurisdiction for cost-effective provision.

Thirdly, centralised provision may lead to lower administration and compliance costs in the financing of public services. For example, using one computer system for the whole country or one revenue collection system serving national and provincial governments may prevent the cost of duplication.

In practice, no country has a completely decentralised or completely centralised system. While the provision of certain goods is preferable at national level, others are best provided at sub-national level. The crucial question is then: what is the optimal degree of fiscal decentralisation? This brings us to the assignment problem.

18.3 Taxing and spending at sub-national level: The assignment issue

The "assignment problem" is concerned with how expenditure and tax functions should be allotted among the various levels of government. The fiscal federalism literature provides broad guidelines on this fundamental issue of how spending and taxation responsibilities should be distributed among national and sub-national governments.

18.3.1 Stabilisation function

There is general consensus that macroeconomic policy should be assigned to central government. Sub-national governments cannot and should not conduct monetary policy. If the power to create money were decentralised to regional entities, there would be strong incentives for sub-national governments to print money to finance public service provision, rather than raising sub-national taxes or imposing user charges. Such behaviour would clearly lead to inflationary pressures, thus adversely affecting the national economy and compromising national government policies for which the particular sub-national government bears no responsibility.

The conventional wisdom in the fiscal federalism literature is that fiscal stabilisation policy would be ineffective at sub-national level. Provincial and local economies tend to be "open" (i.e. they "import" and "export" large shares of what they produce or consume from other provinces or local jurisdictions). If a single sub-national government were to pursue an expansionary fiscal policy, for example, much of the increase in demand would be lost to outside jurisdictions due to the openness of such economies. If, for example, a provincial government were to cut taxes substantially in order to stimulate the provincial economy, most of the newly generated spending would flow out of the provincial economy in payment for goods and services produced elsewhere. The ultimate impact on employment levels in the province would be very small. Fiscal policy by sub-national governments are thus likely to prove impotent since import leakages would be so great as to substantially reduce any multiplier effects. Taxes suitable for macroeconomic stabilisation, such as per-

sonal and corporate income tax, should therefore be centralised (Musgrave, 1983).

18.3.2 Distribution function

In the fiscal federalism literature it is generally argued that only a centralised redistribution policy by central government is likely to be effective. The argument is that any effort to redistribute income by a single sub-national government (e.g. by increasing taxes on high-income earners and firms and spending the proceeds on the poor) would ultimately be self-defeating. There would be an influx of poor migrants into the jurisdiction, attracted by the fiscal benefits (transfer payments or increased public services). This would be accompanied by an exodus of high-income earners and businesses from that jurisdiction. It then becomes more difficult for the jurisdiction to attain its distributional goals, given the dwindling tax base. Sub-national governments may therefore end up in a worse distributional position, which may in fact clash with the redistributory objectives of the national government.

18.3.3 Allocation function

Probably the most compelling economic case for fiscal decentralisation is that it has the potential to secure efficiency gains.

The static arguments linking fiscal decentralisation with improved efficiency include the following:

- Uniform centralised policy forces every region to consume the same mix of taxes and public spending, even though tastes and attitudes may vary widely across regions in a large country with many cultural and ethnic groups. Each decentralised jurisdiction could more closely tailor its service and tax package to the preferences of its citizenry. For instance, the residents of a particular province might want education in a particular language. Politically, decentralisation, which accommodates diversity, may be necessary to induce various regions to remain part of the federation (e.g. Quebec in Canada).

- Different public goods have different spatial characteristics. Some benefit the entire country (e.g. defence) whereas others benefit only a province (e.g. forestry services) or a locality (street lighting). Public services are provided most efficiently by a jurisdiction that has control over the minimum geographic area which would internalise the benefits and costs of such provision.
- Lower-tier governments may have more information about the needs and priorities of their citizens and region-specific conditions and prices than national governments, which could improve programme design and service delivery.
- Diseconomies of scale and increasing bureaucratic inefficiency arise when spending programmes become too large, that is, serve too large a geographical area.

The dynamic efficiency arguments point out that fiscal decentralisation can stimulate innovation. Contestability in the public sector arena may have similar beneficial effects as competition in private markets. Centralisation of functions may mean that national governments may be prone to inertia. With little experimentation, practices within government may become rigid and perpetuate themselves even when the underlying logic for their introduction no longer holds true. Variety in policy design and application at sub-national level is seen as desirable because it diversifies the country's exposure to disastrous policy experiments. Successful policy experiments at sub-national level can be replicated by other tiers of government as best practice and the failures can be discarded.

Improved allocative efficiency in a decentralised system depends heavily on the political and institutional mechanisms through which sub-national governments can be made aware of their electorates' preferences

and are held accountable for their actions. However, in many less developed countries these **democratic structures** are not in place, or if they are nominally in place, *de facto* do not function. Furthermore, sub-national governments may lack capacity and may be prone to corruption. Thus while efficiency gains due to fiscal decentralisation are attainable in principle, whether these are in fact realised depends on how fiscal decentralisation is implemented. In a sense, while fiscal decentralisation can attenuate one form of government failure, it may introduce other forms. The above discussion also makes clear that while a decentralised system may promote efficiency, it may prove detrimental to equity (i.e. redistributory goals) and even compromise stabilisation objectives.

18.3.4 Tax assignment

Tax assignment refers to the assignment of tax sources to different tiers of government. (In the same vein **expenditure assignment** refers to the assignment of expenditure functions to different tiers of government.) Intuitively tax assignment should complement expenditure assignment. In principle, the more the spending responsibilities assigned to a particular level of government, the more the tax revenue sources assigned to it should be. The greater the difference between expenditure and tax assignments, the greater the dependence of sub-national governments will be on grants from national government in order to meet their spending obligations, and the less the ability of the electorate will be to enforce fiscal accountability.

In determining the most appropriate tax assignment, two important factors for consideration are equity (ensuring vertical and horizontal equity among individual tax payers as well as across regions) and efficiency (minimising the cost of collection and compliance, as well as minimising any market distortions). In the light of equity and efficiency, Musgrave (1983) proposes the following assignment guidelines:

- Progressive redistributive taxes should be assigned to the national government (e.g. personal and corporate income taxes).
- Taxes appropriate for macroeconomic stabilisation should likewise be centralised (e.g. value-added tax and personal income tax). As its corollary, taxes assigned to the sub-national governments should be less sensitive to economic and business fluctuations, that is, should be cyclically stable (e.g. motor vehicle taxes).
- Unequal tax bases among jurisdictions should be assigned to the national government (e.g. mining tax).
- Taxes on mobile factors of production should be centralised (e.g. corporate income tax or value-added tax where companies are able to shift the accounting base of the tax to lower-tax jurisdictions).
- Residence-based taxes such as excise taxes should be assigned to the provinces.
- The local authorities should levy taxes on immobile factors of production such as property taxes.
- All levels of government may charge user charges and benefit taxes.

18.4   Tax competition versus tax harmonisation

When different sub-national governments impose different tax rates, then citizens and firms may react by moving to jurisdictions with lower tax rates. **Tax competition** occurs when sub-national governments adjust their tax rates (lower) to attract mobile factors of production (notably capital) from other jurisdictions. **Tax harmonisation** occurs when sub-national governments coordinate their tax policies (for instance, by limiting the degree of variation in tax rates levied, or by defining the tax bases in a uniform way).

Initially tax competition was regarded as distortionary, non-neutral and leading to sub-optimal outcomes – and to be rectified by tax harmonisation. The rationale was that if one province decides to pursue a competitive tax strategy, the other provinces would respond likewise. This "beggar-thy-neighbour" downward spiral as provinces attempt to undercut each other could eventually lead to identical but sub-optimally low tax rates on mobile production factors. In addition, the distribution of mobile factors (particularly capital) would be distorted. Uncoordinated tax policies could therefore lead to market distortions as regards mobile factors of production as well as tradable goods and services.

More recent thinking sees tax competition as a positive influence and efficiency enhancing. Decentralised tax powers could promote innovation, as sub-national governments would be able to experiment with various fiscal packages. In the public sector analogue of private market competition and discipline, policy successes could be emulated elsewhere and failures abandoned. It could also permit sub-national governments to tailor tax mixes to their citizens' preferences and furthermore encourage accountability. If governments are providing services that individuals and firms want and are willing to pay for, then the adverse effects of tax competition may be limited. If government overspends and tries to place the tax burden on those who do not benefit, then tax competition may be construed as a positive spur to increased government responsiveness. One reason for the about-face is the intensifying global competition. With international mobility of capital, if investment is merely displaced to another region, at least it remains within the country instead of migrating across national borders.

18.5   Borrowing powers and debt management at sub-national level

Sub-national governments generally have more limited capacity than central government in issuing debt obligations. In the interest of coordinated macroeconomic policy and the achievement of overall macroeconomic objectives, there must be a central government supervision of the debt operations of sub-national governments. Because the national economy is larger and more diverse, central government can absorb those shocks a single region would find too great to deal with.

Another related aspect of sub-national debt is fiscal exposure, which refers to the total amount of both the direct liabilities of government (e.g. bonds) and the contingent liabilities (e.g. government guarantees). Sub-national borrowing requires an active market in government securities assisted by bond-rating agencies. Fiscally irresponsible behaviour of sub-national governments is then penalised by increased interest rates. The discipline of the market may however be undermined by contagion effects and negative pecuniary externalities. **Financial contagion** refers to a situation where a financial crisis in one government, or regarding one particular type of financial instrument, triggers a loss of confidence in investors, which precipitates similar crises in other similar governments or similar classes of financial instruments. In this context, one province's inability to service debt could cause loss of investor confidence in other provinces. Provincial tax bases are narrower and more elastic than national tax bases due to factor mobility. An adverse shock may render a province unable to service its debt, precipitating a financial panic. The perception that the financial panic is contagious might impose a negative externality on the other provinces. Alternatively, the higher interest rates in response to increased perceived risk will affect all the provinces.

Effective market discipline on the borrowing activities of provinces assumes, however, that private agents have sufficient information to assess provincial risk profiles accurately and so on. For instance, if sub-national governments do not have substantial own tax revenue sources, potential bor-

rowers and bond-rating agencies will set their interest rates based on their perceptions of the terms under which tax-sharing or intergovernmental grants are likely to be made. In less developed countries payments to sub-national governments are often suspended when central governments run into financial problems. In practice, information asymmetries are rife, creating the conditions for moral hazard behaviour.

Moral hazard occurs in a situation where the actions of one party to a contract cannot be monitored by the other party or parties to the contract. This permits opportunistic behaviour on the part of the party whose actions are "hidden", to the detriment of the other less informed parties. A classical example of moral hazard is in the insurance market where drivers (whose levels of care cannot be observed by the insurance company) start to drive more recklessly once fully insured. Moral hazard behaviour and sub-national debt are described below.

In the instance of sub-national debt, moral hazard entails that one party (the lending institution) may behave in fiscally imprudent or risky ways, such as by extending risky loans to provincial governments of dubious creditworthiness, knowing that the debt will be either explicitly or implicitly guaranteed by the other party (the national government). To complicate the problem, provincial governments know that the national government is explicitly or implicitly underwriting their debt, and therefore also have an incentive to act fiscally imprudently. There is thus moral hazard between the lender and the provincial government as well as between the provincial and national governments.

Even if a government explicitly refuses to bail out a sub-national government, this may have very little credibility with markets. Although it would be best for a government to say in advance that it will not bail out sub-national governments in such an eventuality, it has every incentive to renege on its undertaking. In other words, no matter how emphatically national government refuses to aid bankrupt provinces, there will always be a strong incentive for the government to assist sub-national governments should they get into financial trouble. The long-run costs of impassively standing by while a sub-national government fails may be so great that national governments invariably act as the government of last resort.

Anticipating this behaviour, markets would react as if national government had implicitly underwritten sub-national government lending. The implicit guarantee by central government (which generally has a better credit rating than sub-national governments) will mean that sub-national governments will be able to borrow on more favourable terms than would have applied otherwise, encouraging increased debt.

In addition, under these circumstances moral hazard behaviour by creditors could exacerbate the situation. The closer a sub-national government is to financial crisis and the more liabilities it accumulates, the more likely it is that the national government will have to step in and bail it out. Banks and financial institutions, anticipating this, may lend more rather than less to sub-national government. This may result in even more unsustainable sub-national debt, which could have a destabilising effect on the macro economy.

Because political circumstances render it untenable in most cases for a central government to allow a sub-national government to go bankrupt, national government may ultimately find itself liable for any default on public debt no matter which tier of government does the borrowing. This would apply even if the actual letter of the debt contract exempts the national government from any liability. This would suggest a need for national government regulation in order to allow sub-national borrowing but under conditions that will minimise national government risk. In an international setting, irre-

sponsible behaviour by or on behalf of a sub-national government could harm the country's credibility and credit rating, and thus impose a negative externality on other spheres of government.

18.6 Intergovernmental grants

Intergovernmental grants are transfer payments from one sphere of government (e.g. national) to another sphere of government (e.g. a provincial or local government). Intergovernmental grants may be unconditional or conditional. **Unconditional grants** may be spent by recipient governments as they see fit. **Conditional grants** must be spent on the specific service stipulated by the grantor (i.e. the sphere of government which is making the grant).

Grants may also be matching or non-matching. In a **matching grant**, the grantor government will match a certain percentage of each rand of spending by the sub-national government on the same activity. A **non-matching grant** is just a lump-sum allocation which does not depend on the level of sub-national expenditure.

18.6.1 Unconditional non-matching grants

An unconditional non-matching grant is a lump-sum transfer to sub-national government on which no constraints are placed as to how it is to be spent. The recipient government may spend it on any public good or service, or provide tax relief to its citizens. This grant acts to increase the income of the recipient government, but does not alter the relative price of any particular public good. A non-matching grant is in effect an income supplement. A **block grant** in the South African context refers to a type of unconditional non-matching grant where a global lump sum is transferred to a sub-national government to be spent at its discretion. This is also referred to as **revenue sharing**.

The effect of introducing such a grant is

illustrated in Figure 18.1 below. We measure spending on the grant-aided public good in rand on the horizontal axis. Spending on all other public goods is measured on the vertical axis. The line AB shows the government's budget constraint before receiving a grant. The line CD shows the government's new budget constraint after receiving the grant. I_0 and I_1 are the indifference curves of the median voter, indicating society's preferences.

Point E_0 shows the initial equilibrium, which could be thought of as reflecting the median voter's preferences (i.e. preferred combination of grant-aided and other public goods). An unconditional grant (of BD rand) shifts the recipient government's budget constraint from AB to CD. The new equilibrium is at E_1, signifying a higher level of social welfare. There is an increase in public good expenditure by the sub-national government (GH). This increase is, however, less than the amount of the grant (BD). Unconditional grants, because they may be spent on any public good or to finance tax breaks, have the least stimulatory effect on the recipient government's consumption of the grant-aided public good.

18.6.2 Conditional non-matching grants

Conditional non-matching grants give recipient governments a given amount of funds (without sub-national matching) provided that these funds are spent on a particular purpose. For example, a conditional grant might be for spending on health care only. As shown in Figure 18.2, the sub-national government's budget line will therefore shift

Figure 18.1 Unconditional non-matching grant

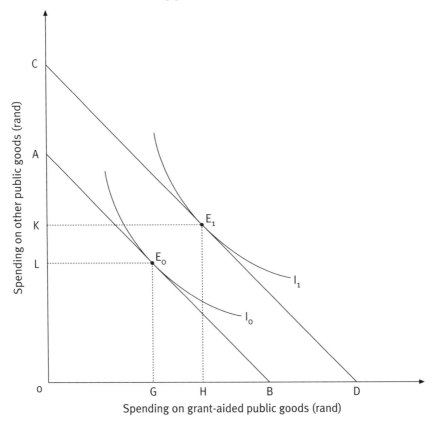

Spending on other public goods (rand)

Spending on grant-aided public goods (rand)

outwards by the amount of the grant (*AF*) from the original budget line *AB* to the post-grant budget line *AFD*.

From the sub-national government's perspective, *OJ* (equal to *AF*) of the granted aided good is "free". Therefore at the new equilibrium E_1, at least *OJ* of the grant-aided public good will be produced and consumed. Note that this particular community can still reduce its own spending on the grant-aided good as long as the full grant (i.e. *AF*) is spent as prescribed. At E_1, therefore, the extra spending on the subsidised good is less than the grant because part of the initial spending on the subsidised good by the sub-national government was diverted to the other goods. Such grants are most appropriate to subsidise activities considered low priority by sub-national govern-

ments but considered to be high priority activities by national government.

18.6.3 Conditional matching grants (open-ended)

Matching conditional grants, which are cost-sharing arrangements, may be open-ended or closed-ended. With open-ended matching grants the national government pays some proportion of the cost of providing a particular public good or service. The sub-national government provides the rest of the funds needed. It therefore, in effect, reduces the price of that particular public service (say health care) for the recipient government. Since the grant is open-ended, the sub-national government can use as much of the grant at the new price, so long as it matches the national government contribution by the stated percentage.

Figure 18.2 Conditional non-matching grant

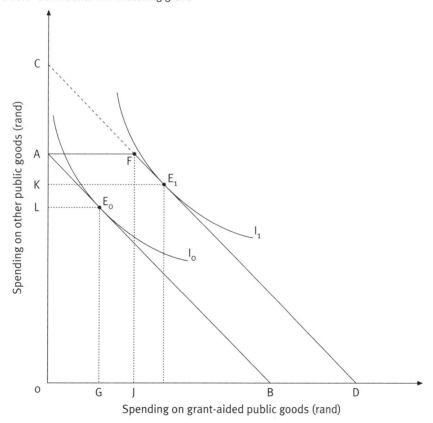

Spending on other public goods (rand)

Spending on grant-aided public goods (rand)

As shown in Figure 18.3 below, a $33\frac{1}{3}$ per cent subsidy on health care provision or expenditure (i.e. R2 of sub-national government funds for each R1 of grant) would rotate the budget line outwards from AB to AD. (If the slope of the original budget line was 1, then the slope of the budget constraint after the grant would be flatter at $\frac{2}{3}$, reflecting the change in the relative price of the two goods. The public good subsidised by the grant becomes relatively cheaper.) Because of this cost-sharing arrangement, at any level of other goods and services, the sub-national government can afford 50 per cent more health care services. As in the case of a selective tax on income (see Chapter 11, Section 11.4.1) a grant that changes the relative price of public goods has an income and a substitution effect.

The income effect in this case entails that the public (as represented by the sub-national government) is better off and can thus consume more of both the grant-aided and the other public goods. The substitution effect involves the substitution of the grant-aided good for other public goods. The net of the income and substitution effects determines the position of E_1, the new equilibrium. As long as E_1 lies to the right of E_0, more of the subsidised public good is purchased. Both the income and substitution effects would prompt the sub-national government to increase expenditure on the public good.

If E_1 lies to the left of E_0, the income effect dominates the substitution effect to such an extent that less of the subsidised good is purchased than before the grant (i.e. the sub-

Figure 18.3 Conditional matching grant (open ended)

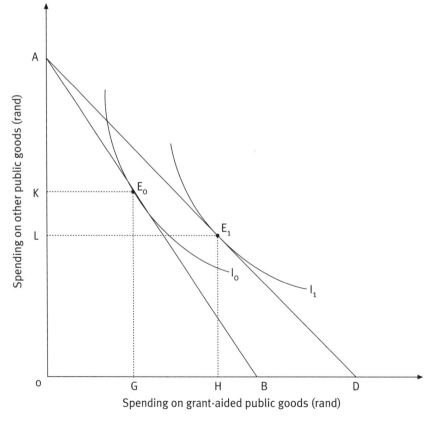

Spending on other public goods (rand)

Spending on grant-aided public goods (rand)

sidised good or service is an inferior or Giffen good or service).

In general, open-ended matching grants are regarded as most appropriate for correcting inefficiencies in public good production which result from positive externalities (Shah, 1994). Positive externalities, or benefit spillovers, occur when the provision of goods and services by one sub-national government benefits other sub-national governments, which do not however bear the cost of provision. In this case there would be an incentive for the sub-national government to under-provide that public good or service unless it was subsidised. Note that open-ended matching grants may benefit richer sub-national governments more than poorer ones who might not be able to match national government expenditure. Geometrically it

can be shown that if E_1 were to lie directly above E_0, the cost to the sub-national government of the new bundle of public goods would be the same as the pre-grant combination. The response of a poor community to a conditional grant may well be to seek a combination of goods that does not increase or even decrease the total cost in respect of all public goods, that is, E_1 will be directly above or even to the left of E_0.

18.6.4 Conditional matching grants (closed-ended)

There are also closed-ended matching grants where the national government pays some proportion of the cost of providing a particular public good or service, up to a certain limit. The effect of a closed-ended matching grant is illustrated in Figure 18.4.

Figure 18.4 Conditional matching grant (closed-ended)

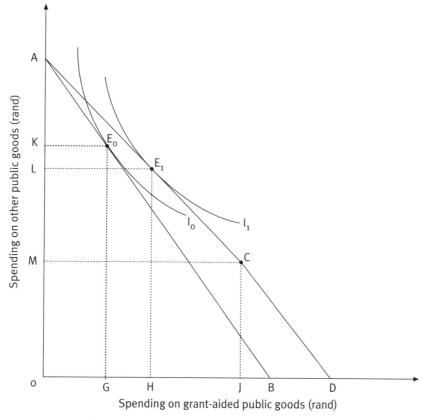

When there is a $33\frac{1}{3}$ per cent subsidy on (say) health care up to a limit, the budget line will move from AB to ACD. Costs of health care provision will be shared along AC until the subsidy limit (at spending level OJ) is reached. Beyond the subsidy limit, health care is unsubsidised and the subnational government faces the full price of provision, hence the steeper slope of the section CD of the budget line. At the new equilibrium E_1, more health care will be provided than would have been the case without the grant.

Grantor governments prefer closed-ended matching transfers because this allows them to retain control over their budgets.

18.6.5 The rationale for intergovernmental grants

The main arguments for intergovernmental transfers are summarised below. The design of the grant should be appropriate to the objective it seeks to attain.

- Fiscal imbalances between expenditure needs and revenue generation capacities of sub-national government can be addressed. Under circumstances where it is not feasible to devolve increased tax powers to sub-national government, **unconditional non-matching grants** (i.e. block grants) should be considered. Sometimes revenue is collected at national level and then transferred to sub-national governments as block grants to address fiscal imbalances. This is known as **revenue sharing**.
- To ensure minimum standards in the provision of public goods and services across the nation, **conditional non-matching grants** are appropriate.
- To compensate for benefit spillovers, **conditional matching transfers** (open-ended) are suitable. The rate of subsidisation should reflect the degree of benefit spillover.
- To assist sub-national governments finan-

cially while promoting expenditures on an activity considered by the national government to be of a high priority, but at the same time affording the national government better control over its own budget, a **conditional matching grant** (closed-ended) may be considered.

18.7 Intergovernmental issues in South Africa

18.7.1 Constitutional issues

Expenditure assignment

The South African Constitution establishes a state with three spheres of government: national, provincial and local. It assigns to each of these three spheres of government certain powers or functions. These competences may be **concurrent** (shared responsibility of national and provincial governments) or **exclusive** (sole responsibility and discretion of the province, or sole responsibility of national government). Functional areas of concurrent legislative competencies are listed in Schedule 4 of the Constitution. Exclusive provincial responsibilities are detailed in Schedule 5.

Schedule 5 of the constitution specifies that certain expenditure responsibilities be devolved completely to provincial sphere (e.g. provincial roads and abattoirs). Others (as described in Schedule 4) are administered jointly as concurrent competencies (e.g. primary and secondary education and health). Some functions remain at national level (e.g. foreign affairs and defence).

Provincial legislation in respect of these Schedule 5 functions takes precedence over national legislation, except when national legislation is necessary to establish national norms and standards, to maintain economic unity, to protect the common market in respect of the mobility of goods, services, capital and labour or to promote economic activities across provincial borders. Thus provinces do have a limited degree of fiscal (and political) autonomy but this is weighed up against national interest.

Local government competences are detailed in part B of Schedule 4 and Schedule 5. Examples of concurrent functions of local government include air pollution, electricity and gas reticulation, municipal health services, etc. Exclusive local government competences include beaches and amusement facilities, cleansing, dog licensing, local amenities, sport facilities and roads.

Revenue assignment and borrowing powers

The Constitution permits a province to impose taxes, levies and duties other than income tax, value-added tax, general sales tax, and rates on property or customs duties. Most productive taxes are reserved for national government.

A **province** may also levy flat-rate surcharges on the tax bases of any tax (including individual income tax), levy or duty imposed by national legislation except corporate income tax, value-added tax, rates on property and customs duties.

Provinces may levy these taxes providing they do not prejudice national economic policies, economic activities across provincial boundaries and national goods and service or factor mobility. Additional own revenue[1] raised by provinces or municipalities may not be deducted from their share of revenue raised nationally, or from other allocations made out of national government revenue. This is to provide an incentive for provinces to increase their tax effort.

To supplement own revenues and fiscal transfers from national government through the revenue sharing formula (see Section 18.7.2), provinces are also empowered to raise loans. The Municipal Finance Management Act (2002) outlines the conditions under which provinces may borrow.

Loans may be raised only to finance capital expenditure (e.g. bridges and other infrastructure) and not for current expenditure (e.g. wages). The only exception to the ban on borrowing to finance current expenditure is for bridging finance, in which case such loans must be redeemed within twelve months. No national government guarantee is available in respect of provincial borrowing.

Local governments are entitled by the Constitution to impose rates on property and surcharges on fees for services provided by or on behalf of the municipality (e.g. for electricity or sewerage). Municipalities are also allowed to borrow, subject to the same restrictions as the provinces which were described above.

18.7.2 Intergovernmental transfers and the Financial and Fiscal Commission

In South Africa most taxes are raised at national level because collection is easier to administer and it avoids the duplication associated with a more decentralised system. However, the Constitution assigns provinces certain responsibilities for the delivery of goods and services, either individually or jointly with national government. There is an imbalance between the expenditure mandate of sub-national levels of government and the financial resources that they can raise on their own account. This mismatch arose because the capacity of the provinces to raise revenue for themselves independently of national government is very limited. For most provinces, income raised within the province as "own revenue" (mainly from car licences and hospital fees) amounts to less than 5 per cent of the provincial budget (see FFC 1996). In terms of tax assignment criteria the scope to expand the provincial revenue base is thus limited.

The Constitution states that provinces are

---

1 Here own revenue is taken to refer to revenue raised within the province or on behalf of the province. These include provincial taxes, user charges, licence fees, etc.

entitled to an equitable share of the revenue collected nationally, in line with their new expenditure responsibilities and functions. The process by which government incomes are pooled and subsequently divided among national and sub-national governments is referred to as **revenue sharing**.

The Financial and Fiscal Commission (FFC) is an independent body established in terms of the Constitution, to make impartial recommendations to the legislative authorities on financial and fiscal matters such as: equitable allocations to the three tiers of government from the national revenue pool; intentions of provincial governments to levy taxes and surcharges; raising of loans by lower tier governments; and the criteria to be used for these purposes.

We now focus on the process of making equitable allocations to national, provincial and local government from nationally collected revenues.

The vertical division of revenue

The allocation of funds from nationally collected revenue entails first a vertical division of such revenue between the national, provincial and local spheres of government. The vertical division of revenue for 2001/02-2004/05 is depicted in Table 18.1. First a "top slice", which consists mainly of funds to service the debt and a contingency reserve, is subtracted from the nationally collected revenue pool. The remainder is then split among the national, provincial and local spheres. Note that the national share includes the budgets for national departments but excludes conditional grants to provinces and local government.

From Table 18.1 it can be seen that 40,5 per cent of the remaining revenue pool after the "top slice" went to finance the national government in 2002/03, a share that was expected to drop marginally to 40,2 per cent in two years' time. Provincial governments received 55,8 per cent of total revenue after

Table 18-1 Vertical division of revenue in South Africa, 2001/02-2004/05, R billion

Financial item		2001/02	2002/03	2003/04	2004/05
Total national budget expenditure		262,6	287,9	311,2	334,6
Less top slice, of which					
Debt service cost		47,5	47,5	49,9	52,4
Contingency reserve		–	3,3	5,0	9,0
Resources to be divided		215,1	237,1	256,4	273,1
National share[a]	R billion	87,3	96,1	103,3	109,9
	% of total to be divided	40,6	40,5	40,3	40,2
Provincial share[b]	R billion	121,2	132,4	142,8	152,4
	% of total to be divided	56,4	55,8	55,7	55,8
Local government share[b]	R billion	6,5	8,6	10,2	10,9
	% of total to be divided	3,0	3,6	4,0	4,0

Notes: Due to rounding totals may not add up.
          [a] Excluding conditional grants to provincial and local national government.
          [b] Including conditional grants from national government
Source: National Treasury (2002a)

the top slice (their "equitable share" which is an unconditional grant as well as conditional grants from national government). It was envisaged that the provincial share would remain constant between 2002/03 and 2004/05. Local government received only 3,6 per cent after the top slice in 2002/03. While the FFC formulae were regarded as important inputs in the calculation of these vertical divisions, the Commission's recommendations apparently were not decisive. The Government regards the *vertical* division of funds between the different spheres of government as a policy judgement that reflects the relative priority of functions assigned to each sphere of government and not something that can be captured in a formula (Ministry of Finance 1999: 59).

The horizontal division of revenue

The vertical split is then followed by a horizontal division of the pool of resources available among the nine provinces and the 284 municipalities. To ensure that each provincial government receives an equitable allocation in order to meet its constitutional expenditure obligations, the FFC (1996) proposed a revenue sharing formula for the horizontal division of resources among the nine provinces over a three to five year period. The FFC asserts that formula funding is more objective and less prone to manipulation by politicians and civil servants. In addition it would enable provinces to predict with greater certainty the revenues that would accrue to them over the period the formula was in force. The formula is mainly population-driven with the population in a province being an indicator of the fiscal need of the province. It is also weighted in favour of rural people as a proxy for backlogs and for poverty. The formula aims at equalising rural weighted spending per capita across the provinces.

However, the FFC is only an advisory body and its recommendations are not binding on the Budget Council which actually makes the division of revenues. The Budget Council (see Chapter 17, Box 17.1) consists of the Minister of Finance and the nine provincial MECs for Finance, with the FFC as observers. The actual formula used by the Budget Council to determine each province's equitable share is based on the provinces' demographic and economic profiles. It consists of the following:

- An **education share** (41%), based on the average size of the school-age population and the number of learners actually enrolled.
- A **health share** (19%), based on the proportion of the population without private health insurance.
- A **social security component** (18%), based on the estimate of people entitled to social security grants (elderly, disabled, and children).
- A **basic share** (7%), based on each province's share of the total population of the country.
- A **backlog component** (3%), based on the distribution of capital needs as captured in the schools register of needs, the audit of hospital facilities and the share of rural population in each province.
- An **economic output share** (7%), based on the distribution of total remuneration in the country.
- An **institutional grant** (5%), equally divided among the provinces.

The formula determines the equitable share that is given to the provinces as an unconditional block grant. In order to determine the total allocation for each province, the conditional grants, which each province receives from national government, must be added to the equitable share. Table 18.2 shows the budgeted allocations to the provinces for 2002/03.

As will be illustrated later, local governments are (in aggregate) not as reliant as provinces on transfers from other spheres of government. There is however substantial variation among municipalities. Some poorer municipalities rely on grants for up to 37% of their income, while some urban municipalities raise 98% of their own income (National Treasury, 2002a:264). Transfers to the local sphere include unconditional equitable share grants, conditional grants and grants in kind (eg the Water Services Operating Subsidy). Conditional grants are generally for municipal infrastructure and other capital expenditure, for capacity building or in support of restructuring.

The individual municipality's claim to nationally collected revenue depends not only on the total size of the vertical division, but also on the nature of the horizontal division among municipalities. The FFC formula, which is the basis of the method used by the Department of Provincial and Local Government and the National Treasury to distribute the equitable share, bases the claim for a share on the relative needs of jurisdictions, after taking the tax capacity into account. The purpose of the formula is to provide financial assistance to those municipalities that cannot provide basic services to the poor from their own tax base.

Essentially, the local government equitable share formula consists of two components: an institutional grant (I grant) to support administrative capacity in local governments, and a basic services grant (S grant) which supports basic service provision to poor households. The I grant is derived from variables such as degree of economies of scale in operating costs, average monthly income per capita, population of the municipality, and a poverty threshold etc. The S grant depends on the number of households in a municipality as well as the annual per capita cost of providing basic services to households in poverty.

The introduction of free basic services at municipal level has created upward pressure on the local government equitable share.

Table 18.2 Budgeted provincial allocations for 2002/03

Province	Equitable share[a]		Conditional share		Total	
	Rbn	% of total	Rbn	% of total	Rbn	% of total
Eastern Cape	20,5	17,2	1,0	11,7	22,0	16,6
Free State	7,9	6,7	0,9	7,5	8,9	6,8
Gauteng	18,2	15,3	3,4	26,9	21,7	16,4
KwaZulu-Natal	24,3	20,4	2,1	16,5	26,4	20,0
Mpumalanga	8,4	7,1	0,7	5,4	9,1	6,9
Northern Cape	2,9	2,4	0,2	1,9	3,1	2,4
Northern Province	16,1	13,5	1,2	9,7	17,4	13,1
North West	9,9	8,4	0,7	5,3	10,6	8,1
Western Cape	10,9	9,1	1,9	15,2	12,8	9,7
Total	**119,5**	**100,0**	**12,9**	**100,0**	**132,4**	**100,0**

Notes: Due to rounding totals may not add up.

  [a] The equitable share is an unconditional grant which provinces can allocate as they see fit. Conditional grants from national to provincial governments include conditional grants for health, for local government as a transitionary measure and other supplementary allocations

Source: National Treasury (2002a)

18.7.3 Provincial financing issues

Until recently, provinces were only spending agencies for the national government, disbursing funds according to the policies and priorities determined at national level. In the past, provinces were treated in much the same way as national departments with regard to the budget. They were concerned mainly with implementation of national policy. They could not set their own priorities nor did they have much accountability – problems could always be blamed on national government. Estimating and evaluating expenditures across functions and provinces were done by government officials in Pretoria, with little regard for provincial priorities. Under the provisions of the new Constitution the provincial governments have much more latitude to determine their own spending patterns.

Provincial budgets should therefore increasingly embody the provincial governments' responses to regional challenges and opportunities for development within the nine provinces. Under these circumstances coordination between the spheres of government in setting expenditure priorities becomes crucial, so that differing needs can be provided for without jeopardising national goals.

However, the nine provinces have vastly differing capacities for financial management and expenditure control. Accountability and efficiency thus depends on the strengthening of managerial and administrative capacity in all – especially the weaker – provinces. Given South Africa's history of government overspending (see the discussion of efficiency in Section 17.5.3 of Chapter 17), sound financial management is particularly important so that provinces can perform the spending functions devolved to them without the risk of provincial overspending. Provincial overspending would of course jeopardise national deficit targets and other stabilisation objectives.

It is also important that the share of national revenue received by the province be adequate to fulfil provincial spending obligations. If financing is not commensurate with the new distribution of responsibilities across spheres of government, this could also lead to persistent pressures for provincial overspending.

Probably one of the most pressing challenges facing provincial government is the need to diversify their tax bases and reduce dependence on national government. Provinces in South Africa have very little own revenue capacity in comparison with sub-national governments in other countries and thus are fiscally highly dependent on central government. Currently, provincial own revenues are generally less than 5 per cent of provincial expenditure. These are derived mainly from motor vehicle licenses, hospital fees and gambling proceeds.

There are concerns that the over-reliance on funding from central government could undermine provincial fiscal autonomy. Furthermore, there is a weak link between the revenue raising responsibility, which is mainly at the national level, and the responsibility for the spending decisions, which is provincial. This could dilute fiscal accountability in the sense that provincial executives are not called upon to justify expenditure patterns to provincial electorates as **taxpayers**. This could also induce perverse incentives such as inefficient increases in expenditure, since costs are *de facto* being shifted onto national government, as well as deviation from provincial electorate preferences. Fiscal federalism's supposed benefit of allocative efficiency is thus weaker. Tax legislation has recently been passed which should allow provinces limited leeway to extend their tax bases.

The FFC has proposed that provinces be allowed to "piggy-back" a provincial surcharge on the national personal income tax. For a number of technical reasons, it is unlikely that provincial governments will be able to implement a surcharge on the personal income tax in the near future, although they may elect to levy smaller taxes in terms of the Provincial Taxation Regulation Process Act of 2001. If provinces were empowered to tax, this would probably only benefit the better-off provinces, which have viable tax bases (e.g. Gauteng, Western Cape and possibly KwaZulu-Natal).

18.7.4 Local government financing issues

Unlike the provinces, local government in aggregate has a more substantial tax base and the 284 municipalities which make up the local government sphere generate more than 90 per cent of their aggregate budget as own revenues. Government transfers are therefore a much smaller percentage of local government revenue than at the provincial level. See also Box 18.1.

18-1

Local government finances in 2001/02

In the 2001/02 local government financial year, municipal operating budgets amounted to R52.7 billion. In addition municipalities budgeted R11.7 billion on their capital budgets. Local government capital expenditures are financed through historical operating surpluses, own revenues, loans, contributions from district municipalities and conditional grants and other transfers from national and provincial governments .

The key operating expenditures included personnel expenditure (34%), bulk purchases such as electricity bought from ESKOM and retailed to residents and bulk purchases in connection with water and sewerage service provision (27%). Other operating expenditures (such as general expenses and administration and interest and redemption on loans amount to 39% of operating budgets in aggregate.

The main sources of revenue for municipalities were (National Treasury 2002a: 169-170):

- gross income from electricity, water and sewerage charges and other bulk services (55%%)

- property rates (21%)
- regional service levies (7%)
- intergovernmental grants, subsidies and other sources (17%)

At the end of the third quarter of 1998, outstanding debt owed to municipalities amounted to R16 billion. Revenue management remains one of the weaknesses of municipal government.

There are three main categories of municipalities: metropolitan councils, district councils and local councils. There is considerable variation in terms of revenue and expenditure patterns both within and across these categories.

The key issue confronting local governments is sustainability. A culture of non-payment has lead to the accumulation of arrears and squeezed the revenue side of municipal budgets. One of the challenges of local government is to improve financial management to ensure that budgets are adhered to. This would include the introduction of uniform accounting standards and compliance with GAMAP (Generally Accepted Municipal Accounting Practices). Financial reporting systems also tend to be weak (for instance National Treasury received budget information from only 244 of the 284 municipalities).

Since 1994, local governments have been undergoing a fundamental transformation, which culminated in the redemarcation of municipalities in December 2000. The number of municipalities has been reduced from 843 to 284. Other important changes include the reassignment of functions between district and local municipalities, the impact of the restructuring of the electricity industry, devolution of health and certain public transport functions, the funding of free basic services, and the introduction of a new property rates system. It would be important to assess the impact of all these factors cumulatively on local government finance. At present, however, there are too many transformation processes which are still either under way or newly completed for the true financial position of individual municipalities to be determined at this stage.

Important concepts

bloc grant

conditional grants

expenditure assignment

financial contagion

fiscal federalism

inter-governmental fiscal relations

inter-governmental grants

matching grant

non-matching grant

revenue-sharing

spatial externalities

tax assignment

tax competition

tax harmonisation

sub-national government

unconditional grants

Self-assessment exercises

18.1 The fiscal federalism literature contends that stabilisation and distribution functions are best performed at national level, whereas allocative functions are best performed at sub-national level. Can you explain why?

18.2 Explain the assumptions and main arguments of the Tiebout model.

18.3 "A fiscally decentralised system is always more efficient and more equitable than a fiscally centralised system." Discuss.

18.4 To ensure minimum educational standards across all provinces, what kind of intergovernmental grant would be most suitable? Why? Illustrate your answer by means of a diagram.

18.5 "Tax competition by sub-national governments always has negative effects." Do you agree?

18.6 Should provincial debt be formally guaranteed by the national government? Why (not)?

18.7 How does the South African expenditure and revenue assignment compare with the guidelines of fiscal federalism theory?

18.8 What are the key issues and trends in provincial and local government finances in South Africa?

References

Abedian, I. & Biggs, M. (eds.). 1998. *Economic globalization and fiscal policy.* Cape Town: Oxford University Press.

Abedian, I. & Standish. 1984. An analysis of the sources of growth in state expenditure in South Africa 1920-1982. *South African Journal of Economics*, 52(4): 391-408.

Alence, R. 1998. *The economic policy-making process in South Africa: Report on a survey of an informed panel,* late 1997. Pretoria: Human Science Research Council.

Anderson, G.M. 1991. The fiscal significance of user charges and earmarked taxes: a survey. In: Richard E. Wagner (ed.). 1991. *Charging for Government: user charges and earmarked taxes in principle and practice.* London and New York: Routledge. 13-34.

Ardington, E. & Lund, F. 1995. *Pensions and development: How the social security system can complement programmes of reconstruction and development.* Development Paper 61. Midrand: Development Bank of Southern Africa.

Arrow, K.J. 1951. *Social choice and individual values.* New York: John Wiley.

Arrow, K.J. 1962. The economic implications of learning by doing. *Review of Economic Studies*, 29.

Atkinson, A.B. & Stiglitz, J.E. 1980. *Lectures on Public Economics.* Maidenhead UK: McGraw-Hill.

Bahl, R. 1998. Land versus property taxes in developing and transition countries. Paper presented at a conference on land value taxation in contemporary societies hosted by the Lincoln Institute of Land Policy, 11-13 January 1998. Phoenix.

Bannock, G. Baxter, R.E. & Rees, R. 1971. *The Penguin Dictionary of Economics.* London/New York: Allen Lane/The Viking Press.

Baumol, W.J. 1982. *Contestable markets and the theory of industry structure.* San Diego: Harcourt.

Baumol, W.J. 1967. Macro-economics of unbalanced growth: the anatomy of urban crisis. *American Economic Review*, 57 (June): 415-426.

Becker, G.S. 1985. Public policies, pressure groups, and dead weight costs. *Journal of Public Economics*, 28(3): 329-347.

Bird, R.M. 1971. Wagners "law" of expanding state activity. *Public Finance*, 26(1): 1-26.

Bird, R.M. 1992. *Tax policy and economic development.* Baltimore: Johns Hopkins.

Black, P.A. 1981. Injection leakages, trade repercussions and the regional multiplier. *Scottish Journal of Political Economy*, 28(3).

Black, P.A. 1993. Affirmative Action: rational response to a changing environment. *South African Journal of Economics*, 61(4).

Black, P.A. 1996a. Affirmative Action in South Africa: rational discrimination according to Akerlof? *South African Journal of Economics*, 64(1): 74-82.

Black, P.A. 1996b. A theory of the regional accelerator. *Journal for Studies in Economics and Econometrics*, 20(2): 25-30.

Black, P.A. & Dollery, B.E. 1992. *Leading issues*

in South African Microeconomics: Selected readings. Halfway House: Southern.

Black, P.A. & Saxby, G. 1996. Differential investment multipliers: an application of Weiss and Gooding. South African Journal of Economic and Management Sciences, 9(4).

Boadway, R.W. & Wildasin, D.E. 1984. Public sector economics. 2nd edition. Boston: Little, Brown and Co.

Boadway, R. & Shah, A. 1995. Perspectives on the role of investment incentives in developing countries. In: Shah, A. (ed.). Fiscal incentives for investment and innovation. Washington: World Bank.

Bohm, P. 1978. Social efficiency. London: Macmillan.

Borcherding, T.E. (ed.). 1977. Budgets and bureaucrats. Durham: Duke University Press.

Boskin, M.J. (ed.). 1996. Frontiers of tax reform. Stanford: Hoover Institution Press.

Bracewell-Milnes B. 1991. The Case for Earmarked Taxes: Government spending and Public Choice, Part 2: Earmarking in Britain: Theory and Practice. London: Institute of Economic Affairs.

Brennan, G. & Buchanan. J.M. 1980. The power to tax: analytical foundations of a fiscal federalism constitution. Cambridge, New York: Cambridge University Press.

Bromberger, N. 1982. Government policies affecting the distribution of income, 1940-1980. In: Schrire R. (ed.). 1982. South Africa: public policy perspectives. Cape Town: Juta. 165-203.

Brown, C.V. & Jackson, P.M. 1990. Public sector economics. Oxford: Basil Blackwell.

Browne, G.W.G. 1975. Fiscal policy in South Africa. In: Lombard, J.A. (ed.). Economic policy in South Africa. Cape Town: HAUM. 1-25.

Browne, G.W.G. 1983. Fifty years of public finance. South African Journal of Economics, 51(1) March: 134-173.

Browning, E.K. & Browning, J.M. 1994. Public finance and the price system. 4th edition. New York: Macmillan.

Buchanan, J.M., Tollison, R.D. & Tullock, G. (eds.). 1980. Towards a theory of the rent-seeking society. College Station: Texas A & M University Press.

Buchanan, J.M. & Tullock, G. 1962. The calculus of consent. Ann Arbor Mich.: Universit of Michigan Press.

Bundy, C. 1988. The rise and fall of the South African peasantry. 2nd edition. Cape Town: David Philip.

Calitz, E. 1986. Aspekte van die vraagstuk van staatsbestedingsprioriteite met spesiale verwysing na die Republiek van Suid-Afrika: 'n funksioneel-ekonomiese ondersoek. D Com thesis. Stellenbosch: University of Stellenbosch.

Calitz, E. 1988. Public expenditure in South Africa: an assessment of trends and the process of determining priorities. Journal for Studies in Economics and Econometrics, 12(2): 25-35.

Calitz, E. 1997. Aspects of the performance of the South African economy. South African Journal of Economics, 65(3): 314-333.

Case, A. & Deaton, A. Forthcoming. School inputs and educational outcomes in South Africa. Quarterly Journal of Economics.

Central Statistical Service. 1996. Living in South Africa: Selected findings of the 1995 October household survey. Pretoria.

Chia, N.C. & Whalley, J. 1995. Patterns in investment: tax incentives among developing countries. In: Shah, A. (ed.). Fiscal incentives for investment and innovation. Washington: World Bank.

Cnossen, S. 1990. The case for selective taxes on goods and services in developing countries. In: Bird, R. & Oldman, O. (eds.). Taxation in developing countries. 4th edition. Baltimore: Johns Hopkins. 344-355.

Coase, R. 1960. The problem of social cost. Journal of Law and Economics, 3:1-44.

Cohen, J.M. & Cohen, M.J. 1960. The Penguin Dictionary of Quotations. New York: Penguin.

Dahlman, C.J. 1979. The problem of externality. *Journal of Law & Economics*, April, 22: 141-162.

Dasgupta, A.K. & Pearce, D.W. 1974. *Cost-benefit analysis: theory and practice*. London: Macmillan Press.

Demsetz, H. 1982. Barriers to entry. *American Economic Review*, 72: 47-57.

Department of Housing. 1995 & 1996. *Annual Reports*. Pretoria: Department of Housing.

Department of Finance. Various years. *Budget Review*. Pretoria.

Department of Finance. 1996. *Macroeconomic strategy on growth, employment and redistribution*. Pretoria.

Department of Finance. Various years. *Budget Survey*. Pretoria.

Department of Finance. Various years. *Statistical/Economic Reviews in connection with the Budget Speech*. Pretoria.

Department of Finance. 1998. *Budget Review 1998*. Pretoria.

Department of Finance. 1999a. *Budget Review 1999*. Pretoria.

Department of Finance. 1999b. *National Expenditure Survey 1999*. Pretoria: Government Printer.

Department of Welfare. 1997. *White Paper for Social Welfare*. Pretoria: Government Printer.

Deran, E. 1965. Earmarking and expenditures: a survey and a new test. *National Tax Journal*. 18(December): 354-61.

De Wulf, L. 1975. Fiscal incidence studies in developing countries: Survey and critique. *IMF Staff Working Papers*. 22(1) March: 61-131.

De Villiers, A.P. 1996. Effektiwiteit van Suid-Afrika se onderwysstelsel: 'n ekonomiese analise. PhD thesis. Stellenbosch: University of Stellenbosch.

Döckel, J.A. & Calitz, E. 1988. Die Bestaansreg van buitebegrotingsfondse. *Journal of Studies in Economics and Econometrics*, 12(3): 31-39.

Döckel, J.A. & Seeber, A.V. 1978. The behaviour of government expenditure in

South Africa. *South African Journal of Economics*, 46(4): 337-351.

Dornbusch, R. & Draghi, M. (eds.). 1990. *Public debt management: theory and history*. Cambridge: Cambridge University Press.

Dornbusch, R., Fischer, S., Mohr, P. & Rogers, C. 1994. *Macroeconomics*. 3rd edition. Johannesburg: Lexicon.

Downs, A. 1957. *An economic theory of democracy*. New York: Harper & Row.

Easson, A.J. 1992. *Tax incentives for foreign direct investment in developing countries*. Australian Tax Forum, 9: 387-439.

F.F.C. 1996. The Financial and Fiscal Commission's recommendations for the allocation of financial resources to the national Government and the provincial Governments for the 1997/98 financial year. Midrand: Financial and Fiscal Commission.

Faria, A.G.A. 1005. Source versus residence principle; Relief from double taxation; Aspects of tax treaties; International capital flows. In: Shome, P. (ed.). 1995. *Tax policy handbook*. IMF: Washington.

Fourie, L.J., Falkena, H.B. & Kok, W.J. (eds.). 1999. *Student guide to the South African financial system*. 2nd edition. Johannesburg: International Thomson Publishing (Southern Africa).

Fourie, F.C.v.N. 1997. *How to think and reason in macroeconomics*. Kenwyn: Juta.

Franzsen, R. 1997. The current status of property taxation in South Africa: legislation and practice. Paper presented at a policy-oriented conference hosted by the Centre for Business Law (Unisa) and the Financial and Fiscal Commission, 23-25 July 1997. Pretoria.

Franzsen Commission. 1968. *First Report of the Commission of Inquiry into fiscal and monetary policy in South Africa* (Chairman: D.G. Franzsen). RP 24/1969. November 1968. Pretoria: Government Printer.

Freeman, A.M. 1983. *Intermediate microeconomic analysis*. New York: Harper.

Frey, B.S. 1978. *Modern political economy.* Oxford: Martin Robertson.

Friedman, M. 1966. *Essays in positive economics.* Chicago: University of Chicago Press.

Gillis, M., Shoup, C.S. & Sicat, G.P. (eds.). 1990. *Value added taxation in developing countries.* Washington: World Bank.

Harberger, A.C. 1962. The incidence of the corporation income tax. *Journal of Political Economy,* 70(3): 215-240.

Hayek, F.A. 1960. *The constitution of liberty.* London: Routledge & Kegan Paul.

Heyns, J.v.d.S. 1996. The theory and practice of tax earmarking: implications for South Africa. *Journal of Studies in Economics and Econometrics,* 20(1): 35-58.

Hockman, H.M. & Rodgers, J.D. 1969. *Pareto optimal redistribution.* American Economic Review, 59(4), Part 1: 531-541.

Harrod, R. 1952. *Economic essays.* New York: Harcourt, Brace & Co.

Hyman, D.N. 1999. *Public finance: a contemporary application of theory to policy.* 6th edition. Fort Worth: Dryden.

International Monetary Fund. 2000 & 2001. *Government finance statistics yearbook.* Washington: IMF.

Janisch, C.A. 1996. An analysis of the burdens and benefits of taxes and government expenditure in the South African economy for the year 1993/94. Unpublished Masters dissertation. Pietermaritzburg: University of Natal.

Katz Commission. 1994. *Interim Report of the Commission of Inquiry into certain aspects of the tax structure of South Africa* (Chairman: M.M. Katz). Pretoria: Government Printer.

Katz Commission. 1995. *Third Interim Report of the Commission of Inquiry into certain aspects of the tax structure of South Africa* (Chairman: M.M. Katz). Pretoria: Government Printer.

Katz Commission. 1997a. *Fourth Interim Report of the Commission of Inquiry into certain aspects of the tax structure of South Africa* (Chairman: M.M. Katz). Pretoria: Government Printer.

Katz Commission. 1997b. *Fifth Interim Report of the Commission of Inquiry into certain aspects of the Tax Structure of South Africa* (Chairman: MM Katz). Pretoria: Government Printer.

Khalilzadeh-Shirazi, J. & Shah, A. 1991. *Tax policy in developing countries.* Washington: World Bank.

Klasen, S. 1996. Poverty and inequality in South Africa. *Mimeo.* (Accepted for publication in Social Indicator Research.) Cambridge: Centre for History and Economics: Kings College.

Kruger, J.J. 1992. State provision of social security: some theoretical, comparative and historical perspectives with reference to South Africa. Masters thesis. Stellenbosch: University of Stellenbosch.

Lachman, D. & Bercuson, K. 1992. *Economic policies for a new South Africa.* IMF Occasional Paper 91. Washington DC: International Monetary Fund.

Leach, D.F. 1997, Concentration – profits monopoly vs efficiency debate: South African evidence, *Contemporary Economic Policy,* 15(2); 12-23.

Leibenstein, H. 1966. Allocative efficiency vs X-efficiency. *American Economic Review,* 56(3): 392-415.

Leibenstein, H. 1978. General X-efficiency theory and economic development. New York: Oxford University Press.

Leistner, G.M.E. 1968. Table insert. *Africa Institute Bulletin,* VI(6): 175-7.

Lim, D. 1993. Recent trends in the size and growth of government in developing countries. In: Gemmell, N. (ed.). *The growth of the public sector: theories and international evidence.* Aldershot: Edward Elgar. 34-50.

Lipsey, R.G. & Chrystal, K.A. 1995. *An introduction to positive economics.* 8th edition. New York: Oxford.

Lund Committee. 1996. *Report of the Lund Committee on child and family support.* Pretoria: Government Printer.

Margo Commission. 1987. *Report of the*

Commission of Inquiry into the tax structure of the Republic of South Africa (Chairman: C.S. Margo). RP34/1987. Pretoria: Government Printer.

McCleary, W. 1991. The earmarking of government revenue: a review of some World Bank experience. *The World Bank Research Observer*, 6(1) (January): 81-103.

McGrath, M.D. 1983. The distribution of personal income in South Africa in selected years over the period from 1945 to 1980. PhD thesis. Durban: University of Natal.

McGrath, M.D., Janish, C. & Horner, C. 1997. *Redistribution through the fiscal system in the South African economy*. Paper presented at the Conference of the Economic Society of South Africa, Potchefstroom, 8 September.

Meltzer, A.H. & Richard, S.F. 1981. A rational theory of the size of government. *Journal of Political Economy*, 89(5): 914-927.

Meth, C., Naidoo, R. & Shipman, B. 1996. *Report of the Task Team on unemployment insurance and related coverage issues*. Pretoria: Department of Labour.

Minister of Finance. Various years. *Budget Speech*. Pretoria.

Ministry of Finance. 1997. *Medium Term Budget Policy Statement 1997*. Pretoria.

Ministry of Finance. 1999. *Medium Term Budget Policy Statement 1998*. Pretoria.

Mintz, J.M. & Seade, J. 1991. Cashflow or income: the choice of base for company taxation. *The World Bank Observer*, 6(2): 177-190.

Mohr, P., Fourie, L. & associates. 2000. 2nd edition. *Economics for South African students*. Pretoria: JL van Schaik.

Mouton Committee. 1992. *Report of the Committee of Investigation into a retirement provision system for South Africa*. Vols. 1 & 2. Pretoria: Department of Finance.

Musgrave, R.A. 1959. *The theory of public finance: a study in public economy*. Tokyo: McGraw-Hill.

Musgrave, R.A. 1969. *Fiscal systems*. New Haven: Yale University Press.

Musgrave, R. 1983. Who should tax, where and what? In: McClure, C.E. (ed.). *Tax assignment in federal countries*. Canberra: Australian National University Press.

Musgrave, R.A. 1987. Public finance. In: Eatwell, J., Milgate, M. & Newman, P. (eds.). 1987. *The new Palgrave*. New York: McMillan Press. 1055-1061.

Musgrave, R.A. & Musgrave, P.B. 1989. *Public finance in theory and practice*. 5th edition. New York: McGraw-Hill.

National Treasury. 2002a. *Budget Review 2002*. Pretoria.

National Treasury. 2002b. *Estimates of National Expenditure 2002*. Pretoria.

Native Economic Commission. 1932. *Report of the Native Economic Commission 1930-32*. Government Printer: Pretoria.

Nattrass, J. 1988. *The South African economy: its growth and change*. 2nd edition. Cape Town: Oxford.

Newbery, D. & Stern, N. (eds.). 1987. *The theory of taxation for developing countries*. Washington: World Bank.

Niskanen, W.A. 1971. *Bureaucracy and representative government*. Chicago: Aldine-Atherton.

Niskanen, W.A. 1974. Non-market decision making: the peculiar economics of bureaucracy. *American Economic Review*, 57(2): 293-321.

Nozick, R. 1974. *Anarchy, state and utopia*. New York: Basic Books.

Oates, W.E. 1985. Searching for Leviathan: an empirical study. *American Economic Review*, 75: 748-57.

Olson, M. 1965. *The logic of collective action*. Cambridge: Harvard University Press.

Organisation for Economic Co-operation and Development (OECD). 1988. *Taxation of net wealth, capital transfers and capital gains on individuals*. Paris: OECD.

Ouattara, A.D. 1997. Globalization's challenges for Africa. *IMF Survey*, 9 June.

Peacock, A.T. & Wiseman, J. 1967. *The growth of public expenditure in the United Kingdom*. London: George Allen & Unwin.

Pigou, A.C. 1950. *The economics of welfare*, 5th edn. London: MacMillan.

Ramsey, F.P. 1927. A contribution to the theory of taxation. *Economic Journal*, 37: 47-61.

Rawls, J. 1971. *A theory of justice*. Cambridge, Mass.: Harvard University Press.

Reader's Digest. 1994. *Illustrated history of South Africa: the real story*. 3rd edition. Cape Town: Reader's Digest.

Republic of South Africa. 1987. *White paper on privatisation and deregulation in the Republic of South Africa*. WPG-87. Pretoria: Government Printer.

Republic of South Africa. 1998. *White paper on local government*: issued by Ministry of Provincial Affairs and Constitutional Development, Pretoria.

Richardson, J. 1986. The local historian's encyclopedia. 2nd edition. London: Historical Publications.

Rodrik, D. 1996. Understanding economic policy reform. *Journal of Economic Literature*, 34(1) March: 9-41.

Romer, P.M. 1986. Increasing returns and long-run growth. *Journal of Political Economy*, 94, October.

Rosen, H.S. 2002. *Public finance*. 6th edition. New York: McGraw-Hill.

Rosenthal, L. 1983. Subsidies to the personal sector. In: Millward, R., Parker, D., Rosenthal, L., Sumner, M.T. & Topham, N. (eds.). 1983. *Public sector economics*. London and New York: Longman. 78-128.

Rostow, W.W. 1971. *Politics and the stages of growth*. Cambridge: Cambridge University Press.

Sadka, E. & Tanzi, V. 1993. A tax on gross assets of enterprises as a form of presumptive taxation. *IBFD Bulletin*, February 1993: 66-73.

Saldru. 1994. *South Africans rich and poor: Baseline Household Statistics*. Cape Town: Saldru.

Samuelson, P.A. 1954. A diagrammatic exposition of the theory of public expenditure. *Review of Economics & Statistics*, vol 37.

Samuelson, P.A. 1955. A diagrammatic exposition of a theory of public expenditure. *Review of Economics and Statistics*, 37(November): 350-356.

Sandford, C. & Hasseldine, J. 1992. *The compliance costs of business taxes in New Zealand*. Wellington: Institute of Policy Studies, Victoria University.

Saunders, P. & Klau, F. 1985. The role of the public sector: causes and consequences of the growth of government. *OECD Economic Studies*, 4 (special edition): 11-239.

Schumpeter, J. 1955. *Capitalism, socialism and democracy*. 4th edition. London: Allen & Unwin.

Shah, A. 1994. The reform of intergovernmental fiscal relations in developing and emerging market economies. *Policy and Research Series 23*. Washington DC: World Bank.

Shah, A. 1995. Introduction to fiscal incentives for investment and innovation. In: Shah, A. (ed.). *Fiscal incentives for investment and innovation*. Washington DC: World Bank.

Schumpeter, J. 1954. *Capitalism, socialism and democracy*, 4th ed, London: Allen & Unwin.

Shome, P. & Schutte, C. 1993. Cashflow tax. *IMF Working Paper*, WP/93/2, Fiscal Affairs Department. Washington: IMF.

Skinner, J. 1991. If agricultural land taxation is so efficient, why is it so rarely used? *The World Bank Economic Review*, 5(1): 113-133.

Siebrits, F.K. 1998. Government spending in an international perspective. In: Abedian, I. & Biggs, M. (eds.). *Economic globalization and fiscal policy*. Cape Town: Oxford University Press. 305-336.

Slemrod, J. & Sorum, N. 1984. The compliance cost of the U.S. individual income tax system. *National Tax Journal*, 38(4).

Smith Committee. 1995. *Report of the Committee on strategy and policy re-view of retirement provision in South Africa*. Pretoria: Department of Finance.

Social and Economic Planning Council.

1944. *Report of the Social and Economic Planning Council on Social Security, Welfare Services and the National Income*. Report no. 2. Pretoria: Government Printer.

Social Security Committee. 1944. *Report of the Committee on Social Security*. Pretoria: Government Printer.

South Africa Foundation. 1998. Big and Small Business in South Africa: Where the Twine Meets. *SAF Viewpoint*, December.

South African Reserve Bank. Various issues. *Quarterly Bulletin*.

Spandau, A.M.K.M. 1971. Income distribution and economic growth in South Africa. Doctoral thesis. Pretoria: University of South Africa.

Statistics South Africa. 1997. *Earning and spending in South Africa: selected findings of the 1995 income and expenditure survey*. Pretoria: Statistics South Africa.

Statistics South Africa. 2001. *South Africa in transition: selected findings from the October Household Survey of 1999 and changes that have occurred between 1995 and 1999*, Pretoria.

Steenekamp, T.J. 1994. Moet armes belasting betaal? *South African Journal of Economics*, 62(4): 371-392.

Steenekamp, T.J. 1996. Some aspects of corporate taxation in South Africa: the Katz Commission. *South African Journal of Economics*, 64(1): 1-19.

Stiglitz, J. 1998. More instruments and broader goals: moving towards the post-Washington consensus. The Annual WIDER 1998 Lecture. Helsinki.

Strydom, P.D.F. 1987. Structural imbalances in the South African economy. Paper delivered at the 1987 Conference of the Economic Society of South Africa. Pretoria.

Sunley, E.M. 1989. *The treatment of companies under cashflow taxes: some administrative, transitional, and international issues*. Working paper 189 of Country Economics Department, Washington: World Bank.

Tanzi, V. 1995. *Taxation in an integrating world*. Washington DC: Brookings.

Tanzi, V. 1996. Globalization, tax competition and the future of tax systems. IMF Working Paper WP/96/141. Washington DC: IMF.

Tanzi, V. & Schuknecht, L. 1995. The growth of government and the reform of the state in industrial countries. IMF Working Paper 95/130. Washington DC: International Monetary Fund.

Teja, R.S. 1991. *The case for earmarked taxes, government spending and public choice, Part 1: an American perspective, theory and an example*. London: Institute of Economic Affairs.

Terreblanche, S.J. 1978. Moontlike fiskale struktuur in 'n alternatiewe konstitusionele model in Suid-Afrika (with English summary). In: Benyon, J.A. (ed.). *Constitutional change in South Africa*. Pietermaritzburg: University of Natal. 190-224.

Theron Commission. 1976. *Verslag van die Kommissie van Ondersoek na aangeleenthede rakende die Kleurlingbevolkingsgroep*. RP38/1976. Pretoria: Government Printer.

Tiebout , C.M. 1956. A pure theory of local expenditures. *Journal of Political Economy*, 64(October): 416-424.

Todaro, M.P. 1997. *Economic Development*. 6th edition. New York: Longman.

Tomlinson Commission. 1955. *Summary of the Report of the Commission for the socio-economic development of the Bantu areas within the Union of South Africa*. UG61/1955. Pretoria: Government Printer.

United Nations. 1997. *Human Development Report*. New York: Oxford University Press.

Toumanoff, P.G. 1984. A positive analysis of the theory of market failure. *Kyklos*, 37(4): 529-541.

Van der Berg, S. 1989. Long-term economic trends and development prospects in South Africa. *African Affairs*. 88(351): 181-203.

Van der Berg, S. 1991. Redirecting government expenditure. In: Moll, P., Nattrass, N. & Loots, L. (eds.). 1991. *Redistribution: How can it work in South Africa?* Cape Town: David Philip. 74-85.

Van der Berg, S. 1992. Social reform and the reallocation of social expenditures. In Schrire, R. (ed.). 1992. *Wealth or poverty? Critical choices for South Africa.* Cape Town: Oxford. 121-142.

Van Heerden, J.H. 1996. The distribution of personal wealth in South Africa. *South African Journal of Economics*, 64(4): 278-292.

Wagner, A. 1883. Three extracts on public finance. In: Musgrave, R.A. & Peacock, A.T. (eds.). 1958. *Classics in the theory of public finance.* London: Macmillan.

Weiss, J. 1995. *Economic policy in developing countries: the reform agenda.* Prentice Hall/Harvester Wheatsheaf.

Whiteford, A. & McGrath, M. 1994. Inequality in the size distribution of income in South Africa. Occasional Papers 10. Stellenbosch: Stellenbosch Economic Project.

World Bank. 1991. *Lessons of tax reform.* Washington: World Bank.

World Bank. 1994. *World development report 1994.* Washington: World Bank.

World Bank. 1995. Key indicators of poverty in South Africa. Prepared for the Reconstruction and Development Programme Office. Pretoria: Government Printer.

Index